The Voluntaryist Handbook
A COLLECTION OF ESSAYS, EXCERPTS, AND QUOTES

Organized by
Keith Knight

THE VOLUNTARYIST HANDBOOK
A COLLECTION OF ESSAYS, EXCERPTS, AND QUOTES

First Edition, 2022

© 2022 Keith Knight

Cover design by TopLobsta.com

Edited by Keith Knight

Ebook design by Mike Dworski

Published in the United States of America by
The Libertarian Institute
612 W. 34th St.
Austin, TX 78705

LibertarianInstitute.org

ISBN-13: 978-1-7336473-9-7
ISBN-10: 1-7336473-9-2:

To Edward Stringham, Ph.D., a man who values truth, freedom, morality, and leading by example.

Table of Contents

Introduction	i
Terms	iii
1 What Is the Free Market?	1
Murray N. Rothbard, Ph.D.	
2 One Moral Standard for All	6
Sheldon Richman	
3 Coercivists and Voluntarists	9
Donald J. Boudreaux, Ph.D.	
4 Three Thought Experiments	12
Jason Brennan, Ph.D.	
5 Do We Ever Really Get Out of Anarchy?	13
Alfred G. Cuzán, Ph.D.	
6 What It Means to Be an Anarcho-Capitalist	22
Stephan Kinsella, J.D.	
7 Six Questions for Statists	25
Stefan Molyneux, M.A.	
8 The Argument for Free Markets: Morality vs. Efficiency	28
Walter E. Williams, Ph.D.	
9 Social Cooperation	38
Sheldon Richman	
10 The Central Banking Scam	41
Patrick MacFarlane, J.D.	
11 Homelessness, Regulation, and Minimum Wage	44
12 The Right and Wrong of Compulsion by the State (Excerpts)	54
Auberon Herbert	
13 War, Peace, and the State	58
Murray N. Rothbard, Ph.D.	

14 No Treason (Excerpts)   70
    Lysander Spooner

15 How Private Governance Made the Modern World Possible   74
    Edward P. Stringham, Ph.D.

16 The Misplaced Fear of "Monopoly"   79
    Thomas E. Woods, Jr., Ph.D.

17 Privatize the Roads   84
    Walter Block, Ph.D.

18 The Utilitarian Case for Voluntaryism   88
    Danny Duchamp

19 Marxist and Austrian Class Analysis   91
    Hans-Hermann Hoppe, Ph.D.

20 Is 'Equality' a Worthy Goal?   109
    Bradley Thomas

21 How I Changed My Mind on Intellectual Property   112
    Isaac Morehouse

22 The Case for Libertarian Anarchism: Responses to Ten Objections 116
    Roderick T. Long, Ph.D.

23 The Reluctant Anarchist   134
    Joseph Sobran, B.A.

24 Individualism vs. War   142
    Scott Horton

25 I Was a Police Officer, Now I'm a Voluntaryist   145
    Shepard Oakley

26 On the Ultimate Justification of the Ethics of Private Property   148
    Hans-Hermann Hoppe, Ph.D.

27 Persuasion vs. Force   154
    Mark Skousen, Ph.D. and Jo Ann Skousen

28 The Most Dangerous Superstition (Excerpts)   161
    Larken Rose

29 Can Anarcho-Capitalism Work?	163
Llewellyn H. Rockwell, Jr.	
30 Chaos Theory (Excerpts)	168
Robert P. Murphy, Ph.D.	
31 The "Power Vacuum" Argument	170
Larken Rose	
32 So, Tell Me, 'Do You Hate the State?'	173
Peter R. Quiñones	
33 Government Itself Is Immoral	175
James Corbett	
34 The Obviousness of Anarchy	178
John Hasnas, Ph.D.	
35 Economics in One Lesson (Excerpts)	202
Henry Hazlitt	
36 How Markets Have Delivered More Economic Equality	204
Antony Sammeroff	
37 The State Is Too Dangerous to Tolerate (Excerpts)	207
Robert Higgs, Ph.D.	
38 An Invisible Enemy Turned Inward	209
Clint Russell	
39 A Right-Wing Critique of the Police State	211
Llewellyn H. Rockwell, Jr.	
40 The Only Police Reform That Matters	213
Jason Brennan, Ph.D.	
41 Welfare Before the Welfare State	215
Joshua Fulton, B.A.	
42 Fallacies You Need to Be Told About	220
Michael Huemer, Ph.D.	
43 The Anti-Capitalist Ideology of Slavery	230
Phillip W. Magness, Ph.D.	

44 From Marine to Voluntaryist	235
Shane Hazel	
45 The Law (Excerpts)	237
Frédéric Bastiat	
46 How Government Solved the Health Care Crisis	240
Roderick T. Long, Ph.D.	
47 The Imposers and the Imposed Upon	244
Jeff Deist	
48 Agorism (Quotes)	254
49 What Must Be Done (Excerpt)	257
Hans-Hermann Hoppe, Ph.D.	
50 Quotes	269
Afterword	301
Permissions	303
Acknowledgements	304

Introduction

There exist two blatant contradictions which roughly ninety-nine percent of intellectuals, journalists, and voters erroneously believe.

On the one hand, they say that the free market must be regulated in order to prevent monopolies. It is assumed that these monopolies would have such great power over the market that their customers would be forced to settle for products far more expensive than, and inferior to, those that would be offered under competitive market conditions. On the other hand, these intellectuals, journalists, and voters explicitly advocate that one group (government) monopolize the money supply, policing, courts, taxation, legislation, compulsory education, and a myriad of other things that we may consider to be vitally important.

Second, the vast majority of people recognize the moral legitimacy of the biblical commandments "Thou Shalt Not Steal" and "Thou Shalt Not Murder." Yet, when it comes to the practices of taxation and war, these principles are blatantly disregarded by almost everyone. If taxation is not theft, why can only governments do such a thing? Why not simply allow all organizations, companies, clubs, churches, or individuals to issue taxes?

It should therefore come as no surprise that governments are infamous for delivering poor quality. Imagine a restaurant where you had to pay regardless of whether they brought food to your table.

Likewise, war is simply a euphemism for theft-funded mass murder, a blatant crime that we would never dismiss if non-government actors were to engage in it.

What if justice required us not to have double standards? This book seeks to dispel the belief that morality applies differently to government employees. If it is immoral for me to do something — say, conscript people to perform labor against their will — how can I justifiably vote for a representative to do such a thing on my behalf?

Many real criticisms apply to the free market: greed, envy, dog-eat-dog mentalities, short-sightedness, etc. The problem with all of those criticisms is that they apply many times over to the state, since, by definition, *the state does not face competition* and *one cannot opt out of funding it*. While voluntarily funded competing organizations may have shortcomings, they are preferable to the coercively funded monopolies of the state.

The following collection of essays, excerpts, and quotes has given me the intellectual capacity to stop hating people based on arbitrary differences and to focus on what really matters. Should I achieve my ends in life violently with threats, or voluntarily with persuasion?

The corporate press will explicitly seek to divide people of goodwill based on gender, income, race, nationality, and any numerous other interchangeable sources of division to suit their agenda. No longer should we tolerate such an obvious scam.

These passages, which can be read in any order, are what convinced me to abandon statism and embrace voluntaryism.

Terms

Voluntaryism
The moral position which maintains that no peaceful person can justly be submitted to the control of others, in the absence of his or her own consent.

Libertarianism
The moral position which maintains that it is illegitimate to initiate aggression against non-aggressors.

Anarchy
From the Greek prefix *an*, "without, in the absence of" and the Greek noun *archon*, "master, ruler." *Anarchy* does not mean "without rules"; it literally means "without rulers, without masters."

Communism
The abolition of private property.

Socialism
The institutionalized interference with, or aggression against, private property and private property claims.

Capitalism
A social system based on the explicit recognition of private property, and non-aggressive contractual exchanges between private property owners.

Free Market
A summary description of all voluntary exchanges that take place in a given economic environment.

Original Appropriation
A process by which previously unowned natural resources, particularly land, become the property of a person or group of persons.

Contract
Consensual title transfer between two or more parties.

Exchange
A voluntary interaction between two individuals in which both forfeit ownership of an object to the other, to the benefit of both.

Economics
The study of purposeful behavior applied to the use of scarce resources which have alternative uses.

Scarcity/Scarce
Limited with respect to the ends that resources could possibly serve.

Property
A term describing anything over which a party has legal title, affording owners certain enforceable rights over said scarce resources.

Political Authority
The hypothesized moral property in virtue of which governments may coerce people in certain ways not permitted to anyone else and in virtue of which citizens must obey governments in situations in which they would not be obligated to obey anyone else.

Non-Aggression Principle
An ethical stance which asserts that aggression is inherently illegitimate. *Aggression* is defined as the initiation of physical force against persons or property, the threat of such, or fraud upon persons or their property. In contrast to pacifism, the non-aggression principle does not preclude violent self-defense. The principle is a deontological (or rule-based) ethical stance.

Self-Ownership
Also known as "sovereignty of the individual" or "individual sovereignty"; the concept of property in one's own person, expressed as the moral or natural right of a person to have bodily integrity and be the exclusive controller of his or her own body and life.

Ownership
The recognized right of one party to exclude another from scarce resources.

State
That organization in society which attempts to maintain a monopoly of the use of force and violence in a given territorial area; in particular, it is the only organization in society that obtains its revenue not by voluntary contribution or payment for services rendered, but by coercion.

1
What Is the Free Market?

Murray N. Rothbard, Ph.D.

Murray Newton Rothbard (1926–1995) was an economist, scholar, intellectual, and polymath who made major contributions in economics, political philosophy (libertarianism in particular), economic history, and legal theory. He developed and extended the Austrian School of economics based on the earlier pioneering work of Ludwig von Mises, Ph.D.

"Free Market" is a summary term for an array of exchanges that take place in society. Each exchange is undertaken as a voluntary agreement between two people or between groups of people represented by agents. These two individuals (or agents) exchange two economic goods, either tangible commodities or nontangible services. Thus, when I buy a newspaper from a news dealer for fifty cents, the news dealer and I exchange two commodities: I give up fifty cents, and the news dealer gives up the newspaper. Or if I work for a corporation, I exchange my labor services, in a mutually agreed way, for a monetary salary; here the corporation is represented by a manager (an agent) with the authority to hire.

Both parties undertake the exchange because each expects to gain from it. Also, each will repeat the exchange next time (or refuse to) because his expectation has proved correct (or incorrect) in the recent past. Trade, or exchange, is engaged in precisely because both parties benefit; if they did not expect to gain, they would not agree to the exchange.

This simple reasoning refutes the argument against free trade typical of the "mercantilist" period of sixteenth- to eighteenth-century Europe, and classically expounded by the famed sixteenth-century French essayist Montaigne. The mercantilists argued that in any trade, one party can benefit only at the expense of the other, that in every transaction there is a winner and a loser, an "exploiter" and an "exploited." We can immediately see the fallacy in this still-popular viewpoint: the willingness and even eagerness to trade means that both parties benefit. In modern game-theory jargon, trade is a win-win situation, a "positive-sum" rather than a "zero-sum" or "negative-sum" game.

How can both parties benefit from an exchange? Each one values the two goods or services differently, and these differences set the scene for an exchange. I, for example, am walking along with money in my pocket but no newspaper; the news dealer, on the other hand, has plenty of newspapers but is anxious to acquire money. And so, finding each other, we strike a deal.

Two factors determine the terms of any agreement: how much each participant values each good in question, and each participant's bargaining skills. How many cents will exchange for one newspaper, or how many Mickey Mantle baseball cards will swap for a Babe Ruth, depends on all the participants in the newspaper market or the baseball card market — on how much each one values the cards as compared to the other goods he could buy. These terms of exchange, called "prices" (of newspapers in terms of money, or of Babe Ruth cards in terms of Mickey Mantles), are ultimately determined by how many newspapers, or baseball cards, are available on the market in relation to how favorably buyers evaluate these goods. In shorthand, by the interaction of their supply with the demand for them.

Given the supply of a good, an increase in its value in the minds of the buyers will raise the demand for the good, more money will be bid for it, and its price will rise. The reverse occurs if the value, and therefore the demand, for the good falls. On the other hand, given the buyers' evaluation, or demand, for a good, if the supply increases, each unit of supply — each baseball card or loaf of bread — will fall in value, and therefore, the price of the good will fall. The reverse occurs if the supply of the good decreases.

The market, then, is not simply an array, but a highly complex, interacting latticework of exchanges. In primitive societies, exchanges are all barter or direct exchange. Two people trade two directly useful goods, such as horses for cows or Mickey Mantles for Babe Ruths. But as a society develops, a step-by-step process of mutual benefit creates a situation in which one or two broadly useful and valuable commodities are chosen on the market as a medium of indirect exchange. This money-commodity, generally but not always gold or silver, is then demanded not only for its own sake, but even more to facilitate a re-exchange for another desired commodity. It is much easier to pay steelworkers not in steel bars, but in money, with which the workers can then buy whatever they desire. They are willing to accept money because they know from experience and insight that everyone else in the society will also accept that money in payment.

The modern, almost infinite latticework of exchanges, the market, is made possible by the use of money. Each person engages in specialization, or a division of labor, producing what he or she is best at. Production begins with natural resources, and then various forms of machines and capital goods, until finally, goods are sold to the consumer. At each stage of production from natural resource to consumer good, money is voluntarily exchanged for capital goods, labor services, and land resources. At each step of the way, terms of exchanges, or prices, are determined by the voluntary interactions of suppliers and demanders. This market is "free" because choices, at each step, are made freely and voluntarily.

What Is the Free Market?

The free market and the free price system make goods from around the world available to consumers. The free market also gives the largest possible scope to entrepreneurs, who risk capital to allocate resources so as to satisfy the future desires of the mass of consumers as efficiently as possible. Saving and investment can then develop capital goods and increase the productivity and wages of workers, thereby increasing their standard of living. The free competitive market also rewards and stimulates technological innovation that allows the innovator to get a head start in satisfying consumer wants in new and creative ways.

Not only is investment encouraged, but perhaps more important, the price system, and the profit-and-loss incentives of the market, guide capital investment and production into the proper paths. The intricate latticework can mesh and "clear" all markets so that there are no sudden, unforeseen, and inexplicable shortages and surpluses anywhere in the production system.

But exchanges are not necessarily free. Many are coerced. If a robber threatens you with "Your money or your life," your payment to him is coerced and not voluntary, and he benefits at your expense. It is robbery, not free markets, that actually follows the mercantilist model: the robber benefits at the expense of the coerced. Exploitation occurs not in the free market, but where the coercer exploits his victim. In the long run, coercion is a negative-sum game that leads to reduced production, saving, and investment, a depleted stock of capital, and reduced productivity and living standards for all, perhaps even for the coercers themselves.

Government, in every society, is the only lawful system of coercion. Taxation is a coerced exchange, and the heavier the burden of taxation on production, the more likely it is that economic growth will falter and decline. Other forms of government coercion (*e.g.*, price controls or restrictions that prevent new competitors from entering a market) hamper and cripple market exchanges, while others (prohibitions on deceptive practices, enforcement of contracts) can facilitate voluntary exchanges.

The ultimate in government coercion is socialism. Under socialist central planning the socialist planning board lacks a price system for land or capital goods. As even socialists like Robert Heilbroner now admit, the socialist planning board therefore has no way to calculate prices or costs or to invest capital so that the latticework of production meshes and clears. The current Soviet experience, where a bumper wheat harvest somehow cannot find its way to retail stores, is an instructive example of the impossibility of operating a complex, modern economy in the absence of a free market. There was neither incentive nor means of calculating prices and costs for hopper cars to get to the wheat, for the flour mills to receive and process it, and so on down through the large number of stages needed to reach the ultimate consumer in Moscow or Sverdlovsk. The investment in wheat is almost totally wasted.

Market socialism is, in fact, a contradiction in terms. The fashionable discussion of market socialism often overlooks one crucial aspect of the market. When two goods are indeed exchanged, what is really exchanged is the property titles in those goods. When I buy a newspaper for fifty cents, the seller and I are exchanging property titles: I yield the ownership of the fifty cents and grant it to the news dealer, and he yields the ownership of the newspaper to me. The exact same process occurs as in buying a house, except that in the case of the newspaper, matters are much more informal, and we can all avoid the intricate process of deeds, notarized contracts, agents, attorneys, mortgage brokers, and so on. But the economic nature of the two transactions remains the same.

This means that the key to the existence and flourishing of the free market is a society in which the rights and titles of private property are respected, defended, and kept secure. The key to socialism, on the other hand, is government ownership of the means of production, land, and capital goods. Thus, there can be no market in land or capital goods worthy of the name.

Some critics of the free market argue that property rights are in conflict with "human" rights. But the critics fail to realize that in a free-market system, every person has a property right over his own person and his own labor, and that he can make free contracts for those services. Slavery violates the basic property right of the slave over his own body and person, a right that is the groundwork for any person's property rights over nonhuman material objects. What's more, all rights are human rights, whether it is everyone's right to free speech or one individual's property rights in his own home.

A common charge against the free-market society is that it institutes "the law of the jungle," of "dog eat dog," that it spurns human cooperation for competition, and that it exalts material success as opposed to spiritual values, philosophy, or leisure activities. On the contrary, the jungle is precisely a society of coercion, theft, and parasitism, a society that demolishes lives and living standards. The peaceful market competition of producers and suppliers is a profoundly cooperative process in which everyone benefits, and where everyone's living standard flourishes (compared to what it would be in an unfree society). And the undoubted material success of free societies provides the general affluence that permits us to enjoy an enormous amount of leisure as compared to other societies, and to pursue matters of the spirit. It is the coercive countries with little or no market activity, notably under communism, where the grind of daily existence not only impoverishes people materially, but deadens their spirit.

Further Reading

Ballvé, Faustino, *Essentials of Economics*, 1963.
Hazlitt, Henry, *Economics in One Lesson*, 1946.
Mises, Ludwig von, *Economic Freedom and Interventionism*, edited by Bettina Greaves, 1990.
Rockwell, Llewellyn, Jr. (Ed.), *The Economics of Liberty*, 1990.
Rockwell, Llewellyn, Jr. (Ed.), *The Free Market Reader*, 1988.
Rothbard, Murray N., *Power and Market: Government and the Economy*, 2nd ed., 1977.
Rothbard, Murray N., *What Has Government Done to Our Money?*, 4th ed., 1990.

2
One Moral Standard for All

Sheldon Richman
The Future of Freedom Foundation
2013

Sheldon Richman is the Executive Editor of the Libertarian Institute and a Contributing Editor at Antiwar.com.

Libertarians make a self-defeating mistake in assuming that their fundamental principles differ radically from most other people's principles. Think how much easier it would be to bring others to the libertarian position if we realized that they already agree with us in substantial ways.

What am I talking about? It's quite simple. Libertarians believe that the initiation of force is wrong. So do the overwhelming majority of nonlibertarians. They, too, think it is wrong to commit offenses against person and property. I don't believe they abstain merely because they fear the consequences (retaliation, prosecution, fines, jail, lack of economic growth). They abstain because they sense deep down that it is wrong, unjust, improper. In other words, even if they never articulate it, they believe that other individuals are ends in themselves and not merely means to other people's ends. They believe in the dignity of individuals. As a result, they perceive and respect the moral space around others. (This doesn't mean they are consistent, but when they are not, at least they feel compelled to rationalize.)

That's the starting point of the libertarian philosophy, at least as I see it. (I am not a calculating consequentialist, or utilitarian, but neither am I a rule-worshiping deontologist. Rather, I am comfortable with the Greek approach to morality, eudaimonism, which, as Roderick Long writes, "means that virtues like prudence and benevolence play a role in determining the content of justice, but also — via a process of mutual adjustment — that justice plays a role in determining the content of virtues like prudence and benevolence." In this view, justice, or respect for rights, like the other virtues, is a *constitutive*, or internal, means — rather than an instrumental means — to the ultimate end of all action, flourishing, or the good life.)

Libertarians differ from others in that they apply the same moral standard to all people's conduct. Others have a double standard, the live-and-let-live standard for "private" individuals and another, conflicting one for government personnel. All we have to do is get people to see this and all will be well.

Okay, I'm oversimplifying a bit. But if I'm close to right, you'll have to admit that the libertarian's job now looks much more manageable. Socrates would walk through the agora in Athens pointing out to people that they unwittingly held contradictory moral positions. By asking them probing questions, he nudged them into adjusting their views until they were brought into harmony, with the nobler of their views holding sway. (Does this mean that agoraphobia began as a fear of being accosted by a Greek philosopher in a public place?) This harmonization is known as reflective equilibrium, though Long emphasizes the *activity*, reflective equilibration, rather than the end state.

So it remains only for libertarians to engage in a series of thought experiments to win others over to their position. For example, if I would properly be recognized as an armed robber were I to threaten my neighbors into giving me a percentage of their incomes so that I might feed the hungry, house the homeless, and provide pensions for the retired, why aren't government officials similarly recognized? If I can't legally impose mandates on people, as the Affordable Care Act does, why can Barack Obama and members of Congress do so? If I can't forcibly forbid you to use marijuana or heroin or cocaine, why can DEA agents do it?

Those officials are human beings. You are a human being. I am a human being. So we must have the same basic rights. Therefore, what you and I may not do, *they* may not do. The burden of rebuttal is now on those who reject the libertarian position.

Undoubtedly the nonlibertarian will respond that government officials were duly elected by the people according to the Constitution, or hired by those so elected. Thus they may do what is prohibited to you and me. This reply is inadequate. If you and I admittedly have no right to tax and regulate others, how could we delegate a nonexistent right to someone else through an election? Obviously, we can't. (Frédéric Bastiat pointed this out in *The Law*.)

That's the nub of the libertarian philosophy right there. No one has the right to treat people merely as means — no matter how noble the end. *No one*. The implication is that if you want someone's cooperation, you must use persuasion (such as offering to engage in a mutually beneficial exchange), not force. That principle must be applicable to all human beings on pain of contradiction.

This argument should have particular appeal for advocates of equality — for what better embodies their ideal than the libertarian principle, which establishes the most fundamental equality of all persons? I don't mean equality of outcome, equality of income, equality of opportunity, equality under the law, or equality of freedom. I mean something more basic: what

Long calls equality of *authority*. You can find it in John Locke (*Second Treatise of Government*, chapter 2, section 6):

> Being all equal and independent, no one ought to harm another in his life, health, liberty or possessions... And, being furnished with like faculties, sharing all in one community of nature, there cannot be supposed any such subordination among us that may authorise us to destroy one another, as if we were made for one another's uses...

"Unless it be to do justice on an offender," Locke continued, no one may "take away, or impair the life, or what tends to the preservation of the life, the liberty, health, limb, or goods of another."

Long traces out a key implication of this idea: "Lockean equality involves not merely equality before legislators, judges, and police, but, far more crucially, equality with legislators, judges, and police."

One moral standard for all, no exceptions, no privileges. That's a fitting summation of the libertarian philosophy. The good news is that most people are more than halfway there.

3
Coercivists and Voluntarists

Donald J. Boudreaux, Ph.D.
Foundation for Economic Education

Professor Donald J. Boudreaux is a Senior Fellow with the F.A. Hayek Program for Advanced Study in Philosophy, Politics, and Economics at the Mercatus Center at George Mason University. He is a Professor of Economics (and former Economics Department chair) at George Mason University. He specializes in globalization and trade, law and economics, and antitrust economics.

Categorizing a political position according to some simple left-right scale of values leaves something to be desired. Political views cover such a wide variety of issues that it is impossible to describe adequately any one person merely by identifying where he sits on a lone horizontal line.

Use of the single left-right scale makes impossible a satisfactory description of libertarian (and classical-liberal) attitudes toward government. Libertarians oppose not only government direction of economic affairs, but also government meddling in the personal lives of peaceful people. Does this opposition make libertarians "rightists" (because they promote free enterprise) or "leftists" (because they oppose government meddling in people's private affairs)? As a communications tool, the left-right distinction suffers acute anemia.

Nevertheless, despite widespread dissatisfaction with the familiar left-right — "liberal-conservative" — lingo, such use continues. One reason for its durability is convenience. Never mind that all-important nuances are ignored when describing someone as being, say, "to the right of Richard Nixon" or "to the left of Lyndon Johnson." The description takes only seconds and doesn't tax the attention of nightly news audiences.

Therefore, no practical good is done by lamenting the mass media's insistence on using a one-dimensional tool for describing political views. A better strategy for helping to improve political discussion is to devise a set of more descriptive terms.

There is much to be said for a suggestion offered by Professor Richard Gamble, who teaches history at Palm Beach Atlantic University. Gamble proposes that instead of describing someone as either "left" or "right," or "liberal" or "conservative," we describe him as being either a *centralist* or a *decentralist*. This "centralist-decentralist" language would be a vast improvement over the muddled "left-right" language.

Unfortunately, "centralist-decentralist" language contains its own potential confusion — namely, "decentralist" might be taken to mean someone who is indifferent to what Clint Bolick calls "grassroots tyranny." Is there an even better set of labels for a one-dimensional political spectrum? I think so: "coercivist-voluntarist."

At one end of this spectrum are coercivists. Coercivists believe that all order in society must be consciously designed and implemented by a sovereign government power. Coercivists cannot fathom how individuals without mandates from above can ever pattern their actions in a way that is not only orderly, but also peaceful and productive. For the coercivist, direction by sovereign government is as necessary for the creation of social order as the meticulous craftsmanship of a watchmaker is necessary for the creation of a watch.

At the other end of the spectrum are voluntarists. Voluntarists understand two important facts about society that coercivists miss. First, voluntarists understand that social order is inevitable without coercive direction from the state as long as the basic rules of private property and voluntary contracting are respected. This inevitability of social order when such rules are observed is the great lesson taught by Adam Smith, Ludwig von Mises, F.A. Hayek, and all of the truly great economists through the ages.

Second, voluntarists understand that coercive social engineering by government — far from promoting social harmony — is fated to *ruin* existing social order. Voluntarists grasp the truth that genuine and productive social order is possible only when each person is free to pursue his own goals in his own way, constrained by no *political* power. Coercive political power is the enemy of social order because it is unavoidably arbitrary — bestowing favors for reasons wholly unrelated to the values the recipients provide to their fellow human beings. And even if by some miracle the exercise of political power could be shorn of its arbitrariness, it can never escape being an exercise conducted in gross ignorance. It is a simpleton's fantasy to imagine that all the immense and detailed knowledge necessary for the successful central direction of human affairs can ever be possessed by government.

Society emerges from the cooperation of hundreds of millions of people, each acting on the basis of his own unique knowledge of individual wants, talents, occupations, and circumstances. No bureaucrat can know enough about software design to outperform Bill Gates, or enough about retailing to successfully second-guess the folks at Wal-Mart, or enough about any of the millions of different industries to outdo people who are highly specialized in their various trades.

Coercivists and Voluntarists

The coercivist-voluntarist vocabulary is superior to the left-right, or liberal-conservative, vocabulary at distinguishing liberty's friends from its foes. Support for high taxes and intrusive government commercial regulation is a "liberal" trait. A supporter of high taxes and regulation is also, however, properly labeled a coercivist. But note: no less of a coercivist is the conservative who applauds government regulation of what adults voluntarily read, view, or ingest. Both parties believe that social order will deteriorate into chaos unless government coercion overrides the myriad private choices made by individuals.

Voluntarists are typically accused of endorsing complete freedom of each individual from all restraints. This accusation is nonsense. While they oppose heavy reliance upon *coercively* imposed restraints, sensible voluntarists do not oppose restraints *per se*. Voluntarists, in contrast to coercivists, recognize that superior restraints on individual behavior emerge decentrally and peaceably. Parents restrain their children. Neighbors use both formal and informal means to restrain each other from un-neighborly behaviors. The ability of buyers to choose where to spend their money restrains businesses from abusing customers.

A free society is chock-full of such decentrally and noncoercively imposed restraints. Indeed, it is the voluntary origins of such restraints that make them more trustworthy than coercively imposed restraints. A voluntary restraint grows decentrally from the give and take of everyday life and is sensitive to all the costs and benefits of both the restraint itself and of the restrained behavior. But a coercive restraint too often is the product not of that give and take of all affected parties but, instead, of political deals. And political deals are notoriously biased toward the wishes of the politically well-organized while ignoring the wishes of those unable to form effective political coalitions. What's more, members of the political class often free themselves from the very restraints they foist upon others. Coercively imposed restraints are not social restraints at all; rather, they are arbitrary commands issued by the politically privileged.

The true voluntarist fears nothing as much as he fears coercive power — whether exercised by those on the "left" or the "right."

4
Three Thought Experiments

Jason Brennan, Ph.D.
Political Philosophy: An Introduction
2016

Jason Brennan is the Robert J. and Elizabeth Flanagan Family Chair and Professor of Strategy, Economics, Ethics, and Public Policy at the McDonough School of Business at Georgetown University. He specializes in political philosophy and applied ethics.

Imagine Virtuous Vani cares deeply about others and is willing to do whatever it takes to save lives. She believes that processed sugar is a scourge killing Americans. So one day she packs a pistol, invades the local 7-Eleven, and declares, "This here gun says you can't sell Big Gulps anymore."

Principled Peter believes that you don't give enough money to charity. You're living high while people die. One day he sends you an email: "FYI: I hacked into your bank account. I transferred a third of it to poor single moms."

Decent Dani thinks you should buy American rather than German cars. After all, your fellow citizens provide you with roads, schools, and police. You owe them some business. He finds you shopping at a foreign dealer, pulls out a Taser, and says, "You know what? I'll let you buy that BMW, but only if you first pay me $3,000."

You'd probably regard Vani, Peter, and Dani as criminals. How dare they treat you like that? You'd want the police to arrest them.

But there's a puzzle here. While the police would indeed arrest Vani, Peter, and Dani, they're also happy to help other people — bureaucrats in Washington, Berlin, or Ottawa — do the same things Vani, Peter, and Dani want to do. So this set of examples suggests a few questions: What, if anything, explains why it's wrong for Peter to take a third of your income but not wrong for the government tax office to do so? What, if anything, justifies the Food and Drug Administration in determining what you can and can't eat but forbids Vani from doing so? In general, governments claim the right to do things ordinary people may not do. What, if anything, justifies that?

This is one of the central questions in political philosophy.

5
Do We Ever Really Get Out of Anarchy?

Alfred G. Cuzán, Ph.D.
Journal of Libertarian Studies

Alfred G. Cuzán is a distinguished university Professor of Political Science at the University of West Florida.

Introduction

A major point of dispute among libertarian theorists and thinkers today as always revolves around the age-old question of whether man can live in *total* anarchy or whether the minimal state is absolutely necessary for the maximization of freedom. Lost in this dispute is the question of whether man is *capable* of getting out of anarchy at all. Can we really abolish anarchy and set up a Government in its place? Most people, regardless of their ideological preferences, simply assume that the abolition of anarchy is possible, that they live under Government and that anarchy would be nothing but chaos and violence.[1]

The purpose of this paper is to question this venerated assumption and to argue that the escape from anarchy is impossible, that we always live in anarchy, and that the real question is what kind of anarchy we live under, market anarchy or non-market (political) anarchy. Further, it is argued that political anarchies are of two types — hierarchical or plural. The more pluralist political anarchy is, the more it resembles market anarchy. The performance of hierarchical and plural anarchies is evaluated in terms of their ability to minimize the level of force in society. It is shown that plural anarchies are much less violent than hierarchical anarchies. We conclude that the real question libertarians must solve is not whether minimalism or anarchy, but which type of anarchy, market or political, hierarchical or plural, is most conducive to the maximization of freedom.

I.

Anarchy is a social order without Government, subject only to the economic laws of the market. Government is an agent external to society, a "third party" with the power to coerce all other parties to relations in society into accepting its conceptions of those relations. The idea of Government as an agent external to society is analogous to the idea of God as an intervener in human affairs. For an atheist, a good analogy might be to assume that omnipotent Martians fill the role we usually ascribe to Government, *i.e.*, an external designer and enforcer of rules of behavior by which everyone subject to those rules *must* abide.

However, that the idea of Government exists is no proof of its empirical existence.[2] Few of us would be convinced by an argument such as: "I believe the idea of God is possible, therefore God exists." Yet such is the structure of the argument which underlies all assumptions about the existence of Government. That societies may have some form of organization they call the "government" is no reason to conclude that those "governments" are empirical manifestations of the *idea* of Government.

A closer look at these earthly "governments" reveals that they do not get us out of anarchy at all. They simply replace one form of anarchy by another and hence do not give us real Government. Let's see how this is so.

Wherever earthly "governments" are established or exist, anarchy is officially prohibited for all members of society, usually referred to as subjects or citizens. They can no longer relate to each other on their own terms — whether as merchants at a port or a vigilante unit and its prey in the open desert or the streets of Newark, N.J. Rather, all members of society must accept an external "third party" — a government — into their relationships, a third party with the coercive powers to enforce its judgments and punish detractors.

For example, when a thief steals my wallet at a concert, I am legally required to rely on the services of members of a third party to catch him (policemen), imprison him (jailers), try him (prosecutors, judges, even "public" defenders), judge him (trial by a group of individuals coerced into jury duty by the courts), and acquit or punish him (prisons, hangmen). At most, I am legally authorized to catch him, but I am prohibited from settling the account myself. Such prohibitions have reached tragi-comic proportions, as when government punishes victims of crime for having defended themselves beyond the limits authorized by "law." In short, I or any other citizen or subject must accept the rulings of government in our relations with others. We are required to abide by the law of this "third party."

However, such a "third party" arrangement for society is non-existent among those who exercise the power of government themselves. In other words, there is no "third party" to make and enforce judgments among the individual members who make up the third party itself. The rulers still remain in a state of anarchy *vis-à-vis* each other. They settle disputes *among themselves*, without regard for a Government (an entity outside themselves). Anarchy still exists. Only whereas without government it was market or natural anarchy, it is now a *political* anarchy, an anarchy inside power.[3]

Take, for example, the rulers of our own Federal government. It is a group composed of congressmen, judges, a president and a vice-president, top-level bureaucrats in civilian and military agencies, and their armies of assistants who together oversee the work of the millions of public employees who man the several Federal bureaucracies. These individuals together make and enforce laws, edicts, regulations and vast arrays of orders of all kinds by which all members of society must abide.

Yet, in their relations among each other, they remain largely "lawless." Nobody *external to the group* writes and enforces rules governing the relations among them. At most, the rulers are bound by flexible constraints imposed by a "constitution" which they, in any case, interpret and enforce among and upon themselves. The Supreme Court, after all, is only a *branch* of the government, composed of people appointed by and subjected to pressures from other members of the government. Moreover, their decisions are enforced by some *other* branch of the government, the executive, over whom the judges have no power, only authority. Further, the Congress, through vocal pressures and the manipulation of budgetary allocations to the judiciary, also exercises pressures which the judges must contend with. Similarly, congressmen have no "third party" arbiters either among themselves or in their relations with the executive. Furthermore, even the various Federal bureaucracies and all their component parts are without a "third party" to govern their relations, internally or externally. In short, looking *inside* the government reveals that the rulers remain in a state of anarchy among themselves. They live in a political anarchy.

The anarchic relations of government officials can be illustrated in the following example: Suppose that a congressman manages to divert streams of moneys from the government's flows to his private estate. This is a crime, theft, the stealing of money. But from whom? From you or me? Only in the sense that we were coerced into contributing to the public treasury which the congressman viewed as booty. It was no longer ours, it belonged to someone else. But who? Why, the members of the government who have the power to allocate those flows of resources.

In short, the congressman stole from *other* government officials — congressmen, bureaucrats, a president, etc. But what is done about the crime? Is the congressman publicly accused, indicted, and tried for his crime like an ordinary citizen who steals from another citizen? Sometimes; but what usually happens is a flurry of political maneuverings at high levels; mutual threats are delivered behind closed doors and forces marshalled against each other; occasional battles take place in which either reputations are destroyed, money changes hands, or resource flows or access to them are altered.

The hue and cry is soon forgotten, the congressman receives a "clean bill of health" by the prosecution, or the charges are dismissed or not pressed, and the congressman wins re-election at the polls. Occasionally, if the infractor was a weak or declining public figure, or one much hated by his colleagues, he is brought before the courts, tried, and given a minimal or even a suspended sentence. In most instances, small fish near the bottom of the bureaucracies are sacrificed for the crimes higher-ups either directed, profited from or sanctioned. But make no mistake: no "third party," no Government, ever made or enforced a judgment. The rulers of the government themselves literally took the law into their own hands and produced what outside the government would be considered "vigilante justice."

In short, society is *always* in anarchy. A government only abolishes anarchy among what are called "subjects" or "citizens," but among those who rule, anarchy prevails.

Figure 1 illustrates this situation. The circle on the left shows a state of true or market or natural anarchy, in which all members of society relate to each other in strictly bilateral transactions without third party intervention. The circle on the right shows the situation prevalent under government. In the higher compartment we see individuals whose relations among each other are no longer bilateral. All relations are legally "triangular," in that all members of society are forced to accept the rule of government in their transactions. However, in the lower compartment, inside the "government" itself, relations among the rulers remain in anarchy.

Fig. 1

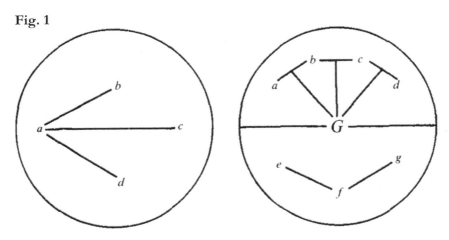

II.

Having shown that anarchy is not completely abolished by government but reserved, so to speak, for the rulers only, among whom it is the prevailing condition, it is proper to inquire whether this is beneficial for society. Its proponents and defenders claim that without government society would be in a state of intolerable violence. Thus it is logical to inquire whether the effect of government is to increase, reduce, or in no way affect the level of violence in society.

Is political anarchy less violent than natural or market anarchy? Minimalists argue that it is, provided government is strictly confined to the

Do We Ever Really Get Out of Anarchy?

role of acting as a third party in property disputes. While government necessarily involves the use of limited violence, minimalists say, the level of violence in a minimal state would be lower than that in natural anarchy.

Fig. 2

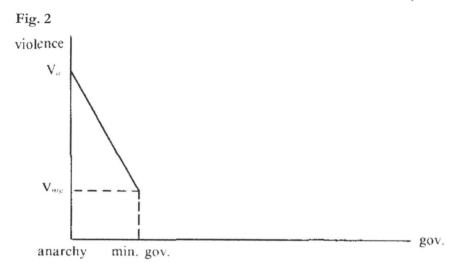

Figure 2 illustrates the minimalist idea. By providing the amount of government of the minimal state, the level of violence in society drops below the level in natural anarchy. Presumably, judging from the vociferous anti-interventionist stand of the minimalists, if government grows beyond the size of a limited state, either there are no further gains in reducing violence — and thus more government is pointless and costly in other ways — and/or beyond a certain size the level of violence in society rises to meet or perhaps surpass the amount of natural violence. (See Figure 3.)

Fig. 3 *

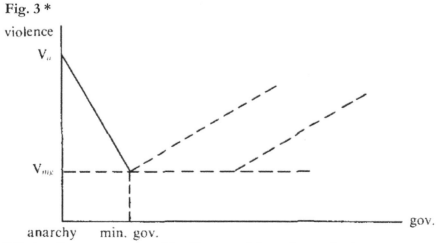

* Broken lines represent possible effects on violence from enlarging government beyond the minimal state.

That violence under political anarchy might exceed the violence of market anarchy is not inconceivable. Hitler's concentration camps and Stalin's Gulags are evidence of violence in such proportions that one could hardly venture to say that natural anarchy would be *worse* than that. Similarly, the political anarchy of nation-states has produced interstate violence on such a scale that it must give pause even to the most devoted disciple of Hobbes.[4]

A third view is possible and theoretically the most interesting. This view says that the relation between government (the substitution of political for market anarchy) and violence, is qualified by a third element, the *structure* of the government, measured along a centralization dimension. The more authoritative powers are dispersed among numerous political units, the more pluralistic the government. The more centralized the structure, *i.e.*, the more authoritative powers are concentrated, the more hierarchical the government. Note that the more hierarchical the government, the more government is run on the assumption of an ultimate arbiter. In other words, the more centralized the structure, the greater the effort to *create* a single "third party" inside the government itself in the form of a God-like figure such as a Hitler, Stalin, Mao or Castro. Such a "third party," however, remains in complete anarchy from the rest of his countrymen and the rest of the world.

The more plural the politics of a country, the more the rulers behave without any reference to a "third party" and thus the more society resembles natural anarchy. The less plural or more hierarchical the politics of a country, the more society appears to be ruled by a truly "external" element, a God-like figure sent from the heavens of history, religion or ideology.

A cursory glance at contemporary societies and recent history shows that, empirically, it is precisely those societies ruled by such earthly personifications of Government where the level of violence in the form of political repression, coercion and intimidation is highest. In contrast, violence is lowest in societies with highly pluralistic politics, such as Switzerland. This is true even in the "communist" world: the more pluralistic communist politics of Poland or Yugoslavia are less violent than the more hierarchical politics of the Soviet Union. Similarly, in the Western world, the more pluralistic politics of the United States are less violent than those of Italy, where politics are much more hierarchical.

But why would the degree of centralization determine whether political anarchy is violent in hierarchical states such as China or Cuba, and relatively peaceful in pluralist states such as India and Costa Rica? The answer may be simply in the fact that centralized states are more likely to make mistakes than decentralized states.[5] Political mistakes are in the form of *wrong* or *false* conceptions about the nature of bilateral relations in society and in politics, such as conceptions held about the relation between worker and capitalist in communist states. If judgments are wrong, they are not voluntarily accepted by one or both of the parties to the transactions. Under those conditions, the only way for the rulers to enforce their "third party" conceptions is to use force, which, under different conditions, will or will not be resisted by the opposition.

In a pluralist government, wrong conceptions about bilateral relations in society are less likely to occur. This is because there are numerous units independently interacting with each other and with the citizens and subjects, so that more and better information about the effect of these judgments on bilateral relations exist. Moreover, wrong conceptions are more easily checked as various autonomous political units, each capable of marshalling political resources of their own, confront each other in a successive series of political transactions.

In a hierarchical government, however, not even the members of the government are permitted to settle disputes among themselves. *All* relations are subjected to the judgment of some supreme leader. Such a leader must maintain a vast network of spies and enforcers to accomplish such a superhuman feat. Of course, one man's ability to control the behavior of others is quite limited, and so even in Hitler's Germany, truly Machiavellian, feudalistic deals were made right under the Fuehrer's nose. Naturally, such arrangements were prohibited so everyone lived in a state of fearful insecurity, not knowing when his enemies would succeed in turning Hitler against him.[6]

Whether this explanation is a good one or not, we still have with us the *explanandum*, i.e., the fact that hierarchical politics are more violent than pluralist politics. But if society with a pluralist political anarchy experiences less violence than societies with a hierarchical or "governed" government, isn't it logical to inquire whether natural anarchy is less violent than political anarchy? Why should the relation between government and violence be curvilinear? Isn't it possible that it is upward sloping *all* the way, so that government always produces more violence than the market?

Summary and Conclusion

We have shown that anarchy, like matter, never disappears — it only changes form. Anarchy is either market anarchy or political anarchy. Pluralist, decentralized political anarchy is less violent than hierarchical political anarchy. Hence, we have reason to hypothesize that market anarchy could be less violent than political anarchy. Since market anarchy can be shown to outperform political anarchy in efficiency and equity in *all other respects*,[7] why should we expect anything different now? Wouldn't we be justified to expect that market anarchy produces less violence in the enforcement of property rights than political anarchy? After all, the market is the best economizer of all — wouldn't it also economize on violence better than government does, too?

NOTES

1. Even Gordon Tullock writes, "If, as I believe is correct, people under anarchy are every bit as selfish as they are now, we would have the Hobbesian jungle..." From the point of view of this paper, it is interesting that in the very next sentence he adds: "...[W]e would be unable to distinguish a fully corrupt government from no government." Gordon Tullock, "Corruption and Anarchy," in Gordon Tullock (Ed.) *Further Explorations in the Theory of Anarchy* (Blacksburg, Virginia: University Publications, 1974).

2. Paul Craig Roberts, in *Alienation and the Soviet Economy* (Albuquerque: University of New Mexico Press, 1971), argues similarly that to be able to conceive of central planning is no proof of its empirical possibility. Roberts shows that formally planned economies like the Soviet Union are not centrally planned at all, but are plural economies guided by non-market signals. Roberts' conclusion that central planning does not exist is analogous to my own conclusion that Government does not exist either. I am grateful to Murray Rothbard for pointing out the parallels in the two arguments.

While the body of this paper was being typed, I read Michael Bakunin *God and the State* (New York: Dover Publications, 1970), and was struck by the similarities between Bakunin's argument against God and my argument against Government. This is not surprising, since many assumptions used to justify government refer to man's evil nature. It's as if government took God's place on earth to keep evil humans in line. That governments are themselves made up of ordinary human beings who remain in a state of anarchy among themselves seems to have escaped those who adhere to this view.

3. Of course, the rulers of any government have as their power base interest groups in and *out* of government. The leaders of non-governmental interest groups often hold the key to the political survival of even the most powerful politicians. Hence, the strict dichotomy between governmental and non-governmental members of society breaks down. Around the edges of government, many private individuals live in a state of anarchy *vis-à-vis* government officials. George Meany is probably as good an example as any. I am indebted to my colleague Cal Clark for pointing this out.

Also living in anarchy *vis-à-vis* government officials are all those members of underground criminal organizations which supply consumers with a vast array of illegal goods and services. That the CIA made deals with top gangsters to carry out some of its missions should not come as a surprise. Most police departments probably have similar relations with local crime chiefs.

4. This is an argument which Murray Rothbard makes and which implies

that true archists should logically favor a single world government in order to abolish anarchy among nation-states. Yet few of them do. (Murray Rothbard, in letter to the author, September 21, 1978; and Walter Block, in letter to the author, October 26, 1978.)

5. See Gordon Tullock, *The Politics of Bureaucracy* (Washington, D.C.: The Public Affairs Press, 1965), for a full theoretical development of this idea.

6. See Albert Speer, *Inside the Third Reich* (New York: Avon Books, 1970), Part II.

7. Murray Rothbard, *Power and Market* (Kansas City: Sheed Andrews and McMeel, Inc., 1970).

*Many thanks to Murray Rothbard and Walter Block for their encouragement and comments on an earlier draft of this paper. My colleagues Cal Clark, Stew Ropp and Paul Sagal of New Mexico State University also provided helpful criticisms. Janet Garcia gracefully typed the manuscript.

6
What It Means to Be an Anarcho-Capitalist

Stephan Kinsella, J.D.
LewRockwell.com
2004

> Stephan Kinsella is an attorney and libertarian writer in Houston. He was previously General Counsel for Applied Optoelectronics, Inc., a partner with Duane Morris, and Adjunct Law Professor at South Texas College of Law.

Libertarian opponents of anarchy are attacking a straw man. Their arguments are usually utilitarian in nature and amount to "but anarchy won't *work*" or "we *need* the (things provided by the) state." But these attacks are confused at best, if not disingenuous. To be an anarchist does not mean you think anarchy will "work" (whatever that means); nor that you predict it will or "can" be achieved. It is possible to be a pessimistic anarchist, after all. To be an anarchist only means that you believe that aggression is not justified, and that states necessarily employ aggression. And, therefore, that states, and the aggression they necessarily employ, are unjustified. It's quite simple, really. It's an ethical view, so no surprise it confuses utilitarians.

Accordingly, anyone who is not an anarchist must maintain either: (a) aggression is justified; or (b) states (in particular, minimal states) do not necessarily employ aggression.

Proposition (b) is plainly false. States always tax their citizens, which is a form of aggression. They always outlaw competing defense agencies, which also amounts to aggression. (Not to mention the countless victimless crime laws that they inevitably, and without a single exception in history, enforce on the populace. Why minarchists think minarchy is even possible boggles the mind.)

As for (a), well, socialists and criminals also feel aggression is justified. This does not make it so. Criminals, socialists, and anti-anarchists have yet to show how aggression — the initiation of force against innocent victims — is justified. No surprise; it is not possible to show this. But criminals don't feel compelled to justify aggression; why should advocates of the state feel compelled to do so?

Conservative and minarchist-libertarian criticism of anarchy on the grounds that it won't "work" or is not "practical" is just confused. Anarchists don't (necessarily) predict anarchy will be achieved — I for one don't think it will. But that does not mean states are justified.

Consider an analogy. Conservatives and libertarians all agree that private crime (murder, robbery, rape) is unjustified, and "should" not occur. Yet no matter how good most men become, there will always be at least some small element who will resort to crime. Crime will always be with us. Yet we still condemn crime and work to reduce it.

Is it logically possible that there could be no crime? Sure. Everyone could voluntarily choose to respect others' rights. Then there would be no crime. It's easy to imagine. But given our experience with human nature and interaction, it is safe to say that there will always be crime. Nevertheless, we still proclaim crime to be evil and unjustified, in the face of the inevitability of its recurrence. So to my claim that crime is immoral, it would just be stupid and/or insincere to reply, "but that's an impractical view" or "but that won't work," "since there will always be crime." The fact that there will always be crime — that not everyone will voluntarily respect others' rights — does not mean that it's "impractical" to oppose it; nor does it mean that crime is justified. It does not mean there is some "flaw" in the proposition that *crime is wrong*.

Likewise, to my claim that the state and its aggression is unjustified, it is disingenuous and/or confused to reply, "anarchy won't work" or is "impractical" or "unlikely to ever occur."[1] The view that the state is unjustified is a normative or ethical position. The fact that not enough people are willing to respect their neighbors' rights to allow anarchy to emerge, *i.e.*, the fact that enough people (erroneously) support the legitimacy of the state to permit it to exist, does not mean that the state, and its aggression, are justified.[2]

Other utilitarian replies like "but we need a state" do not contradict the claim that states employ aggression and that aggression is unjustified. It simply means that the state-advocate does not mind the initiation of force against innocent victims — *i.e.*, he shares the criminal/socialist mentality. The private criminal thinks his own need is all that matters; he is willing to commit violence to satisfy his needs; to hell with what is right and wrong. The advocate of the state thinks that his opinion that "we" "need" things justifies committing or condoning violence against innocent individuals. It is as plain as that. Whatever this argument is, it is not libertarian. It is not opposed to aggression. It is in favor of something else — making sure certain public "needs" are met, despite the cost — but not peace and cooperation. The criminal, gangster, socialist, welfare-statist, and even minarchist all share this: they are willing to condone naked aggression, for *some* reason. The details vary, but the result is the same — innocent lives are trampled by physical assault. Some have the stomach for this; others are more civilized

— libertarian, one might say — and prefer peace over violent struggle.

As there are criminals and socialists among us, it is no surprise that there is a degree of criminal-mindedness in most people. After all, the state rests upon the tacit consent of the masses, who have erroneously accepted the notion that states are legitimate. But none of that means the criminal enterprises condoned by the masses are justified.

It's time for libertarians to take a stand. Are you for aggression, or against it?

NOTES

1. Another point: in my view, we are about as likely to achieve minarchy as we are to achieve anarchy. *I.e.*, both are remote possibilities. What is striking is that almost every criticism of "impracticality" that minarchist hurl at anarchy is also true of minarchy itself. Both are exceedingly unlikely. Both require massive changes in views among millions of people. Both rest on presumptions that most people simply don't care much about.

2. Though the case for anarchy does not depend on its likelihood or "feasibility," any more than the case against private crime depends on there never being any acts of crime, anarchy is clearly possible. There is anarchy among nations, for example. There is also anarchy within government, as pointed out in the seminal and neglected *Journal of Libertarian Studies* article by Alfred G. Cuzán, "Do We Ever Really Get Out of Anarchy?" Cuzán argues that even the government itself is in anarchy, internally — the President does not literally force others in government to obey his comments, after all; they obey them voluntarily, due to a recognized, hierarchical structure. Government's (political) anarchy is not a good anarchy, but it demonstrates anarchy is possible — indeed, that we never really get out of it. And Shaffer makes the insightful point that we are in "anarchy" with our neighbors. If most people did not already have the character to voluntarily respect most of their neighbors' rights, society and civilization would be impossible. Most people are good enough to permit civilization to occur, despite the existence of some degree of public and private crime. It is conceivable that the degree of goodness could rise — due to education or more universal economic prosperity, say — sufficient to make support for the legitimacy of states evaporate. It's just very unlikely.

7
Six Questions for Statists

Stefan Molyneux, M.A.
Practical Anarchy: The Freedom of the Future
2017

Stefan Molyneux is the founder and host of Freedomain.

When considering statist objections to anarchic solutions, the six questions below are most useful.

1. Does the government actually *solve* the problem in question?

People often say that government courts "solve" the problem of injustice. However, these courts can take many years to render a verdict — and cost the plaintiff and defendant hundreds of thousands of dollars or more. Government courts are also used to harass and intimidate, creating a "chilling effect" for unpopular opinions or groups. Thus I find it essential to question the embedded premises of statism: Do State armies actually defend citizens? Does State policing actually protect private property? Does State welfare actually solve the problem of poverty? Does the war on drugs actually solve the problem of addiction and crime? Do State prisons actually rehabilitate prisoners and reduce crime?

It can be very tempting to fall into the trap of thinking that the existing statist approach is actually a solution — but I try to avoid taking that for granted, since it is so rarely the case.

2. Can the criticism of the anarchic solution be equally applied to the statist solution?

One of the most common objections to a stateless society is the fear that a political monopoly could somehow emerge from a free market of competing justice agencies. In other words, anarchism is rejected because it contains the mere *possibility* of political monopoly. However, if political monopoly is such a terrible evil, then a statist society — which is founded on just such a political monopoly — must be rejected even more firmly, just as we would always choose the mere *possibility* of cancer over actually *having* cancer.

3. Is anarchy accepted as a core value in nonpolitical spheres?

In my last book, *Everyday Anarchy*, I pointed out the numerous spheres in society where anarchy is both valued and defended, such as dating, career choices, education and so on. If anarchy is dismissed as "bad" overall, then it also must be "bad" in these other spheres as well. Unless the person criticizing anarchy is willing to advocate for a Ministry of Dating, the value of anarchy in certain spheres must at least be recognized. Thus anarchy cannot be rejected as an overall negative — and its admitted value and productivity must at least be accepted as *potentially* valuable in other spheres as well.

4. Would the person advocating statism perform State functions himself?

Most of us recognize and accept the right to use violence in an extremity of self-defense. Those who support statism recognize that, in this realm, State police merely formalize a right that everyone already has, namely the right of self-defense. A policeman can use force to protect a citizen from being attacked, just as that citizen can use force himself. However, if someone argues that it is moral to use force to take money from people to pay for public schools, would he be willing to use this force *himself*? Would he be willing to go door to door with a gun to extract money for public schools? Would he be willing to extend this right to everyone in society? If not, then he has created two opposing ethical categories — the State police, to whom this use of violence is *moral* — and everyone else, to whom this use of violence is *immoral*. How can these opposing moral categories be justified?

5. Can something be both voluntary and coercive at the same time?

Everyone recognizes that an act cannot be both "rape" and "lovemaking" simultaneously. Rape requires force, because the victim is unwilling; lovemaking does not. Because no action can be both voluntary and coercive at the same time, statists cannot appeal to the principle of "voluntarism" when defending the violence of the State. Statists cannot say that we "agree" to be taxed, and then say that taxation must be coercive. If we agree to taxation, the coercion is unnecessary — if we do not agree to taxation, then we are coerced against our will.

6. Does political organization change human nature?

If people care enough about the poor to vote for state welfare programs, then they will care enough about the poor to fund private charities. If people care enough about the uneducated to vote for state schools, they will care enough to donate to private schools. Removing the State does not fundamentally alter human nature. The benevolence and wisdom that democracy relies on will not be magically transformed into cold selfishness the moment that the State ends. Statism relies on maturity and benevolence on the part of the voters, the politicians, and government workers. If this maturity and benevolence is not present, the State is a mere brutal tyranny, and must be abolished. If the majority of people *are* mature and benevolent — as I believe — then the State is an unnecessary overhead, and far too prone to violent injustices to be allowed to continue. In other words, people cannot be called "virtuous" only when it serves the statist argument, and then "selfish" when it does not.

There are a number of other principles, which are more specific to particular circumstances, but the six described above will show up repeatedly.

8
The Argument for Free Markets: Morality vs. Efficiency

Walter E. Williams, Ph.D.

Walter Edward Williams (1936–2020) was an American economist, commentator, and academic.

"Freedom can be preserved only if it is treated as a supreme principle which must not be sacrificed for any particular advantage."

– F.A. Hayek

Freedom's First Principle

Freedom's first principle is: *Each person owns himself.* The transition from socialism to capitalism and the preservation of capitalism require what philosopher David Kelley calls the entrepreneurial outlook on life, which he describes, in part, as "a sense of self-ownership, a conviction that one's life is one's own, not something for which one must answer to some higher power."[1] Once we accept self-ownership as a first principle, we readily discover what constitutes just and unjust conduct. Unjust conduct is simply any conduct that violates an individual's property rights in himself when he himself has not infringed upon the property rights of others. Therefore, acts like murder, rape, and theft, whether done privately or collectively, are unjust because they violate private property. There is broad consensus that government-sponsored murder and rape are unjust; however, not as much consensus is reached regarding theft. Theft being defined as forcibly taking the rightful property of one person for the benefit of another.

For individual freedom to be viable, it must be a part of the shared values of a society, and there must be an institutional framework to preserve it against encroachments by majoritarian or government will. Constitutions and laws alone cannot guarantee the survival of personal freedom as is apparent where Western-style constitutions and laws have been exported to countries not having a tradition of individual freedom. U.S. articulation of the right to individual autonomy is enunciated in our Declaration of Independence:

The Argument for Free Markets: Morality vs. Efficiency

> We hold these truths to be self-evident, that all men are created equal, that they are endowed by the Creator with certain unalienable rights, that among these are life, liberty and the pursuit of happiness.

That statement, which played such an important role in the rebellion against England and in the establishment of the U.S. Constitution, was the outgrowth of libertarian ideas of such thinkers as John Locke, Montesquieu, and Sir William Blackstone.

Even in societies with a tradition of freedom, such as the United States, the values supporting that freedom have suffered erosion and have proven an insufficient safeguard against encroachment by the state. As is so often the case, political liberty (democracy) has been used to redistribute income and wealth. The redistributive state, in turn, has had a stifling effect on economic liberty and has reduced individual freedom.

Ultimately, the struggle to achieve and preserve freedom must take place in the habits and minds of individuals. And, as admonished by the Constitution of the State of North Carolina (Art. I, Sec. 35), "The frequent reference to fundamental principles is absolutely necessary to preserve the blessings of liberty." It is those fundamental principles that deliver economic efficiency and wealth, not the other way around. Fundamental moral principles or values are determined in the arena of civil society. Values such as thrift, hard work, honesty, trust and cooperative behavior, based on shared norms, are the keys to improving the human condition and provide the undergirding for a free market economy. Just as important are such social institutions as respect for private property, sanctity of contracts, educational institutions, clubs, charities, churches, and families. All those institutions provide the glue to hold society together in terms of common values and provide for the transmission of those values to successive generations. Too often informal institutions and local networks are trivialized and greater favor is given to the intellectual's narrow conception of what constitutes knowledge and wisdom.

The importance of informal networks such as friends, church members, neighbors, and families cannot be underestimated — as demonstrated in the following example of small proprietorships.[2] The critical determinants of a proprietor's success are perseverance, character, ability, and other personal characteristics. Banks seldom finance the establishment of such business. Most small businesses are financed through friends and family. The reason is that those are the people who have the lowest cost in acquiring the necessary information about the proprietor's characteristics deemed critical for success. Also, friends and family, who lend the proprietor money, have a personal stake in the business and have an incentive to moderate their likely bias in favor of the borrower. Clearly, a formal lending institution could query friends and relatives. However, the information obtained would have greater bias because friends and relatives would not have sufficient stake in the business to offset any personal bias they had in favor of the borrower.

Institutions and Wealth

F.A. Hayek refers to the rules of several property determined by traditions and values. Those rules consisted in what David Hume called "the stability of possessions," "transference by consent," and "the keeping of promises."[3] Nations that have respected the rules of several property have produced social and economic climates far more conducive to the welfare of their citizens than nations that have failed to respect property rights. People in countries with larger amounts of economic freedom, such as the United States, Canada, Australia, Hong Kong, Japan, and Taiwan, are far richer and have greater human rights protections than people in countries with limited free markets such as Russia, Albania, China, and every country in Africa.

The role of private property and free markets in creating wealth is often overlooked. Factors such as natural-resource endowment, population size, and previous conditions (colonialism) are claimed to explain wealth. Yet those factors cannot explain human betterment. The United States and Canada have relatively small populations, abundant natural resources, and are wealthy. However, if low population density and abundant natural resources were adequate explanations of wealth, one would expect the former Soviet Union and countries on the continents of Africa and South America to be wealthy. Instead, the former Soviet Union, Africa, and South America are home to many of the world's poorest and most miserable people.

A history of colonialism is often given as an excuse for poverty but that is a bogus hypothesis. The world's richest country, the United States, was formerly a colony. Canada, Australia, and New Zealand were colonies — and Hong Kong remains a colony. A far better explanation of wealth are the values and traditions that produce the rules of several property. Economics is not an independent variable whose laws are unaffected by the institutional framework within which it operates. Economic efficiency is a by-product of pre-existing cultural and moral norms.

The Intellectual Defense of Liberty

All too often defenders of free-market capitalism base their defense on the demonstration that capitalism is more efficient in terms of resource allocation and, hence, leads to a larger bundle of goods than socialism and other forms of statism. However, as Milton Friedman frequently points out, economic efficiency and greater wealth should be promoted as simply a side-benefit of free markets. The intellectual defense of free-market capitalism should focus on its moral superiority. In other words, even if free enterprise were not more efficient than other forms of human organization, it is morally superior because it is rooted in voluntary relationships rather than force and coercion, and it respects the sanctity of the individual.

The wealth created by free-market capitalism also cultivates civil society. For most of human history, individuals have had to simply eke out a living. With the rise of capitalism and the concomitant rise in human productivity, people were able to satisfy their physical needs with less and less time. Economic progress made it possible for people to have the time to develop spiritually and culturally. The rise of capitalism enabled the gradual extension of civilization to greater and greater numbers of people. As the wealth of nations grew, people had the means to become educated in the liberal arts and to gain greater knowledge about the world around them. The rise of capitalism enabled ordinary people to attend the arts, afford recreation, and contemplate more fulfilling and interesting life activities, and engage in other culturally enriching activities that were formerly only within the purview of the rich.

Demystification of the State

A.V. Dicey wrote:

> The beneficial effect of State intervention, especially in the form of legislation, is direct, immediate, and so to speak visible, whilst its evil effects are gradual and indirect, and lie outside our sight... Hence the majority of mankind must almost of necessity look with undue favour upon government intervention. This natural bias can be counteracted only by the existence, in a given society... of a presumption or prejudice in favour of individual liberty, that is of laissez-faire.[4]

One can hardly determine the casualties of war simply by looking at survivors. We must ask what happened to those whom we do not see. Similarly, when evaluating interventionist public policy, we cannot evaluate it simply by looking at its beneficiaries. We must discover its victims. Most often the victims of public policy are invisible. To garner greater public support against government command and control, we must somehow find a way to make those victims visible.

In all interventionist policy there are those who are beneficiaries and those who are victims. In most cases the beneficiaries are highly visible and the victims are invisible. A good example is the minimum wage law. After enactment of an increase in the minimum wage law, politicians accompanied by television crews readily point to people who have benefitted from the legislation. The beneficiaries are those with a fatter paycheck. Thus, the politician can lay claim to the wisdom of his legislation that increased minimum wages. Moreover, the politician is also a beneficiary since those now earning higher wages will remember him when election time comes around. By parading minimum wage beneficiaries across the stage, those who oppose minimum wage increases can be readily portrayed as having a callous, meanspirited disregard for interests of low-wage workers.

A political strategy of those who support liberty should be that of exposing the invisible victims of minimum wage laws. We need to show those who have lost their jobs, or do not become employed in the first place, because their productivity did not warrant being employed at the minimum wage. We should find a way to demonstrate jobs destroyed by minimum wages such as busboys, gasoline station attendants, and movie ushers. We must show how marginally profitable firms have been forced out of business, though surviving firms may have the same number of employees. We should show how capital was artificially substituted for labor as a result of higher mandated wages and how firms have adjusted their production techniques in order to economize on labor. The particular adjustments firms make in response to higher mandated wages are less important than the fact that adjustments will be made.

A more dramatic example of the invisible victims of interventionist state policy can be found in the regulation of medicines and medical devices, as in the case of the Food and Drug Administration (FDA) in the United States. Essentially, FDA officials can make two types of errors. They can err on the side of undercaution and approve a drug with dangerous unanticipated side effects. Or they can err on the side of overcaution, not approving a useful and safe drug, or creating costly and lengthy drug approval procedures.

Errors on the side of undercaution lead to embarrassment and possibly loss of bureaucratic careers and promotions because the victims of unsafe drugs will be visible through news stories of sick people, congressional investigations, and hearings. However, errors on the side of overcaution, through extensive delay in the approval of drugs — as in the cases of propranolol, Septra, and other drugs — impose virtually no costs on the FDA. Victims of FDA errors on the side of overcaution are mostly invisible to the press, the public, and politicians.

Those victims should be made visible. Once the FDA (or some other approving agency) approves a drug widely used elsewhere with no untoward effects, we should find people who died or needlessly suffered as a result of the FDA's delay. For political efficiency we cannot simply offer intellectual arguments. We must get pictures and stories of FDA victims in an effort to appeal to a sense of fair play, decency, and common sense among the citizenry. But there is also a role for intellectual arguments in the sense of teaching people that any meaningful use of "safe" must see safety as a set of tradeoffs rather than a category. The attempt to get a "safe" drug means that people will die or needlessly suffer during the time it takes to achieve greater safety. That toll must be weighted against the number of people who might die or become ill because of the drug's earlier availability and attendant unanticipated harmful side effects. People should also be taught to understand that if a 100 percent safe drug is ever achieved, it will be the only thing in this world that is 100 percent safe.

Another area of state interventionism, which particularly applies to less developed nations, is restrictive import laws and regulations. Restricting foreign imports as a means to save jobs sounds plausible. Adding to the appeal of restrictive trade policy is the fact that its beneficiaries are highly visible while its victims are invisible.

Using an example of the American experience may suggest a political strategy. Most people fully understand that import restrictions raise the cost of products but may have little understanding of its systemic effects. Arthur Denzau of the Center for the Study of American Business found that "voluntary restraints" on imported steel saved nearly 17,000 jobs in the steel industry. However, the higher steel prices, resulting from the restraints, led to a loss of 52,000 jobs in American steel-using industries. On balance steel restrictions led to a net loss of 35,400 jobs.[5] The process is easy to understand. Caterpillar Company uses steel to produce heavy construction equipment. Trade restrictions caused higher steel prices that in turn raised Caterpillar's production costs. Higher costs made Caterpillar less competitive in both domestic and international markets, which led Caterpillar to downsize its labor force. As a result, we see more Japanese- and Korean-produced heavy equipment in the United States. Importing finished products, by the way, is just another way to import steel.

In addition to causing a net loss of jobs, trade restrictions are costly to consumers. According to estimates, the Reagan administration's "voluntary import restraints" on Japanese cars increased the price of Japanese cars sold in the United States by $900 and increased the price of U.S. cars by $350, for a total cost to American consumers of $4.3 billion. That price tag translates into a cost of $200,000 per year for each job saved in Detroit.[6] It would have been cheaper to have given each Detroit auto worker, laid off by freer trade, a check for $60,000 a year so they could buy a vacation residence in Miami. That way, collectively, we would have been better off to the tune of $140,000 per job saved. Of course, that policy choice would not have been politically feasible because the costs would have been apparent and taxpayers would have refused to pay for the free vacation. It is not only auto workers with whom the nation could have made the trade. According to the Federal Trade Commission, quotas on textile products from Hong Kong cost consumers $34,500 per year for each job saved for American textile workers earning $7,600 to $10,700 annually.[7]

Identifying the invisible victims of trade restrictions may suggest a political strategy to fight such restrictions. One such strategy is to organize companies adversely affected by import restrictions, such as steel-using companies in the case of the U.S. import restrictions on steel.

Justice: Process vs. Results

At the heart of most interventionist policy is a vision of justice. Most often this vision evaluates the presence of justice by looking at results.

Social justice has considerable appeal and as such is used as justification for interventionist statism. There are several criticisms of the concept of social justice that Hayek has answered well, but defenders of personal liberty must make a greater effort to demystify the term and show that justice or fairness cannot be determined by examining results. The results people often turn to in order to determine the presence or absence of justice are educational and occupational status, income, life expectancy, and other socioeconomic factors. But justice or fairness cannot be determined by results. It is a process question.

Consider, for example, that three individuals play a regular game of poker. The typical game outcome is: individual A wins 75 percent of the time, while individuals B and C win 15 percent and 10 percent of the time, respectively. By knowing the game's result, nothing unambiguous can be said about whether there has been "poker justice." Individual A's disproportionate winnings are consistent with his being an astute player, clever cheater, or just plain lucky. The only way one can determine whether there has been poker justice is to examine the game's process. Process questions would include: Did the players play voluntarily? Were the poker rules neutral and unbiasedly applied? Was the game played without cheating? If the process were just, affirmative answers would be given to those three questions and there would be poker justice irrespective of the outcome. Thus, justice is really a process issue.

The most popular justification for the interventionist state is to create or ensure fairness and justice in the distribution of income. Considerable confusion, obfuscation, and demagoguery regarding the sources of income provide statists with copious quantities of ammunition to justify their redistributionist agenda. Income is not distributed. In a free society, income is earned. People serving one another through the provision of goods and services generate income.

We serve our fellow man in myriad ways. We bag his groceries, teach his children, entertain him, and heal his wounds. By doing so, we receive "certificates of performance." In the United States, we call these certificates dollars. Elsewhere they are called pesos, francs, marks, yen, and pounds. Those certificates stand as evidence (proof) of our service. The more valuable our service to our fellow man (as he determines), the greater the number of certificates of performance we receive and hence the greater our claim on goods and services. That free-market process promotes a moral discipline that says: Unless we are able and willing to serve our fellow man, we shall have no claim on what he produces. Contrast that moral discipline to the immorality of the welfare state. In effect the welfare state says: You do not have to serve your fellow man; through intimidation, threats, and coercion, we will take what he produces and give it to you.

The vision that sees income as being "distributed" implies a different scenario for the sources of income never made explicit. The vision that sees income as being distributed differs little from asserting that out there is a dealer of dollars. It naturally leads to the conclusion that if some people have fewer dollars than others, the dollar dealer is unfair; he is a racist, sexist, or a multi-nationalist. Therefore, justice and fairness require a re-dealing (income redistribution) of dollars. That way the ill-gotten gains of the few are returned to their "rightful" owners. That vision is the essence of the results-oriented view of justice underpinning the welfare state.

People who criticize the existing distribution of income as being unfair and demand government redistribution are really criticizing the process whereby income is earned. Their bottom line is that millions of individual decision makers did not do the right thing. Consider the wealth of billionaire Bill Gates, the founder of Microsoft. Gates earned billions because millions of individuals voluntarily spent their money on what they wanted — his products. For someone to say that Gates's income is unfair is the same as saying that the decisions of millions of consumers are wrong. To argue that Gates's income should be forcibly taken and given to others is to say that somehow third parties have a right to preempt voluntary decisions made by millions of traders.

When sources of income are viewed more realistically, we reach the conclusion that low income, for the most part, is a result of people not having sufficient capacity to serve their fellow man well rather than being victims of an unfair process. Low-income people simply do not have the skills to produce and do things their fellow man highly values. Seldom do we find poor highly productive individuals or nations. Those who have low incomes tend to have low skills and education and hence low productive capacity. Our challenge is to make those people (nations) more productive.

Another explanation of low income is that the rules of the game have been rigged. That is, people do have an ability to provide goods and services valued by their fellow man but are restricted from doing so. Among those rules are minimum wage laws, occupational and business licensure laws and regulations, and government-sponsored monopolies. Hence, another argument for free-market capitalism is that it is good for low-income, low-skilled people.

The Vision of Black Markets
We should always keep in mind the resiliency of markets. Despite the efforts of socialist regimes, markets tend to survive to one degree or another; they are an irrepressible part of human nature. As Adam Smith wrote, "It is the necessary... certain propensity in human nature... to truck, barter, and exchange one thing for another."[8] During the 70 years of the Soviet

experiment, with massive attempts to suppress markets (including jail, banishment, and death), markets in one form or another survived. The conditions for the formation of markets are always present and explain their resiliency. Those conditions are: (1) private ownership of property, (2) interaction between people who place different valuations on goods, and (3) individual will and self-interest.

Those conditions give rise to markets be they legal or illegal (black) markets. According to some estimates, up to 84 percent of the Soviet people purchased goods and services through the black market or *fartsovshiki*. The *fartsovshiki* was also a source of additional employment, and hence income, for as many as 20 million Soviet citizens.[9] According to *Automotive News*, 60 percent of Soviet citizens used black-market mechanics for auto repairs and another 30 percent purchased gasoline and parts from black-market distributors.[10]

Soviet officials could never eliminate black markets and one doubts that they wanted to. After all, the Soviet system may have survived as long as it did because some of its more uglier consequences were mitigated by the presence of black markets. Given the periodic shortages of life's necessities such as food and clothing, there may have been uncontrollable social disorder if Soviet citizens had to do without rather than have a black-market outlet to which they could turn to for relief.

The Soviet experience proves that man is by nature a capitalist. The transition from socialism to capitalism requires only that human nature be permitted to flourish.

Conclusion

The struggle to extend and preserve free markets must have as its primary focus the moral argument. State interventionists stand naked before well-thought-out moral arguments for private ownership of property, voluntary exchange, and the parity of markets. People readily understand moral arguments on a private basis — for example, one person does not have the right to use force against another to serve his own purposes. However, people often see government redistribution as an acceptable use of force. In a democratic welfare state that coercion is given an aura of legitimacy. The challenge is to convince people that a majority vote does not establish morality and that free markets are morally superior to other forms of human organization.

NOTES

1. Kelley, D. (1994) "The Entrepreneurial Life." *IOS Journal* 4 (December): 1, 4–6.
2. Sowell, T. (1980) *Knowledge and Decisions*. New York: Basic Books, 25.
3. Hayek, F.A. (1984) "The Origins and Effects of Our Morals: A Problem

for Science." In C. Nishiyama and K.R. Leube (Eds.) *The Essence of Hayek*, 318–30. Stanford, Calif.: Hoover Institution Press, 321.
4. Dicey, A.V. (1914) *Lectures on the Relation between Law and Public Opinion during the Nineteenth Century*. London: Macmillan, 257.
5. Denzau, A. (1987) *How Import Restraints Reduce Employment*. St. Louis: Center for the Study of American Business, Washington University, 12.
6. Tarr, D.G., and Morkre, M.E. (1984) *Aggregate Costs to the United States of Tariffs and Quotas on Imports: General Tariff Cuts and Removal of Quotas on Automobiles, Steel, Sugar, and Textiles*. Washington, D.C.: Federal Trade Commission, Bureau of Economics Staff Report, 57.
7. Morkre, M.E. (1984) *Import Quotas on Textiles: The Welfare Effects of United States Restrictions on Hong Kong*. Washington, D.C.: Federal Trade Commission, Bureau of Economics Staff Report, 27.
8. Smith, A. ([1776] 1976) *An Inquiry into the Nature and Causes of the Wealth of Nations*. Edwin Cannan, ed. Chicago: University of Chicago Press, 17.
9. Galuszka, P. (1989) "The Paradox of Perestroika." *Business Week*, 5 June: 66–67.
10. *Automotive News* (1985) "Auto Black Market Grows in Russia." 5 August.

9
Social Cooperation

Sheldon Richman

Sheldon Richman is the Executive Editor of the Libertarian Institute and a Contributing Editor at Antiwar.com.

At FEE's Advanced Austrian Economics Seminar last summer, more than one speaker mentioned that Ludwig von Mises considered a different title for the book we know as *Human Action*. The other title? *Social Cooperation*.

I've heard that story before, but this time it got me thinking: Would the free-market movement have been perceived differently by the outside world if Mises had used the other title? With the question phrased so narrowly, the answer is probably no. So let's broaden it: Would the free-market movement be perceived differently if its dominant theme was social cooperation rather than (rugged) individualism, self-reliance, independence, and other synonyms we're so fond of?

Maybe.

There's no mystery why that other title occurred to Mises. I haven't tried to make a count, but I would guess that "social cooperation" (or "human cooperation") is the second most-used phrase in the book. The first is probably "division of labor," which is another way of saying "social cooperation." *Human Action* is *about* social cooperation or it isn't about anything at all. The first matter Mises takes up after his opening disquisition on the nature of action itself is... cooperation. He begins, "Society is concerted action, cooperation... It substitutes collaboration for the — at least conceivable — isolated life of individuals. Society is division of labor and combination of labor. In his capacity as an acting animal man becomes a social animal."

It is through cooperation and the division of labor that we all can live better lives. Naturally, Mises laid great stress on the need for peace, since the absence of peace is the breakdown of that vital cooperation. This put Mises squarely in the pacifistic classical-liberal tradition as exemplified by Richard Cobden, John Bright, Frédéric Bastiat, Herbert Spencer, and William Graham Sumner. Mises wrote in *Liberalism*:

> The liberal critique of the argument in favor of war is fundamentally different from that of the humanitarians. It starts from the premise that

not war, but peace, is the father of all things... War only destroys; it cannot create... The liberal abhors war, not, like the humanitarian, in spite of the fact that it has beneficial consequences, but because it has only harmful ones.

Given Mises's orientation it is unsurprising to see him attach so much importance to what he calls the Ricardian Law of Association. This is known as the law of comparative advantage (or cost), which states that two parties can gain from trade even if one is more efficient at making every product they both want.

The key is opportunity cost. A $500-an-hour lawyer who is also the fastest, most accurate typist in the world will likely find it advantageous to hire a typist. Why? Because every hour the lawyer spends typing instead of practicing law costs him $500 minus what he would have paid a typist. The typist faces no such opportunity cost. So lawyer and typist both benefit by cooperating. This is true of groups (countries) too. People will discover the benefits of concentrating on what, comparatively, they make most efficiently (or least inefficiently) and trading with others. As a result more total goods will be produced.

This law is an important part of the argument for free international trade because it answers the objection that a national group that can't make anything as efficiently (absolutely) as others will be left out of the world economy. But Mises understood that the law of comparative advantage was merely an application of the broader *law of association*. As he wrote in *Human Action*:

> The law of association makes us comprehend the tendencies which resulted in the progressive intensification of human cooperation. We conceive what incentive induced people not to consider themselves simply as rivals in a struggle for the appropriation of the limited supply of means of subsistence made available by nature. We realize what has impelled them and permanently impels them to consort with one another for the sake of cooperation. Every step forward on the way to a more developed mode of the division of labor serves the interests of all participants... The factor that brought about primitive society and daily works toward its progressive intensification is human action that is animated by the insight into the higher productivity of labor achieved under the division of labor.

This seemingly simple idea leads to counterintuitive conclusions. As a result of expanding cooperation, human beings compete to *produce*, not to *consume*. Mises expressed this with my favorite sentence in *Human Action*: "The fact that my fellow man wants to acquire shoes as I do, does not make it harder for me to get shoes, but easier." The expansion of cooperation also means dealing with strangers at great distance — a further incentive for peace.

Unfortunately the emphasis on cooperation is not what nonlibertarians are likely to "know" about free-market economics and the normative freedom philosophy. They are more apt to associate these with "rugged individualism" than "social cooperation." I have no doubt that a major reason for this is that our opponents who know better *want* the public to have a distorted sense of the genuinely liberal worldview. When President Bill Clinton declared (disingenuously) in his 1996 state of the union address, "The era of big government is over," he followed up that sentence with this: "But we can't go back to the era of fending for yourself." But human beings have always been social/political animals. There was no era when men and women fended for themselves individually. The choice is between free and forced association.

Of course libertarians and free-market advocates do emphasize the importance of the division of labor. Nevertheless we are partly responsible for the public misperception. Our rhetoric too often implies atomism, however inadvertently. (The appropriate individualism is molecular individualism.) I understand the value of the terms "individualism," "self-reliance," and "independence," but we should realize that they can easily lead to undesirable caricatures. Let's not encourage anyone to think that the libertarian ideal is Ted Kaczynski minus the mail bombs.

We're all grappling with an uncertain future. Social cooperation unquestionably makes that task easier than if we attempted to go it alone. That's why individuals formed mutual-aid (fraternal) organizations. Besides camaraderie, these groups provided what the welfare state feebly and coercively supposes to provide today: islands of relative security in a sea of uncertainty.

If people support the welfare state, don't be puzzled. It's because they cannot see a better voluntarist alternative. That's where libertarians come in.

We libertarians might have an easier time persuading others if we emphasized that freedom produces ever-more innovative ways to cooperate for mutual benefit and that when government dominates life, social cooperation is imperiled.

10
The Central Banking Scam

Patrick MacFarlane, J.D.
Libertarian Institute

Patrick MacFarlane is a Wisconsin attorney in private practice and the host of the "Liberty Weekly" podcast at LibertyWeekly.net.

Oddly enough, the one question that finally brought me to anarchy was: "Where does money come from?"

It was perplexing to me that the answer to such a simple question could be so simple, yet so complex — and, moreover, *absurd*.

So? Where *does* money come from?

I found that the short answer is that new money is created by either 1) artificial bank credit expansion through the fractional-reserve lending process; or 2) the Central Bank prints it (It then uses the newly printed money to buy assets from private banks and adds said assets to its balance sheet). In both instances, new money is conjured, being created out of thin air, and injected into the economy through various means, thus eroding the purchasing power of those not privileged enough to enjoy the new money.

In other words, a state-enabled cartel of banks counterfeits it.

As Murray Rothbard explained in *The Case Against the Fed*, the counterfeiting process is enabled through the institution of Central Banking:

> The Central Bank has always had two major roles: (1) to help finance the government's deficit; and (2) to cartelize the private commercial banks in the country, so as to help remove the two great market limits on their expansion of credit, on their propensity to counterfeit: a possible loss of confidence leading to bank runs; and the loss of reserves should any one bank expand its own credit. For cartels on the market, even if they are to each firm's advantage, are very difficult to sustain unless government enforces the cartel. In the area of fractional-reserve banking, the Central Bank can assist cartelization by removing or alleviating these two basic free-market limits on banks' inflationary expansion credit.[1]

Central Banking is incredibly damaging to the economy.

In short, the Central Bank's manipulation of interest rates sends false signals to businessmen, causing malinvestments in high-order capital goods, "which could only be prosperously sustained through lower time preferences and greater savings and investments."[2]

The "boom" signifies this period of malinvestment. Therefore, the resulting "bust" that rocks & shocks the nation, is the market clearing out the "wastes and errors of the boom." Of course, the common people, seduced by the false promises of a "booming" economy do not receive a bailout, as do the private friends of government. The result is a massive transfer of wealth from the people and into the coffers of the state and their private-sector cronies.

Not only is the entire institution of Central Banking steeped in counterfeit and fraud, but it also encourages irresponsible behavior. Central banking gives the illusion of pooled resources where scrupulous toil and savings have created none. Therefore, artificially cheap credit encourages high time preference throughout society: get something for nothing today and shift the cost to future generations.

An additional driver of this high time preference behavior is inflation. Inflation is the increase in the money supply that occurs when the Central Bank prints more money. Inflation is usually signified by rising prices. From the point of view of consumers, why save money when it will be worth half as much in ten years?

Aside from siphoning wealth from the people and encouraging high time preference behavior, Central Banks facilitate one of the vilest operations of the State apparatus.

In chapter 4 of *End the Fed*, Ron Paul identifies this most destructive consequence of central banking:

> It is no coincidence that the century of total war coincided with the century of central banking. When governments had to fund their own wars without a paper money machine to rely upon, they economized on resources. They found diplomatic solutions to prevent war, and after they started a war, they ended it as soon as possible.[3]

To better explain how the above process occurs, consider a simpler example:[4]

The King of Ruritania decides that he does not care for the King of neighboring Moldovia. In preparation for his invasion of Moldovia, the Ruritanian King requisitions of his finance minister an accounting of the royal treasury.

Alas for the King, the royal coffers are bare. He may not be able to finance his new war! In response, the King issues a royal decree: all the official coinage of the land is to be recalled for reminting.

Once the currency is collected, the King melts the coinage down, removes ten percent of the silver content in each coin, and replaces it with nickel. The King then remints the new coins and fills the royal coffers the ten percent surplus of new coins. Suddenly, the King's coffers are full, and the people are ten percent less wealthy. This process is called "debasing the currency."

Since the invention of the printing press, the State has been able to replace hard money with paper deposit tickets, untether the hard reserves to those deposit tickets through legislation, and purchase assets with printed deposit tickets. The process becomes a bit more evolved, but money is created through the magic of the lending process.

Poof.

With the above answers in tow, it became clear to me that the Central Banking institution lies at the very core of the state apparatus. Without monopoly rights to print fiat currency, many of the State's most destructive endeavors would be logistically impossible. This newfound knowledge of this immoral practice hardened my natural skepticism of the state.

Even more perplexing than the answers I found regarding central banking, were the questions they evoked: how is the truth so well hidden from everyone? Why does no one even think to ask where money comes from? Why didn't we learn about something so important in school? If a question this profound is so well hidden, is it deliberate?[5] If so, why? What else is being hidden from us?

NOTES

1. Rothbard, Murray N. "The Case Against the Fed," page 58.
2. Murray Rothbard, *America's Great Depression*.
3. *End the Fed*, page 63.
4. This is Rothbard's explanation of coin clipping from *The Mystery of Banking*.
5. It is deliberate. See James Corbett, *Century of Enslavement: The History of the Federal Reserve* and *How Big Oil Conquered the World*.

11
Homelessness, Regulation, and Minimum Wage

> There exists a clear bridge between what is ideologically sound, and what works in the real world. Homelessness, regulation, and exploitation are three areas where government believers most often say, "To hell with the logic of voluntaryism! These things are important." Voluntaryists agree that these are important issues, which is why leaving them in the hands of the government, a coercively funded monopoly, is the worst approach to solving them. The following is a collection of quotes which will help to explain why those who desire regulation out of their concerns for homelessness and exploitation, should instead embrace voluntaryism.

The very same people who say that government has no right to interfere with sexual activity between consenting adults believe that the government has every right to interfere with economic activity between consenting adults.
– Thomas Sowell, Ph.D., "Looking for That Elusive Escalator to Success," *Sun Sentinel*, Jan. 2000.

Any statute or administrative regulation necessarily makes actions illegal that are not overt initiations of crimes or torts according to libertarian theory. Every statute or administrative rule is therefore illegitimate and itself invasive and a criminal interference with the property rights of noncriminals.
– Murray N. Rothbard, Ph.D., *Economic Controversies* (2011, Mises Institute), p. 406.

The annual cost of federal regulations in the United States increased to more than $1.75 trillion in 2008. Had every U.S. household paid an equal share of the federal regulatory burden, each would have owed $15,586 in 2008. By comparison, the federal regulatory burden exceeds by 50 percent private spending on health care, which equaled $10,500 per household in 2008. While all citizens and businesses pay some portion of these costs, the distribution of the burden of regulations is quite uneven. The portion of regulatory costs that falls initially on businesses was $8,086 per employee in 2008. Small businesses, defined as firms employing fewer than 20 employees, bear the largest burden of federal regulations. As of 2008, small businesses face an annual regulatory cost of $10,585 per employee, which is 36 percent higher than the regulatory cost facing large firms (defined as firms with 500 or more employees).

– Nicole V. Crain and W. Mark Crain,
"The Impact of Regulatory Costs on Small Firms"
(2010, Lafayette College), p. iv.

At a cost that ranges from $10,000 to $50,000, tiny homes like the Matchbox could help to ease the shortage of affordable housing in the capital city. Heating and cooling costs are negligible. Rainwater catchment systems help to make the homes self-sustaining. They're an attractive option to the very sort of residents who the city attracts in abundance: single, young professionals without a lot of stuff, who aren't ready to take on a large mortgage.

But tiny houses come with one enormous catch: they're illegal, in violation of several codes in Washington, D.C.'s Zoning Ordinance. Among the many requirements in the 34 chapters and 600 pages of code are mandates defining minimum lot size, room sizes, alleyway widths, and "accessory dwelling units" that prevent tiny houses from being anything more than a part-time residence.

– Todd Krainin, "Jay Austin's Beautiful, Illegal Tiny House,"
Reason, Aug. 2014.

Elvis Summers crowdfunded $100k & built dozens of $1,200 tiny houses for the homeless. Then the city seized them.

Each night, tens of thousands of people sleep in tent cities crowding the palm-lined boulevards of Los Angeles, far more than any other city in the nation. The homeless population in the entertainment capital of the world has hit new record highs in each of the past few years.

But a 39-year-old struggling musician from South L.A. thought he had a creative fix. Elvis Summers, who went through stretches of homelessness himself in his 20s, raised over $100,000 through crowdfunding campaigns last spring. With the help of professional contractors and others in the community who sign up to volunteer through his nonprofit, Starting Human, he has built dozens of solar-powered, tiny houses to shelter the homeless since.

Summers says that the houses are meant to be a temporary solution that, unlike a tent, provides the secure foundation residents need to improve their lives. "The tiny houses provide immediate shelter," he explains. "People can lock their stuff up and know that when they come back from their drug treatment program or court or finding a job all day, their stuff is where they left it."

Each house features a solar power system, a steel-reinforced door, a camping toilet, a smoke detector, and even window alarms. The tiny structures cost Summers roughly $1,200 apiece to build.

L.A. city officials, however, had a different plan to address the crisis. A decade after the city's first 10-year plan to end homelessness withered in 2006, Mayor Eric Garcetti announced in February a $1.87 billion proposal to get all L.A. residents off the streets, once and for all. He and the City Council aim to build 10,000 units of permanent housing with supportive services over the next decade. In the interim, they are shifting funds away from temporary and emergency shelters.

Councilmember Curren Price, who represents the district where Summers's tiny houses were located, does not believe they are beneficial either to the community or to the homeless people housed in them. "I don't really want to call them houses. They're really just boxes," says Price. "They're not safe, and they impose real hazards for neighbors in the community."

Most of Summers's tiny houses are on private land that has been donated to the project. A handful had replaced the tents that have proliferated on freeway overpasses in the city. Summers put them there until he could secure a private lot to create a tiny house village similar to those that already exist in Portland, Seattle, Austin, and elsewhere. "My whole issue and cause is that something needs to be done right now," Summers emphasizes.

But the houses, nestled among dour tent shantytowns, became brightly colored targets early this year for frustrated residents who want the homeless out of their backyards. Councilmember Price was bombarded by complaints from angry constituents.

In February, the City Council responded by amending a sweeps ordinance to allow the tiny houses to be seized without prior notice. On the morning of the ninth, just as the mayor and council gathered at City Hall to announce their new plan to end homelessness, police and garbage trucks descended on the tiny homes, towing three of them to a Bureau of Sanitation lot for disposal. Summers managed to move eight of the threatened houses into storage before they were confiscated, but their residents were left back on the sidewalk.

— Justin Monticello,
"This L.A. Musician Built $1,200 Tiny Houses for the Homeless,"
Reason, Dec. 2016.

What Makes Wages Rise

The buyers do not pay for the toil and trouble the worker took nor for the length of time he spent in working. They pay for the products.

The better the tools are which the worker uses in his job, the more he can perform in an hour, the higher is, consequently, his remuneration. What makes wages rise and renders the material conditions of the wage earners more satisfactory is improvement in the technological equipment. American wages are higher than wages in other countries because the capital invested per head of the worker is greater and the plants are thereby in the position to use the most efficient tools and machines.

What is called the American way of life is the result of the fact that the United States has put fewer obstacles in the way of saving and capital accumulation than other nations.

The economic backwardness of such countries as India consists precisely in the fact that their policies hinder both the accumulation of domestic capital and the investment of foreign capital. As the capital required is lacking, the Indian enterprises are prevented from employing sufficient quantities of modern equipment, are therefore producing much less per man-hour and can only afford to pay wage rates which, compared with American wage rates, appear as shockingly low.

There is only one way that leads to an improvement of the standard of living for the wage-earning masses, viz., the increase in the amount of capital invested. All other methods, however popular they may be, are not only futile, but are actually detrimental to the well-being of those they allegedly want to benefit.

– Ludwig von Mises, Ph.D., "Wages, Unemployment, and Inflation," *Christian Economics*, March 1958.

The Implications of Self-Ownership
Some people might say, "Well, the problem is, if we can sell kidneys, then really desperately poor people would sell their kidneys — and richer people wouldn't — and you'd exploit them." Part of my response is to say, "If you have a person who's in such dire straits that their best option is to sell a kidney, and you take that away from them, you're a horrible human being who doesn't care about social justice. Your moral sense is completely warped, I hope you're not voting." It's a forceful thing to say, but it's true... this is a horrible thing for that human being to have to do, but also it's their best option, which means if you take that away, they're gonna do something even worse than that — so by hypothesis, you don't want to take that away.

– Jason Brennan, Ph.D., Professor and author of *Markets Without Limits*, from an episode of Keith Knight's "Don't Tread on Anyone" podcast.

Top 3 Ways "Sweatshops" Help the Poor Escape Poverty

The *New York Times* recently reported on the case of Nokuthula Masango, an employee at a clothing factory in New Castle, South Africa. Masango works long hours in tough conditions all for only $36 per week. If that sounds low, it is, even by South African standards where the legal minimum wage is $57 per week. Many people would describe Masango's factory as a sweatshop, and many would say that the owners of the sweatshop are treating Masango and their other employees unfairly. Now in this video I don't want to try to fully settle the question of whether sweatshops treat their workers unfairly or not. Let's grant for the sake of argument that they do. The point I want to make here is that even if sweatshop workers are treated unfairly, there are three points to be made in defense of sweatshops.

First, it's important to remember that the exchange between the worker and her employer is mutually beneficial, even when it's unfair. Sweatshops make their employees better off even if they don't make them as much better off as critics think they should. Consider sweatshop wages. As you might recall, Masango earned $36 a week at her sweatshop job. Compare this with her friend, who lost her job at a sweatshop after it was closed for violating minimum-wage laws and had to find work as a nanny. That friend wound up earning just $14 a month, less than 12 percent of what Masango earned. And this wage gap is typical of sweatshop jobs relative to other jobs in the domestic economy. Studies have shown sweatshop jobs often pay three to seven times the wages paid elsewhere in the economy.

So even if we think the conditions of sweatshop labor are unfair, relative to their other alternatives, sweatshop labor is a very attractive option for workers in the developing world. And this is why those workers are often so eager to accept so-called sweatshop jobs. Now no one on either side of the debate defends forced labor, but so long as sweatshop labor is voluntary, even in a weak sense of being free from physical coercion, workers would only take a job in a sweatshop when that job is better for them than any of their other alternatives. This is true even if we grant that sweatshop workers' freedom is often limited in a variety of unjust ways by their government or by the so-called coercion of poverty.

Coercion constrains options, but as long as workers are free to choose from within their constrained set of options, we can expect them to select those jobs that offer the best prospects of success. And when given the choice between working in a sweatshop or working on a farm or working elsewhere in the urban economy, workers consistently choose the sweatshop job.

The second point to be made in defense of sweatshops is this: Even if you think sweatshop labor is unfair, it is a bad idea to prohibit it. Think of it this way: People only take sweatshop jobs because they're desperately poor and low on options. But, taking away sweatshops does nothing to eliminate that poverty or to enhance their options. In fact, it only reduces them further, taking away what workers themselves regard as the best option they have.

Now, of course, most anti-sweatshop activists aren't trying to shut down factories, but sometimes well-intentioned actions have unintended consequences. The layoffs faced by Masango's friend are a stark demonstration of this. That friend was fired because the owners of her factory decided it would be better to stop doing business altogether than to pay the legal minimum wage. And while you can make it illegal for factories to pay low wages, you cannot make it illegal for them to pay no wages by shutting down altogether.

The third and final point is this. It's better to do something to help the problem of global poverty than it is to do nothing. And sweatshops are doing something to help. They're giving people jobs that pay better than their other alternatives, and they're contributing to a process of economic development that has the potential to affect dramatic increases in living standards. Most of us, on the other hand, do nothing to improve the lives of these workers, and that includes American companies that don't outsource their production at all but instead give their jobs to U.S. workers, who by global standards are already some of the world's wealthiest people.

So take the perspective of one of the world's poor for a moment and ask yourself which looks better to you: The American company that outsources to a sweatshop or the American company that, because of its high-minded moral principles, doesn't? Maybe the sweatshop is run by people who are greedy and shallow in their motivations and maybe the other company is run by people with the purest of intentions. But good intentions don't get you a job and they don't feed your family. So which looks better now?

– Matt Zwolinski, Ph.D.,
"Top 3 Ways Sweatshops Help the Poor Escape Poverty,"
Learn Liberty, June 2012.

Is Price Gouging Immoral? Should It Be Illegal?

A hurricane hits your town and the power is out. Your child is diabetic, and you need power to keep her insulin refrigerated. You're desperate, but perhaps you're in luck. I have an electrical generator that I'm willing to sell you, and you have the $800 that generators like mine typically cost. The only problem is I don't want to sell it to you for $800 — I want $1,300. Now, as it turns out, my offer would be illegal in the majority of U.S. states, about 34 of which have statutes that prohibit price gouging. That practice is usually defined as raising prices on certain kinds of goods to an unfair or excessively high level during an emergency. So there's really no question about what the law would do to me if I made an offer like this to you.

But even if the law is clear, the moral status of price gouging is not. Is price gouging always immoral? And whether it is or not, should it be illegal? Let's look at the question of morality first. Is asking $1,300 for the generator morally wrong? Of course, you'd rather buy it from me for $800, but there are three reasons why my charging a higher price isn't obviously wrong. First, remember, you don't have to buy it from me for $1,300. If that's more than you think the generator is worth, you're free to walk on by. If you do decide to pay, it's because you believe you're getting more value out of the generator than you do from the $1,300 you gave up for it. In other words, you're coming away from the deal with more than you gave up. The second: ask yourself what would happen if I did charge only $800 for the generator. Remember, you aren't the only person who needs electric power in this situation. If the price was lower, would the generator still have been there when you tried to buy it, or would someone else have snatched it up before you ever had a chance?

This leads directly to the third point, which is that high prices do more than just line seller's pockets. They also affect how buyers and sellers behave. For buyers, high prices reduce demand and encourage conservation. They lead buyers to ask themselves whether they really need that generator or hotel room or whether they can do without. And by doing so, they allow at least some of those resources to be conserved for other people who might need them more and therefore are willing to pay more. And for sellers, high prices encourage people to bring more goods to where they're needed. If generators can be bought in an area not affected by the hurricane for $800 and resold later for $1,300, that creates a profit incentive for people to bring generators from where they're less needed to where they're more needed to get them to where they'll do more good for people who need them most.

All of this leads to a surprising conclusion. Even someone who can't afford to pay $1,300 for a generator benefits from a system in which sellers are allowed to charge that price. That's because the profit motive the debt system creates encourages competition, which increases supply and ultimately drives down prices to a more affordable level for everyone. Now, it's true that when price gouging is legal, some people won't be able to afford the higher prices that result. But ask yourself, what alternative institutions would do better? When price gouging is prohibited, goods usually go to whoever shows up first. If you care about distributive justice, is that really a better system?

I think there are good reasons to doubt that price gouging is immoral. But suppose you're not convinced. Suppose you think price gouging is exploitative and wrong. Should it be illegal? The answer, even if we assume that price gouging is immoral is almost certainly that it should not be illegal. If price gouging is wrong, it's because it hurts people in vulnerable situations. But then, the last thing you want to do is hurt those vulnerable people even more. Remember, the only reason price gouging occurs is because a disaster causes demand for certain goods to go up or supply to go down with the result that there isn't enough stuff to go around.

Antigouging laws don't do anything to address this underlying shortage. In fact, they make it worse by destroying incentives for conservation and increased supply. So even if you think that price gouging is morally wrong and that merchants should refuse to engage in it, making it illegal doesn't make sense. It hurts the very people who need our help most.

– Matt Zwolinski, Ph.D.
"Is Price Gouging Immoral? Should It Be Illegal?"

Homelessness, Regulation, and Minimum Wage

Learn Liberty, April 2012.

Question: If business is not regulated, wouldn't the environment be destroyed?

Answer: Our greatest polluter is the government (*i.e.*, U.S. military), not corporate America. Putting government in charge of protecting the environment is like asking the fox to guard the hen house. The most polluted countries in the world are those where government had total control of the environment, such as Eastern Europe before the fall of the Berlin Wall. Government is just as dangerous to our environment as it is to the wealth of our nation — it is the proverbial wolf in sheep's clothing. If your neighbor dumps garbage on your lawn, he or she should clean it up and compensate you for any damages. Similarly, if a business or government agency causes harm, they should make it right again. Today, restitution rarely happens. Businesses pay fines to the government, not to the victim; government polluters simply claim sovereign immunity and walk away. Regulation isn't working. We need to replace it with restitution.

– Mary J. Ruwart, Ph.D., *Short Answers to the Tough Questions* (2012, SunStar Press), p. 48.

What is zoning? It is a government program that consists of mandatory rules, regulations, and laws that prevent or inhibit low-income housing from being built within a community. It obviously doesn't occur to Sanders that builders cannot build low-cost housing for the poor in Seattle when zoning laws prohibit them from doing so.

The situation is aggravated by the fact that the poor are locked out of the labor market by the government's mandatory minimum wage. Suppose, for example, that a homeless man is willing to work for $5 an hour and that an employer is willing to hire him at that price. They can't make the deal because the law makes it illegal for them to enter into that consensual transaction...

The minimum wage law is the reason why there has been a chronic, permanent unemployment rate of 30–40 percent among black teenagers for years.

I grew up in Laredo, Texas, which the Census Bureau in the 1950s labeled the poorest city in the United States. Laredo did not have zoning. We had a family friend who was a builder. His specialty? Building low-income housing for the poor. He once explained to me that he would travel into Mexico (Laredo is situated on the border) and purchase low-cost building supplies, which enabled him to build low-priced housing that served poor people. His places were always super-clean, super-nice, super-maintained, and super-sold out.

Was my friend doing this out of a sense of altruism and love for the poor? On the contrary. He was doing it to make money. He was the classic example

of what people on the left call a no-good, capitalist, profit-seeking, bourgeois swine. And my friend was a wealthy man because poor people loved his housing.
— Jacob Hornberger, "The Cure for Homelessness"
(2018, The Future of Freedom Foundation).

There's no reason to trust activist government because the people in charge can be expected, time and again, to back those with power and influence over those without... It's important to avoid comparing idealized State practice with imaginary worst-case practice in the government's absence... Both charity and mutual aid are more viable than government-run antipoverty programs, more able to help poor people, precisely because those programs have high administrative costs. (Thanks to Tom Woods for this point.) Programs supported freely by people in the government's absence would not feature such high costs. Because donors could choose among multiple programs, there would be persistent pressure for administrative costs to be reduced... Governments raise the cost of being poor. Building codes and zoning regulations raise the cost of housing and so make it harder for people to find inexpensive homes. Some people are forced to live without permanent housing at all, while others must spend much larger fractions of their incomes on housing than they otherwise would. As for food, that's also more expensive thanks to agricultural tariffs and import quotas. In the absence of government policies that make meeting their basic needs unnecessarily expensive, poor people would have more disposable income and would be more economically secure.
— Gary Chartier, Ph.D. "Government Is No Friend of the Poor"
(2012, Foundation for Economic Education).

During the 20 years before the War on Poverty was funded, the portion of the nation living in poverty had dropped to 14.7% from 32.1%. Since 1966, the first year with a significant increase in anti-poverty spending, the poverty rate reported by the Census Bureau has been virtually unchanged.
— Phil Gramm and John F. Early, "Government Can't Rescue the Poor,"
The Wall Street Journal, Oct. 2018.

...[W]hy don't all workers make the minimum wage?... The obvious answer is that competition would prevent this absurd outcome.
— Robert P. Murphy, Ph.D., *The Politically Incorrect Guide to Capitalism*
(2007, Regnery Publishing), p. 24.

Minimum wage legislation decreases the likelihood that people with few skills and little experience will be able to get their foot in the door and enter the labor market to gain on-the-job experience. Notice how the state has no problem with students at Universities working thousands of hours a year for

$0.00, in the form of classwork, homework, and studying.

Many see this when it comes to healthcare, food, housing, books — the higher the cost of those items, the more difficult it is for those with lower incomes to access those goods and services. Higher wages result in fewer employers, fewer choices for employees, fewer businesses, less consumer choice, and higher prices than would otherwise exist.

It is often the people who can offer me no career, no products, and no services, who tell me that I am being exploited by those voluntarily offering me those things.* If an employer offering me $1.00 an hour is bad, your offering me $0.00 is worse — not to mention, I get no on-the-job experience.

*Anarcho-communists do not recognize people's freedom to contract voluntarily; therefore, they are seeking to rule over others, and cannot logically be considered anarchists in principle, even though the first "anarchists" were communists. If the first mathematicians declared that 2 + 2 = 32, that would not make 2 + 2 = 32.

– Patrick MacFarlane, J.D.

12
The Right and Wrong of Compulsion by the State (Excerpts)

Auberon Herbert
The Right and Wrong of Compulsion by the State
1885

> Auberon Herbert (1838–1906) was an English radical individualist who was influenced by the work of Herbert Spencer. With a group of other late Victorian classical liberals, he was active in such organizations as the Personal Rights and Self-Help Association and the Liberty and Property Defense League. He formulated a system of "thorough" individualism that he described as "voluntaryism."

Each man and woman are to be free to direct their faculties and their energies, according to their own sense of what is right and wise, in every direction, except one. They are not to use their faculties for the purpose of forcibly restraining their neighbor from the same free use of his faculties. (p. 1)

It is not by tying a man's hands that you shall make him skillful in any craft, especially that difficult one of living well and wisely. (p. 3)

...[E]ven if you believed that you could make men wise and good by depriving them of liberty of action, you have no right to do so. Who has given you a commission to decide what your brother man shall or shall not do? Who has given you charge of his life and his faculties and his happiness as well as of your own? Perhaps you think yourself wiser and better fitted to judge than he is; but so did all those of old days — kings, emperors, and heads of dominant churches — who possessed power, and never scrupled to compress and shape their fellow-men as they themselves thought best, by means of that power. (p. 5)

We are fast getting rid of emperors and kings and dominant churches, as far as the mere outward form is concerned, but the soul of these men and these institutions is still living and breathing within us. (p. 6)

...I must reply to you that your majority has no more rights over the body or mind of a man than either the bayonet-surrounded emperor or the infallible church. (p. 6)

One person will wish to regulate the mass of men in matters of religion; another in education; another in philosophy; another in art; another in

The Right and Wrong of Compulsion by the State (Excerpts)

matters of trade; another in matters of labor; another in matters of contract; another in matters of amusement. One person will desire to regulate the people in a few matters, and give freedom in many; another to give freedom in few and regulate in many. There is no possibility of permanent human agreement in the matter, where once you have ceased to stand on any definite principle, where once you have sanctioned the use of force for certain undefined needs of the moment. (p. 9)

Until they have done this, until they have found some law by which they can distinguish the right from the wrong use of power, by which they can justly satisfy not only their own minds but the minds of others, they are simply leaving in suspension the greatest matter that affects human beings; they are like men who start to make their passage over the wide seas, without chart or compass, and hopefully remark that the look of the waters, the face of the sky, and the direction of the wind will at any special moment tell them what course they ought to steer. (p. 10)

No man is acting consciously and with distinct self-guidance, no man possesses a fixed goal and purpose in life, until he has brought the facts of his daily existence under the arrangement of general principles. Until he has done this, the facts of life will use and command him; he will not use and command them. (p. 11)

But apart from this influence on character, which freedom and state-regulation must respectively exercise, the answer which every man finds it in his soul to make to this great question, "By what title do men exercise power over each other?" must decide for him the general course of his own life. (p. 13)

And now let us look a little more closely into the rights of the individual. I claim that he is by right the master of himself and of his own faculties and energies. If he is not, who is? Let us suppose that A having no rights over himself, B and C, being in a majority, have rights over him. But we must assume an equality in these matters, and if A has no rights over himself, neither can B and C have any rights over themselves. To what a ridiculous position are we then brought! B and C having no rights over themselves, have absolute rights over A; and we should have to suppose in this most topsy-turvy of worlds that men were walking about, not owning themselves, as any simple-minded person would naturally conclude that they did, but owning some other of their fellow-men; and presently in their turn perhaps to be themselves owned by some other. Look at it from another point of view. You tell me a majority has a right to decide as they like for their fellow-men. What majority? 21 to 20? 20 to 5? 20 to 1? But why any majority? What is there in numbers that can possibly make any opinion or decision better or more valid, or which can transfer the body and mind of one man into the keeping of another man? Five men are in a room. Because three men take one view and two another, have the three men any moral right to enforce their view on the other two men? What magical power comes over the three men that because they are one more in number than the two men, therefore they suddenly become possessors of the minds and bodies of these others? As long as they were two to two, so long we may suppose each man remained master of his own mind and body; but from the moment that another man, acting Heaven only knows from what motives, has joined himself to one party or the other, that party has become straightway possessed of the souls and bodies of the other party. Was there ever such a degrading and indefensible superstition? (pp. 14–15)

If the fact of being in a majority, if the fact of the larger number carries this extraordinary virtue with it, does a bigger nation possess the right to decide by a vote the destiny of a smaller nation? (p. 16)

You deny the rights of the individual to regulate and direct himself. But you suddenly acknowledge and exaggerate these rights as soon as you have thrown the individual into that mass which you call the majority. (p. 16)

I do not think that it is possible to find a perfect moral foundation for the authority of any government, be it the government of an emperor or a republic. (p. 19)

...I see that the exercise of these energies and faculties depends upon the observance of the universal law that no man shall by force restrain another man in the use of his faculties. (p. 19)

Just as the individual has rights of self-preservation, as regards the special man who commits a wrong against him, so has a government — which is the individual in mass — exactly the same rights, neither larger nor smaller, as regards the whole special class of those who employ violence. (p. 20)

When we propose to use force against the capitalist because he forces his work-people to accept certain terms, we are confusing the two meanings which belong to the word force. We are confusing together direct and indirect force. *Direct compulsion*, by whomsoever exercised, is only a remnant of that barbarous state when emperors and dominant churches used men according to their own ideas. *Indirect compulsion* is a condition of life to which we have always been, and always shall be, necessarily subject; it is inseparably bound up with our joint existence in the world. The richest and most powerful man lives under indirect compulsion as well as the poorest and feeblest... mischief (that) arises when you make the existence of indirect compulsion a ground for employing direct compulsion. (pp. 22–23)

In exactly the same way he who uses direct force to combat indirect force only restrains one injury by inflicting another of a graver kind, places the fair-minded people as well as the unfair-minded people on the side of oppression, and, by thus equalizing the actions of the good and bad, indefinitely delays the development of those moral influences to which we can alone look as the solvent of that temper that makes men use harshly the indirect power resting in their hands. (p. 24)

The Right and Wrong of Compulsion by the State (Excerpts)

Private property and free trade stand on exactly the same footing, both being essential and indivisible parts of liberty, both depending upon rights, which no body of men, whether called governments or anything else, can justly take from the individual. (p. 30)

If I tie a man's hands, and take from him his purse, I evidently constrain both his will and his actions. If I sell a man a loaf professing to be made only of wheat, and in reality made partly of potatoes, I constrain his will so that his actions are constrained. My fraud is force in disguise. (p. 33)

Now, a man's property is the result of the exercise of his faculties; is an inseparable part of himself and his faculties: and therefore, whenever his property is injured, his faculties are interfered with, and his will about himself, his faculties, his actions, and his property, constrained. (p. 34)

There are good reasons for remonstrating with him, or reasoning with him, or persuading him, or entreating him; but not for compelling him, or visiting him with any evil in case he do otherwise. (p. 40)

But our great uniform systems, by which the state professes to serve the people, necessarily exclude difference and variety; and in excluding difference and variety, exclude also the means of improvement. I ought to show how untrue is the cry against competition. I ought to show that competition has brought benefits to men tenfold — nay, a hundredfold — greater than the injuries it has inflicted; that every advantage and comfort of civilized life has come from competition; and that the hopes of the future are inseparably bound up with the still better gifts which are to come from it and it alone. I ought to show, even if this were not so, even if competition were not a power fighting actively on your side, that still your efforts would be vain to defeat or elude it. I ought to show that all external protection, all efforts to place forcibly that which is inferior on the same level as that which is superior, is a mere dream, born of our ignorance of nature's methods. (pp. 63–64)

There are none of the good things of life, from the highest to the lowest, that will not come to the people when once they gain the clearness of mind to see the moral bounds that they ought to set to the employment of force, when they gain the loyally steadfast purpose to employ their energies only within such bounds. (p. 67)

Indeed, you will find, as you examine this matter, that all ideas of right and wrong must ultimately depend upon the answer that you give to my question, "Have twenty men — just because they are twenty — a moral title to dispose of the minds and bodies and possessions of ten other men, just because they are ten?" (p. 69)

13
War, Peace, and the State

Murray N. Rothbard, Ph.D.
Egalitarianism as a Revolt Against Nature and Other Essays
1963

Murray Newton Rothbard (1926–1995) was an economist, scholar, intellectual, and polymath who made major contributions in economics, political philosophy (libertarianism in particular), economic history, and legal theory. He developed and extended the Austrian School of economics based on the earlier pioneering work of Ludwig von Mises, Ph.D.

The libertarian movement has been chided by William F. Buckley, Jr., for failing to use its "strategic intelligence" in facing the major problems of our time. We have, indeed, been too often prone to "pursue our busy little seminars on whether or not to demunicipalize the garbage collectors" (as Buckley has contemptuously written), while ignoring and failing to apply libertarian theory to the most vital problem of our time: war and peace. There *is* a sense in which libertarians have been utopian rather than strategic in their thinking, with a tendency to divorce the ideal system which we envisage from the realities of the world in which we live. In short, too many of us have divorced theory from practice, and have then been content to hold the pure libertarian society as an abstract ideal for some remotely future time, while in the concrete world of today we follow unthinkingly the orthodox "conservative" line. To live liberty, to begin the hard but essential strategic struggle of changing the unsatisfactory world of today in the direction of our ideals, we must realize and demonstrate to the world that libertarian theory can be brought sharply to bear upon all of the world's crucial problems. By coming to grips with these problems, we can demonstrate that libertarianism is not just a beautiful ideal somewhere on Cloud Nine, but a tough-minded body of truths that enables us to take our stand and to cope with the whole host of issues of our day.

Let us then, by all means, use our strategic intelligence. Although, when he sees the result, Mr. Buckley might well wish that we had stayed in the realm of garbage collection. Let us construct a libertarian theory of war and peace.

The fundamental axiom of libertarian theory is that no one may threaten or commit violence ("aggress") against another man's person or property.

Violence may be employed only against the man who commits such violence; that is, only defensively against the aggressive violence of another.[1]

In short, no violence may be employed against a non-aggressor. Here is the fundamental rule from which can be deduced the entire *corpus* of libertarian theory.[2]

Let us set aside the more complex problem of the State for a while and consider simply relations between "private" individuals. Jones finds that he or his property is being invaded, aggressed against, by Smith. It is legitimate for Jones, as we have seen, to repel this invasion by defensive violence of his own. But now we come to a more knotty question: is it within the right of Jones to commit violence against innocent third parties as a corollary to his legitimate defense against Smith? To the libertarian, the answer must be clearly, no. Remember that the rule prohibiting violence against the persons or property of innocent men is absolute: it holds regardless of the subjective *motives* for the aggression. It is wrong and criminal to violate the property or person of another, even if one is a Robin Hood, or starving, or is doing it to save one's relatives, *or* is defending oneself against a third man's attack. We may understand and sympathize with the motives in many of these cases and extreme situations. We may later mitigate the guilt if the criminal comes to trial for punishment, but we cannot evade the judgment that this aggression is still a criminal act, and one which the victim has every right to repel, by violence if necessary. In short, A aggresses against B because C is threatening, or aggressing against, A. We may understand C's "higher" culpability in this whole procedure; but we must still label this aggression as a criminal act which B has the right to repel by violence.

To be more concrete, if Jones finds that his property is being stolen by Smith, he has the right to repel him and try to catch him; but he has *no* right to repel him by bombing a building and murdering innocent people or to catch him by spraying machine gun fire into an innocent crowd. If he does this, he is as much (or more of) a criminal aggressor as Smith is.

The application to problems of war and peace is already becoming evident. For while war in the narrower sense is a conflict between States, in the broader sense we may define it as the outbreak of open violence between people or groups of people. If Smith and a group of his henchmen aggress against Jones and Jones and his bodyguards pursue the Smith gang to their lair, we may cheer Jones on in his endeavor; and we, and others in society interested in repelling aggression, may contribute financially or personally to Jones's cause. But Jones has *no* right, any more than does Smith, to aggress against anyone else in the course of his "just war": to steal others' property in order to finance his pursuit, to conscript others into his posse by use of violence, or to kill others in the course of his struggle to capture the Smith forces. If Jones should do any of these things, he becomes a criminal as *fully* as Smith, and he too becomes subject to whatever sanctions are meted out against criminality. In fact, if Smith's crime was theft, and Jones should use conscription to catch him, or should kill others in the pursuit, Jones becomes more of a criminal than Smith, for such crimes against another person as enslavement and murder are surely far worse than theft. (For while theft injures the extension of another's personality, enslavement injures, and murder obliterates, that personality itself.)

Suppose that Jones, in the course of his "just war" against the ravages of Smith, should kill a few innocent people, and suppose that he should declaim, in defense of this murder, that he was simply acting on the slogan, "Give me liberty or give me death." The absurdity of this "defense" should be evident at once, for the issue is not whether Jones was willing to risk death personally in his defensive struggle against Smith; the issue is whether he was willing to kill other people in pursuit of his legitimate end. For Jones was in truth acting on the completely indefensible slogan: "Give me liberty or give *them* death" — surely a far less noble battle cry.[3]

The libertarian's basic attitude toward war must then be: it is legitimate to use violence against criminals in defense of one's rights of person and property; it is completely impermissible to violate the rights of *other* innocent people. War, then, is only proper when the exercise of violence is rigorously limited to the individual criminals. We may judge for ourselves how many wars or conflicts in history have met this criterion.

It has often been maintained, and especially by conservatives, that the development of the horrendous modern weapons of mass murder (nuclear weapons, rockets, germ warfare, etc.) is only a difference of *degree* rather than *kind* from the simpler weapons of an earlier era. Of course, one answer to this is that when the degree is the number of human lives, the difference is a very big one.[4] But another answer that the libertarian is particularly equipped to give is that while the bow and arrow and even the rifle can be pinpointed, if the will be there, against actual criminals, modern nuclear weapons cannot. Here is a crucial difference in kind. Of course, the bow and arrow could be used for aggressive purposes, but it could also be pinpointed to use only against aggressors. Nuclear weapons, even "conventional" aerial bombs, cannot be. These weapons are *ipso facto* engines of indiscriminate mass destruction. (The only exception would be the extremely rare case where a mass of people who were all criminals inhabited a vast geographical area.) We must, therefore, conclude that the use of nuclear or similar weapons, or the threat thereof, is a sin and a crime against humanity for which there can be no justification.

This is why the old cliché no longer holds that it is not the arms but the will to use them that is significant in judging matters of war and peace. For it is precisely the characteristic of modern weapons that they cannot be used selectively, cannot be used in a libertarian manner. Therefore, their very existence must be condemned, and nuclear disarmament becomes a good to be pursued for its own sake. And if we will indeed use our strategic intelligence, we will see that such disarmament is not only a good, but the highest political good that we can pursue in the modern world. For just as murder is a more heinous crime against another man than larceny, so mass murder — indeed murder so widespread as to threaten human civilization and human survival itself — is the worst crime that any man could possibly commit. And that crime is now imminent. And the forestalling of massive annihilation is far more important, in truth, than the demunicipalization of garbage disposal, as worthwhile as that may be. Or are libertarians going to wax properly indignant about price control or the income tax, and yet shrug their shoulders at or even positively advocate the ultimate crime of mass murder?

If nuclear warfare is totally illegitimate even for individuals defending themselves against criminal assault, how much more so is nuclear or even "conventional" warfare between States!

It is time now to bring the State into our discussion. The State is a group of people who have managed to acquire a virtual monopoly of the use of violence throughout a given territorial area. In particular, it has acquired a monopoly of aggressive violence, for States generally recognize the right of individuals to use violence (though not against States, of course) in self-defense.[5] The State then uses this monopoly to wield power over the inhabitants of the area and to enjoy the material fruits of that power. The State, then, is the only organization in society that regularly and openly obtains its monetary revenues by the use of *aggressive* violence; all other individuals and organizations (except if delegated that right by the State) can obtain wealth only by peaceful production and by voluntary exchange of their respective products. This use of violence to obtain its revenue (called "taxation") is the keystone of State power. Upon this base the State erects a further structure of power over the individuals in its territory, regulating them, penalizing critics, subsidizing favorites, etc. The State also takes care to arrogate to itself the compulsory monopoly of various critical services needed by society, thus keeping the people in dependence upon the State for key services, keeping control of the vital command posts in society and also fostering among the public the myth that *only* the State can supply these goods and services. Thus the State is careful to monopolize police and judicial service, the ownership of roads and streets, the supply of money, and the postal service, and effectively to monopolize or control education, public utilities, transportation, and radio and television.

Now, since the State arrogates to itself the monopoly of violence over a territorial area, so long as its depredations and extortions go unresisted, there is said to be "peace" in the area, since the only violence is one-way, directed by the State downward against the people. Open conflict within the area only breaks out in the case of "revolutions" in which people resist the use of State power against them. Both the quiet case of the State unresisted and the case of open revolution may be termed "vertical violence": violence of the State against its public or vice versa.

In the modern world, each land area is ruled over by a State organization, but there are a number of States scattered over the earth, each with a monopoly of violence over its own territory. No super-State exists with a monopoly of violence over the entire world; and so a state of "anarchy" exists between the several States. (It has always been a source of wonder, incidentally, to this writer how the same conservatives who denounce as lunatic any proposal for eliminating a monopoly of violence over a given territory and thus leaving private individuals without an overlord, should be equally insistent upon leaving *States* without an overlord to settle disputes between them. The former is always denounced as "crackpot anarchism"; the latter is hailed as preserving independence and "national sovereignty" from "world government.") And so, except for revolutions, which occur only sporadically, the open violence and two-sided conflict in the world takes place *between* two or more States, that is, in what is called "international war" (or "horizontal violence").

Now there are crucial and vital differences between inter-State warfare on the one hand and revolutions against the State or conflicts between private individuals on the other. One vital difference is the shift in geography. In a revolution, the conflict takes place *within* the same geographical area: both the minions of the State and the revolutionaries inhabit the same territory. Inter-State warfare, on the other hand, takes place between two groups, each having a monopoly over its own geographical area; that is, it takes place between inhabitants of different territories. From this difference flow several important consequences: (1) in inter-State war the scope for the use of modern weapons of destruction is far greater. For if the "escalation" of weaponry in an intra-territorial conflict becomes too great, each side will blow itself up with the weapons directed against the other. Neither a revolutionary group nor a State combating revolution, for example, can use nuclear weapons against the other. But, on the other hand, when the warring parties inhabit different territorial areas, the scope for modern weaponry becomes enormous, and the entire arsenal of mass devastation can come into play. A second consequence (2) is that while it is *possible* for revolutionaries to pinpoint their targets and confine them to their State enemies, and thus avoid aggressing against innocent people, pinpointing is far less possible in an inter-State war.[6] This is true even with older weapons; and, of course, with modern weapons there can be no pinpointing whatever. Furthermore, (3) since each State can mobilize all the people and resources in its territory, the other State comes to regard all the citizens of the opposing country as at least temporarily its enemies and to treat them accordingly by extending the war to them. Thus, all of the consequences of inter-territorial war make it almost inevitable that inter-State war will involve aggression by each side against the innocent civilians — the private individuals — of the other. This inevitability becomes absolute with modern weapons of mass destruction.

If one distinct attribute of inter-State war is inter-territoriality, another unique attribute stems from the fact that each State lives by taxation over its subjects. Any war against another State, therefore, involves the increase and extension of taxation-aggression over its own people.[7] Conflicts between private individuals can be, and usually are, voluntarily waged and financed by the parties concerned. Revolutions can be, and often are, financed and fought by voluntary contributions of the public. But State wars can only be waged through aggression against the taxpayer.

All State wars, therefore, involve increased aggression against the State's own taxpayers, and almost all State wars (*all*, in modern warfare) involve the maximum aggression (murder) against the innocent civilians ruled by the enemy State. On the other hand, revolutions are generally financed voluntarily and may pinpoint their violence to the State rulers, and private conflicts may confine their violence to the actual criminals. The libertarian must, therefore, conclude that, while some revolutions and some private conflicts *may* be legitimate, State wars are *always* to be condemned.

Many libertarians object as follows: "While we too deplore the use of taxation for warfare, and the State's monopoly of defense service, we have to recognize that these conditions exist, and while they do, we must support the State in just wars of defense." The reply to this would go as follows: "Yes, as you say, unfortunately States exist, each having a monopoly of violence over its territorial area." What then should be the attitude of the libertarian toward conflicts between these States? The libertarian should say, in effect, to the State: "All right, you exist, but as long as you exist at least confine your activities to the area which you monopolize." In short, the libertarian is interested in reducing as much as possible the area of State aggression against all private individuals. The only way to do this, in international affairs, is for the people of each country to pressure their own State to confine its activities to the area which it monopolizes and not to aggress against other State-monopolists. In short, the objective of the libertarian is to confine any existing State to as small a degree of invasion of person and property as possible. And this means the total avoidance of war. The people under each State should pressure "their" respective States not to attack one another, and, if a conflict should break out, to negotiate a peace or declare a ceasefire as quickly as physically possible.

Suppose further that we have that rarity — an unusually clear-cut case in which the State is actually trying to defend the property of one of its citizens. A citizen of country A travels or invests in country B, and then State B aggresses against his person or confiscates his property. Surely, our libertarian critic would argue, here is a clear-cut case where State A should threaten or commit war against State B in order to defend the property of "its" citizen. Since, the argument runs, the State has taken upon itself the monopoly of defense of its citizens, it then has the obligation to go to war on behalf of any citizen, and libertarians have an obligation to support this war as a just one.

But the point again is that each State has a monopoly of violence and, therefore, of defense only over its territorial area. It has no such monopoly; in fact, it has no power at all, over any other geographical area. Therefore, if an inhabitant of country A should move to or invest in country B, the libertarian must argue that he thereby takes his chances with the State-monopolist of country B, and it would be immoral and criminal for State A to tax people in country A *and* kill numerous innocents in country B in order to defend the property of the traveler or investor.[8]

It should also be pointed out that there is no defense against nuclear weapons (the only current "defense" is the threat of mutual annihilation) and, therefore, that the State *cannot* fulfill any sort of defense function so long as these weapons exist.

The libertarian objective, then, should be, regardless of the specific causes of any conflict, to pressure States not to launch wars against other States and, should a war break out, to pressure them to sue for peace and negotiate a ceasefire and peace treaty as quickly as physically possible. This objective, incidentally, is enshrined in the international law of the eighteenth and nineteenth centuries, that is, the ideal that no State could aggress against the territory of another — in short, the "peaceful coexistence" of States.[9]

Suppose, however, that despite libertarian opposition, war has begun and the warring States are not negotiating a peace. What, then, should be the libertarian position? Clearly, to reduce the scope of assault of innocent civilians as much as possible. Old-fashioned international law had two excellent devices for this: the "laws of war," and the "laws of neutrality" or "neutrals' rights." The laws of neutrality are designed to keep any war that breaks out confined to the warring States themselves, without aggression against the States or particularly the peoples of the other nations. Hence the importance of such ancient and now forgotten American principles as "freedom of the seas" or severe limitations upon the rights of warring States to blockade neutral trade with the enemy country. In short, the libertarian tries to induce neutral States to *remain* neutral in any inter-State conflict and to induce the warring States to observe fully the rights of neutral citizens. The "laws of war" were designed to limit as much as possible the invasion by warring States of the rights of the civilians of the respective warring countries. As the British jurist F.J.P. Veale put it:

> The fundamental principle of this code was that hostilities between civilized peoples must be limited to the armed forces actually engaged...

It drew a distinction between combatants and noncombatants by laying down that the sole business of the combatants is to fight each other and, consequently, that noncombatants must be excluded from the scope of military operations.[10]

In the modified form of prohibiting the bombardment of all cities not in the front line, this rule held in Western European wars in recent centuries until Britain launched the strategic bombing of civilians in World War II. Now, of course, the entire concept is scarcely remembered, the very nature of nuclear war resting on the annihilation of civilians.

In condemning all wars, regardless of motive, the libertarian knows that there may well be varying degrees of guilt among States for any specific war. But the overriding consideration for the libertarian is the condemnation of any State participation in war. Hence his policy is that of exerting pressure on all States not to start a war, to stop one that has begun and to reduce the scope of any persisting war in injuring civilians of either side or no side.

A neglected corollary to the libertarian policy of peaceful coexistence of States is the rigorous abstention from any foreign aid; that is, a policy of nonintervention between States (= "isolationism" = "neutralism"). For any aid given by State A to State B (1) increases tax aggression against the people of country A and (2) aggravates the suppression by State B of its own people. If there are any revolutionary groups in country B, then foreign aid intensifies this suppression all the more. Even foreign aid to a revolutionary group in B — more defensible because directed to a voluntary group opposing a State rather than a State oppressing the people — must be condemned as (at the very least) aggravating tax aggression at home.

Let us see how libertarian theory applies to the problem of *imperialism,* which may be defined as the aggression by State A over the people of country B, and the subsequent maintenance of this foreign rule. Revolution by the B people against the imperial rule of A is certainly legitimate, provided again that revolutionary fire be directed only against the rulers. It has often been maintained — even by libertarians — that Western imperialism over undeveloped countries should be supported as more watchful of property rights than any successor native government would be. The first reply is that judging what might follow the *status quo* is purely speculative, whereas existing imperialist rule is all too real and culpable. Moreover, the libertarian here begins his focus at the wrong end — at the alleged benefit of imperialism to the native. He should, on the contrary, concentrate first on the Western taxpayer, who is mulcted and burdened to pay for the wars of conquest, and then for the maintenance of the imperial bureaucracy. On this ground alone, the libertarian must condemn imperialism.[11]

Does opposition to all war mean that the libertarian can never countenance change — that he is consigning the world to a permanent freezing of unjust regimes? Certainly not. Suppose, for example, that the hypothetical state of "Waldavia" has attacked "Ruritania" and annexed the western part of the country. The Western Ruritanians now long to be reunited with their Ruritanian brethren. How is this to be achieved? There is, of course, the route of peaceful negotiation between the two powers, but suppose that the Waldavian imperialists prove adamant. Or, libertarian Waldavians can put pressure on their government to abandon its conquest in the name of justice. But suppose that this, too, does not work. What then? We must still maintain the illegitimacy of Ruritania's mounting a war against Waldavia. The legitimate routes are (1) revolutionary uprisings by the oppressed Western Ruritanian people, and (2) aid by private Ruritanian groups (or, for that matter, by friends of the Ruritanian cause in other countries) to the Western rebels — either in the form of equipment or of volunteer personnel.[12]

We have seen throughout our discussion the crucial importance, in any present-day libertarian peace program, of the elimination of modern methods of mass annihilation. These weapons, against which there can be no defense, assure maximum aggression against civilians in any conflict with the clear prospect of the destruction of civilization and even of the human race itself. Highest priority on any libertarian agenda, therefore, must be pressure on all States to agree to general and complete disarmament down to police levels, with particular stress on nuclear disarmament. In short, if we are to use our strategic intelligence, we must conclude that the dismantling of the greatest menace that has ever confronted the life and liberty of the human race is indeed far more important than demunicipalizing the garbage service.

We cannot leave our topic without saying at least a word about the domestic tyranny that is the inevitable accompaniment of war. The great Randolph Bourne realized that "war is the health of the State."[13] It is in war that the State really comes into its own: swelling in power, in number, in pride, in absolute dominion over the economy and the society. Society becomes a herd, seeking to kill its alleged enemies, rooting out and suppressing all dissent from the official war effort, happily betraying truth for the supposed public interest. Society becomes an armed camp, with the values and the morale — as Albert Jay Nock once phrased it — of an "army on the march."

The root myth that enables the State to wax fat off war is the canard that war is a defense *by* the State *of* its subjects. The facts, of course, are precisely the reverse. For if war is the health of the State, it is also its greatest danger. A State can only "die" by defeat in war or by revolution. In war, therefore, the State frantically mobilizes the people to fight for *it* against another State, under the pretext that *it* is fighting for them. But all this should occasion no surprise; we see it in other walks of life. For which categories of crime does the State pursue and punish most intensely — those against private citizens or those against *itself?* The gravest crimes in the State's lexicon are almost invariably not invasions of person and property, but dangers to its *own* contentment: for example, treason, desertion of a soldier to the enemy, failure to register for the draft, conspiracy to overthrow the government. Murder is pursued haphazardly unless the victim be a *policeman,* or *Gott soll hüten,* an assassinated Chief of State; failure to pay a private debt is, if anything, almost encouraged, but income tax evasion is punished with utmost severity; counterfeiting the State's money is pursued far more relentlessly than forging private checks, etc. All this evidence demonstrates that the State is far more interested in preserving its own power than in defending the rights of private citizens.

A final word about conscription: of all the ways in which war aggrandizes the State, this is perhaps the most flagrant and most despotic. But the most striking fact about conscription is the absurdity of the arguments put forward on its behalf. A man must be conscripted to defend his (or someone else's?) liberty against an evil State beyond the borders. Defend his liberty? How? By being coerced into an army whose very *raison d'être* is the expunging of liberty, the trampling on all the liberties of the person, the calculated and brutal dehumanization of the soldier and his transformation into an efficient engine of murder at the whim of his "commanding officer"?[14] Can any conceivable foreign State do anything worse to him than what "his" army is now doing for his alleged benefit? Who is there, O Lord, to defend him against his "defenders"?

NOTES

1. There are some libertarians who would go even further and say that no one should employ violence even in defending himself against violence. However, even such Tolstoyans, or "absolute pacifists," would concede the defender's right to employ defensive violence and would merely urge him not to exercise that right. They, therefore, do not disagree with our proposition. In the same way, a libertarian temperance advocate would not challenge a man's right to drink liquor, only his wisdom in exercising that right.

2. We shall not attempt to justify this axiom here. Most libertarians and even conservatives are familiar with the rule and even defend it; the problem is not so much in arriving at the rule as in fearlessly and consistently pursuing its numerous and often astounding implications.

3. Or, to bring up another famous antipacifist slogan, the question is not whether "we would be willing to use force to prevent the rape of our sister," but whether, to prevent that rape, we are willing to kill innocent people and perhaps even the sister herself.

4. William Buckley and other conservatives have propounded the curious moral doctrine that it is no worse to kill millions than it is to kill one man.

The man who does either is, to be sure, a murderer; but surely it makes a huge difference how many people he kills. We may see this by phrasing the problem thus: after a man has already killed one person, does it *make any difference* whether he stops killing now or goes on a further rampage and kills many dozen more people? Obviously, it does.

5. Professor Robert L. Cunningham has defined the State as the institution with "a monopoly on initiating open physical coercion." Or, as Albert Jay Nock put it similarly if more caustically, "The State claims and exercises the monopoly of crime... It forbids private murder, but itself organizes murder on a colossal scale. It punishes private theft, but itself lays unscrupulous hands on anything it wants."

6. An outstanding example of pinpointing by revolutionaries was the invariable practice of the Irish Republican Army, in its later years, of making sure that only British troops and British government property were attacked and that no innocent Irish civilians were injured. A guerrilla revolution not supported by the bulk of the people, of course, is far more likely to aggress against civilians.

7. If it be objected that a war *could* theoretically be financed solely by a State's lowering of nonwar expenditures, then the reply still holds that taxation remains greater than it *could* be without the war effect. Moreover, the purport of this article is that libertarians should be opposed to government expenditures *whatever* the field, war or nonwar.

8. There is another consideration which applies rather to "domestic" defense within a State's territory: the less the State can successfully defend the inhabitants of its area against attack by criminals, the *more* these inhabitants may come to learn the inefficiency of state operations, and the more they will turn to non-State methods of defense. Failure by the State to defend, therefore, has educative value for the public.

9. The international law mentioned in this paper is the old-fashioned libertarian law as had voluntarily emerged in previous centuries and has nothing to do with the modern statist accretion of "collective security." Collective security forces a maximum escalation of every local war into a worldwide war — the precise reversal of the libertarian objective of *reducing* the scope of any war as much as possible.

10. F.J.P. Veale, *Advance to Barbarism* (Appleton, Wis.: C.C. Nelson, 1953), p. 58.

11. Two other points about Western imperialism: first, its rule is not nearly so liberal or benevolent as many libertarians like to believe. The only property rights respected are those of the Europeans; the *natives* find their best lands stolen from them by the imperialists and their labor coerced by violence into working the vast landed estates acquired by this theft. Second, another myth holds that the "gunboat diplomacy" of the turn of the century was a heroic libertarian action in defense of the property rights of Western

investors in backward countries. Aside from our above strictures against going beyond any State's monopolized land area, it is overlooked that the bulk of gunboat moves were in defense, *not* of private investments, but of Western holders of government bonds. The Western powers coerced the smaller governments into increasing tax aggression on their own people, in order to pay off foreign bondholders. By no stretch of the imagination was this an action on behalf of private property — quite the contrary.

12. The Tolstoyan wing of the libertarian movement could urge the Western Ruritanians to engage in *nonviolent* revolution, for example, tax strikes, boycotts, mass refusal to obey government orders or a general strike — especially in arms factories. *Cf.* the work of the revolutionary Tolstoyan, Bartelemy De Ligt, *The Conquest of Violence: An Essay on War and Revolution* (New York: Dutton, 1938).

13. See Randolph Bourne, "Unfinished Fragment on the State," in *Untimely Papers* (New York: B.W. Huebsch, 1919).

14. To the old militarist taunt hurled against the pacifist: "Would you use force to prevent the rape of your sister?" the proper retort is: "Would you rape your sister if ordered to do so by your commanding officer?"

14
No Treason (Excerpts)

Lysander Spooner
1867

Lysander Spooner (1808–1887) was an American individualist anarchist and legal theorist.

That two men have no more natural right to exercise any kind of authority over one, than one has to exercise the same authority over two. A man's natural rights are his own, against the whole world; and any infringement of them is equally a crime, whether committed by one man, or by millions; whether committed by one man, calling himself a robber (or by any other name indicating his true character), or by millions, calling themselves a government. (Part 1, Sec 2)

To say that majorities, as such, have a right to rule minorities, is equivalent to saying that minorities have, and ought to have, no rights, except such as majorities please to allow them. (Part 1, Sec 2)

The principle that the majority have a right to rule the minority, practically resolves all government into a mere contest between two bodies of men, as to which of them shall be masters, and which of them slaves; a contest, that — however bloody — can, in the nature of things, never be finally closed, so long as man refuses to be a slave. (Part 1, Sec 2)

Clearly this individual consent is indispensable to the idea of treason; for if a man has never consented or agreed to support a government, he breaks no faith in refusing to support it. And if he makes war upon it, he does so as an open enemy, and not as a traitor that is, as a betrayer, or treacherous friend. All this, or nothing, was necessarily implied in the Declaration made in 1776. If the necessity for consent, then announced, was a sound principle in favor of three millions of men, it was an equally sound one in favor of three men, or of one man. If the principle was a sound one in behalf of men living on a separate continent, it was an equally sound one in behalf of a man living on a separate farm, or in a separate house. (Part 1, Sec 4)

Thus the whole Revolution turned upon, asserted, and, in theory, established, the right of each and every man, at his discretion, to release himself from the support of the government under which he had lived. And this principle was asserted, not as a right peculiar to themselves, or to that time, or as applicable only to the government then existing; but as a universal right of all men, at all times, and under all circumstances. George the Third called our ancestors traitors for what they did at that time. (Part 1, Sec 4)

The necessity for the consent of "the people" is implied in this declaration. The whole authority of the Constitution rests upon it. If they did not consent, it was of no validity. Of course it had no validity, except as between those who actually consented. No one's consent could be presumed against him, without his actual consent being given, any more than in the case of any other contract to pay money, or render service. (Part 2, Sec 1)

Furthermore, those who originally agreed to the Constitution, could thereby bind nobody that should come after them. They could contract for nobody but themselves. They had no more natural right or power to make political contracts, binding upon succeeding generations, than they had to make marriage or business contracts binding upon them. (Part 2, Sec 1)

Any one man, or any number of men, have had a perfect right, at any time, to refuse his or their further support; and nobody could rightfully object to his or their withdrawal. (Part 2, Sec 1)

A traitor is a betrayer — one who practices injury, while professing friendship. (Part 2, Sec 2)

But it is obvious that, in truth and in fact, no one but himself can bind any one to support any government. And our Constitution admits this fact when it concedes that it derives its authority wholly from the consent of the people. And the word treason is to be understood in accordance with that idea. (Part 2, Sec 3)

One essential of a free government is that it rest wholly on voluntary support. And one certain proof that a government is not free, is that it coerces more or less persons to support it, against their will. (Part 2, Sec 6)

The Constitution has no inherent authority or obligation. It has no authority or obligation at all, unless as a contract between man and man. And it does not so much as even purport to be a contract between persons now existing. It purports, at most, to be only a contract between persons living eighty years ago. And it can be supposed to have been a contract then only between persons who had already come to years of discretion, so as to be competent to make reasonable and obligatory contracts. Furthermore, we know, historically, that only a small portion even of the people then existing were consulted on the subject, or asked, or permitted to express either their consent or dissent in any formal manner. Those persons, if any, who did give their consent formally, are all dead now. Most of them have been dead forty, fifty, sixty, or seventy years. And the constitution, so far as it was their contract, died with them. They had no natural power or right to make it obligatory upon their children. It is not only plainly impossible, in the nature of things, that they could bind their posterity, but they did not even attempt to bind them. That is to say, the instrument does not purport to be an agreement between any body but "the people" then existing; nor does it, either expressly or impliedly, assert any right, power, or disposition, on their part, to bind anybody but themselves. (Part 6, Sec 1)

Those who vote for the unsuccessful candidates cannot properly be said to have voted to sustain the Constitution. (Part 6, Sec 2)

The fact is that the government, like a highwayman, says to a man: "Your money, or your life." ...The highwayman takes solely upon himself the responsibility, danger, and crime of his own act. He does not pretend that he has any rightful claim to your money, or that he intends to use it for your own benefit. He does not pretend to be anything but a robber. (Part 6, Sec 3)

"The government" — that is, the agent of a secret band of robbers and murderers, who have taken to themselves the title of "the government," and have determined to kill everybody who refuses to give them whatever money they demand. (Part 6, Sec 3)

[E]very man who puts money into the hands of a "government" (so called), puts into its hands a sword which will be used against him, to extort more money from him, and also to keep him in subjection to its arbitrary will. (Part 6, Sec 3)

[W]hy should they wish to protect him, if he does not wish them to do so? (Part 6, Sec 3)

The Constitution was not only never signed by anybody, but it was never delivered by anybody, or to anybody's agent or attorney. It can therefore be of no more validity as a contract, than can any other instrument that was never signed or delivered. (Part 6, Sec 4)

A man is none the less a slave because he is allowed to choose a new master once in a term of years. (Part 6, Sec 6)

He has the same right to resist them, and their agents, that he has to resist any other trespassers. (Part 6, Sec 6)

If the people of this country wish to maintain such a government as the Constitution describes, there is no reason in the world why they should not sign the instrument itself, and thus make known their wishes in an open, authentic manner; in such manner as the common sense and experience of mankind have shown to be reasonable and necessary in such cases; and in such manner as to make themselves (as they ought to do) individually responsible for the acts of the government. (Part 6, Sec 7)

But this tacit understanding (admitting it to exist) cannot at all justify the conclusion drawn from it. A tacit understanding between A, B, and C, that they will, by ballot, depute D as their agent, to deprive me of my property, liberty, or life, cannot at all authorize D to do so. He is none the less a robber, tyrant, and murderer, because he claims to act as their agent, than he would be if he avowedly acted on his own responsibility alone. (Part 6, Sec 8)

I have evidence satisfactory to myself, that there exists, scattered throughout the country, a band of men, having a tacit understanding with each other, and calling themselves "the people of the United States," whose general purposes are to control and plunder each other, and all other persons in the country, and, so far as they can, even in neighboring countries; and to kill every man who shall attempt to defend his person and property against their schemes of plunder and dominion. (Part 6, Sec 11)

15

How Private Governance Made the Modern World Possible

Edward P. Stringham, Ph.D.

Edward Peter Stringham is the Davis Professor of Economic Organizations and Innovation at Trinity College, and Editor of *The Journal of Private Enterprise*.

What makes markets, and especially advanced contracts, possible? Most social scientists, including a high percentage of libertarian ones, describe the world as fraught with prisoners' dilemmas (the idea that collaborators would be better off working together, but they each have an incentive to cheat) that can only be solved by government. For example, Israel Kirzner suggests that markets need "governmental, extra-market enforcement" stating that that without "enforceability of contract... the market cannot operate." Similarly Mancur Olson states that without "institutions that enforce contracts impartially" a society will "lose most of the gains from transactions (like those in the capital market) that require impartial third-party enforcement."[1]

But in many cases government officials do not have the knowledge, incentive or ability to enforce contracts or property rights in a low cost way.[2] Consider parties contracting in third world countries where trials take more than a decade. Or consider parties in the first world making a contract where time is of the essence or a lot of money is at stake. Who wants to get large resources tied up in a trial that can take months or years? Or consider making a low value exchange where the cost of going to trial vastly exceeds the value of a transaction. Or consider making a transaction across political boundaries which makes establishing jurisdiction for a trial difficult. At a minimum using courts or government law enforcers requires time and resources, and as practical matter entire classes of contracts are effectively unenforceable.

Judges, police, and regulators are a *deus ex machina*. Government is often dysfunctional and crowds out private sources of order, or it is simply absent or too costly to use. That means parties can either live with their problems or attempt to solve them. In some cases solutions have yet to be found or are too difficult to implement. Such is the world. But quite often solving problems is a profit opportunity and the more at stake, the more potentially profitable the solutions. Throughout history we can see lots of examples of private parties benefiting by figuring out better ways of facilitating exchange or protecting property rights. These protections of the market come not from government but from the market.

In his theory of clubs, James Buchanan argued that we should not assume that goods either must be private goods for one person or public goods for everyone in society, but instead a high percentage of goods are club goods that fall somewhere in between.[3] One of the most important but underappreciated types of club goods is private governance, the various forms of private enforcement, self-governance, or self-regulation among private groups or individuals that fill a void that government enforcement cannot. A country club or a night club not only provide a physical space for leisure, but they also have rules of entry and conduct. The same is true of places of business or living like shopping malls, apartment complexes, stock exchanges, and financial intermediaries. eBay, for example, is a club that facilitates trade with reputation mechanisms and dispute resolution services. It evaluates the marginal benefits and marginal costs of having various rules or dispute resolution mechanisms and seeks to make its market as attractive as possible. American Express is another type of club that helps ensure that consumers get what they pay for and merchants get paid. Most people don't think of their credit card as a rule enforcing club, but it is. A merchant that overcharges customers or a customer who does not pay his bills gets kicked out of the club and that encourages honest behavior.

Private governance helps protect property rights and facilitate trade in everything from the simplest to the world's most advanced markets. It operates in markets where government theoretically can enforce contracts and where government explicitly refuses to enforce contracts. Let us consider some examples.

In all of the world's first major stock markets, government officials considered much of the trading as a form of gambling or speculation used to manipulate prices. In the first stock market in seventeenth century Amsterdam, government refused to enforce all but the simplest securities contracts. After the founding of the Dutch East India Company in 1602 a secondary market for shares emerged among brokers who began specializing in trading stocks. Officials soon passed edicts outlawing their nascent market, but stockbrokers continued trading and developed many sophisticated transactions including forward contracts, short sales, and options. How is that possible? Instead of formal rules, stockbrokers relied on reciprocity and reputation mechanisms to encourage contractual compliance. In contrast to the one shot prisoners' dilemma story, most business is repeated and brokers had to be reliable if they wanted others to do business with them. Not only would a defaulter sour his relationship with his trading partner, but he would be boycotted by everyone else who found out. Reputation thus served as a substitute to formal rules. The market was wildly successful and helped finance the Dutch Golden Age. Some estimates put the market capitalization of the Dutch East India Company in current dollars at $7 trillion. Modern New Yorkers can thank the Dutch East India Company for financing Henry Hudson's first voyage to New York's North River (the Hudson River) and the Dutch West India Company for founding New Amsterdam (New York).[4]

The stock market in England had many similarities. In eighteenth century London officials banned stockbrokers from the Royal Exchange and also refused to enforce most contracts. The market persisted anyway with brokers meeting in coffeehouses around Change Alley. Adam Smith described how time bargains (forward contracts) were unenforceable but people made them and abided by them anyway. He stated, "A dealer is afraid of losing his character, and is scrupulous in observing every engagement. When a person makes 20 contracts in a day, he cannot gain so much by endeavouring to impose on his neighbours, as the very appearance of a cheat would make him lose." If someone defaulted, brokers would label them a lame duck and brokers eventually began writing the names of defaulters on a blackboard. Later brokers decided to transform Jonathan's Coffeehouse into a private club that could create and enforce rules. The club, later known as New Jonathan's, The Stock Subscription Room, and then The Exchange or The Stock Exchange, had membership requirements and rules for dealing with default. They adopted as their motto "My word is my bond."

One can see a similar history in New York about a century later. Early stockbrokers met in the Tontine Tavern and Coffeehouse which in 1797 adopted a "Constitution and Nominations of the Subscribers." In 1817 others founded the New York Stock and Exchange Board, *i.e.*, the New York Stock Exchange, which had more formal membership requirements and rules. Brokers added different resolutions over the years, and by the 1860s, in addition to blacklisting those who did not follow through with their contracts, to make sure everyone was proper they had rules prohibiting "indecorous language" (suspension for a week), fines for "smoking in the Board-room, or in the ante-rooms" (five dollars), and fines for "standing on tables or chairs" (one dollar). By 1865 the initiation fee was $3,000 and by 1868 one's membership seat became a valuable property right that could be sold to potential members. They also created listing requirements for firms that wanted to be traded on the "big board." The New York Stock Exchange always had to compete for business and throughout the years faced competition from the Open Board of Brokers (merged with the New York Stock Exchange in 1869), the Curb Market and its more formal outgrowth, the New York Curb Exchange (founded in 1921 and renamed the American Stock Exchange in 1953), the Consolidated Stock Exchange of New York (founded in the 1880s), and regional exchanges including the Boston Exchange and Philadelphia Stock Exchange (founded in 1834 and 1754, respectively, the latter in London Coffee House). By creating a set of rules to make stock markets more attractive to investors, they helped finance the growth of American business.

In modern times the largest and most advanced markets are also backed by private governance. Consider derivatives contracts, some of which can entail unlimited downside risk and even the best legal system cannot recover an infinite amount. Even the notional value of contracts traded through the Chicago Mercantile Exchange, Chicago Board of Trade and the New York Mercantile Exchange exceeds $10 trillion per year, the contracts go without a hitch. When two parties make a trade through these exchanges, they are not actually making a contract with each other but making separate contracts with the futures exchange. The futures exchange acts as an intermediary and assumes and manages risks for its customers. Rather than allowing any contract to occur and then attempting to enforce it ex post, they have various rules and margin requirements that specify what trades can be made. The risk management from these exchanges eliminates the "need" to have any of these contracts enforced in court.

Other financial intermediaries also assume and manage risks on behalf of customers. When doing business with PayPal or with most credit cards, if fraudsters make bogus transactions or attempt to take money out of an account PayPal is on the hook. By 2001 fraudsters were stealing more [than] $10 million from PayPal per month at a time when its gross annual revenue per year was only $14 million. At first PayPal contacted the FBI and found that it was of little help. After seeing the evidence, the FBI asked questions such as "What's a banner ad?" These government officials were not at the forefront of technology, but even if they were, they still would have been powerless against anonymous fraudsters on the other side of the globe. Rather than sitting around and hoping that government would solve the problems, PayPal came up with private solutions to deal with fraud before it occurred. They developed human-assisted artificial intelligence to monitor accounts, search for suspicious activity, and temporarily or permanently suspend accounts. By assuming and managing risks on behalf of customers, PayPal transformed what many people assume must be legal questions into risk management questions. When parties can deal with problems ex ante, ex post contract enforcement is not the "necessity" that theorists like Kirzner or Olson assume.

Private governance is responsible for creating order not just in basic markets but also in the world's most sophisticated markets, including stock markets, futures markets, and electronic commerce. The role of private governance in enabling stock markets and modern capitalism is one of the least known but most important achievements in the history of the world. Private governance also protects contracts and property rights in scores of other markets. Private governance can be found working in ancient and modern societies, in small and large groups, among friends and strangers, and for simple and extremely complex transactions. It often exists alongside, and in many cases in spite of, government legal efforts. I document more examples in my book *Private Governance: Creating Order in Economic and Social Life* published by Oxford University Press.

Friedrich Hayek used the word "marvel" to describe the price system and its role in coordinating disparate individuals.[5] The mechanisms of private governance are just as miraculous and responsible for creating order in markets. As Thomas Paine writes:

> Great part of that order which reigns among mankind is not the effect of government. It has its origin in the principles of society and the natural constitution of man. It existed prior to government, and would exist if the formality of government was abolished. The mutual dependence and reciprocal interest which man has upon man, and all the parts of civilised community upon each other, create that great chain of connection which holds it together.[6]

The invisible hand analogy in economics sheds light on underappreciated processes of coordinating behavior, and the study of private governance sheds light on similarly underappreciated mechanisms for creating order. Private governance works behind the scenes so most people miss it, but it makes the modern world possible.

NOTES

1. Kirzner, Israel M. 2000. *The Driving Force of the Market: Essays in Austrian Economics*. New York: Routledge, p. 83. Olson, Mancur. 1996. "Big Bills Left on the Sidewalk: Why Some Nations Are Rich, and Others Poor." *Journal of Economic Perspectives*, 10(2): 3–24, p. 22.

2. Galanter and Williamson label the common worldview that all cooperation and trade depend on third party enforcement as legal centralism. Galanter, Marc 1981. "Justice in Many Rooms: Courts, Private Ordering, and Indigenous Law." *Journal of Legal Pluralism*, 19: 1–47. Williamson, Oliver E. 1983. "Credible Commitments: Using Hostages to Support Exchange." *American Economic Review*, 73(4): 519–40.

3. Buchanan, James M. 1965. "An Economic Theory of Clubs." *Economica*, 32: 1–14.

4. These paragraphs draw from my research in my book: Edward Stringham. 2015. *Private Governance: Creating Order in Economic and Social Life*. New York and Oxford: Oxford University Press.

5. Hayek, Friedrich A. 1945. "The Use of Knowledge in Society." *American Economic Review*, 35(4): 519–30.

6. Paine, Thomas. 1791 [1906]. *Rights of Man*. London: J.M. Dent, p. 84.

16
The Misplaced Fear of "Monopoly"

Thomas E. Woods, Jr., Ph.D.
The Future of Freedom Foundation
2012

Tom Woods is a *New York Times* bestselling author of 12 books, including *The Politically Incorrect Guide to American History* and *Meltdown*. He is a Senior Fellow at the Ludwig von Mises Institute.

Those of us who get drawn, often against our better judgment, into Internet debates soon discover that the case against the market economy in the popular mind boils down to a few major claims. Here I intend to dissect one of them: under the unhampered market we'd be at the mercy of vicious monopolists.

This fear can be attributed in part, no doubt, to the cartoon history of the 19th century virtually all of us were exposed to in school. There we learned that rapacious "robber barons" gained overwhelming market share in their industries by means of all sorts of underhanded tricks, and then, once secure in their position, turned around and fleeced the helpless consumer, who had no choice but to pay the high prices that the firms' "monopoly" position made possible.

This version of events is so deeply embedded in Americans' brains that it is next to impossible to dislodge it, no matter the avalanche of evidence and argument applied against it.

Historian Burton Folsom made an important distinction, in his book *The Myth of the Robber Barons*, between political entrepreneurs and market entrepreneurs. The political entrepreneur succeeds by using the implicit violence of government to cripple his competitors and harm consumers. The market entrepreneur, on the other hand, makes his fortune by providing consumers with products they need at prices they can afford, and maintains and expands his market share by remaining innovative and responsive to consumer demand.

It is only the political entrepreneur who deserves our censure, but both types are indiscriminately attacked in the popular caricature that has deformed American public opinion on the subject.

Andrew Carnegie, for instance, almost single-handedly reduced the price of steel rails from $160 per ton in 1875 to $17 per ton nearly a quarter century later. John D. Rockefeller pushed the price of refined petroleum down from more than 30¢ per gallon to 5.9¢ in 1897. Cornelius Vanderbilt, operating earlier in the century, reduced fares on steamboat transit by 90, 95, and even 100 percent. (On trips for which a fare was not charged, Vanderbilt earned his money by selling concessions on board.)

These are benefactors of mankind to be praised, not villains to be condemned.

To be sure, there are caveats, as there always are in history. For a time, Carnegie did support steel tariffs. Since he substantially reduced the price of steel rails, though, this political position of his did not harm the consumer. Other critics will point to the Carnegie and Rockefeller Foundations and the dubious causes those institutions have supported. Their objection is irrelevant to the specific question of whether the men themselves, in their capacity as entrepreneurs, improved the American standard of living. That question is not even debatable.

Mainstream economics identifies monopolists by their behavior: they earn premium profits by restricting output and raising prices. Was that behavior evident in the industries where monopoly was most frequently alleged to have existed? Economist Thomas DiLorenzo, in an important article in the *International Review of Law and Economics*, actually bothered to look. During the 1880s, when real GDP rose 24 percent, output in the industries alleged to have been monopolized for which data were available rose 175 percent in real terms. Prices in those industries, meanwhile, were generally falling, and much faster than the 7 percent decline for the economy as a whole. We've already discussed steel rails, which fell from $68 to $32 per ton during the 1880s; we might also note the price of zinc, which fell from $5.51 to $4.40 per pound (a 20 percent decline), and refined sugar, which fell from 9¢ to 7¢ per pound (22 percent). In fact, this pattern held true for all 17 supposedly monopolized industries, with the trivial exceptions of castor oil and matches.

In other words, the story we thought we knew from our history class was a fake.

Predatory Pricing

Beyond the appeal to specific examples from history, critics of the market propose plausible-sounding scenarios in which firms might be able to harm consumer welfare. Larger firms can afford to lower their prices, even below cost, as long as it takes to drive their smaller competitors out of business, the major argument runs. Once that task is accomplished, the larger firms can raise their prices and take advantage of consumers who no longer have any choice but to buy from them. That strategy on the part of larger firms is known as "predatory pricing."

The Misplaced Fear of "Monopoly"

Dominick Armentano, professor emeritus of economics at the University of Hartford, surveyed scores of important antitrust cases and failed to uncover a single successful example of predatory pricing. Chicago economist George Stigler noted that the theory has fallen into disfavor in professional circles: "Today it would be embarrassing to encounter this argument in professional discourse."

There is a reason for that disfavor. The strategy is suicidal.

For one thing, a large firm attempting predatory pricing must endure losses commensurate with its size. In other words, a firm holding, say, 90 percent of the market competing with a firm holding the remaining 10 percent of the market suffers losses on its 90 percent market share. Economist George Reisman correctly wonders what is supposed to be so brilliant and irresistible about a strategy that involves having a firm — albeit one with nine times the wealth and nine times the business — lose money at a rate nine times as great as the losses suffered by its competitors.

The dominant firm, should it somehow succeed in driving all competitors from the market, must now drive prices back up, to enjoy its windfall, without at the same time encouraging new entrants (who will be attracted by the prospect of charging those high prices themselves) into the field. Then the predatory-pricing strategy must begin all over again, further postponing the moment when the hoped-for premium profits kick in. New entrants into the field will be in a particularly strong position, since they can often acquire the assets of previous firms at fire-sale prices during bankruptcy proceedings.

During the period of the below-cost pricing, meanwhile, consumers tend to stock up on the unusually inexpensive goods. This factor means it will take still longer for the dominant firm to recoup the losses it incurred from the predatory pricing.

A chain-store variant of the predatory-pricing model runs like this: chain stores can draw on the profits they earn in other markets to sustain them while they suffer losses in a new market where they are trying to eliminate competitors by means of predatory pricing.

But imagine a nationwide chain of grocery stores, which we'll call MegaMart. Let's stipulate that MegaMart has a thousand locations across the country and $1 billion of capital invested. That comes out to $1 million per store. Those who warn of "monopoly" contend that MegaMart can bring to bear its entire fortune in order to drive all competitors from one particular market into which it wants to expand.

Now for the sake of argument, we'll leave aside the empirical and theoretical problems with predatory pricing we've already established. Let's assume MegaMart really could use its nationwide resources to drive all competitors from the field in a new market, and could even keep all potential competitors permanently out of the market out of sheer terror at being crushed by MegaMart.

Even if we grant all this, it still makes no sense from the point of view of business strategy and economic judgment for MegaMart to adopt the predatory-pricing strategy. Yes, for a time it would enjoy abnormally high profits, and indeed the prospect of those profits explains why MegaMart would even consider this approach. But would the premium profits be high enough for the whole venture to be a net benefit for the company?

George Reisman insists, correctly, that they would not. "Such a premium profit is surely quite limited — perhaps an additional $100,000 per year, perhaps even an additional $500,000 per year, but certainly nothing remotely approaching the profit that would be required to justify the commitment of [the firm's] total financial resources."

Let's suppose that the premium profit that could be reaped by MegaMart after removing all its competitors amounted to $300,000, the average of those two figures. Assume also that the average rate of return in the economy is 10 percent. That means MegaMart can afford to lose $3 million — the capitalized value of $300,000 per year — in order to seize the market for itself. Spending an amount greater than that would be a poor investment, since the firm would earn a lower-than-average rate of return (lower, that is, than 10 percent). For that reason, MegaMart's $1 billion in capital is simply irrelevant.

What follows from this, according to Reisman, is that

> ...[E]veryone contemplating an investment in the grocery business who has an additional $5 million or even just $1 million to put up is on as good a footing as [MegaMart] in attempting to achieve such [premium] profits. For it simply does not pay to invest additional capital beyond these sums. In other words, the predatory-pricing game, if it actually could be played in these circumstances, would be open to a fairly substantial number of players — not just the extremely large, very rich firms, but everyone who had an additional capital available equal to the limited capitalized value of the "monopoly gains" that might be derived from an individual location.

Market Defenses

Coming back to the more general "predatory pricing" claim, one final argument buries it forever. Economist Don Boudreaux invites us to imagine what would happen if Walmart adopted the predatory-pricing strategy and embarked on a price war over pharmaceutical products, with the aim of driving other drug retailers from the market. Who would be harmed by this? Consumers, to be sure, as well as rival drug suppliers.

But there's a less obvious set of victims, and it's they who hold the key to solving the alleged problem. Companies that distribute the drugs to Walmart also stand to lose. Why? Because if Walmart drives competitors from the field and then raises drug prices, which is the whole point of predatory pricing, then fewer drugs will be sold. It's as simple as the law of demand: at a higher price of a good there is a lower quantity demanded. That means a company like Merck, which distributes a lot of drugs to Walmart, will sell less of its product.

Is Merck going to take that lying down? Of course not. Since a successful predatory-pricing strategy for Walmart would mean lower sales and profits for Merck, it has a strong incentive to block Walmart's move. And it can do so by means of minimum- or maximum-resale-price-maintenance contracts. A minimum-resale-price-maintenance agreement establishes a minimum selling price at which a retailer must sell a company's product. Such a minimum would make it impossible for Walmart to engage in predatory pricing in the first place; they would have to sell the product at the stipulated minimum price, at the very least, and could not go any lower. Maximum-resale-price-maintenance agreements would allow a company, once predatory pricing has succeeded — and again, for the sake of argument we set aside all the reasons we've given for why predatory pricing can't work — to limit the extent of the damage. It would forbid a retailer to sell its product above a stipulated price. Walmart's putative "monopoly profits" could not be realized to any great extent under such an arrangement.

In other words, profits all across the structure of production are threatened when one stage, whether retailing or anything else, attempts to reap so-called monopoly profits. You can bet that firms threatened with a reduction in their own profits will be particularly alert to the various ways in which they can prevent the creation of "monopolies."

What about the DeBeers diamond cartel? Surely that is an example of free-market "monopoly," defying the economists' assurances that cartels on a free market tend to be unstable and short-lived. In fact, there has been no free market in diamonds. The South African government nationalized all diamond mines, even ones it hadn't yet discovered. Thus, a property owner who discovers diamonds on his property finds ownership title instantly transferred to the government. Mine operators, in turn, who lease the mines, must get a license from the government. By an interesting happenstance, the licensees have all wound up being either DeBeers itself or operators willing to distribute their diamonds through the DeBeers Central Selling Organization. Miners trying to distribute diamonds in defiance of government restrictions have faced stiff penalties.

In short, opponents of laissez faire have spooked public opinion with a combination of bad history and worse theory. The average person, although in possession of few if any hard facts in support of his unease at the prospect of laissez faire, is nevertheless sure that such a dreadful state of affairs must be avoided, and that our selfless public servants must protect us against the anti-social behavior of the incorrigible predators in the private sector.

17
Privatize the Roads

Walter Block, Ph.D.

Walter Block, Ph.D. is an Austrian school economist and anarcho-libertarian philosopher. He is the Harold E. Wirth Eminent Scholar Chair in Economics and Professor of Economics at Loyola University New Orleans and Senior Fellow at the Ludwig von Mises Institute. The following article is an excerpt from *The Free Market Reader* (Rockwell, Llewellyn, Jr. [Ed.], 1988).

If the government demanded the sacrifice of 50,000 citizens each year, an outraged public would revolt. If a religious sect planned to immolate 523,335 in the next decade, it would be toppled. If a Manson-type cult murdered 790 people to celebrate Memorial Day, the press would demand the greatest manhunt in this country's history.

If we learned of a disease that killed 2,077 children under the age of five each year, or a nursing home that allowed 7,346 elderly people to die each year, no stone would be left unturned to combat the enemy.

If private enterprise were responsible for this butchery, a cataclysmic reaction would ensue: Congressmen would appoint investigative panels, the Justice Department would seek out antitrust violations, corporate executives would be jailed, and there would be growing cries for nationalization.

In fact, the government is indeed responsible for a real-life slaughter of these exact proportions: the toll taken on our nation's roadways. Whether at the local, state, regional, or national level, it is government that builds, runs, manages, administers, repairs, and plans the road network.

While many blame alcohol and excessive speed as causes of highway accidents, they ignore the more fundamental reason of government ownership and control. Ignoring this is like blaming a snafu in a restaurant on the fact that a poorly maintained oven went out, or that the waiter fell on a greasy floor with a loaded tray. Of course the proximate causes of customer dissatisfaction are uncooked meat or food in their laps. Yet how can these factors be blamed by themselves, while the role of the restaurant's management is ignored?

It is the restaurant manager's job to ensure that the ovens are performing satisfactorily, and that the floors are properly maintained. If he fails, the blame rests on his shoulders, not on the ovens or floors. We hold responsible for the murder, the finger on the trigger, not the bullet. If unsafe conditions prevail in a private, multi-story parking lot, or in a shopping mall, the entrepreneur in question is held accountable.

Why then is there apathy to the continuing atrocity of government roads? Why is there no public outcry? Probably because most people do not see any alternative to government ownership. Just as no one "opposes" or "protests" a volcano, which is believed to be beyond the control of man, there are few who oppose governmental roadway control. But it is my contention that to virtually eliminate highway deaths we need to put ownership and control of roads into private hands, and let the entire service be guided by the free market.

The notion of a fully private market in roads, streets, and highways is likely to be rejected out of hand because people feel that government road management is inevitable. Governments have always owned roads, so any other system is unthinkable.

But there is nothing unique about transportation: the economic principles we accept as a matter of course in practically every other arena of human experience apply here too. As always, the advantage enjoyed by the market is the automatic reward and penalty system imposed by profits and losses. When customers are pleased, they continue patronizing those merchants who have served them well. Businesses that succeed in satisfying consumers earn a profit, while entrepreneurs who fail to satisfy them are soon driven to bankruptcy.

The market process governs the production of the bulk of our consumer goods and capital equipment. This same process that brings us fountain pens, frisbees, and fishsticks can also bring us roads.

Why would a company or individual want to build a road or buy an already existing one? For the same reason as in any other business: to earn a profit. The necessary funds would be raised in a similar manner: by floating and issuance of stock, by borrowing, or from past savings of the owner. The risks would be the same: attracting customers and prospering, or failing to do so and going bankrupt. Just as private enterprise rarely gives burgers away for free, use of road space would require payment. A road enterprise would face virtually all of the same problems shared by other businesses: attracting a labor force, subcontracting, keeping customers satisfied, meeting the price of competitors, innovating, borrowing money, expanding, etc.

The road entrepreneur would have to try to contain congestion, reduce traffic accidents, and plan and design new facilities in coordination with already existing highways, as well as in conjunction with the plans of others for new expansion. He would also take over the jobs the government does now like (sometimes) filling potholes, installing road signs and guard rails, maintaining lane markings, repairing traffic signals, and so on for the myriad of "road furniture" that keeps traffic moving.

Under the present system, a road manager has nothing to lose if an accident happens and several people are killed on a government turnpike. A civil servant draws his annual salary regardless of the accident toll piled up on his domain. But if he were a private owner and he had to compete with other road owners, sovereign consumers who care about safety would not patronize his road, and thus the owner would lose money and go bankrupt.

A common objection to private roads is the specter of having to halt every few feet and toss a coin into a tollbox. This simply would not occur on the market. Imagine a commercial golf course operating on a similar procedure: forcing the golfers to wait in line at every hole, or demanding payment every time they took a swipe at the ball. Such an enterprise would very rapidly lose customers and go broke. Private roads would create economies of scale, where it would pay entrepreneurs to buy the toll collections rights from the millions of holders, in order to rationalize the system into one in which fewer toll gates blocked the roads.

One scenario would follow the shopping center model: a single owner or builder would buy a section of territory and build roads and houses. Just as many shopping center builders maintain control over parking lots, malls, and other common areas, the entrepreneur would continue the operation of common areas such as the roads, sidewalks, etc. Tolls for residents, guests, and deliveries might be pegged at low levels, or be entirely lacking, as in modern shopping centers.

Consider a road on which traffic must continuously be moving. If it's owned by one person or company, who either built it or bought the rights of passage from the previous owners, it would be foolish for him to install dozens of toll gates per mile. There now exist inexpensive electrical devices which can register the car or truck passing by any fixed point on the road. As the vehicle passes the check point, an electrical impulse can be transmitted to a computer that can produce one monthly bill for all roads use, and even mail it out automatically. Road payments could be facilitated in as unobtrusive a manner as utility bills are now.

It is impossible to predict the exact shape of an industry that does not exist. I am in no position to set up the blueprint for a future private market in transport. I cannot tell how many road owners there will be, what kind of rules of the road they will set up, how much it will cost per mile, etc. I can say that a competitive market process would lead highway entrepreneurs to seek newer and better ways of providing services to their customers.

Now we come back to the question of safety. Government road managers are doing a terrible job. Consider what transpires when safety is questioned in other forms of transportation to see a corollary. When an airline experiences an accident, passengers think twice before flying that airline and typically it loses customers. Airlines with excellent safety records have discovered that the public is aware of safety and make choices based upon it. An "exploding Pinto" wouldn't stay on a private road long, nor would reckless drivers and potholes.

I don't know all the details of how a future free-market road system might work. But I do know that "there has to be a better way." And it is the free market.

18
The Utilitarian Case for Voluntaryism

Danny Duchamp

Danny Duchamp creates videos and essays on liberty, economics, and philosophy from a consequentialist libertarian perspective.

No position but voluntaryism is defensible from a utilitarian perspective.

Even if I convince you of this, you might respond that you are not a utilitarian, so this does not convince you of voluntaryism. However, you needn't be a utilitarian to be persuaded by utilitarian arguments. Utilitarianism is the proposition that you should do whatever maximizes "utility" or "the fulfillment of human values." You may not think that maximally fulfilling human values is always the right thing to do, but you probably do care about human values at least a little, so it's still worth taking utilitarian analysis into account.

Or perhaps you are a utilitarian. That works too.

Voluntaryism is the proposition that interactions in which both parties consent (trade, games, etc.) are universally preferable to interactions in which one party coerces the other (violence, theft, etc.).

I could plausibly establish the utilitarian justification for voluntaryism simply by referring to the billions lifted out of poverty through voluntary trade over the past couple of centuries. Since 1820, GDP per capita worldwide has increased fifteen-fold,[1] the percentage of people living in extreme poverty (less than $1.90/day, inflation adjusted) has fallen from over 90% to under 10%,[2] and the average person has access to a variety of food, entertainment, and technology that even kings under previous economic systems couldn't dream of. The utilitarian benefits of voluntary trade are so gargantuan that no honest utilitarian could entertain any alternative.

However, this argument doesn't make clear why we can attribute the triumphs of capitalism to voluntaryism. More importantly, it misses the deeper philosophical connection between voluntaryism and utilitarianism. To resolve those issues, let us begin from the perspective of a utilitarian.

The problem with utilitarian analysis is that some values are mutually exclusive. If I eat an apple, you can't eat it too. My value for apple-eating is fulfilled, and yours is not. We therefore must determine who "values it more." Sometimes, this may be intuitively obvious. We probably agree that if I am dying of hunger while you aren't even sure if you'd finish the apple, then I value it more than you. In other situations, it isn't so obvious. If neither of us is starving and both of us like apples, then who values it more? It's hard to say.

Why is it so obvious in the extreme case? Perhaps because we know I would be willing to sacrifice more. If the apple were on a high branch, I would be more willing to climb up to get it. If the apple were for sale, I would be willing to pay more. This understanding, drawn from the extreme case, gives us a way of estimating who values something more when it isn't so obvious. Namely, if I would be willing to pay more for something (in effort, money, or anything else), then I value it more.

Fortunately, this system is largely self-arranging. If one of us currently possesses the apple, and the other values it more, the latter can buy it from the former. Not only does this mean the buyer is better off; the seller must be, too. If the buyer did not value the apple more than the money, he would not have bought. If the seller did not value the money more than the apple, he would not have sold.

It is only *largely* self-arranging because while people are generally incentivized to act in accordance with it, there is an exception: coercion. I might *not* want to buy the apple from you if I can simply take it by force. My values are still fulfilled (I must have valued the apple more than the effort of taking it from you), but yours are not (you must have valued the apple more than the *nothing* you got in return, or you would have just given it to me). We are back at the problem of determining whose values are more important.

In fact, it's worse than that. If I try to take something from you, you will resist, imposing costs on both of us in the form of property damage and bodily harm, in addition to the cost of security you may incur to prevent future acts of coercion. It's not just that voluntary acts tend to raise total utility and coercive acts have no such tendency; coercive acts actually tend to *decrease* total utility.

Thus, voluntaryism gives us a method of determining who gets what in a way that maximizes total utility. If someone appropriates some unowned piece of property from nature, leave him be; he has just increased his utility. If he trades that property with someone else, leave them be; they have both just increased their utility. If, however, he steals or damages the property of someone else, *stop him! He has just reduced total utility!*

If we apply these principles of private ownership and voluntary exchange consistently, we must apply them to "capital goods," which are goods used to produce other goods (tools, machines, companies, etc.). If these goods could be seized at any moment, then you would have little reason to produce them. Conversely, if you can reliably maintain ownership of capital goods, you have a profit incentive to produce them and sell their output to the world. This is how capitalism (the private ownership of capital goods) achieved the unprecedented living standards we discussed at the beginning.

This isn't to say that the world we live in now operates entirely on a voluntary basis. Theft, fraud, murder, and assault still happen regularly. Taxation, war, victimless crime laws, and an endless list of other government actions all violate people's consent every day. Our reasoning tells us that each of these actions should be expected to reduce the total fulfillment of human values. At least to the extent that you care about human values, you should attempt to prevent these coercive actions. In other words, at least to the extent that you are a utilitarian, you should be a voluntaryist.

NOTES

1. "GDP per capita, 1820 to 2018," Our World in Data, Global Change Data Lab, https://ourworldindata.org/grapher/gdp-per-capita-maddison-2020.
2. "World population living in extreme poverty, World, 1820 to 2015," Our World in Data, Global Change Data Lab, https://ourworldindata.org/grapher/world-population-in-extreme-poverty-absolute.

19
Marxist and Austrian Class Analysis

Hans-Hermann Hoppe, Ph.D.

Hans-Hermann Hoppe is an Austrian School economist, a libertarian/anarcho-capitalist philosopher, and Professor Emeritus of Economics at the University of Nevada, Las Vegas. The following article is taken from *The Journal of Libertarian Studies*, Vol. IX, No. 2 (Fall 1990).

I will do the following in this chapter: First, I will present a series of theses that constitute the hard-core of the Marxist theory of history. I claim that all of them are essentially correct. Then I will show how these true theses are derived in Marxism from a false starting point. Finally, I want to demonstrate how Austrianism in the Mises-Rothbard tradition can give a correct but categorically different explanation of their validity.

Let me begin with the hard-core of the Marxist belief system:[1]

(1) "The history of mankind is the history of class struggles."[2] It is the history of struggles between a relatively small ruling class and a larger class of the exploited. The primary form of exploitation is economic: The ruling class expropriates part of the productive output of the exploited or, as Marxists say, "it appropriates a social surplus product and uses it for its own consumptive purposes."

(2) The ruling class is unified by its common interest in upholding its exploitative position and maximizing its exploitatively appropriated surplus product. It never deliberately gives up power or exploitation income. Instead, any loss in power or income must be wrestled away from it through struggles, whose outcome ultimately depends on the class consciousness of the exploited, *i.e.*, on whether or not and to what extent the exploited are aware of their own status and are consciously united with other class members in common opposition to exploitation.

(3) Class rule manifests itself primarily in specific arrangements regarding the assignment of property rights or, in Marxist terminology, in specific "relations of production." In order to protect these arrangements or production relations, the ruling class forms and is in command of the state as the apparatus of compulsion and coercion. The state enforces and helps reproduce a given class structure through the administration of a system of "class justice," and it assists in the creation and the support of an ideological

superstructure designed to lend legitimacy to the existence of class rule.

(4) Internally, the process of competition within the ruling class generates a tendency toward increasing concentration and centralization. A multipolar system of exploitation is gradually supplanted by an oligarchic or monopolistic one. Fewer and fewer exploitation centers remain in operation, and those that do are increasingly integrated into a hierarchical order. Externally (*i.e.*, as regards the international system), this centralization process will (and all the more intensively the more advanced it is) lead to imperialist interstate wars and the territorial expansion of exploitative rule.

(5) Finally, with the centralization and expansion of exploitative rule gradually approaching its ultimate limit of world domination, class rule will increasingly become incompatible with the further development and improvement of "productive forces." Economic stagnation and crises become more and more characteristic and create the "objective conditions" for the emergence of a revolutionary class consciousness of the exploited. The situation becomes ripe for the establishment of a classless society, the "withering away of the state," the replacement of government of men over men by the administration of things[3] and, as its result, unheard-of economic prosperity.

All of these theses can be given a perfectly good justification, as I will show. Unfortunately, however, it is Marxism, which subscribes to all of them, that has done more than any other ideological system to discredit their validity in deriving them from a patently absurd exploitation theory.

What is this Marxist theory of exploitation? According to Marx, such precapitalist social systems as slavery and feudalism are characterized by exploitation. There is no quarrel with this. For after all, the slave is not a free laborer, and he cannot be said to gain from his being enslaved. Rather, in being enslaved his utility is reduced at the expense of an increase in wealth appropriated by the slave master. The interest of the slave and that of the slave owner are indeed antagonistic. The same is true as regards the interests of the feudal lord who extracts a land rent from a peasant who works on land homesteaded by himself (*i.e.*, the peasant). The lord's gains are the peasant's losses. It is also undisputed that slavery as well as feudalism indeed hamper the development of productive forces. Neither slave nor serf will be as productive as they would be without slavery or serfdom.

The genuinely new Marxist idea is that essentially nothing is changed as regards exploitation under capitalism (if the slave becomes a free laborer), or if the peasant decides to farm land homesteaded by someone else and pays rent in exchange for doing so. To be sure, Marx, in the famous chapter 24 of the first volume of his *Kapital*, titled "The So-Called Original Accumulation," gives a historical account of the emergence of capitalism which makes the point that much or even most of the initial capitalist property is the result of plunder, enclosure, and conquest. Similarly, in chapter 25, on the "Modern

Theory of Colonialism," the role of force and violence in exporting capitalism to the, as we would nowadays say, Third World is heavily emphasized. Admittedly, all this is generally correct, and insofar as it is there can be no quarrel with labeling such capitalism exploitative. Yet one should be aware of the fact that here Marx is engaged in a trick. In engaging in historical investigations and arousing the reader's indignation regarding the brutalities underlying the formation of many capitalist fortunes, he actually side-steps the issue at hand. He distracts from the fact that his thesis is really an entirely different one: namely, that even if one were to have "clean" capitalism so to speak (one in which the original appropriation of capital were the result of nothing else but homesteading, work and savings), the capitalist who hired labor to be employed with this capital would nonetheless be engaged in exploitation. Indeed, Marx considered the proof of this thesis his most important contribution to economic analysis.

What, then, is his proof of the exploitative character of a clean capitalism?

It consists in the observation that the factor prices, in particular the wages paid to laborers by the capitalist, are lower than the output prices. The laborer, for instance, is paid a wage that represents consumption goods which can be produced in three days, but he actually works five days for his wage and produces an output of consumption goods that exceeds what he receives as remuneration. The output of the two extra days, the surplus value in Marxist terminology, is appropriated by the capitalist. Hence, according to Marx, there is exploitation.[4]

What is wrong with this analysis?[5] The answer becomes obvious, once it is asked why the laborer would possibly agree to such a deal! He agrees because his wage payment represents present goods — while his own labor services represent only future goods — and he values present goods more highly. After all, he could also decide not to sell his labor services to the capitalist and then map the full value of his output himself. But this would of course imply that he would have to wait longer for any consumption goods to become available to him. In selling his labor services he demonstrates that he prefers a smaller amount of consumption goods now over a possibly larger one at some future date. On the other hand, why would the capitalist want to strike a deal with the laborer? Why would he want to advance present goods (money) to the laborer in exchange for services that bear fruit only later? Obviously, he would not want to pay out, for instance, $100 now if he were to receive the same amount in one year's time. In that case, why not simply hold on to it for one year and receive the extra benefit of having actual command over it during the entire time? Instead, he must expect to receive a larger sum than $100 in the future in order to give up $100 now in the form of wages paid to the laborer. He must expect to be able to earn a profit, or more correctly an interest return. He is also constrained by time preference, *i.e.*, the fact that an actor invariably prefers earlier over later goods, in yet another way. For if one can obtain a larger sum in the future by sacrificing a smaller one in the present, why then is the capitalist not engaged in more saving than he actually is? Why does he not hire more laborers than he does, if each one of them promises an additional interest return? The answer again should be obvious: because the capitalist is a consumer, as well, and cannot help being one. The amount of his savings and investing is restricted by the necessity that he, too, like the laborer, requires a supply of present goods "large enough to secure the satisfaction of all those wants the satisfaction of which during the waiting time is considered more urgent than the advantages which a still greater lengthening of the period of production would provide."[6]

What is wrong with Marx's theory of exploitation, then, is that he does not understand the phenomenon of time preference as a universal category of human action.[7] That the laborer does not receive his "full worth" has nothing to do with exploitation but merely reflects the fact that it is impossible for man to exchange future goods against present ones except at a discount. Contrary to the case of slave and slave master where the latter benefits at the expense of the former, the relationship between the free laborer and the capitalist is a mutually beneficial one. The laborer enters the agreement because, given his time preference, he prefers a smaller amount of present goods over a larger future one; and the capitalist enters it because, given his time preference, he has a reverse preference order and ranks a larger future amount of goods more highly than a smaller present one. Their interests are not antagonistic but harmonious. Without the capitalist's expectation of an interest return, the laborer would be worse off having to wait longer than he wishes to wait; and without the laborer's preference for present goods the capitalist would be worse off having to resort to less roundabout and less efficient production methods than those which he desires to adopt. Nor can the capitalist wage system be regarded as an impediment to the further development of the forces of production, as Marx claims. If the laborer were not permitted to sell his labor services and the capitalist to buy them, output would not be higher but lower, because production would have to take place with relatively reduced levels of capital accumulation.

Under a system of socialized production, quite contrary to Marx's proclamations, the development of productive forces would not reach new heights but would instead sink dramatically.[8] For obviously, capital accumulation must be brought about by definite individuals at definite points in time and space through homesteading, producing and/or saving. In each case it is brought about with the expectation that it will lead to an increase in the output of future goods. The value an actor attaches to his capital reflects the value he attaches to all expected future incomes attributable to its cooperation and discounted by his rate of time preference. If, as in the case of collectively owned factors of production, an actor is no longer granted exclusive control over his accumulated capital and hence over the future income to be derived from its employment, but partial control instead is assigned to non-homesteaders, non-producers, and non-savers, the value for him of the expected income and hence that of the capital goods is reduced. His effective rate of time preference will rise and there will be less homesteading of scarce resources, and less saving for the maintenance of existing resources and the production of new capital goods. The period of production, the roundaboutness of the production structure, will be shortened, and relative impoverishment will result.

If Marx's theory of capitalist exploitation and his ideas on how to end exploitation and establish universal prosperity are false to the point of being ridiculous, it is clear that any theory of history which can be derived from it must be false, too. Or if it should be correct, it must have been derived incorrectly. Instead of going through the lengthier task of explaining all of the flaws in the Marxist argument as it sets out from its theory of capitalist exploitation and ends with the theory of history which I presented earlier, I will take a shortcut here. I will now outline in the briefest possible way the correct — Austrian, Misesian-Rothbardian — theory of exploitation; give an explanatory sketch of how this theory makes sense out of the class theory of history; and highlight along the way some key differences between this class theory and the Marxist one and also point out some intellectual affinities between Austrianism and Marxism stemming from their common conviction that there does indeed exist something like exploitation and a ruling class.[9]

The starting point for the Austrian exploitation theory is plain and simple, as it should be. Actually, it has already been established through the analysis of the Marxist theory: Exploitation characterized the relationship between slave and slave master and serf and feudal lord. But no exploitation was found possible under a clean capitalism. What is the principal difference between these two cases? The answer is: the recognition or non-recognition of the homesteading principle. The peasant under feudalism is exploited because he does not have exclusive control over land that he homesteaded, and the slave because he has no exclusive control over his own homesteaded body. If, contrary to this, everyone has exclusive control over his own body (is a free laborer, that is) and acts in accordance with the homesteading principle, there can be no exploitation. It is logically absurd to claim that a person who homesteads goods not previously homesteaded by anybody else, or who employs such goods in the production of future goods, or who saves presently homesteaded or produced goods in order to increase the future supply of goods, could thereby exploit anybody. Nothing has been taken away from anybody in this process and additional goods have actually been created. And it would be equally absurd to claim that an agreement between different homesteaders, savers and producers regarding their non-exploitatively appropriated goods or services could possibly contain any foul play, then. Instead, exploitation takes place whenever any *deviation* from the homesteading principle occurs. It is exploitation whenever a person successfully claims partial or full control over scarce resources which he has not homesteaded, saved or produced, and which he has not acquired contractually from a previous producer-owner. Exploitation is the expropriation of homesteaders, producers and savers by late-coming non-homesteaders, non-producers, non-savers and non-contractors; it is the expropriation of people whose property claims are grounded in work and contract by people whose claims are derived from thin air and who disregard others' work and contracts.[10]

Needless to say, exploitation thus defined is in fact an integral part of human history. One can acquire and increase wealth either through homesteading, producing, saving, or contracting, or by expropriating homesteaders, producers, savers or contractors. There are no other ways. Both methods are natural to mankind. Alongside homesteading, producing and contracting, there have always been non-productive and non-contractual property acquisitions. And in the course of economic development, just as producers and contractors can form firms, enterprises and corporations, so can exploiters combine to large-scale exploitation enterprises, governments and states. The ruling class (which may again be internally stratified) is initially composed of the members of such an exploitation firm. And with a ruling class established over a given territory and engaged in the expropriation of economic resources from a class of exploited producers, the center of all history indeed becomes the struggle between exploiters and the exploited. History, then, correctly told, is essentially the history of the victories and defeats of the rulers in their attempt to maximize exploitatively appropriated income and of the ruled in their attempts to resist and reverse this tendency. It is in this assessment of history that Austrians and Marxists agree, and it is why a notable intellectual affinity between Austrian and Marxist historical investigations exists. Both oppose a historiography which recognizes only action or interaction, economically and morally all on a par; and both oppose a historiography that instead of adopting such a value-neutral stand thinks that one's own arbitrarily introduced subjective value judgments have to provide the foil for one's historical narratives. Rather, history must be told in terms of freedom and exploitation, parasitism and economic impoverishment, private property and its destruction — otherwise it is told falsely.[11]

While productive enterprises come into or go out of existence because of voluntary support or its absence, a ruling class never comes to power because there is a demand for it, nor does it abdicate when abdication is demonstrably demanded. One cannot say by any stretch of the imagination that homesteaders, producers, savers and contractors have demanded their expropriation. They must be coerced into accepting it, and this proves conclusively that the exploitation firm is not in demand at all. Nor can one say that a ruling class can be brought down by abstaining from transactions with it in the same way as one can bring down a productive enterprise. For the ruling class acquires its income through non-productive and non-contractual transactions and thus is unaffected by boycotts. Rather, what makes the rise of an exploitation firm possible, and what alone can in turn bring it down is a specific state of public opinion or, in Marxist terminology, a specific state of class consciousness.

An exploiter creates victims, and victims are potential enemies. It is possible that this resistance can be lastingly broken down by force in the case of a group of men exploiting another group of roughly the same size. However, more than force is needed to expand exploitation over a population many times its own size. For this to happen, a firm must also have public support. A majority of the population must accept the exploitative actions as legitimate. This acceptance can range from active enthusiasm to passive resignation. But it must be acceptance in the sense that a majority must have given up the idea of actively or passively resisting any attempt to enforce non-productive and non-contractual property acquisitions. The class consciousness must be low, undeveloped and fuzzy. Only as long as this state of affairs lasts is there still room for an exploitative firm to prosper, even if no actual demand for it exists. Only if and insofar as the exploited and expropriated develop a clear idea of their own situation and are united with other members of their class through an ideological movement which gives expression to the idea of a classless society where all exploitation is abolished, can the power of the ruling class be broken. Only if, and insofar as, a majority of the exploited public becomes consciously integrated into such a movement and accordingly displays a common outrage over all non-productive or non-contractual property acquisitions, shows a contempt for everyone who engages in such acts, and deliberately contributes nothing to help make them successful (not to mention actively trying to obstruct them), can its power be brought to crumble.

The gradual abolition of feudal and absolutist rule and the rise of increasingly capitalist societies in Western Europe and the U.S. — and, along with this, unheard-of economic growth and rising population numbers — were the result of an increasing class consciousness among the exploited, who were ideologically molded together through the doctrines of natural rights and liberalism. In this Austrians and Marxists agree.[12] They disagree, however, on the next assessment: The reversal of this liberalization process and steadily increased levels of exploitation in these societies since the last third of the nineteenth century, and particularly pronounced since WW I, are the result of a loss in class consciousness. In fact, in the Austrian view Marxism must accept much of the blame for this development by misdirecting attention from the correct exploitation model of the homesteader-producer-saver-contractor vs. the non-homesteader-producer-saver-contractor to the fallacious model of the wage earner vs. the capitalist, thus muddling things up.[13]

The establishment of a ruling class over an exploited one many times its size by coercion and the manipulation of public opinion (*i.e.*, a low degree of class consciousness among the exploited), finds its most basic institutional expression in the creation of a system of public law superimposed on private law. The ruling class sets itself apart and protects its position as a ruling class by adopting a constitution for their firm's operations. On the one hand, by formalizing the internal operations within the state apparatus as well as its relations *vis-à-vis* the exploited population, a constitution creates some degree of legal stability. The more familiar and popular private law notions are incorporated into constitutional and public law, the more conducive this will be to the creation of favorable public opinion. On the other hand, any constitution and public law also formalizes the exemplary status of the ruling class as regards the homesteading principle. It formalizes the right of the state's representatives to engage in non-productive and non-contractual property acquisitions and the ultimate subordination of private to public law.

Class justice, *i.e.*, a dualism of one set of laws for the rulers and another for the ruled, comes to bear in this dualism of public and private law and in the domination and infiltration of public law over and into private law. It is not because private-property rights are recognized by law, as Marxists think, that class justice is established. Rather, class justice comes into being precisely whenever a legal distinction exists between a class of persons acting under and being protected by public law and another class acting under and being protected instead by some subordinate private law. More specifically then, the basic proposition of the Marxist theory of the state in particular is false. The state is not exploitative because it protects the capitalists' property rights, but because it itself is exempt from the restriction of having to acquire property productively and contractually.[14]

In spite of this fundamental misconception, however, Marxism, because it correctly interprets the state as exploitative (contrary, for instance, to the Public Choice School, which sees it as a normal firm among others),[15] is on to some important insights regarding the logic of state operations. For one thing, it recognizes the strategic function of redistributionist state policies. As an exploitative firm, the state must at all times be interested in a low degree of class consciousness among the ruled. The redistribution of property and income — a policy of *divide et impera* — is the state's means with which it can create divisiveness among the public and destroy the formation of a unifying class consciousness of the exploited. Furthermore, the redistribution of state power itself through democratizing the state constitution and opening up every ruling position to everyone and granting everyone the right to participate in the determination of state personnel and policy is a means for reducing the resistance against exploitation as such. Second, the state is indeed, as Marxists see it, the great center of ideological propaganda and mystification: Exploitation is really freedom; taxes are really voluntary contributions; non-contractual relations are really "conceptually" contractual ones; no one is ruled by anyone but we all rule ourselves; without the state neither law nor security would exist; and the poor would perish, etc. All of this is part of the ideological superstructure designed to legitimize an underlying basis of economic exploitation.[16] And finally, Marxists are also correct in noticing the close association between the state and business, especially the banking elite — even though their explanation for it is faulty. The reason is not that the bourgeois establishment sees and supports the state as the guarantor of private property rights and contractualism. On the contrary, the establishment correctly perceives the state as the very antithesis to private property that it is and takes a close interest in it for this reason. The more successful a business, the larger the potential danger of governmental exploitation, but the larger also the potential gains that can be achieved if it can come under government's special protection and is exempt from the full weight of capitalist competition. This is why the business establishment is interested in the state and its infiltration. The ruling elite in turn is interested in close cooperation with the business establishment because of its financial powers. In particular, the banking elite is of interest because as an exploitative firm the state naturally wishes to possess complete autonomy for counterfeiting.

By offering to cut the banking elite in on its own counterfeiting machinations and allowing them to counterfeit on top of its own counterfeited notes under a regime of fractional reserve banking, the state can easily reach this goal and establish a system of state monopolized money and cartelized banking controlled by the central bank. And through this direct counterfeiting connection with the banking system and by extension the banks' major clients, the ruling class in fact extends far beyond the state apparatus to the very nerve centers of civil society — not that much different, at least in appearance, from the picture that Marxists like to paint of the cooperation between banking, business elites and the state.[17]

Competition within the ruling class and among different ruling classes brings about a tendency toward increasing concentration. Marxism is right in this. However, its faulty theory of exploitation again leads it to locate the cause for this tendency in the wrong place. Marxism sees such a tendency as inherent in capitalist competition. Yet it is precisely so long as people are engaged in a clean capitalism that competition is *not* a form of zero-sum interaction. The homesteader, the producer, saver and contractor do not gain at another's expense. Their gains either leave another's physical possessions completely unaffected or they actually imply mutual gains (as in the case of all contractual exchanges). Capitalism thus can account for increases in absolute wealth. But under its regime no systematic tendency toward relative concentration can be said to exist.[18] Instead, zero-sum interactions characterize not only the relationship between the ruler and the ruled, but also between competing rulers. Exploitation defined as non-productive and non-contractual property acquisitions is only possible as long as there is anything that can be appropriated. Yet if there were free competition in the business of exploitation, there would obviously be nothing left to expropriate. Thus, exploitation requires monopoly over some given territory and population; and the competition between exploiters is by its very nature eliminative and must bring about a tendency toward relative concentration of exploitative firms as well as a tendency toward centralization within each exploitative firm. The development of *states* rather than capitalist firms provides the foremost illustration of this tendency: There are now a significantly smaller number of states with exploitative control over much larger territories than in previous centuries. And within each state apparatus there has in fact been a constant tendency toward increasing the powers of the central government at the expense of its regional and local subdivisions. Yet outside the state apparatus a tendency toward relative concentration has also become apparent for the same reason. Not, as should be clear by now, because of any trait inherent in capitalism, but because the ruling class has expanded its rule into the midst of civil society through the creation of a state-banking-business alliance and in particular the establishment of a system of central banking. If a concentration and centralization of state power then takes place, it is only natural that this be accompanied by a parallel process of relative concentration and cartelization of banking and industry. Along with increased state powers, the associated banking and business establishment's powers of eliminating or putting economic competitors at a disadvantage by means of non-productive and/or non-contractual expropriations increases. Business concentration is the reflection of a "state-ization" of economic life.[19]

The primary means for the expansion of state power and the elimination of rival exploitation centers is war and military domination. Interstate competition implies a tendency toward war and imperialism. As centers of exploitation their interests are by nature antagonistic. Moreover, with each of them — internally — in command of the instrument of taxation and absolute counterfeiting powers, it is possible for the ruling classes to let others pay for their wars. Naturally, if one does not have to pay for one's risky ventures oneself, but can force others to do so, one tends to be a greater risk taker and more trigger-happy than one would otherwise be.[20] Marxism, contrary to much of the so-called bourgeois social sciences, gets the facts right: there is indeed a tendency toward imperialism operative in history; and the foremost imperialist powers are indeed the most advanced capitalist nations. Yet the explanation is once again faulty. It is the *state* as an institution exempt from the capitalist rules of property acquisitions that is by nature aggressive. And the historical evidence of a close correlation between capitalism and imperialism only seemingly contradicts this. It finds its explanation, easily enough, in the fact that in order to come out successfully from interstate wars, a state must be in command of sufficient (in relative terms) economic resources. Ceteris paribus, the state with more ample resources will win. As an exploitative firm, a state is by nature destructive of wealth and capital accumulation. Wealth is produced exclusively by civil society; and the weaker the state's exploitative powers, the more wealth and capital society accumulates. Thus, paradoxical as it may sound at first, the weaker or the more liberal a state is internally, the further developed capitalism is; a developed capitalist economy to extract from makes the state richer; and a richer state then makes for more and more successful expansionist wars. It is this relationship that explains why initially the states of Western Europe, and in particular Great Britain, were the leading imperialist powers, and why in the 20th century this role has been assumed by the U.S.

And a similarly straightforward yet once again entirely non-Marxist explanation exists for the observation always pointed out by Marxists, that the banking and business establishment is usually among the most ardent supporters of military strength and imperial expansionism. It is not because the expansion of capitalist markets requires exploitation, but because the expansion of state protected and privileged business requires that such protection be extended also to foreign countries and that foreign competitors be hampered through non-contractual and non-productive property acquisitions in the same way or more so than internal competition. Specifically, it supports imperialism if this promises to lead to a position of military domination of one's own allied state over another. For then, from a position of military strength, it becomes possible to establish a system of — as one may call it — monetary imperialism. The dominating state will use its superior power to enforce a policy of internationally coordinated inflation. Its own central bank sets the pace in the process of counterfeiting, and the central banks of the dominated states are ordered to use its currency as their own reserves and inflate on top of them. This way, along with the dominating state and as the earliest receivers of the counterfeit reserve currency its associated banking and business establishment can engage in an almost costless expropriation of foreign property owners and income producers. A double layer of exploitation of a foreign state and a foreign elite on top of a national state and elite is imposed on the exploited class in the dominated territories, causing prolonged economic dependency and relative economic stagnation *vis-à-vis* the dominant nation. It is this — very uncapitalist — situation that characterizes the status of the United States and the U.S. dollar and that gives rise to the — correct — charge of U.S. economic exploitation and dollar imperialism?[21]

Finally, the increasing concentration and centralization of exploitative powers leads to economic stagnation and thereby creates the objective conditions for their ultimate demise and the establishment of a classless society capable of producing unheard-of economic prosperity.

Contrary to Marxist claims, this is not the result of any historical laws, however. In fact, no such things as inexorable historical laws as Marxists conceive of them exist.[22] Nor is it the result of a tendency for the rate of profit to fall with an increased organic composition of capital (an increase in the proportion of constant to variable capital, that is), as Marx thinks. Just as the labor theory of value is false beyond repair, so is the law of the tendential fall of the profit rate, which is based on it. The source of value, interest and profit is not the expenditure of labor but of acting, *i.e.*, the employment of scarce means in the pursuit of goals by agents who are constrained by time preference and uncertainty (imperfect knowledge). There is no reason to suppose, then, that changes in the organic composition of capital should have any systematic relation to changes in interest and profit.

Instead, the likelihood of crises which stimulate the development of a higher degree of class consciousness (*i.e.*, the subjective conditions for the overthrow of the ruling class) increases because — to use one of Marx's favorite terms — of the dialectics of exploitation which I have already touched on earlier: Exploitation is destructive of wealth formation. Hence, in the competition of exploitative firms (of states), less exploitative or more liberal ones tend to outcompete more exploitative ones because they are in command of more ample resources. The process of imperialism initially has a relatively liberating effect on societies coming under its control. A relatively more capitalist social model is exported to relatively less capitalist (more exploitative) societies. The development of productive forces is stimulated: economic integration is furthered, division of labor extended, and a genuine world market established. Population figures go up in response, and expectations as regards the economic future rise to unprecedented heights.[23] With exploitative domination taking hold, and interstate competition reduced or even eliminated in a process of imperialist expansionism, however, the external constraints on the dominating state's power of internal exploitation and expropriation gradually disappear. Internal exploitation, taxation and regulation begin to increase the closer the ruling class comes to its ultimate goal of world domination. Economic stagnation sets in and the — worldwide — higher expectations become frustrated. And this — high expectations and an economic reality increasingly falling behind these expectations — is the classical situation for the emergence of a revolutionary potential.[24] A desperate need for ideological solutions to the emerging crises arises, along with a more widespread recognition of the fact that state rule, taxation and regulation — far from offering such a solution — actually constitute the very problem that must be overcome. If in this situation of economic stagnation, crises, and ideological disillusion[25] a positive solution is offered in the form of a systematic and comprehensive libertarian philosophy coupled with its economic counterpart: Austrian economics; and if this ideology is propagated by an activist movement, then the prospects of igniting the revolutionary potential to activism become overwhelmingly positive and promising. Anti-statist pressures will mount and bring about an irresistible tendency toward dismantling the power of the ruling class and the state as its instrument of exploitation.[26]

If and insofar as this occurs, however, this will not mean social ownership of means of production, contrary to the Marxist model. In fact, social ownership is not only economically inefficient as has already been explained; it is incompatible with the idea that the state is "withering away."[27] For if means of production are owned collectively, and if it is realistically assumed that not everyone's ideas as to how to employ these means of production happen to coincide (as if by miracle), then it is precisely socially owned factors of production which require continued state actions, *i.e.*, an institution coercively imposing one person's will on another disagreeing one's. Instead, the withering away of the state, and with this the end of exploitation and the beginning of liberty and unheard-of economic prosperity, means the establishment of a pure private property society regulated by nothing but private law.

NOTES

1. See on the following Karl Marx and Frederic Engels, *The Communist Manifesto* (1848); Karl Marx, *Das Kapital*, 3 vols. (1867; 1885; 1894); as contemporary Marxists, Ernest Mandel, *Marxist Economic Theory* (London: Merlin, 1962); idem, *Late Capitalism* (London: New Left Books, 1975); Paul Baran and Paul Sweezy, *Monopoly Capital* (New York: Monthly Review Press, 1966); from a non-Marxist perspective, Leszek Kolakowski, *Main Currents of Marxism* (Oxford: Clarendon Press, 1995); G. Wetter, *Sowjetideologie heute* (Frankfurt/M.: Fischer, 1962), vol. 1; W. Leonhard, *Sowjetideologie heute* (Frankfurt/M.: Fischer, 1962), vol. 2.

2. Marx and Engels, *The Communist Manifesto* (section 1).

3. *The Communist Manifesto* (section 2, last 2 paragraphs); Frederic Engels, *Von der Autorität*, in Karl Marx and Frederic Engels, *Ausgewählte Schriften*, 2 vols. (East Berlin: Dietz, 1953), vol. 1, p. 606; idem, *Die Entwicklung des Sozialismus von der Utopie zur Wissenschaft*, ibid., vol. 2, p. 139.

4. See Marx, *Das Kapital*, vol. 1; the shortest presentation is his *Lohn, Preis, Profit* (1865). Actually, in order to prove the more specific Marxist thesis that exclusively the owner of labor services is exploited (but not the owner of the other originary factor of production: land), yet another argument would be

needed. For if it were true that the discrepancy between factor and output prices constitutes an exploitative relation, this would only show that the capitalist who rents labor services from an owner of labor, and land services from an owner of land would exploit either labor, or land, or labor and land simultaneously. It is the labor theory of value, of course, which is supposed to provide the missing link here by trying to establish labor as the sole source of value. I will spare myself the task of refuting this theory. Few enough remain today, even among those claiming to be Marxists, who do not recognize the faultiness of the labor theory of value. Rather, I will accept for the sake of argument the suggestion made, for instance, by the self-proclaimed "analytical Marxist" John Roemer (*A General Theory of Exploitation and Class* [Cambridge, Mass.: Harvard University Press, 1982]; idem, *Value, Exploitation and Class* [London: Harwood Academic Publishers, 1985]), that the theory of exploitation can be separated analytically from the labor theory of value; and that a "generalized commodity exploitation theory" can be formulated which can be justified regardless of whether or not the labor theory of value is true. I want to demonstrate that the Marxist theory of exploitation is nonsensical even if one were to absolve its proponents from having to prove the labor theory of value and, indeed, even if the labor theory of value were true. Even a generalized commodity exploitation theory provides no escape from the conclusion that the Marxist theory of exploitation is dead wrong.

5. See on the following Eugen von Böhm-Bawerk, *The Exploitation Theory of Socialism-Communism* (South Holland, Ill.: Libertarian Press, 1975); idem, *Shorter Classics of Böhm-Bawerk* (South Holland, Ill.: Libertarian Press, 1962).

6. Ludwig von Mises, *Human Action* (Chicago: Regnery, 1966), p. 407; see also Murray N. Rothbard, *Man, Economy, and State* (Los Angeles: Nash, 1970), pp. 300–01.

7. See on the time preference theory of interest in addition to the works cited in notes 5 and 6; also Frank Fetter, *Capital, Interest and Rent* (Kansas City: Sheed Andrews and McMeel, 1977).

8. See on the following Hans-Hermann Hoppe, *A Theory of Socialism and Capitalism* (Boston: Kluwer Academic Publishers, 1989); idem, "Why Socialism Must Fail," *Free Market* (July 1988); idem, "The Economics and Sociology of Taxation," *Journal des Economistes et des Etudes Humaines* (1990); *supra* chap. 2.

9. Mises's contributions to the theory of exploitation and class are unsystematic. However, throughout his writings he presents sociological and historical interpretations that are class analyses, if only implicitly. Noteworthy here is in particular his acute analysis of the collaboration between government and banking elite in destroying the gold standard in order to increase their inflationary powers as a means of fraudulent, exploitative income and wealth redistribution in their own favor. See for instance his

Monetary Stabilization and Cyclical Policy (1928) in idem, *On the Manipulation of Money and Credit*, ed. Percy Greaves (Dobbs Ferry, N.Y.: Free Market Books 1978); idem, *Socialism* (Indianapolis: Liberty Fund, 1981), chap. 20; idem, *The Clash of Group Interests and Other Essays* (New York: Center for Libertarian Studies, Occasional Paper Series No. 7, 1978). Yet Mises does not give systematic status to class analysis and exploitation theory because he ultimately misconceives of exploitation as merely an intellectual error which correct economic reasoning can dispel. He fails to fully recognize that exploitation is also and probably even more so a moral-motivational problem that exists regardless of all economic reasoning. Rothbard adds his insight to the Misesian structure of Austrian economics and makes the analysis of power and power elites an integral part of economic theory and historical-sociological explanations; and he systematically expands the Austrian case against exploitation to include ethics in addition to economic theory, *i.e.*, a theory of justice next to a theory of efficiency, such that the ruling class can also be attacked as immoral. For Rothbard's theory of power, class and exploitation, see in particular his *Power and Market* (Kansas City: Sheed Andrews and McMeel, 1977); idem, *For a New Liberty* (New York: Macmillan, 1978); idem, *The Mystery of Banking* (New York: Richardson and Snyder, 1983); idem, *America's Great Depression* (Kansas City: Sheed and Ward, 1975). On important nineteenth-century forerunners of Austrian class analysis, see Leonard Liggio, "Charles Dunoyer and French Classical Liberalism," *Journal of Libertarian Studies* 1, no. 3 (1977); Ralph Raico, "Classical Liberal Exploitation Theory," *Journal of Libertarian Studies* 1, no. 3 (1977); Mark Weinburg, "The Social Analysis of Three Early 19th Century French Liberals: Say, Comte, and Dunoyer," *Journal of Libertarian Studies* 2, no. 1 (1978); Joseph T. Salerno, "Comment on the French Liberal School," *Journal of Libertarian Studies* 2, no. 1 (1978); David M. Hart, "Gustave de Molinari and the Anti-Statist Liberal Tradition," 2 parts, *Journal of Libertarian Studies* 5, nos. 3 and 4 (1981).

10. See on this also Hoppe, *A Theory of Socialism and Capitalism*; idem, "The Justice of Economic Efficiency," *Austrian Economics Newsletter* 1 (1988); *infra* chap. 9; idem, "The Ultimate Justification of the Private Property Ethics," *Liberty* (September 1988): *infra* chap. 10.

11. See on this theme also Lord (John) Acton, *Essays in the History of Liberty* (Indianapolis: Liberty Fund, 1985); Franz Oppenheimer, *System der Soziologie, vol. 2: Der Staat* (Stuttgart: G. Fischer, 1964); Alexander Rüstow, *Freedom and Domination* (Princeton, N.J.: Princeton University Press, 1986).

12. See on this Murray N. Rothbard, "Left and Right: The Prospects for Liberty," in idem, *Egalitarianism as a Revolt Against Nature and Other Essays* (Washington, D.C.: Libertarian Review Press, 1974).

13. All socialist propaganda to the contrary notwithstanding, the falsehood of the Marxist description of capitalists and laborers as

antagonistic classes also comes to bear in certain empirical observations: Logically speaking, people can be grouped into classes in infinitely different ways. According to orthodox positivist methodology (which I consider false but am willing to accept here for the sake of argument), that classification system is better which helps us predict better. Yet the classification of people as capitalists or laborers (or as representatives of varying degrees of capitalist- or laborer-ness) is practically useless in predicting what stand a person will take on fundamental political, social and economic issues. Contrary to this, the correct classification of people as tax producers and the regulated vs. tax consumers and the regulators (or as representatives of varying degrees of tax producer- or consumer-ness) is indeed also a powerful predictor. Sociologists have largely overlooked this because of almost universally shared Marxist preconceptions. But everyday experience overwhelmingly corroborates my thesis: Find out whether or not somebody is a public employee (and his rank and salary), and whether or not and to what extent the income and wealth of a person outside of the public sector is determined by public sector purchases and/or regulatory actions; people will systematically differ in their response to fundamental political issues depending on whether they are classified as direct or indirect tax consumers or as tax producers!

14. Franz Oppenheimer, *System der Soziologie*, vol. 2. pp. 322–23, presents the matter thus:

> The basic norm of the state is power. That is, seen from the side of its origin: violence transformed into might. Violence is one of the most powerful forces shaping society, but is not itself a form of social interaction. It must become law in the positive sense of this term, that is, sociologically speaking, it must permit the development of a system of "subjective reciprocity," and this is only possible through a system of self-imposed restrictions on the use of violence and the assumption of certain obligations in exchange for its arrogated rights; in this way violence is turned into might, and a relationship of domination emerges which is accepted not only by the rulers, but under not too severely oppressive circumstances by their subjects as well, as expressing a "just reciprocity." Out of this basic norm secondary and tertiary norms now emerge as implied in it: norms of private law, of inheritance, criminal, obligational and constitutional law, which all bear the mark of the basic norm of power and domination, and which are all designed to influence the structure of the state in such a way as to increase economic exploitation to the maximum level which is compatible with the continuation of legally regulated domination. The insight is fundamental that "law grows out of two essentially different roots." On the one hand, out of the law of the association of equals, which can be called a "natural right," even if it is no natural right, and on the other hand, out of the law of violence transformed into regulated might, the law of unequals.

On the relation between private and public law, see also F.A. Hayek, *Law, Legislation and Liberty*, 3 vols. (Chicago: University of Chicago Press, 1973–79), esp. vol. 1, chap. 6 and vol. 2, pp. 85–88.

15. See James Buchanan and Gordon Tullock, *The Calculus of Consent* (Ann Arbor: University of Michigan Press, 1962), p. 19.

16. See Hans-Hermann Hoppe, *Eigentum, Anarchie, und Staat* (Opladen: Westdeutscher Verlag, 1987); idem, *A Theory of Socialism and Capitalism*.

17. See Hans-Hermann Hoppe, "Banking, Nation States and International Politics," *Review of Austrian Economics* 4 (1990); *supra* chap. 3; Rothbard, *The Mystery of Banking*, chaps. 15–16.

18. See on this in particular Rothbard, *Man, Economy, and State*, chap. 10, esp. the section "The Problem of One Big Cartel"; also Mises, *Socialism*, chaps. 22–26.

19. See on this Gabriel Kolko, *The Triumph of Conservatism* (Chicago: Free Press, 1967); James Weinstein, *The Corporate Ideal in the Liberal State* (Boston: Beacon Press, 1968); Ronald Radosh and Murray N. Rothbard, eds., *A New History of Leviathan* (New York: Dutton, 1972); Leonard Liggio and James J. Martin, eds., *Watershed of Empire* (Colorado Springs, Colo.: Ralph Myles, 1976).

20. On the relationship between state and war see Ekkehart Krippendorff, *Staat und Krieg* (Frankfurt/M.: Suhrkamp, 1985); Charles Tilly, "War Making and State Making as Organized Crime," in Peter Evans et al., eds., *Bringing the State Back In* (Cambridge: Cambridge University Press, 1985); also Robert Higgs, *Crisis and Leviathan* (New York: Oxford University Press, 1987).

21. On a further elaborated version of this theory of military and monetary imperialism see Hoppe, "Banking, Nation States and International Politics" (*supra* chap. 3).

22. See on this in particular Ludwig von Mises, *Theory and History* (Auburn, AL: Ludwig von Mises Institute, 1985), esp. part 2.

23. It may be noted here that Marx and Engels, foremost in their *Communist Manifesto*, championed the historically progressive character of capitalism and were full of praise for its unprecedented accomplishments. Indeed, reviewing the relevant passages of the Manifesto concludes Joseph A. Schumpeter: "Never, I repeat, and in particular by no modern defender of the bourgeois civilization has anything like this been penned, never has a brief been composed on behalf of the business class from so profound and so wide a comprehension of what its achievement is and what it means to humanity" ("The Communist Manifesto in Sociology and Economics," in idem, *Essays of Joseph A. Schumpeter*, ed. Richard Clemence [Port Washington, N.Y.: Kennikat Press, 1951], p. 293). Given this view of capitalism, Marx went so far as to defend the British conquest of India, for example, as a historically progressive development. See Marx's contributions to the *New*

York Daily Tribune, of June 25, 1853, July 11, 1853, August 8, 1853 (Marx and Engels, *Werke*, vol. 9 [East Berlin: Dietz, 1960]). As a contemporary Marxist taking a similar stand on imperialism see Bill Warren, *Imperialism: Pioneer of Capitalism* (London: New Left Books, 1981).

24. See on the theory of revolution in particular Charles Tilly, *From Mobilization to Revolution* (Reading, Mass.: Addison-Wesley, 1978); idem, *As Sociology Meets History* (New York: Academic Press, 1981).

25. For a neo-Marxist assessment of the present era of "late capitalism" as characterized by "a new ideological disorientation" born out of permanent economic stagnation and the exhaustion of the legitimatory powers of conservatism and social-democratism, (*i.e.*, "liberalism" in American terminology) see Jürgen Habermas, *Die Neue Unübersichtlichkeit* (Frankfurt/M.: Suhrkamp, 1985); also idem, *Legitimation Crisis* (Boston: Beacon Press, 1975); C. Offe, *Strukturprobleme des kapitalistischen Staates* (Frankfurt/M.: Suhrkamp, 1972).

26. For an Austrian-libertarian assessment of the crisis-character of late capitalism and on the prospects for the rise of a revolutionary libertarian class consciousness see Rothbard, "Left and Right"; idem, *For a New Liberty*, chap. 15; idem, *The Ethics of Liberty* (Atlantic Highlands, N.J.: Humanities Press, 1982), part 5.

27. On the internal inconsistencies of the Marxist theory of the state see also Hans Kelsen, *Sozialismus und Staat* (Vienna, 1965).

20
Is 'Equality' a Worthy Goal?

Bradley Thomas
2020

Bradley Thomas is creator of the website EraseTheState.com and author of the book *Tweeting Liberty: Libertarian Tweets to Smash Statists and Socialists*.

Probably the most frequently used non-COVID buzzword in 2020 was the term "social justice." You couldn't escape it. From the George Floyd protests turned riots, even to the world of sports, the notion of social justice and its key component — equality — was everywhere.

I can just imagine the late great Murray Rothbard cringing upon turning on a basketball game only to see the word *equality* emblazoned on the backs of players' jerseys.

Indeed, one of Rothbard's most iconic essays was his 1974 tract entitled "Egalitarianism as a Revolt Against Nature."

Egalitarianism, as defined by Dictionary.com, is the "belief in the equality of all people, especially in political, social, or economic life." So make no mistake, when Rothbard critiqued egalitarianism he had his sights set on the "equality" being espoused by today's social justice movement.

Even in 1974, Rothbard had identified the fact that "equality" was a rallying cry of the Left, and that few were willing to challenge the supposed moral superiority of such desires.

"In no area has the Left been granted justice and morality as extensively and almost universally as in its espousal of massive equality. It is rare indeed in the United States to find anyone, especially any intellectual, challenging the beauty and goodness of the egalitarian ideal," he wrote.

Such broad acceptance led Rothbard to declare that "the goal of equality has for too long been treated uncritically and axiomatically as the ethical ideal," a problem Rothbard set about fixing in his essay.

So, is equality an ethical idea so morally pure that it is beyond questioning?

Rothbard replied to this query: "If an ethical ideal is inherently 'impractical,' that is, if it cannot work in practice, then it is a poor ideal and should be discarded forthwith."

In short, Rothbard insisted there can be no ethical superiority of a nonsensical goal. If the goal of "equality" cannot work because it violates the very nature of man, it should be summarily dismissed.

For the sake of clarity, Rothbard explains just exactly what "equality" means.

"The term has been much invoked but little analyzed. A and B are 'equal' if they are identical to each other with respect to a given attribute," he explained.

For instance, if two people are both exactly six feet tall, they can be said to be equal in height.

As such, Rothbard continues, "There is one and only one way, then, in which any two people can really be 'equal' in the fullest sense: they must be identical in all of their attributes."

Anyone with the faintest acquaintance with reality, however, realizes that the human species, mankind, "is uniquely characterized by a high degree of variety, diversity, differentiation; in short, inequality," as he noted.

Rothbard adds, "The age-old record of inequality seems to indicate that this variability and diversity is rooted in the biological nature of man."

Included in these human inequalities and differences are traits like intelligence, ambition, work ethic, skill sets, ability, etc.

To underscore this point, Rothbard quotes biochemist Roger J. Williams from his 1953 book *Free and Unequal*:

> Individuals differ from each other even in the minutest details of anatomy and body chemistry and physics; finger and toe prints; microscopic texture of hair... character of brain waves... and so on almost *ad infinitum*.
>
> ...[I]t is not only possible but certain that every human being possesses by inheritance an exceedingly complex mosaic, composed of thousands of items, which is distinctive for him alone.

In light of this, Rothbard references the "Iron Law of Oligarchy," the insight that "in every organization or activity, a few (generally the most able and/or the most interested) will end up as leaders, with the mass of membership filling the ranks of followers."

Rothbard observed that the egalitarians would respond to these emerging societal hierarchies by insisting that "culture," and not natural human differences, is to blame for such inequalities.

"Since egalitarians begin with the *a priori* axiom that all people, and hence all groups of peoples, are uniform and equal, it then follows for them that any and all group differences in status, prestige, or authority in society *must* be the result of unjust 'oppression' and irrational 'discrimination,'" he noted.

Eliminate the supposed institutions that generate said "oppression," according to the Left egalitarians, and society will achieve the equality of results that social justice demands. Through this reasoning, the egalitarians have convinced themselves that their goal of equality in society is attainable through the means of changing cultural institutions, such as the market economy and the patriarchy.

What the egalitarians fail to recognize, however, is that the institution responsible for society's greatest oppression is their chosen tool to create "equality": the state.

To be clear, Rothbard by no means assigns all inequality to the diverse and unique nature of individual humans. He, of all people, has pointed out the oppressive nature of the state, and how it dispenses suffering — and favors — in unequal distributions. Calling out the state's role in creating injustices is a worthy pursuit.

Where the egalitarians go wrong, according to Rothbard, is in their complete dismissal of human diversity to explain *any* inequality of outcomes, and their willingness to use unjust means to enforce their ideal of a society comprised of undifferentiated and uniform people.

"At the heart of the egalitarian left," Rothbard wrote, "is the pathological belief that there is no structure of reality," and further that the egalitarians believe that the reality of human diversity "can be transformed by mere wish" or "the mere exercise of human will."

Naturally, to impose this "will" of the egalitarians requires an application of violence and coercion from a powerful ruling elite. "An egalitarian society can only hope to achieve its goals by totalitarian methods of coercion," Rothbard concluded.

This imposition of forced conformity is "anti-human," according to Rothbard, and therefore the goal of egalitarianism — or equality — is a "revolt" against the biological reality of our uniqueness.

From this, Rothbard is able to dispense his final verdict: "Since their methodology and their goals deny the very structure of humanity and of the universe, the egalitarians are profoundly antihuman; and, therefore, their ideology and their activities may be set down as profoundly evil as well."

21
How I Changed My Mind on Intellectual Property

Isaac Morehouse

Isaac Morehouse is the founder and CEO of Crash and the founder of Praxis.

I'd been solidly libertarian for many years the first time I gave thought to "intellectual property" (copyrights and patents) at all. Someone mentioned the protection of property, including intellectual property, as the root of prosperity and freedom. I agreed without hesitation.

It just seemed to make sense. Now and then I would read or hear someone reiterate this position and it always seemed right to me. I had spent a lot of time working through the arguments in favor of private property — both philosophical and economic — and I didn't think IP required any special arguments to augment what I already believed about other forms of property.

Then a quote by Thomas Jefferson caught my eye:

> If nature has made any one thing less susceptible than all others of exclusive property, it is the action of the thinking power called an idea, which an individual may exclusively possess as long as he keeps it to himself; but the moment it is divulged, it forces itself into the possession of every one, and the receiver cannot dispossess himself of it. Its peculiar character, too, is that no one possesses the less, because every other possesses the whole of it. He who receives an idea from me, receives instruction himself without lessening mine; as he who lights his taper at mine, receives light without darkening me.

This bothered me. It kept rattling around in my brain and the more I thought about it, the more it seemed that IP was not just like any other form of property. Indeed, it became clear that IP rights required a new set of arguments; arguments for physical property rights were insufficient in defense of IP. So I started to poke around.

Rethinking Everything

My instincts were so strongly in favor of IP that I began by looking primarily for arguments that would bolster my bias. After all, the people who criticized

IP in my experience were the same people who hated markets and businesses and all individual property, or else people who just wanted to get movies and music without paying for them because they didn't work and had no money. They seemed to be complainers and looters, not thinkers, producers and achievers. They had to be wrong.

Once I began looking for theoretical arguments in favor of IP, I realized that a great many people who were not market-hating hippies or Marxists or welfare queens did not find a credible case for IP. This was a disturbing discovery. The more I looked and read and thought, the more problematic the idea of IP became. It was a philosophical problem.

For starters, how was IP to be defined? Any mental exercise I tried presented insurmountable problems with even defining it reliably. If someone writes a certain combination of words on a page in a certain order, do they own it? What if they never show anyone else? What if someone else with no knowledge of the first person has the same combination of words in mind or on paper? What about simultaneous discovery, which is not infrequent in the history of great ideas?

These puzzles and many others forced me to acknowledge the strange characteristics of IP which made any consistent definition or enforcement impossible. Ideas are non-scarce. They could hardly be defined as property at all. What kind of law makes someone a criminal by adding a chemical to another chemical and selling it, even if they had no idea someone else had done the same and gotten government approval? It began to seem more like a violation of property rights than a protection. Why should my use of my property be confined to things other people have never done before?

The Slow Change

I read many more articles and had many late night discussions on the theory of IP over the course of about a year. I came to the unhappy conclusion that ideas were not property, IP was impossible to define, and therefore enforcement was a game of favoritism fraught with all the rent-seeking problems that any regulatory hurdle presents. I didn't like IP because it was not a coherent concept. But I still believed it was necessary.

I maintained a philosophical disbelief in IP and a pro-IP policy position for some time. Even though it seemed an incoherent concept, I could not wrap my head around how innovation would occur absent patents. I didn't care much for copyrights, and I thought trademark issues could be handled via fraud protection, market pressure and contractually without recourse to special IP laws.

But patents seemed an absolute must. It was the production of prescription drugs that got me. I failed to see any possible way in which advanced pharmaceuticals could be produced in a world without IP. Though I was not a pure consequentialist, this concern was enough for me to resist a strict anti-IP position even though I couldn't justify it philosophically.

The IP issue was never (and is still not today) the most interesting issue to me, so I let it be. It only occasionally came up, and I was content to somewhat awkwardly debunk it in theory but support it in practice. My quest for IP consistency was shelved as my intellectual journey took me elsewhere.

The more I learned about economics and political philosophy, the more ridiculous and far-fetched the state became — even a minimal state — and my ideas grew more radical. When I ran out of arguments for the existence of the state — both moral and practical — IP reared its head again. Someone asked me if I thought any form of IP could survive without the state's initiation of force. I could not conceive of any way in which it could.

How Would It Work in Practice?

This left me in a weird place. I had been dragged, again kicking and screaming, to a disbelief in the state as an ethical or practical form of social organization, yet I had always believed that without state created patents, major innovations would cease. Then I came across Boldrin and Levine's "Against Intellectual Monopoly." I read it and my eyes were opened. I wondered how I could have been so dull and lacking in imagination and a grasp of history!

They argued not from a philosophical standpoint, but from a practical and historical standpoint that, far from spurring innovation, IP was one of the greatest stranglers of progress. In fact, the entire purpose of IP laws has been from the beginning to restrict innovation and experimentation and ensure the benefits of good ideas are concentrated on privileged groups, not according to how much they help consumers, but by how well they navigate the bureaucracy.

It was all so simple and obvious; I wondered how I could have missed it. I marveled at how I got by for so long with a worldview so full of the inconsistent and unexplainable. How could I see so clearly that occupational licensing didn't protect consumers but instead protected the big industry players who lobbied for it while failing to see the same about IP?

Upon reflection, it seems the reason my belief in IP was so strong was because it was planted in intellectual soil that had been cultivated since childhood to see the world as on the brink of chaos and disaster, only held together and kept sane by the force of law. Life on this planet was the Hobbesian jungle, and in every facet — from basic survival to usable language to a medium of exchange to innovation and common decency — we needed the strong arm of Leviathan to keep us on track.

When I began to realize how utopian this view of the state was, and how complex the real world was with all its intersecting norms and institutions, it became possible at last to see what should have been rather obvious; that ideas needn't be held hostage in order to be put to use and that the incentive to innovate needs no special nudge from the state.

This is how I came full circle on the issue of IP. I don't want or expect you to read this and be convinced I'm right. I haven't even really presented any arguments. I do hope, however, that you may be inspired to keep an open and inquiring mind and the topic and keep poking around.

If you do, check out Boldrin and Levine's book on the practical case against IP, and Stephan Kinsella's ["How Intellectual Property Hampers the Free Market"] on the theoretical case. Think about your instinctual position on the issue and ask yourself what worldview it comes from.

Don't assume anyone who doesn't favor IP is a property-hating socialist. And for goodness sake, enjoy the process!

22
The Case for Libertarian Anarchism: Responses to Ten Objections

Roderick T. Long, Ph.D.

Roderick Long is a Professor of Philosophy at Auburn University. This is a transcription of an informal talk at the Ludwig von Mises Institute, given at the Mises University, August 6, 2004, during a session called the "Mises Circle."

I want to talk about some of the main objections that have been given to libertarian anarchism and my attempts to answer them. But before I start giving objections and trying to answer them, there is no point in trying to answer objections to a view unless you have given some positive reason to hold the view in the first place. So, I just want to say briefly what I think the positive case is for it before going on to defend it against objections.

THE CASE FOR LIBERTARIAN ANARCHISM

Problems with Forced Monopoly

Think about it this way. What's wrong with a shoe monopoly? Suppose that I and my gang are the only ones that are legally allowed to manufacture and sell shoes — my gang and anyone else that I authorize, but nobody else. What's wrong with it? Well, first of all, from a moral point of view, the question is: why us? What's so special about us? Now in this case, because I've chosen *me*, it is more plausible that I ought to have that kind of monopoly, so maybe I should pick a different example! But still, you might wonder, where do I and my gang get off claiming this right to make and sell something that no one else has the right to make and sell, to provide a good or service no one else has the right to provide. At least as far as you know, I'm just another mortal, another human like unto yourselves (more or less). So, from a moral standpoint I have no more right to do it than anyone else.

Then, of course, from a pragmatic, consequentialist standpoint — well, first of all, what is the likely result of my and my gang having a monopoly on shoes? Well, first of all, there are incentive problems. If I'm the only person who has the right to make and sell shoes, you're probably not going to get the shoes from me very cheaply. I can charge as much as I want, as long as I don't charge so much that you just can't afford them at all or you decide you're happier just not having the shoes. But as long as you're willing and able, I'll charge the highest price that I can get out of you — because you've got no competition, nowhere else to go. You also probably shouldn't expect the shoes to be of particularly high quality, because, after all, as long as they're barely serviceable, and you still prefer them to going barefoot — then you have to buy them from me.

In addition to the likelihood that the shoes are going to be expensive and not very good, there's also the fact that my ability to be the only person who makes and sells shoes gives me a certain leverage over you. Suppose that I don't like you. Suppose you've offended me in some way. Well, maybe you just don't get shoes for a while. So, there's also abuse-of-power issues.

But, it's just not the incentive problem, because, after all, suppose that I'm a perfect saint and I will make the best shoes I possibly can for you, and I'll charge the lowest price I possibly can charge, and I won't abuse my power at all. Suppose I'm utterly trustworthy. I'm a prince among men (not in Machiavelli's sense). There is still a problem, which is: how do I know exactly that I'm doing the best job I can with these shoes? After all, there's no competition. I guess I could poll people to try to find out what kind of shoes they seem to want. But there are lots of different ways I could make shoes. Some of them are more expensive ways of making them, and some are less expensive. How do I know, given that there's no market, and there's really not much I can do in the way of profit and loss accounting? I just have to make guesses. So even if I'm doing my best, the quantity I make, the quality I make may not be best suited to satisfy people's preferences, and I have a hard time finding these things out.

Government is a Forced Monopoly

So those are all reasons not to have a monopoly on the making and selling of shoes. Now, *prima facie* at least, it seems as though those are all good reasons for anyone not to have a monopoly in the provision of services of adjudicating disputes, and protecting rights, and all the things that are involved in what you might broadly call the enterprise of law. First of all, there's the moral question: why does one gang of people get the right to be the only ones in a given territory who can offer certain kinds of legal services or enforce certain kinds of things? And then there are these economic questions: what are the incentives going to be? Once again, it's a monopoly. It seems likely that with a captive customer base they're going to charge higher prices than they otherwise would and offer lower quality. There might even be the occasional abuse of power. And then, even if you manage to avoid all those problems, and you get all the saintly types into the government, there's still the problem of how do they know that the particular way that they're providing legal services, the particular mix of legal services they're offering, the particular ways they do it, are really the best ones? They just try to figure out what will work. Since there's no competition, they don't have much way of knowing whether what they're doing is the most successful thing they could be doing.

So, the purpose of those considerations is to put the burden of proof on the opponent. So this is the point, then, when the opponent of competition in legal services has to raise some objections.

Ten Objections to Libertarian Anarchism

(1) Government Is Not a Coercive Monopoly
Now, one objection that's sometimes raised isn't so much an objection to anarchism as an objection to the moral argument for anarchism: well, look, it's not really a *coercive* monopoly. It's not as though people haven't consented to this because there's a certain sense in which people have consented to the existing system — by living within the borders of a particular territory, by accepting the benefits the government offers, and so forth, they have, in effect, consented. Just as if you walk into a restaurant and sit down and say, "I'll have a steak," you don't have to explicitly mention that you are agreeing to pay for it; it's just sort of understood. By sitting down in the restaurant and asking for the steak, you are agreeing to pay for it. Likewise, the argument goes, if you sit down in the territory of this given state, and you accept benefits of police protection or something, then you've implicitly agreed to abide by its requirements. Now, notice that even if this argument works, it doesn't settle the pragmatic question of whether this is the best working system.

But I think there is something dubious about this argument. It's certainly true that if I go onto someone else's property, then it seems like there's an expectation that as long as I'm on their property I have to do as they say. I have to follow their rules. If I don't want to follow their rules, then I've got to leave. So, I invite you over to my house, and when you come in I say, "You have to wear the funny hat." And you say, "What's this?" And I say, "Well, that's the way it works in my house. Everyone has to wear the funny hat. Those are my rules." Well, you can't say, "I won't wear the hat but I'm staying anyway." These are my rules — they may be dumb rules, but I can do it.

Now suppose that you're at home having dinner, and I'm your next-door-neighbor, and I come and knock on your door. You open the door, and I come in and I say, "You have to wear the funny hat." And you say, "Why is this?" And I say, "Well, you moved in next door to me, didn't you? By doing that, you sort of agreed." And you say, "Well, wait a second! When did I agree to this?"

I think that the person who makes this argument is already assuming that the government has some legitimate jurisdiction over this territory. And then they say, well, now, anyone who is in the territory is therefore agreeing to the prevailing rules. But they're assuming the very thing they're trying to prove — namely that this jurisdiction over the territory is legitimate. If it's not, then the government is just one more group of people living in this broad general geographical territory. But I've got my property, and exactly what their arrangements are I don't know, but here I am in my property and they don't own it — at least they haven't given me any argument that they do — and so, the fact that I am living in "this country" means I am living in a certain geographical region that they have certain pretensions over — but the question is whether those pretensions are legitimate. You can't assume it as a means to proving it.

Another thing is, one of the problems with these implicit social contract arguments is that it's not clear what the contract is. In the case of ordering food in a restaurant, everyone pretty much knows what the contract is. So you could run an implicit consent argument there. But no one would suggest that you could buy a *house* the same way.

There are all these rules and things like that. When it's something complicated no one says, "You just sort of agreed by nodding your head at some point," or something. You have to find out what it is that's actually in the contract; what are you agreeing to? It's not clear if no one knows what exactly the details of the contract are. It's not that persuasive.

Okay, well, most of the arguments I'm going to talk about are pragmatic, or a mixture of moral and pragmatic.

(2) Hobbes: Government Is Necessary for Cooperation

Probably the most famous argument against anarchy is Hobbes. Hobbes' argument is: well, look, human cooperation, social cooperation, requires a structure of law in the background. The reason we can trust each other to cooperate is because we know that there are legal forces that will punish us if we violate each other's rights. I know that they'll punish me if I violate your rights, but they'll also punish you if you violate my rights. And so I can trust you because I don't have to rely on your own personal character. I just have to rely on the fact that you'll be intimidated by the law. So, social cooperation requires this legal framework backed up by force of the state.

Well, Hobbes is assuming several things at once here. First he's assuming that there can't be any social cooperation without law. Second, he's assuming that there can't be any law unless it's enforced by physical force. And third, he's assuming you can't have law enforced by physical force unless it's done by a monopoly state.

But all those assumptions are false. It's certainly true that cooperation can and does emerge, maybe not as efficiently as it would with law, but without law. There's Robert Ellickson's book *Order Without Law* where he talks about how neighbors manage to resolve disputes. He offers all these examples about what happens if one farmer's cow wanders onto another farmer's territory and they solve it through some mutual customary agreements and so forth, and there's no legal framework for resolving it. Maybe that's not enough for a complex economy, but it certainly shows that you can have some kind of cooperation without an actual legal framework.

Second, you can have a legal framework that isn't backed up by force. An example would be the Law Merchant in the late Middle Ages: a system of commercial law that was backed up by threats of boycott. Boycott isn't an act of force. But still, you've got merchants making all these contracts, and if you don't abide by the contract, then the court just publicizes to everyone: "this person didn't abide by the contract; take that into account if you're going to make another contract with them."

And third, you can have formal legal systems that do use force that are not monopolistic. Since Hobbes doesn't even consider that possibility, he doesn't really give any argument against it. But you can certainly see examples in history. The history of medieval Iceland, for example, where there was no one center of enforcement. Although there was something that you might perhaps call a government, it had no executive arm at all. It had no police, no soldiers, no nothing. It had a sort of a competitive court system. But then enforcement was just up to whoever. And there were systems that evolved for taking care of that.

(3) Locke: Three "Inconveniences" of Anarchy

Okay, well, more interesting arguments are from Locke. Locke argues that anarchy involves three things he calls "inconveniences." And "inconvenience" has a somewhat more weighty sound in 17th century English than it does in modern English, but still his point in calling it "inconveniences," which still is a bit weaker, was that Locke thought that social cooperation could exist somewhat under anarchy. He was more optimistic than Hobbes was. He thought, on the basis of moral sympathies on the one hand and self-interest on the other, cooperation could emerge.

He thought there were three problems. One problem, he said, was that there wouldn't be a general body of law that was generally known, and agreed on, and understood. People could grasp certain basic principles of the law of nature. But their applications and precise detail were always going to be controversial. Even libertarians don't agree. They can agree on general things, but we're always arguing with each other about various points of fine detail. So, even in a society of peaceful, cooperative libertarians, there are going to be disagreements about details. And so, unless there's some general body of law that everyone knows about so that they can know what they can count on being able to do and what not, it's not going to work. So that was Locke's first argument. There has to be a generally known universal body of law that applies to everyone that everyone knows about ahead of time.

Second, there is a power-of-enforcement problem. He thought that without a government you don't have sufficiently unified power to enforce. You just have individuals enforcing things on their own, and they're just too weak, they're not organized enough, they could be overrun by a gang of bandits or something.

Third, Locke said the problem is that people can't be trusted to be judges in their own case. If two people have a disagreement, and one of them says, "Well, I know what the law of nature is and I'm going to enforce it on you," well, people tend to be biased, and they're going to find most plausible the interpretation of the law of nature that favors their own case. So, he thought that you can't trust people to be judges in their own case; therefore, they should be morally required to submit their disputes to an arbitrator. Maybe in cases of emergency they can still defend themselves on-the-spot, but for other cases where it's not a matter of immediate self-defense, they need to delegate this to an arbitrator, a third party — and that's the state.

So Locke thinks that these are three problems you have under anarchy, and that you wouldn't have them under government or at least under the right kind of government. But I think that it's actually exactly the other way around. I think that anarchy can solve all three of those problems, and that the state, by its very nature, cannot possibly solve them.

So let's first take the case of universality, or having a universally known body of law that people can know ahead of time and count on. Now, can that emerge in a non-state system? Well, in fact, it did emerge in the Law Merchant precisely because the states were not providing it. One of the things that helped to bring about the emergence of the Law Merchant is the individual states in Europe each had different sets of laws governing merchants. They were all different. And a court in France wouldn't uphold a contract made in England under the laws of England, and vice versa. And so, the merchants' ability to engage in international trade was hampered by the fact that there wasn't any uniform system of commercial law for all of Europe. So the merchants got together and said, "Well, let's just make some of our own. The courts are coming up with these crazy rules, and they're all different, and they won't respect each other's decisions, so we'll just ignore them and we'll set up our own system." So this is a case in which uniformity and predictability were produced by the market and not by the state. And you can see why that's not surprising. It's in the interest of those who are providing a private system to make it uniform and predictable if that's what the customers need.

It's for the same reason that you don't find any triangular ATM cards. As far as I know, there's no law saying that you can't have a triangular ATM card, but if anyone tried to market them, they just wouldn't be very popular because they wouldn't fit into the existing machines. When what people need is diversity, when what people need is different systems for different people, the market provides that. But there are some things where uniformity is better. Your ATM card is more valuable to you if everyone else is using the same kind as well or a kind compatible with it so that you can all use the machines wherever you go; and therefore, the merchants, if they want to make a profit, they're going to provide uniformity. So the market has an incentive to provide uniformity in a way that government doesn't necessarily.

On the question of having sufficient power for organizing for defense — well, there's no reason you can't have organization under anarchy. Anarchy doesn't mean that each person makes their own shoes. The alternative to government providing all the shoes is not that each person makes their own shoes. So, likewise, the alternative to government providing all the legal services is not that each person has to be their own independent policeman. There's no reason that they can't organize in various ways. In fact, if you're worried about not having sufficient force to resist an aggressor, well, a monopoly government is a much more dangerous aggressor than just some gang of bandits or other because it's unified all this power in just one point in the whole society.

But I think, most interestingly, the argument about being a judge in your own case really boomerangs against Locke's argument here. Because first of all, it's not a good argument for a monopoly because it's a fallacy to argue from *everyone should submit their disputes to a third party* to *there should be a third party that everyone submits their disputes to*. That's like arguing from *everyone likes at least one TV show* to *there's at least one TV show that everyone likes*. It just doesn't follow. You can have everyone submitting their disputes to third parties without there being some one third party that everyone submits their disputes to. Suppose you've got three people on an island. A and B can submit their disputes to C, and A and C can submit their disputes to B, and B and C can submit their disputes to A. So you don't need a monopoly in order to embody this principle that people should submit their disputes to a third party.

But moreover, not only do you not need a government, but a government is precisely what doesn't satisfy that principle. Because if you have a dispute with the government, the government doesn't submit that dispute to a third party. If you have a dispute with the government, it'll be settled in a government court (if you're lucky — if you're unlucky, if you live under one of the more rough-and-ready governments, you won't ever even get as far as a court). Now, of course, it's better if the government is itself divided, checks-and-balances and so forth. That's a little bit better, that's closer to there being third parties, but still they are all part of the same system; the judges are paid by tax money and so forth. So, it's not as though you can't have better and worse approximations to this principle among different kinds of governments. Still, as long as it's a monopoly system, by its nature, it's in a certain sense lawless. It never ultimately submits its disputes to a third party.

(4) Ayn Rand: Private Protection Agencies Will Battle

Probably the most popular argument against libertarian anarchy is: well, what happens if (and this is Ayn Rand's famous argument) I think you've violated my rights and you think you haven't, so I call up my protection agency, and you call up your protection agency — why won't they just do battle? What guarantees that they won't do battle? To which, of course, the answer is: well, nothing *guarantees* they won't do battle. Human beings have free will. They can do all kinds of crazy things. They might go to battle. Likewise, George Bush might decide to push the nuclear button tomorrow. They might do all sorts of things.

The question is: what's likely? Which is likelier to settle its disputes through violence: a government or a private protection agency? Well, the difference is that private protection agencies have to bear the costs of their own decisions to go to war. Going to war is expensive. If you have a choice between two protection agencies, and one solves its disputes through violence most of the time, and the other one solves its disputes through arbitration most of the time — now, you might think, "I want the one that solves its disputes through violence — that sounds really cool!" But then you look at your monthly premiums. And you think, well, how committed are you to this Viking mentality? Now, you might be so committed to the Viking mentality that you're willing to pay for it; but still, it is more expensive. A lot of customers are going to say, "I want to go to one that doesn't charge all this extra amount for the violence." Whereas, governments — first of all, they've got captive customers, they can't go anywhere else — but since they're taxing the customers anyway, and so the customers don't have the option to switch to a different agency. And so, governments can externalize the costs of their going to war much more effectively than private agencies can.

(5) Robert Bidinotto: No Final Arbiter of Disputes

One common objection — this is one you find, for example, in Robert Bidinotto, who's a Randian who's written a number of articles against anarchy (he and I have had sort of a running debate online about this) — his principal objection to anarchy is that under anarchy, there's no final arbiter in disputes. Under government, some final arbiter at some point comes along and resolves the dispute one way or the other. Well, under anarchy, since there's no one agency that has the right to settle things once and for all, there's no final arbiter, and so disputes, in some sense, never end, they never get resolved, they always remain open-ended.

So what's the answer to that? Well, I think that there's an ambiguity to the concept here of a final arbiter. By "final arbiter," you could mean the final arbiter in what I call the Platonic sense. That is to say, someone or something or some institution that somehow absolutely guarantees that the dispute is resolved forever; that absolutely guarantees the resolution. Or, instead, by "final arbiter" you could simply mean some person or process or institution or something-or-other that more or less reliably guarantees most of the time that these problems get resolved.

Now, it is true, that in the Platonic sense of an absolute guarantee of a final arbiter — in that sense, anarchy does not provide one. But neither does any other system. Take a minarchist constitutional republic of the sort that Bidinotto favors. Is there a final arbiter under that system, in the sense of something that absolutely guarantees ending the process of dispute forever? Well, I sue you, or I've been sued, or I am accused of something, whatever — I'm in some kind of court case. I lose. I appeal it. I appeal it to the Supreme Court. They go against me. I lobby the Congress to change the laws to favor me. They don't do it. So then I try to get a movement for a Constitutional Amendment going. That fails, so I try and get people together to vote in new people in Congress who will vote for it. In some sense it can go on forever. The dispute isn't over.

But, as a matter of fact, most of the time most legal disputes eventually end. Someone finds it too costly to continue fighting. Likewise, under anarchy — of course there's no guarantee that the conflict won't go on forever. There are very few guarantees of that ironclad sort. But that's no reason not to expect it to work.

(6) Property Law Cannot Emerge from the Market

Another popular argument, also used often by the Randians, is that market exchanges presuppose a background of property law. You and I can't be making exchanges of goods for services, or money for services, or whatever, unless there's already a stable background of property law that ensures us the property titles that we have. And because the market, in order to function, presupposes existing background property law, therefore, that property law cannot itself be the product of the market. The property law must emerge — they must really think it must emerge out of an infallible robot or something — but I don't know exactly what it emerges from, but somehow it can't emerge from the market.

But their thinking this is sort of like: first, there's this property law, and it's all put in place, and no market transactions are happening — everyone is just waiting for the whole legal structure to be put in place. And then it's in place — and now we can finally start trading back and forth. It certainly is true that you can't have functioning markets without a functioning legal system; that's true. But it's not as though first the legal system is in place, and then on the last day they finally finish putting the legal system together —

then people begin their trading. These things arise together. Legal institutions and economic trade arise together in one and the same place, at one and the same time. The legal system is not something independent of the activity it constrains. After all, a legal system again is not a robot or a god or something separate from us. The existence of a legal system consists in people obeying it. If everyone ignored the legal system, it would have no power at all. So it's only because people generally go along with it that it survives. The legal system, too, depends on voluntary support.

I think that a lot of people — one reason that they're scared of anarchy is they think that under government it's as though there's some kind of guarantee that's taken away under anarchy. That somehow there's this firm background we can always fall back on that under anarchy is just gone. But the firm background is just the product of people interacting with the incentives that they have. Likewise, when anarchists say people under anarchy would probably have the incentive to do this or that, and people say, "Well, that's not good enough! I don't just want it to be likely that they'll have the incentive to do this. I want the government to absolutely guarantee that they'll do it!"

But the government is just people. And depending on what the constitutional structure of that government is, it's likely that they'll do this or that. You can't design a constitution that will guarantee that the people in the government will behave in any particular way. You can structure it in such a way so that they're more likely to do this or less likely to do this. And you can see anarchy as just an extension of checks-and-balances to a broader level.

For example, people say, "What guarantees that the different agencies will resolve things in any particular way?" Well, the U.S. Constitution says nothing about what happens if different branches of the government disagree about how to resolve things. It doesn't say what happens if the Supreme Court thinks something is unconstitutional but Congress thinks it doesn't, and wants to go ahead and do it anyway. Famously, it doesn't say what happens if there's a dispute between the states and the federal government. The current system where once the Supreme Court declares something unconstitutional, then the Congress and the President don't try to do it anymore (or at least not quite so much) — that didn't always exist. Remember when the Court declared what Andrew Jackson was doing unconstitutional, when he was President, he just said, "Well, they've made their decision, let them enforce it." The Constitution doesn't say whether the way Jackson did it was the right way. The way we do it now is the way that's emerged through custom. Maybe you're for it, maybe you're against it — whatever it is, it was never codified in law.

(7) Organized Crime Will Take Over

One objection is that under anarchy organized crime will take over. Well, it might. But is it likely? Organized crime gets its power because it specializes in things that are illegal — things like drugs and prostitution and so forth. During the years when alcohol was prohibited, organized crime specialized in the alcohol trade. Nowadays, they're not so big in the alcohol trade. So the power of organized crime to a large extent depends on the power of government. It's sort of a parasite on government's activities. Governments by banning things create black markets. Black markets are dangerous things to be in because you have to worry both about the government and about other dodgy people who are going into the black market field. Organized crime specializes in that. So, organized crime I think would be weaker, not stronger, in a libertarian system.

(8) The Rich Will Rule
Another worry is that the rich would rule. After all, won't justice just go to the highest bidder in that case, if you turn legal services into an economic good? That's a common objection. Interestingly, it's a particularly common objection among Randians, who suddenly become very concerned about the poor impoverished masses. But under which system are the rich more powerful? Under the current system or under anarchy? Certainly, you've always got some sort of advantage if you're rich. It's good to be rich. You're always in a better position to bribe people if you're rich than if you're not; that's true. But, under the current system, the power of the rich is magnified. Suppose that I'm an evil rich person, and I want to get the government to do something-or-other that costs a million dollars. Do I have to bribe some bureaucrat a million dollars to get it done? No, because I'm not asking him to do it with his own money. Obviously, if I were asking him to do it with his own money, I couldn't get him to spend a million dollars by bribing him any less than a million. It would have to be at least a million dollars and one cent. But people who control tax money that they don't themselves personally own, and therefore can't do whatever they want with, the bureaucrat can't just pocket the million and go home (although it can get surprisingly close to that). All I have to do is bribe him a few thousand, and he can direct this million dollars in tax money to my favorite project or whatever, and thus the power of my bribe money is multiplied.

Whereas, if you were the head of some private protection agency and I'm trying to get you to do something that costs a million dollars, I'd have to bribe you more than a million. So, the power of the rich is actually less under this system. And, of course, any court that got the reputation of discriminating in favor of millionaires against poor people would also presumably have the reputation of discriminating for billionaires against millionaires. So, the millionaires would not want to deal with it all of the time. They'd only want to deal with it when they're dealing with people poorer, not people richer. The reputation effects — I don't think this would be too popular an outfit.

Worries about poor victims who can't afford legal services, or victims who die without heirs (again, the Randians are very worried about victims dying without heirs) — in the case of poor victims, you can do what they did in Medieval Iceland. You're too poor to purchase legal services, but still, if someone has harmed you, you have a claim to compensation from that person. You can sell that claim, part of the claim or all of the claim, to someone else. Actually, it's kind of like hiring a lawyer on a contingency fee basis. You can sell to someone who is in a position to enforce your claim. Or, if you die without heirs, in a sense, one of the goods you left behind was your claim to compensation, and that can be homesteaded.

(9) Robert Bidinotto: The Masses Will Demand Bad Laws

Another worry that Bidinotto has — and this is sort of the opposite of the worry that the rich will rule — is: well, look, isn't Mises right, that the market is like a big democracy, where there is consumer sovereignty, and the masses get whatever they want? That's great when it's refrigerators and cars and so forth. But surely that's not a good thing when it's *laws*. Because, after all, the masses are a bunch of ignorant, intolerant fools, and if they just get whatever laws they want, who knows what horrible things they will make.

Of course, the difference between economic democracy of the Mises sort and political democracy is: well, yeah, they get whatever they want, but they're going to have to pay for it. Now, it's perfectly true that if you have people who are fanatical enough about wanting to impose some wretched thing on other people, if you've got a large enough group of people who are fanatical enough about this, then anarchy might not lead to libertarian results.

If you live in California, you've got enough people who are absolutely fanatical about banning smoking, or maybe if you're in Alabama, and it's homosexuality instead of smoking they want to ban (neither one would ban the other, I think) — in that case, it might happen that they're so fanatical about it that they would ban it. But remember that they are going to have to be paying for this. So when you get your monthly premium, you see: well, here's your basic service — protecting you against aggression; oh, and then here's also your extended service, and the extra fee for that — peering in your neighbors' windows to make sure that they're not — either the tobacco or the homosexuality or whatever it is you're worried about. Now the really fanatical people will say, "Yes, I'm going to shell out the extra money for this." (Of course, if they're that fanatical, they're probably going to be trouble under minarchy, too.) But if they're not that fanatical, they'll say, "Well, if all I have to do is go into a voting booth and vote for these laws restricting other people's freedom, well, heck, I'd go in, it's pretty easy to go in and vote for it." But if they actually have to *pay* for it — "Gee, I don't know. Maybe I can reconcile myself to this."

(10) Robert Nozick and Tyler Cowen: Private Protection Agencies Will Become a *de facto* Government

Okay, one last consideration I want to talk about. This is a question that originally was raised by Robert Nozick and has since been pushed farther by Tyler Cowen. Nozick said: Suppose you have anarchy. One of three things will happen. Either the agencies will fight — and he gives two different scenarios of what will happen if they fight. But I've already talked about what happens if they fight, so I'll talk about the third option. What if they don't fight? Then he says, if instead they agree to these mutual arbitration contracts and so forth, then basically this whole thing just turns into a government. And then Tyler Cowen has pushed this argument farther. He said what happens is that basically this forms into a cartel, and it's going to be in the interest of this cartel to sort of turn itself into a government. And any new agency that comes along, they can just boycott it.

Just as it's in your interest if you come along with a new ATM card that it be compatible with everyone else's machines, so if you come along with a brand new protection agency, it is in your interest that you get to be part of this system of contracts and arbitration and so forth that the existing ones have. Consumers aren't going to come to you if they find out that you don't have any agreements as to what happens if you're in a conflict with these other agencies. And so, this cartel will be able to freeze everyone out.

Well, could that happen? Sure. All kinds of things could happen. Half the country could commit suicide tomorrow. But, is it likely? Is this cartel likely to be able to abuse its power in this way? The problem is cartels are unstable for all the usual reasons. That doesn't mean that it's impossible that a cartel succeed. After all, people have free will. But it's unlikely because the very incentives that lead you to form the cartel also lead you to cheat on it — because it's always in the interest of anyone to make agreements outside the cartel once they are in it.

Bryan Caplan makes a distinction between self-enforcing boycotts and non-self-enforcing boycotts. Self-enforcing boycotts are ones where the boycott is pretty stable because it's a boycott against, for example, doing business with people who cheat their business partners. Now, you don't have to have some iron resolve of moral commitment in order to avoid doing business with people who cheat their business partners. You have a perfectly self-interested reason not to do business with those people.

But think instead of a commitment not to do business with someone because you don't like their religion or something like that, or they're a member of the wrong protection agency, one that your fellow protection agencies told you not to deal with — well, the boycott might work. Maybe enough people (and maybe everyone) in the cartel is so committed to

The Case for Libertarian Anarchism: Responses to Ten Objections

upholding the cartel that they just won't deal with the person. Is that possible? Yes. But, if we assume that they formed the cartel out of their own economic self-interest, then the economic self-interest is precisely what leads to the undermining because it's in their interest to deal with the person, just as it's always in your interest to engage in mutually beneficial trade.

QUESTION PERIOD

Anyway, those are some of the objections and some of my replies, and I'll open it up.

Q1: My chief concern about anarchism is: why can't you say that government is just another division of labor? Because it could be that some people are better or possess natural capabilities that are more suited to ruling over others. I'm not saying anarchy cannot work, but solely from empirical evidence, the fact that none of the industrialized regions in the world are in a state of anarchy, nor have they ever been for long in a state of anarchy says something about perhaps the stability or viability of complex human societies in the present state. And also, going back to what I said earlier, you can conceive of the relationship between the ruler and the ruled as just another common division of labor. Some people possess leadership abilities that are better able to organize people than others. Some people lack that.

RL: On the division-of-labor point, to the extent the division of labor is voluntary — if you're better at something-or-other than I am, and so you do it, and then I buy the services from you — as long as it's voluntary, that's fine. But when we're talking about division of labor and some people are better at ruling than other people — well, if I *consent* to your ruling me — maybe I'm hiring you as my advisor because I think you're better at making decisions than I am, so I make one last decision which is to hire you as my advisor, and from then on, I do what you say — that's not government; you're my employee, you're an employee that I follow very religiously. But, ruling implies ruling people without their consent. That the division of labor is beneficial to everyone involved doesn't seem to apply in cases where one group is forcing the other to accept its services. And on the question of why we don't see any industrialized country that has anarchy — of course, we also don't see any industrialized county that has monarchy. But then industrialized countries haven't been around all that long. There was a time when people said every civilized country (or just about every civilized country) is a monarchy. You find people in the seventeenth and eighteenth centuries saying: look, all the civilized countries are monarchies; democracy would never work. And by saying democracy would never work, they meant not just that it would have these various bad results in the long run; they just thought it would completely fall apart into chaos in a matter of months. Whatever you may think of democracy, it was more viable than they predicted. It could last longer, at any rate, than they predicted. So, things are in flux. There was a time when it was all monarchies. Now it's all semi-oligarchical democracies. The night is young.

Q2: Roderick, surely we all appreciate the wonderful work that you do here at the Mises Institute, but Ludwig von Mises wasn't an anarchist. So, I was wondering if you could tell us more about your institute and the Molinari Institute.

RL: Mises wasn't really a Misesian! [*laughter*] Well, I have my own think tank. It is somewhat smaller than this one. I'm not sure whether it has a physical size. It does consist of more than one person. The board of directors is three people. So, it's three people plus a website. Someday it will rule the Earth — in an anarchic way. Right now mostly what it does is put up various libertarian and anarchist classics on the website. There's an offshoot of it — the Molinari Society, which is the same three people plus one more. Insofar as, as Hayek said, social facts consist in people's attitudes toward them, the more people who think that it exists, the more it exists. The whole thing exists a little bit more because we got affiliated with the American Philosophical Association. The Molinari Society is hosting a session at the American Philosophical Association meetings in December. So it is actually going to be a Molinari event in December involving the three-people-plus-another-one. So that's the grand and glorious progress. Its mission is to overthrow the government. We've applied for tax-exempt status from the government. (We'll see just how dumb they are! We worded the description somewhat differently when we sent in the forms.)

Q3: I was going to bolster the point you made about the Randian objection that market transactions require some sort of legal background to them. The fact that there are black markets belies this. If you're a cocaine dealer and you get ripped off by your middleman, you certainly can't go to a court and say "Go arrest him, he didn't give me the cocaine he was supposed to..."

RL: I'm sure someone's tried it...

Q3: ...Now, of course, this very easily can lead to violence, but don't forget that there are people actively trying to stop you, not just that they're not letting you arbitrate, they're actively stopping you from doing it.

RL: David Friedman makes the argument that one of the main functions of the Mafia is to serve as something like a court system for criminals. That's not all it does, but the Mafia takes an interest in what sorts of criminal goings-on are going on in its territory — because it wants its cut, but it also doesn't want gangs having shoot-outs with each other in its territory. If you've got a conflict, you agreed to some kind of criminal deal with someone and they cheated you, and it happened in the jurisdiction of some particular Mafia group, they'll take an interest in that as long as you're providing your cut. If they're not cooperating, the Mafia will act as something kind of court-like and policelike. They're sort of cops for criminals.

Q4: What will prevent protection companies from becoming a protection racket?

RL: Well, other protection companies. If it succeeds in doing it, then it's become a government. But during the time it's trying to do it, it hasn't yet become a government, so we assume there are still other agencies around, and it's in those other agencies' interest to make sure that this doesn't happen. Could it become a protection racket? In principle, could protection agencies evolve into government? Some could. I think probably historically some have. But the question is: is that a likely or inevitable result? I don't think so because there is a check-and-balance against it. Checks-and-balances can fail in anarchy just like they can fail under constitutions. But there is a check-and balance against it which is the possibility of calling in other protection agencies or someone starting another protection agency before this thing has yet had a chance to acquire that kind of power.

Q5: Who best explains the origin of the state?

RL: Well, there's a popular nineteenth-century theory of the origin of the state that you find in a number of different forms. It's in Herbert Spencer, it's in Oppenheimer, and you find it in some of the French liberals like Comte and Dunoyer, and Molinari — who wasn't really French, he was Belgian ("I am not a Frenchie, I'm a Belgie!"). This theory — they had different versions of it, but it's all pretty similar — was that what happens is that one group conquers another group. Often the theory was that a sort of hunter-marauder group conquers an agricultural group. In Molinari's version of it what happens is: first, they just go and kill people and grab their stuff. And then gradually they figure out: well, maybe we should wait and not kill them because we want them to grow more stuff next time we come back. So instead, we'll just come and grab their stuff and not kill them, and then they'll grow some more stuff, and next year we'll be back. And then they think, well, if we take all their stuff, then they won't have enough seed corn to grow it, or they won't have any incentive to grow it — they'll just run away or something — so we won't take everything. And finally, they think: we don't have to keep going away and coming back. We can just move in. And then gradually, over time, you get a ruling class and a ruled class. At first, the ruling class and the ruled class may be ethnically different because they were these different tribes. But even if, over time, the tribes intermarry and there's no longer any difference in the compositions, they still have got the same structure of a ruling group and a ruled group. So that was one popular theory of the origin of the state, or at least the origin of many states. I think another origin you can see of some states or state-like things is in the same sort of situation but in cases where they succeed in fending off the invaders. Some local group within the invaded group says: we're going to specialize in defense — we're going to specialize in defending the rest of you guys against these invaders. And they succeed. If you look at the history of England, I think this is what happens with the English monarchy. Before the Norman Conquest, the earliest English monarchs were war leaders whose main job was national defense. They had very little to do within the country. They were primarily directed against foreign invaders. But it was a monopoly. (Now, the question is how they got that monopoly. I'm not so sure.) But once they got it, they gradually started getting involved more and more in domestic control as well.

Q6: Hector, Murray's story about Hector? It's very much similar to this story, and it's on the web, and it's just a beautiful story.

RL: Which story about Hector is this?

Q6: The first one about why do we have to leave, let's just stay there...

RL: Oh, yeah.

Q6: Murray did a beautiful job on that, and I would recommend it.

RL: What's that in?

Q6: It's on LewRockwell.com.

RL: It's one of the Rothbard articles on there? Okay.

Q6: I wanted to buttress your thesis in several ways. One, another argument in favor of anarchy is that if you really favor the government, you have to favor world government because right now there's anarchy between governments, and we can't have that if you want government. Very few people favor world government, and it's incompatible with the case against anarchy.

RL: There has to be a *final* final arbiter.

Q6: Another buttress is the issue about negotiations. The way that the time zones came up and the way that the standard gauge for railroads came up was through negotiations between railroad companies.

RL: And the internet. Some of that is legal, but other aspects are just customary.

Q6: And another support is this thing about the cartel. At one time the National Basketball Association had eight teams and they wouldn't allow any other people to come in, so they started the ABA (the American Basketball Association, with the red-white-and-blue ball). So if you had this cartel that wouldn't let other people in, they could start another cartel.

RL: What happened to them?

Q6: They eventually merged. Now there are like thirty teams in the NBA. And if that's too few, yet another league can come up.

RL: The crucial point is that in the Austrian definition of competition it's not number of competing firms, it's the free entry. As long as it's possible to start another one, that can have the same effect as actually doing it.

Q6: In addition to the dissolution of a cartel, you can have other cartels competing against the first cartel.

RL: Did the XFL have any good effect? [*laughter*]

Q6: I wanted to ask a question. In your answer to the first question, where

you said you were appointing him as your guide — does this mean you take my side —
RL: No.
Q6: — on alienability?
RL: No, no. That's why I said he was the employee rather than the owner. I believe in inalienable rights.
Q6: He's an employee, yet you can't fire him...
RL: No, I can fire him. He's my advisor, I always will follow him — but I haven't given up my right to fire him.

23

The Reluctant Anarchist

Joseph Sobran, B.A.

Joe Sobran (1946–2010) received his B.A. in English from Eastern Michigan University and pursued graduate studies in English, specializing in Shakespeare. From 1969 to 1970 he taught English on a fellowship and lectured on Shakespeare. From 1972 to 1993, he wrote for *National Review*. The following passage is reprinted and expanded from *Sobran's*, December 2002, pages 3–6.

My arrival (very recently) at philosophical anarchism has disturbed some of my conservative and Christian friends. In fact, it surprises me, going as it does against my own inclinations.

As a child I acquired a deep respect for authority and a horror of chaos. In my case the two things were blended by the uncertainty of my existence after my parents divorced and I bounced from one home to another for several years, often living with strangers. A stable authority was something I yearned for.

Meanwhile, my public-school education imbued me with the sort of patriotism encouraged in all children in those days. I grew up feeling that if there was one thing I could trust and rely on, it was my government. I knew it was strong and benign, even if I didn't know much else about it. The idea that some people — Communists, for example — might want to overthrow the government filled me with horror.

G.K. Chesterton, with his usual gentle audacity, once criticized Rudyard Kipling for his "lack of patriotism." Since Kipling was renowned for glorifying the British Empire, this might have seemed one of Chesterton's "paradoxes"; but it was no such thing, except in the sense that it denied what most readers thought was obvious and incontrovertible.

Chesterton, himself a "Little Englander" and opponent of empire, explained what was wrong with Kipling's view: "He admires England, but he does not love her; for we admire things with reasons, but love them without reason. He admires England because she is strong, not because she is English." Which implies there would be nothing to love her for if she were weak.

Of course Chesterton was right. You love your country as you love your mother — simply because it is *yours*, not because of its superiority to others, particularly superiority of power.

This seems axiomatic to me now, but it startled me when I first read it. After all, I was an American, and American patriotism typically expresses itself in superlatives. America is the freest, the mightiest, the richest, in short the *greatest* country in the world, with the greatest form of government — the most democratic. Maybe the poor Finns or Peruvians love their countries too, but heaven knows why — they have so little to be proud of, so few "reasons." America is also the most *envied* country in the world. Don't all people secretly wish they were Americans?

That was the kind of patriotism instilled in me as a boy, and I was quite typical in this respect. It was the patriotism of supremacy. For one thing, America had never lost a war — I was even proud that America had created the atomic bomb (providentially, it seemed, just in time to crush the Japs) — and this is why the Vietnam War was so bitterly frustrating. Not the dead, but the defeat! The end of history's great winning streak!

As I grew up, my patriotism began to take another form, which it took me a long time to realize was in tension with the patriotism of power. I became a philosophical conservative, with a strong libertarian streak. I believed in government, but it had to be "limited" government — confined to a few legitimate purposes, such as defense abroad and policing at home. These functions, and hardly any others, I accepted, under the influence of writers like Ayn Rand and Henry Hazlitt, whose books I read in my college years.

Though I disliked Rand's atheism (at the time, I was irreligious, but not anti-religious), she had an odd appeal to my residual Catholicism. I had read enough Aquinas to respond to her Aristotelian mantras. Everything had to have its own nature and limitations, including the state; the idea of a state continually growing, knowing no boundaries, forever increasing its claims on the citizen, offended and frightened me. It could only end in tyranny.

I was also powerfully drawn to Bill Buckley, an explicit Catholic, who struck the same Aristotelian note. During his 1965 race for mayor of New York, he made a sublime promise to the voter: he offered "the internal composure that comes of knowing there are rational limits to politics." This may have been the most futile campaign promise of all time, but it would have won my vote!

It was really this Aristotelian sense of "rational limits," rather than any particular doctrine, that made me a conservative. I rejoiced to find it in certain English writers who were remote from American conservatism — Chesterton, of course, Samuel Johnson, Edmund Burke, George Orwell, C.S. Lewis, Michael Oakeshott.

In fact I much preferred a literary, contemplative conservatism to the activist sort that was preoccupied with immediate political issues. During the Reagan years, which I expected to find exciting, I found myself bored to death by supply-side economics, enterprise zones, "privatizing" welfare programs, and similar principle-dodging gimmickry. I failed to see that "movement" conservatives were less interested in principles than in Republican victories. To the extent that I did see it, I failed to grasp what it meant.

Still, the last thing I expected to become was an anarchist. For many years I didn't even know that serious philosophical anarchists existed. I'd never heard of Lysander Spooner or Murray Rothbard. How could society survive at all without a state?

Now I began to be critical of the U.S. Government, though not very. I saw that the welfare state, chiefly the legacy of Franklin Roosevelt's New Deal, violated the principles of limited government and would eventually have to go. But I agreed with other conservatives that in the meantime the urgent global threat of Communism had to be stopped. Since I viewed "defense" as one of the proper tasks of government, I thought of the Cold War as a necessity, the overhead, so to speak, of freedom. If the Soviet threat ever ceased (the prospect seemed remote), we could afford to slash the military budget and get back to the job of dismantling the welfare state.

Somewhere, at the rainbow's end, America would return to her founding principles. The Federal Government would be shrunk, laws would be few, taxes minimal. That was what I thought. Hoped, anyway.

I avidly read conservative and free-market literature during those years with the sense that I was, as a sort of late convert, catching up with the conservative movement. I took it for granted that other conservatives had already read the same books and had taken them to heart. Surely we all wanted the same things! At bottom, the knowledge that there were rational limits to politics. Good old Aristotle. At the time, it seemed a short hop from Aristotle to Barry Goldwater.

As is fairly well known by now, I went to work as a young man for Buckley at *National Review* and later became a syndicated columnist. I found my niche in conservative journalism as a critic of liberal distortions of the U.S. Constitution, particularly in the Supreme Court's rulings on abortion, pornography, and "freedom of expression."

Gradually I came to see that the conservative challenge to liberalism's jurisprudence of "loose construction" was far too narrow. Nearly everything liberals wanted the Federal Government to do was unconstitutional. The key to it all, I thought, was the Tenth Amendment, which forbids the Federal Government to exercise any powers not specifically assigned to it in the Constitution. But the Tenth Amendment had been comatose since the New Deal, when Roosevelt's Court virtually excised it.

This meant that nearly all Federal legislation from the New Deal to the Great Society and beyond had been unconstitutional. Instead of fighting liberal programs piecemeal, conservatives could undermine the whole lot of them by reviving the true (and, really, obvious) meaning of the Constitution. Liberalism depended on a long series of usurpations of power.

Around the time of Judge Robert Bork's bitterly contested (and defeated) nomination to the U.S. Supreme Court, conservatives spent a lot of energy arguing that the "original intent" of the Constitution must be conclusive. But they applied this principle only to a few ambiguous phrases and passages that bore on specific hot issues of the day — the death penalty, for instance. About the *general* meaning of the Constitution there could, I thought, be no doubt at all. The ruling principle is that whatever the Federal Government isn't authorized to do, it's forbidden to do.

That alone would invalidate the Federal welfare state and, in fact, nearly all liberal legislation. But I found it hard to persuade most conservatives of this. Bork himself took the view that the Tenth Amendment was unenforceable. If he was right, then the whole Constitution was in vain from the start.

I never thought a constitutional renaissance would be easy, but I did think it could play an indispensable role in subverting the legitimacy of liberalism. Movement conservatives listened politely to my arguments, but without much enthusiasm. They regarded appeals to the Constitution as rather pedantic and, as a practical matter, futile — not much help in the political struggle. Most Americans no longer even remembered what *usurpation* meant. Conservatives themselves hardly knew.

Of course they were right, in an obvious sense. Even conservative courts (if they could be captured) wouldn't be bold enough to throw out the entire liberal legacy at once. But I remained convinced that the conservative movement had to attack liberalism at its constitutional root.

In a way I had transferred my patriotism from America as it then was to America as it had been when it still honored the Constitution. And when had it crossed the line? At first I thought the great corruption had occurred when Franklin Roosevelt subverted the Federal judiciary; later I came to see that the decisive event had been the Civil War, which had effectively destroyed the right of the states to secede from the Union. But this was very much a minority view among conservatives, particularly at *National Review*, where I was the only one who held it.

I've written more than enough about my career at the magazine, so I'll confine myself to saying that it was only toward the end of more than two happy decades there that I began to realize that we *didn't* all want the same things after all. When it happened, it was like learning, after a long and placid marriage, that your spouse is in love with someone else, and has been all along.

Not that I was betrayed. I was merely blind. I have no one to blame but myself. The Buckley crowd, and the conservative movement in general, no more tried to deceive me than I tried to deceive them. We all assumed we were on the same side, when we weren't. If there is any fault for this misunderstanding, it is my own.

In the late 1980s I began mixing with Rothbardian libertarians — they called themselves by the unprepossessing label "anarcho-capitalists" — and even met Rothbard himself. They were a brilliant, combative lot, full of challenging ideas and surprising arguments. Rothbard himself combined a profound theoretical intelligence with a deep knowledge of history. His magnum opus, *Man, Economy, and State*, had received the most unqualified praise of the usually reserved Henry Hazlitt — in *National Review*!

I can only say of Murray what so many others have said: never in my life have I encountered such an original and vigorous mind. A short, stocky New York Jew with an explosive cackling laugh, he was always exciting and cheerful company. Pouring out dozens of big books and hundreds of articles, he also found time, heaven knows how, to write (on the old electric typewriter he used to the end) countless long, single-spaced, closely reasoned letters to all sorts of people.

Murray's view of politics was shockingly blunt: the state was nothing but a criminal gang writ large. Much as I agreed with him in general, and fascinating though I found his arguments, I resisted this conclusion. I still wanted to believe in constitutional government.

Murray would have none of this. He insisted that the Philadelphia convention at which the Constitution had been drafted was nothing but a "coup d'etat," centralizing power and destroying the far more tolerable arrangements of the Articles of Confederation. This was a direct denial of everything I'd been taught. I'd never heard anyone suggest that the Articles had been preferable to the Constitution! But Murray didn't care what anyone thought — or what everyone thought. (He'd been too radical for Ayn Rand.)

Murray and I shared a love of gangster films, and he once argued to me that the Mafia was preferable to the state, because it survived by providing services people actually wanted. I countered that the Mafia behaved like the state, extorting its own "taxes" in protection rackets directed at shopkeepers; its market was far from "free." He admitted I had a point. I was proud to have won a concession from him.

Murray died a few years ago without quite having made an anarchist of me. It was left to his brilliant disciple, Hans-Hermann Hoppe, to finish my conversion. Hans argued that no constitution could restrain the state. Once its monopoly of force was granted legitimacy, constitutional limits became mere fictions it could disregard; nobody could have the legal standing to enforce those limits. The state itself would decide, by force, what the constitution "meant," steadily ruling in its own favor and increasing its own power. This was true *a priori*, and American history bore it out.

What if the Federal Government grossly violated the Constitution? Could states withdraw from the Union? Lincoln said no. The Union was "indissoluble" unless all the states agreed to dissolve it. As a practical matter, the Civil War settled that. The United States, plural, were really a single enormous state, as witness the new habit of speaking of "it" rather than "them."

So the people are bound to obey the government even when the rulers betray their oath to uphold the Constitution. The door to escape is barred. Lincoln in effect claimed that it is not our rights but the state that is "unalienable." And he made it stick by force of arms. No transgression of the Constitution can impair the Union's inherited legitimacy. Once established on specific and limited terms, the U.S. Government is forever, even if it refuses to abide by those terms.

As Hoppe argues, this is the flaw in thinking the state can be controlled by a constitution. Once granted, state power naturally becomes absolute. Obedience is a one-way street. Notionally, "We the People" create a government and specify the powers it is allowed to exercise over us; our rulers swear before God that they will respect the limits we impose on them; but when they trample down those limits, our duty to obey them remains.

Yet even after the Civil War, certain scruples survived for a while. Americans still agreed in principle that the Federal Government could acquire new powers only by constitutional amendment. Hence the postwar amendments included the words "Congress shall have power to" enact such and such legislation.

But by the time of the New Deal, such scruples were all but defunct. Franklin Roosevelt and his Supreme Court interpreted the Commerce Clause so broadly as to authorize virtually any Federal claim, and the Tenth Amendment so narrowly as to deprive it of any inhibiting force. Today these heresies are so firmly entrenched that Congress rarely even asks itself whether a proposed law is authorized or forbidden by the Constitution.

In short, the U.S. Constitution is a dead letter. It was mortally wounded in 1865. The corpse can't be revived. This remained hard for me to admit, and even now it pains me to say it.

Other things have helped change my mind. R.J. Rummel of the University of Hawaii calculates that in the twentieth century alone, states murdered about 162,000,000 million of their own subjects. This figure doesn't include the tens of millions of foreigners they killed in war. How, then, can we speak of states "protecting" their people? No amount of private crime could have claimed such a toll. As for warfare, Paul Fussell's book *Wartime* portrays battle with such horrifying vividness that, although this wasn't its intention, I came to doubt whether any war could be justified.

My fellow Christians have argued that the state's authority is divinely given. They cite Christ's injunction "Render unto Caesar the things that are Caesar's" and St. Paul's words, "The powers that be are ordained of God." But Christ didn't say which things — if any — belong to Caesar; his ambiguous words are far from a command to give Caesar whatever he claims. And it's notable that Christ never told his disciples either to establish a state or to engage in politics. They were to preach the Gospel and, if rejected, to move on. He seems never to have imagined the state as something they could or should enlist on their side.

At first sight, St. Paul seems to be more positive in affirming the authority of the state. But he himself, like the other martyrs, died for *defying* the state, and we honor him for it; to which we may add that he was on one occasion a jailbreaker as well. Evidently the passage in Romans has been misread. It was probably written during the reign of Nero, not the most edifying of rulers; but then Paul also counseled slaves to obey their masters, and nobody construes this as an endorsement of slavery. He may have meant that the state and slavery were here for the foreseeable future, and that Christians must abide them for the sake of peace. Never does he say that either is here forever.

St. Augustine took a dim view of the state, as a punishment for sin. He said that a state without justice is nothing but a gang of robbers writ large, while leaving doubt that any state could ever be otherwise. St. Thomas Aquinas took a more benign view, arguing that the state would be necessary even if man had never fallen from grace; but he agreed with Augustine that an unjust law is no law at all, a doctrine that would severely diminish any known state.

The essence of the state is its legal monopoly of force. But force is subhuman; in words I quote incessantly, Simone Weil defined it as "that which turns a person into a thing — either corpse or slave." It may sometimes be a necessary evil, in self-defense or defense of the innocent, but nobody can have by right what the state claims: an exclusive privilege of using it.

It's entirely possible that states — organized force — will always rule this world, and that we will have at best a choice among evils. And some states are worse than others in important ways: anyone in his right mind would prefer living in the United States to life under a Stalin. But to say a thing is inevitable, or less onerous than something else, is not to say it is good.

For most people, *anarchy* is a disturbing word, suggesting chaos, violence, antinomianism — things they hope the state can control or prevent. The term *state,* despite its bloody history, doesn't disturb them. Yet it's the state that is truly chaotic, because it means the rule of the strong and cunning. They imagine that anarchy would naturally terminate in the rule of thugs. But mere thugs can't assert a plausible *right* to rule. Only the state, with its propaganda apparatus, can do that. This is what *legitimacy* means. Anarchists obviously need a more seductive label.

"But what would you replace the state with?" The question reveals an inability to imagine human society without the state. Yet it would seem that an institution that can take 200,000,000 lives within a century hardly needs to be "replaced."

Christians, and especially Americans, have long been misled about all this by their good fortune. Since the conversion of Rome, most Western rulers have been more or less inhibited by Christian morality (though, often enough, not so you'd notice), and even warfare became somewhat civilized for centuries; and this has bred the assumption that the state isn't necessarily an evil at all. But as that morality loses its cultural grip, as it is rapidly doing, this confusion will dissipate. More and more we can expect the state to show its nature nakedly.

For me this is anything but a happy conclusion. I miss the serenity of believing I lived under a good government, wisely designed and benevolent in its operation. But, as St. Paul says, there comes a time to put away childish things.

24
Individualism vs. War

Scott Horton
Antiwar.com
2005

Scott Horton is director of the Libertarian Institute, editorial director of Antiwar.com, and author of *Enough Already: Time to End the War on Terrorism*.

Chris Hedges is a Pulitzer Prize-winning veteran foreign correspondent, having covered foreign conflicts in Argentina, El Salvador, Nicaragua, Colombia, Guatemala, Bosnia, Iraq, Sudan, Algeria, India, Israel/Palestine, Turkey, and Kosovo for the *New York Times*, *Dallas Morning News*, *Christian Science Monitor*, and National Public Radio. Based on this experience, he authored the books *War is a Force that Gives Us Meaning* and *What Every Person Should Know About War*.

War is ultimately about collectivism. During crisis, individuality fades in favor of team effort. During violent conflict, particularly between governments, the world becomes, especially it seems for Americans, a giant, bloody football game: our team versus theirs, us versus them, good versus evil. Go, team, go.

This, of course, leads to all sorts of fallacious thinking, such as "Death to them is not like death to us," "We have to let them bomb us so they won't know we've broken the codes," "Using nuclear bombs on civilians saved lives," "Everything changed on September 11th," and "Don't you understand that we are at war?" The last two are usually intended as a blanket permission slip for the state to break any law, tell any lie, and kill any person — so long as it's to protect "us" from "them."

In George Orwell's nightmarish dystopia *1984*, the world is divided into three empires in a state of perpetual warfare, because "the consciousness of being at war, and therefore in danger, makes the handing-over of all power to a small caste seem the natural, unavoidable condition of survival." Every so often, a bomb falls in a lower-class neighborhood and kills enough people to remind them that they are at war and need Big Brother to protect them.

Hedges describes patriotism in his book as merely a "thinly veiled form of collective self-worship." As Randolph Bourne said in 1918, "War is the Health of the State":

Individualism vs. War

> The moment war is declared... the mass of the people, through some spiritual alchemy, become convinced that they have willed and executed the deed themselves. They then, with the exception of a few malcontents, proceed to allow themselves to be regimented, coerced, deranged in all the environments of their lives, and turned into a solid manufactory of destruction toward whatever other people may have, in the appointed scheme of things, come within the range of the Government's disapprobation. The citizen throws off his contempt and indifference to Government, identifies himself with its purposes, revives all his military memories and symbols, and the State once more walks, an august presence, through the imaginations of men. Patriotism becomes the dominant feeling, and produces immediately that intense and hopeless confusion between the relations which the individual bears and should bear toward the society of which he is a part. The patriot loses all sense of the distinction between State, nation, and government.

The "few malcontents" during America's wars have always provoked the wrath of the state. From John Adams's Alien and Sedition Acts to Lincoln's filling of military prisons with journalists and other dissenters to the terrible Wilsonian purges of Bourne's day, through the Cold War presidents' COINTELPRO and recent intimidation of antiwar protesters, the "good of the whole" has always outweighed the rights of the individual from the state's point of view.

Hedges says that war is a narcotic, in fact a more powerful addiction than any drug. Our government is hooked on it, and it's destroying our country. For example, our so-called representatives in congress just made the supposedly temporary parts of the unconstitutional PATRIOT Act permanent.

Other negative components and long-lasting side effects of war collectivism are racism and the corruption of language. As in the mass slaughter of "Tutsis" by "Hutus" (these were ethnicities essentially invented by the Dutch, according to ethnologist Luc de Heusch) in Rwanda in 1994, all that is necessary to convince people that it's perfectly okay to torture and murder is to repeat over and over again that "the enemy" (meaning, of course, many people) is in fact not human at all, but "cockroaches," "nips," "gooks," "krauts," "ay-rabs" or "hajis."

As the *New York Times* quotes an unidentified member of the U.S. Army's 337th Company, which was in charge of interrogations of prisoners at Bagram Air Force base in Afghanistan where at least two men were murdered in custody:

> We were pretty much told that they were nobodies, that they were just enemy combatants... I think that giving them the distinction of soldier would have changed our attitudes toward them. A lot of it was based on

racism, really. We called them "hajis," and that psychology was really important.

It's amazing what a little dehumanization can accomplish. Perfectly nice kids, turned into torturers by their government's crafty use of language.

During the Bosnian war, Hedges says in *War Is a Force That Gives Us Meaning*:

> Many Muslims called the Serbs "Chetnicks," the Serbian irregulars in World War II, who slaughtered many Muslims. Muslims, for many Serbs in Bosnia, were painted as Islamic fundamentalists. The Croats, to the Serbs and Muslims, were branded "Ustache," the fascist quislings who ruled Croatia during World War II. And there were times when, in interviews, it was hard to know if people were talking about what happened a few months ago or a few decades ago. It all merged into one huge mythic campaign.

A mythic campaign that cost 250,000 real lives.

Hedges says that if you add it all up, there have only been 99 years of recorded human history where there was not a war going on somewhere, so our odds aren't that great, it's true, but the supposed usefulness of war has been shown to be false time and again. Invasion is no way to obtain resources; it costs much less to simply pay for what is needed. The death and destruction only ensure new enemies for the future.

If mankind is to have a future, it will be a future of individualism. If the politicians of the world continue to act as though "their" countries can only be successful at the expense of others, we are doomed. There are just too many nuclear bombs on this planet to be able to maintain perpetual war without eventual catastrophe.

War is not glorious, it is not heroic — war is death. If our society is out to spread the Anglo-American tradition of individual liberty, property rights, and open markets, let's start by acting out our own creed as an example to the rest, and start treating the people of earth, and each other, like what we are: people.

25

I Was a Police Officer, Now I'm a Voluntaryist

Shepard Oakley

Shepard Oakley is a husband, grandfather, and semi-retired entrepreneur.

Scumbags would frequently get my blood boiling when they refused to respect my authority or when they would break the law. I had become a cop for a handful of reasons, with the top five being: I would be able to drive fast legally, I would only get into fights that I knew I (and my team) would win, I would get decent pay for someone from my caste, I would receive great benefits, and I wanted to help people.

Let's chat about the last, but not the least, reason mentioned above. Yes, I wanted to help people. I recall at age four, as my mother was breaking up with her boyfriend Adam, he grabbed her by the hair and threw her to the muddy ground by his farm driveway in Tennessee. I saw other family violence in neighbors, and at age ten, an old man french-kissed me. I developed a personal policy that I didn't like bad people hurting weak people.

I thought law enforcement would be a good way to help. So, I started my career by getting my foot in the door as a meter mister and a community service officer, first in my little Rocky Mountain town, and then in a beach town in Southern California.

I applied to be a police officer at many law enforcement agencies, but the first to hire me was the Orange County Sheriff's Department in Southern California. After a six-month boot-camp-style academy, I started my seven-year stint working as a jailer, which was a requisite of becoming a patrol deputy. Within two years, I was tired of the industrial jail complex system and transferred back to the beach town where I had been a meter mister, now as a sworn police trainee. Six months later, I was fired for having a "Midwestern Mennonite" lack of street smarts.

One example of this lack of street smarts was my failure to catch on to which kind of Mexican should be pulled over. When I was told to pull Mexicans over — because why would they be in a rich white community? — I started doing so, but then I had to be taught that illegal immigrant dishwashers were not the kind of Mexicans that should be pulled over. Instead, first- and second-generation Chicanos with shaved heads and gang attire, especially the ones rolling four deep in an old Impala, were the proper targets.

I applied at 15 agencies, starting the afternoon that I was fired, and the first to offer me a job was my little town back in the Rockies. I spent six and a half years there, working patrol, investigations, bike patrol, horse patrol, and on the SWAT team, ending up as the Sniper Team Leader. I developed a specialty in communications-related areas, crisis negotiation, child forensic interviewing, and criminal interrogations. Also, I got to drive fast, and because of the badge on my chest and radio on my hip, I never "lost a fight." Oh yeah, and in my almost nine years in the system, no criminal really tried to hurt me.

I bought into the silly notion that I was "risking my life every day" to keep people safe, and it took many years for me to realize that peaceful people (free market folks) died at higher rates than cops. I proudly stood up alongside other cops and military when invited to do so at spaghetti dinner fundraisers so that the citizenry could clap and show their respect for the brave men that kept them safe and free. I even started a police officer's association (read: union-lite) in my agency.

Prior to reaching ten years as a sworn cop, I was the subject of an IA (Internal Affairs) Investigation. I was frustrated that my decision and actions on the night in question, which I still believe were right, were being called into question, and I decided to call it quits. This was the beginning of my full-time entrepreneurship journey. By now I had a B.S. degree in social science and some good prospects in the executive protection and security consulting arena.

Soon after quitting, I tried for the county sheriff position but wasn't selected. Then, through involvement in Ron Paul's 2008 presidential race, I learned things that led me to be more introspective. I read books, listened to lectures and podcasts, and attended conventions. I thought, I studied logic and reason, and I contemplated morality. Exciting stuff, right? The former Shepard wouldn't have thought so, but the new me viewed these things as being of utmost importance.

Do you also think that this higher-level thinking is one of the most important things that good people ought to engage in?

I hope I have properly introduced myself so that I can effectively hint at some of what my life experiences have taught me and how I have acquired my worldview. Let's look back at the first paragraph of this piece, and I will rip it apart. What did I think a "scumbag" consisted of? Well, you know, gang bangers, tweakers, potheads, child molesters, murderers, and hippies. I don't have the space here. However, I now realize how horribly wrong I was about "scumbags." My worldview had changed, and now I realized that being honest, making sure all interactions with others are voluntary and respecting private property are about the only foundational things necessary to be eligible to escape the label of "scumbag."

My curiosity also led me to read books like *The Most Dangerous Superstition*, where I learned about the myth of "authority." How many good people who displayed "contempt of cop" attitudes had I treated unfairly because they refused to respect my authority, a thing that didn't even exist? I am sorry.

I drove fast, and it arguably wasn't always completely necessary. There is a lot of gray area in law enforcement. For example, when arresting a person for driving under the influence, how many pounds of pressure should be applied in a wristlock? There isn't really a clear line between what is necessary to keep control and adding an extra ounce because of adrenaline or frustration. In law enforcement, when a handful of cops wrestle a belligerent drunk's hands behind his back, this is later referred to as a "fight." When I was a cop, I really thought this was an honest notion. Now I know better.

Pay and benefits? Back when I was a cop, it cost a bit over $100k a year to keep each cop on the road. This included training, vehicles, salary, uniforms, etc. I later realized that my time as a cop had cost someone over a million dollars. Who was that person, and did he agree to pay? I have realized that it was not a single person; rather, it was a bunch of hard-working people who pay extortion fees. I was also financially supported by inflation-causing printing of money by central banks, which I learned more about in *The Creature from Jekyll Island*. Steal a million bucks from good people, much?

I am sorry to those against whom I initiated violence either by ticketing or arresting for victimless crimes, and to those who had money extorted through taxation to pay for me. I continue to make amends as best I can by writing books and producing video and audio content about morality, and by living a good and moral life. I used to be a true scumbag; now I am a Voluntaryist.

26
On the Ultimate Justification of the Ethics of Private Property

Hans-Hermann Hoppe, Ph.D.

Hans-Hermann Hoppe is an Austrian School economist, a libertarian/anarcho-capitalist philosopher, and Professor Emeritus of Economics at the University of Nevada, Las Vegas. The following passage is reprinted from *Liberty* 2, no. 1 (1988).

Ludwig von Mises, in his masterpiece *Human Action*, presents and explains the entire body of economic theory as implied in, and deducible from, one's conceptual understanding of the meaning of action (plus that of a few general, explicitly introduced assumptions about the empirical reality in which action is taking place). He calls this conceptual knowledge the "axiom of action," and he demonstrates in which sense the meaning of action from which economic theory sets out, *i.e.*, of values, ends, and means, of choice, preference, profit, loss, and cost, must be considered *a priori* knowledge. It is not derived from sense impressions but from reflection (one does not see actions but rather interprets certain physical phenomena as actions!). Most importantly, it cannot possibly be invalidated by any experience whatsoever, because any attempt to do so would already presuppose the existence of action and an actor's understanding of the categories of action (experiencing something is, after all, itself an intentional action!).

Thus having reconstructed economics as, in the last resort, derived from an *a priori* true proposition, Mises can claim to have provided an ultimate foundation of economics. He terms a so-founded economics "praxeology," the logic of action, in order to emphasize the fact that its propositions can be definitively proven by virtue of the indisputable action-axiom and the equally indisputable laws of logical reasoning (such as the laws of identity and contradiction) — completely independent, that is, of any kind of empirical testing (as employed, for instance, in physics).

However, though his idea of praxeology and his construction of an entire body of praxeological thought places him among the greats of the modern Western tradition of rationalism in its search for certain foundations, Mises does not think that another claim of this tradition can be made good: the claim that there are also foundations in ethical matters. According to Mises

On the Ultimate Justification of the Ethics of Private Property

there exists no ultimate justification for ethical propositions in the same sense as there exists one for economic propositions. Economics can inform us whether or not certain means are appropriate for bringing about certain ends, yet whether or not the ends can be regarded as just can neither be decided by economics nor by any other science. There is no justification for choosing one rather than another end. In the last resort, which end is chosen is arbitrary from a scientific point of view and is a matter of subjective whim, incapable of any justification beyond the mere fact of simply being liked.

Many libertarians have followed Mises on this point. Like Mises, they have abandoned the idea of a rational foundation of ethics. As he does, they make as much as possible out of the economic proposition that the libertarian private property ethic produces a higher general standard of living than any other one; that most people actually prefer higher over lower standards of living; and hence, that libertarianism should prove highly popular. But ultimately, as Mises certainly knew, such considerations can only convince somebody of libertarianism who has already accepted the "utilitarian" goal of general wealth maximization. For those who do not share this goal, they have no compelling force at all. Thus, in the final analysis, libertarianism is based on nothing but an arbitrary act of faith.

In the following I outline an argument that demonstrates why this position is untenable, and how the essentially Lockean private property ethic of libertarianism can ultimately be justified. In effect, this argument supports the natural rights position of libertarianism as espoused by the other master thinker of the modern libertarian movement, Murray N. Rothbard — above all in his *Ethics of Liberty*. However, the argument establishing the ultimate justification of private property is different from the one typically offered by the natural rights tradition. Rather than this tradition, it is Mises, and his idea of praxeology and praxeological proofs, who provides the model.

I demonstrate that *only* the libertarian private property ethic can be justified argumentatively, because it is the praxeological presupposition of argumentation as such; and that any deviating, nonlibertarian ethical proposal can be shown to be in violation of this demonstrated preference. Such a proposal can be made, of course, but its propositional content would contradict the ethic for which one demonstrated a preference by virtue of one's own act of proposition-making, *i.e.*, by the act of engaging in argumentation as such.

For instance, one can say "people are and always shall be indifferent towards doing things," but this proposition would be belied by the very act of proposition-making, which in fact would demonstrate subjective preference (of saying this rather than saying something else or not saying anything at all). Likewise, nonlibertarian ethical proposals are falsified by the reality of actually proposing them.

To reach this conclusion and to properly understand its importance and logical force, two insights are essential.

First, it must be noted that the question of what is just or unjust — or for that matter the even more general question of what is a valid proposition and what is not — only arises insofar as I am, and others are, capable of propositional exchanges, *i.e.*, of argumentation. The question does not arise *vis-à-vis* a stone or fish because they are incapable of engaging in such exchanges and of producing validity claiming propositions. Yet if this is so — and one cannot deny that it is without contradicting oneself, as one cannot argue the case that one cannot argue — then any ethical proposal as well as any other proposition must be assumed to claim that it is capable of being validated by propositional or argumentative means. (Mises, too, insofar as he formulates economic propositions, must be assumed to claim this.)

In fact, in producing *any* proposition, overtly or as an internal thought, one demonstrates one's preference for the willingness to rely on argumentative means in convincing oneself or others of something. There is then, trivially enough, no way of justifying anything unless it is a justification by means of propositional exchanges and arguments. However, then it must be considered the ultimate defeat for an ethical proposal if one can demonstrate that its content is logically incompatible with the proponent's claim that its validity be ascertainable by argumentative means. To demonstrate any such incompatibility would amount to an impossibility proof, and such proof would constitute the most deadly defeat possible in the realm of intellectual inquiry.

Second, it must be noted that argumentation does not consist of free-floating propositions but is a form of action requiring the employment of scarce means; and that the means which a person demonstrates as preferring by engaging in propositional exchanges are those of private property.

For one thing, no one could possibly propose anything, and no one could become convinced of any proposition by argumentative means, if a person's right to make exclusive use of his physical body were not already presupposed. It is this recognition of each other's mutually exclusive control over one's own body which explains the distinctive character of propositional exchanges that, while one may disagree about what has been said, it is still possible to agree at least on the fact that there is disagreement. It is also obvious that such a property right to one's own body must be said to be justified *a priori*, for anyone who tried to justify any norm whatsoever would already have to presuppose the exclusive right of control over his body as a valid norm simply in order to say, "I propose such and such." Anyone disputing such a right would become caught up in a practical contradiction since arguing so would already imply acceptance of the very norm which he was disputing.

Furthermore, it would be equally impossible to sustain argumentation for any length of time and rely on the propositional force of one's arguments if one were not allowed to appropriate in addition to one's body other scarce means through homesteading action (by putting them to use before somebody else does), and if such means and the rights of exclusive control regarding them were not defined in objective physical terms.

For if no one had the right to control anything at all except his own body, then we would all cease to exist and the problem of justifying norms simply would not exist. Thus, by virtue of the fact of being alive, property rights to other things must be presupposed to be valid. No one who is alive could argue otherwise.

Moreover, if a person did not acquire the right of exclusive control over such goods by homesteading action, *i.e.*, by establishing an objective link between a particular person and a particular scarce resource before anybody else had done so, but if instead late-comers were assumed to have ownership claims to goods, then *no one would be allowed to do anything with anything* as one would have to have all of the late-comers' consent prior to ever doing what one wanted to do. Neither we, nor our forefathers, nor our progeny could, do, or will survive if one were to follow this rule. In order for any person — past, present, or future — to argue anything it must be possible to survive then and now, and in order to do just this property rights cannot be conceived of as being "timeless" and nonspecific regarding the number of people involved. Rather, property rights must be thought of as originating as a result of specific individuals acting at definite points in time. Otherwise, it would be impossible for anyone to first say anything at a definite point in time and for someone else to be able to reply. Simply saying that the first-user-first-owner rule of libertarianism can be ignored or is unjustified implies a contradiction, for one's being able to say so must presuppose one's existence as an independent decision-making unit at a given point in time.

Finally, acting and proposition-making would also be impossible, if the things acquired through homesteading were not defined in objective, physical terms (and if correspondingly, aggression were not defined as an invasion of the physical integrity of another person's property), but in terms of subjective values and evaluations. While every person can have control over whether or not his actions cause the *physical* integrity of something to change, control over whether or not one's actions affect the *value* of someone's property rests with other people and their evaluations. One would have to interrogate and come to an agreement with the entire world population to make sure that one's planned actions would not change another person's evaluations regarding his property. Surely, everyone would be long dead before this was accomplished. Moreover, the idea that property values should be protected is argumentatively indefensible, for even in order to argue so it must be presupposed that actions must be permitted *prior* to any actual agreement. (If they were not one could not even make this proposition.) If they are permitted, however, this is only possible because of objective borders of property, *i.e.*, borders which every person can recognize as such on his own without having to agree first with anyone else with respect to one's system of values and evaluations.

By being alive and formulating any proposition, one demonstrates that any ethic except the libertarian private property ethic is invalid. If this were not so and late-comers had to have legitimate claims to things or things owned were defined in subjective terms, no one could possibly survive as a physically independent decision-making unit at any given point in time. Hence, no one could ever raise any validity claiming proposition.

This concludes my *a priori* justification of the private property ethic. A few comments regarding a topic already touched upon earlier, the relationship of this "praxeological" proof of libertarianism to the utilitarian and to the natural rights position, shall complete the discussion. As regards the utilitarian position, the proof contains its ultimate refutation. It demonstrates that simply in order to propose the utilitarian position, exclusive rights of control over one's body and one's homesteaded goods already must be presupposed as valid. More specifically, as regards the consequentialist aspect of libertarianism, the proof shows its praxeological impossibility: the assignment of rights of exclusive control cannot be dependent on certain outcomes. One could never act and propose anything unless private property rights existed prior to a later outcome. A consequentialist ethic is a praxeological absurdity. Any ethic must instead be "aprioristic" or instantaneous in order to make it possible that one can act here and now and propose this or that rather than having to suspend acting until later. Nobody advocating a wait-for-the-outcome ethic would be around to say anything if he took his own advice seriously. Also, to the extent that utilitarian proponents are still around, they demonstrate through their actions that their consequentialist doctrine is and must be regarded as false. Acting and proposition-making require private property rights now and cannot wait for them to be assigned only later.

As regards the natural rights position, the praxeological proof, generally supportive as it is of the former's position concerning the possibility of a rational ethic and in full agreement with the conclusions reached within this tradition (specifically, by Murray N. Rothbard), has at least two distinctive advantages. For one thing, it has been a common quarrel with the natural rights position, even on the part of otherwise sympathetic observers, that the concept of human nature is far too diffuse to allow the derivation of a determinate set of rules of conduct. The praxeological approach solves this problem by recognizing that it is not the wider concept of human nature but the narrower one of propositional exchanges and argumentation which must serve as the starting point in deriving an ethic. Moreover, there exists an *a priori* justification for this choice insofar as the problem of true and false, of right and wrong, does not arise independent of propositional exchanges. No one, then, could possibly challenge such a starting point without contradiction. Finally, it is argumentation which requires the recognition of private property, so an argumentative challenge of the validity of the private property ethic is praxeologically impossible.

Second, there is the logical gap between "is-" and "ought-statements" which natural rights proponents have failed to bridge successfully — except for advancing some general critical remarks regarding the ultimate validity of the fact-value dichotomy. Here the praxeological proof of libertarianism has the advantage of offering a completely value-free justification of private property. It remains entirely in the realm of is-statements and never tries to derive an "ought" from an "is." The structure of the argument is this: (a) justification is propositional justification — *a priori* true is-statement; (b) argumentation presupposes property in one's body and the homesteading principle — *a priori* true is-statement; and (c) then, no deviation from this ethic can be argumentatively justified — *a priori* true is-statement. The proof also offers a key to an understanding of the nature of the fact-value dichotomy: Ought-statements cannot be derived from is-statements. They belong to different logical realms. It is also clear, however, that one cannot even state that there *are* facts and values if no propositional exchanges exist, and that this practice of propositional exchanges in turn presupposes the acceptance of the private property ethic as valid. In other words, cognition and truth-seeking as such have a normative foundation, and the normative foundation on which cognition and truth rest is the recognition of private property rights. (p. 339)

27
Persuasion vs. Force

Mark Skousen, Ph.D. and Jo Ann Skousen

Mark Skousen has written for *The Wall Street Journal*, *Forbes*, and *The Christian Science Monitor*, and has made regular appearances on CNBC's "Kudlow & Co.," Fox News, and C-SPAN's "Book TV." Jo Ann is the Festival Director for the Anthem Libertarian Film Festival and the Entertainment Editor for *Liberty* magazine. A version of this essay originally appeared in the September 1991, issue of *Liberty* magazine.

Sometimes a single book or even a short cogent essay can change an individual's entire outlook on life. For Christians, it is the *New Testament*. For radical socialists, Karl Marx and Friedrich Engels' *The Communist Manifesto* is revolutionary. For libertarians, Ayn Rand's *Atlas Shrugged* is pivotal. For economists, Ludwig von Mises' *Human Action* can be mind-changing.

Recently I came across a little essay in a book called *Adventures of Ideas*, by Alfred North Whitehead, the British philosopher and Harvard professor. The essay, "From Force to Persuasion," had a profound effect upon me. Actually what caught my attention was a single passage on page 83. This one small excerpt in a 300-page book changed my entire political philosophy.

Here's what it says:

> The creation of the world — said Plato — is the victory of persuasion over force... Civilization is the maintenance of social order, by its own inherent persuasiveness as embodying the nobler alternative. The recourse to force, however unavoidable, is a disclosure of the failure of civilization, either in the general society or in a remnant of individuals...
>
> Now the intercourse between individuals and between social groups takes one of these two forms: force or persuasion. Commerce is the great example of intercourse by way of persuasion. War, slavery, and governmental compulsion exemplify the reign of force.

Professor Whitehead's vision of civilized society as the triumph of persuasion over force should become paramount in the mind of all civic-minded individuals and government leaders. It should serve as the guideline for the political ideal.

Let me suggest, therefore, a new political creed: The triumph of persuasion over force is the sign of a civilized society.

Surely this is a fundamental principle to which most citizens, no matter where they fit on the political spectrum, can agree.

Too Many Laws

Too often lawmakers resort to the force of law rather than the power of persuasion to solve a problem in society. They are too quick to pass another statute or regulation in an effort to suppress the effects of a deeprooted problem in society rather than seeking to recognize and deal with the real cause of the problem, which may require parents, teachers, pastors, and community leaders to convince people to change their ways.

Too often politicians think that new programs requiring new taxes are the only way to pay for citizens' retirement, health care, education or other social needs. "People just aren't willing to pay for these services themselves," they say, so they force others to pay for them instead.

Supreme Court Justice Oliver Wendell Holmes once said, "Taxation is the price we pay for civilization." But isn't the opposite really the case? Taxation is the price we pay for failing to build a civilized society. The higher the tax level, the greater the failure. A centrally planned totalitarian state represents a complete defeat for the civilized world, while a totally voluntary society represents its ultimate success.

Thus, legislators, ostensibly concerned about poverty and low wages, pass a minimum wage law and establish a welfare state as their way to abolish poverty. Yet poverty persists, not for want of money, but for want of skills, capital, education, and the desire to succeed.

The community demands a complete education for all children, so the state mandates that all children attend school for at least ten years. Winter Park High School, which two of our children attend, is completely fenced in. Students need a written excuse to leave school grounds and an official explanation for absences. All the gates except one are closed during school hours, and there is a permanent guard placed at the only open gate to monitor students coming and going. Florida recently passed a law that takes away the driver's license of any student who drops out of high school. Surely, they say, that will eliminate the high dropout rate for students.

But suppressing one problem only creates another. Now students who don't want to be in school are disrupting the students who want to learn. The lawmakers forget one thing. Schooling is not the same as education.

Many high-minded citizens don't like to see racial, religious or sexual discrimination in employment, housing, department stores, restaurants, and clubs. Yet instead of persuading people in the schools, the churches and the media that discrimination is inappropriate behavior and morally repugnant, law-makers simply pass civil rights legislation outlawing discrimination, as though making hatred illegal can instantly make it go away. Instead, forced integration often intensifies the already-existing hostilities. Does anyone wonder why discrimination is still a serious problem in our society?

Is competition from the Japanese, the Germans and the Brazilians too stiff for American industry? We can solve that right away, says Congress. No use trying to convince industry to invest in more productive labor and capital, or voting to reduce the tax burden on business. No, they'll just impose import quotas or heavy duties on foreign products and force them to "play fair." Surely that will make us more competitive, and keep American companies in business.

Drugs, Guns, and Abortion

Is the use of mind-altering drugs a problem in America? Then let's pass legislation prohibiting the use of certain high-powered drugs. People still want to use them? Then let's hire more police to crack down on the drug users and drug dealers. Surely that will solve the problem. Yet such laws never address the fundamental issue, which would require analyzing why people misuse drugs and discovering ways they can satisfy their needs in a nondestructive manner. By outlawing illicit drugs, we fail to consider the underlying cause of increased drug or alcohol misuse among teenagers and adults, and we fail to accept the beneficial uses of such drugs in medicine and healthcare. I salute voluntary efforts in communities to deal with these serious problems, such as "no alcohol" high school graduation parties and drug-awareness classes. Tobacco is on the decline as a result of education, and drug use could abate as well if it were treated as a medical problem rather than a criminal one.

Abortion is a troublesome issue, we all agree on that. Whose rights take precedence, the baby's or the mother's? When does life begin, at conception or at birth?

Political conservatives are shocked by the millions of legal killings that take place every year in America and around the world. How can we sing "God Bless America" with this epidemic plaguing our nation? So, for many conservatives the answer is simple: Ban abortions! Force women to give birth to their unexpected and unwanted babies. That will solve the problem. This quick fix will undoubtedly give the appearance that we have instantly solved our national penchant for genocide.

Wouldn't it be better if we first tried to answer the all-important questions, "Why is abortion so prevalent today, and how can we prevent unwanted pregnancies?" Or, once an unwanted pregnancy occurs, how can we persuade people to examine alternatives, including adoption?

Crime is another issue plaguing this country. There are those in society who want to ban handguns, rifles and other firearms, or at least have them tightly controlled and registered, in an attempt to reduce crime. We can solve the murder and crime problem in this country, they reason, simply by passing a law taking away the weapons of murder. No guns, no killings. Simple, right?

Yet they only change the outward symptoms, while showing little interest in finding ways to discourage a person from becoming criminal or violent in the first place.

Legislators should be slow to pass laws to protect people against themselves. While insisting on a woman's "right to choose" in one area, they deny men and women the right to choose in every other area. Unfortunately, they are all too quick to act. Drivers aren't wearing their seatbelts? Let's pass a mandatory seatbelt law. Motorcyclists aren't wearing helmets? Let's mandate helmets. We'll force people to be responsible!

More Than Just Freedom

How did we get into this situation, where lawmakers feel compelled to legislate personal behavior "for our own good"? Often we only have ourselves to blame.

The lesson is clear: If we are going to preserve what personal and economic freedom we have left in this country, we had better act responsibly, or our freedom is going to be taken away. Too many detractors think that freedom is nothing more than the right to act irresponsibly. They equate liberty with libertine behavior: that the freedom to choose whether to have an abortion means that they should have an abortion, that the freedom to take drugs means that they should take drugs, that the legalization of gambling means that they should play the roulette wheel.

It is significant that Professor Whitehead chose the word "persuasion," not simply "freedom," as the ideal characteristic of the civilized world. The word "persuasion" embodies both freedom of choice and responsibility for choice. In order to persuade, you must have a moral philosophy, a system of right and wrong, which you govern yourself. You want to persuade people to do the right thing not because they have to, but because they want to.

There is little satisfaction from doing good if individuals are mandated to do the right thing. Character and responsibility are built when people voluntarily choose right over wrong, not when they are forced to do so. A soldier will feel a greater sense of victory if he enlists in the armed forces instead of being drafted. And high school students will not comprehend the joy of service if it is mandated by a community-service requirement for graduation.

Admittedly, there will be individuals in a free society who will make the wrong choices, who will become drug addicts and alcoholics, who will refuse to wear a safety helmet, who will hurt themselves playing with firecrackers, and who will drop out of high school. But that is the price we must pay for having a free society, where individuals learn from their mistakes and try to build a better world.

In this context, let us answer the all-important question, "Liberty and morality: can we have both?" The answer is, absolutely yes! Not only can we have both, but we must have both, or eventually we will have neither. As Sir James Russell Lowell said, "The ultimate result of protecting fools from their folly is to fill the planet full of fools."

Our motto should be, "We teach them correct principles, and they govern themselves."

Freedom without responsibility only leads to the destruction of civilization, as evidenced by Rome and other great civilizations of the past. As Alexis de Tocqueville said, "Despotism may govern without faith, but liberty cannot." In a similar vein, Henry Ward Beecher added, "There is no liberty to men who know not how to govern themselves." And Edmund Burke wrote, "What is liberty without wisdom and without virtue?"

Today's political leaders demonstrate their low opinion of the public with every social law they pass. They believe that, if given the right to choose, the citizenry will probably make the wrong choice. Legislators do not think any more in terms of persuading people; they feel the need to force their agenda on the public at the point of a bayonet and the barrel of a gun, in the name of the IRS, the SEC, the FDA, the DEA, the EPA, or a multitude of other ABCs of government authority.

A Challenge to All Lovers of Liberty

My challenge to all lovers of liberty today is to take the moral high ground. Our cause is much more compelling when we can say that we support drug legalization, but do not use mind altering drugs. That we tolerate legal abortion, but choose not to abort our own future generations. That we support the right to bear arms, but do not misuse handguns. That we favor the right of individuals to meet privately as they please, but do not ourselves discriminate.

In the true spirit of liberty, Voltaire [sic] once said, "I disapprove of what you say, but I will defend to the death your right to say it." If we are to be effective in convincing others of the benefits of a tolerant world, we must take the moral high ground by saying, "We may disapprove of what you do, but we will defend to the death your right to do it."

In short, my vision of a responsible free society is one in which we discourage evil, but do not prohibit it. We make our children and students aware of the consequences of drug abuse and other forms of irresponsible behavior. But after all our persuading, if they still want to use harmful drugs, that is their privilege. In a free society, individuals must have the right to do right or wrong, as long as they don't threaten or infringe upon the rights or property of others. They must also suffer the consequences of their actions, as it is from consequences that they learn to choose properly.

We may discourage prostitution or pornography by restricting it to certain areas and to certain ages, but we will not jail or fine those who choose to participate in it privately. If an adult bookstore opens in our neighborhood, we don't run to the law and pass an ordinance, we picket the store and discourage customers. If our religion asks us not to shop on Sunday, we don't pass Sunday "blue" laws forcing stores to close, we simply don't patronize them on Sunday. If we don't like excessive violence and gratuitous sex on TV, we don't write the Federal Communications Commission, we join boycotts of the advertiser's products. Several years ago the owners of 7-Eleven stores removed pornographic magazines from their stores, not because the law required it, but because a group of concerned citizens persuaded them. These actions reflect the true spirit of liberty.

Lovers of liberty should also be strong supporters of the institutions of persuasion, such as churches, charities, foundations, private schools and colleges, and private enterprise. They should engage in many causes of their own free will and choice. They should not rely on the institutions of force, such as government agencies, to carry out the cause of education and the works of charity and welfare. It is not enough simply to pay your taxes and cast your vote and think you've done your part.

It is the duty of every advocate of human liberty to convince the world that we must solve our problems through persuasion and not coercion. Whether the issue is domestic policy or foreign policy, we must recognize that passing another regulation or going to war is not necessarily the only solution to our problems. Simply to pass laws prohibiting the outward symptoms of problems is to sweep the real problems under the rug. It may hide the dirt for a while, but it doesn't dispose of the dirt properly or permanently.

Liberty Under Law

This approach does not mean that laws would not exist. People should have the freedom to act according to their desires, but only to the extent that they do not trample on the rights of others. Rules and regulations, such as traffic laws, need to be established and enforced by private and public institutions in order for a free society to exist. There should be stringent laws against fraud, theft, murder, pollution, and the breaking of contracts, and those laws should be effectively enforced according to the classic principle that the punishment should fit the crime. The full weight of the law should be used to fine and imprison the perpetrators, to compensate the victims, and to safeguard the rights of the innocent. Yet within this legal framework, we should permit the maximum degree of freedom in allowing people to choose what they think, act and do to themselves without harming others.

Convincing the public of our message, that "persuasion instead of force is the sign of a civilized society," will require a lot of hard work, but it can be rewarding. The key is to make a convincing case for freedom, to present the facts to the public so that they can see the logic of our arguments, and to develop a dialogue with those who may be opposed to our position. Our emphasis must be on educating and persuading, not on arguing and name-calling. For we shall never change our political leaders until we change the people who elect them.

A Vision of an Ideal Society

Martin Luther King, Jr. gave a famous sermon at the Lincoln Memorial in the mid-1960s. In it, King said that he had a dream about the promised land. Well, I too have a vision of an ideal society.

I have a vision of world peace, not because the military have been called in to maintain order, but because we have peace from within and friendship with every nation.

I have a vision of universal prosperity and an end to poverty, not because of foreign aid or government-subsidized welfare, but because each of us has productive, useful employment where every trade is honest and beneficial to both buyer and seller, and where we eagerly help the less fortunate of our own free will.

I have a vision of an inflation-free nation, not because of wage and price controls, but because our nation has an honest money system.

I have a vision of a crime-free society, not because there's a policeman on every corner, but because we respect the rights and property of others.

I have a vision of a drug-free America, not because harmful drugs are illegal, but because we desire to live long, healthy, self-sustaining lives.

I have a vision of an abortion-free society, not because abortion is illegal, but because we firmly believe in the sanctity of life, sexual responsibility, and family values.

I have a vision of a pollution-free and environmentally sound world, not because of costly controls and arbitrary regulations, but because private enterprise honors its stewardship and commitment to developing rather than exploiting the earth's resources.

I have a vision of a free society, not because a benevolent dictator commands it, but because we love freedom and the responsibility that goes with it.

The following words, taken from an old Protestant hymn whose author is fittingly anonymous, express the aspiration of every man and every woman in a free society:

> Know this, that every soul is free
> To choose his life and what he'll be;
> For this eternal truth is given
> That God will force no man to heaven.
> He'll call, persuade, direct aright,
> And bless with wisdom, love, and light,
> In nameless ways be good and kind,
> But never force the human mind.

28
The Most Dangerous Superstition (Excerpts)

Larken Rose

> Larken Rose is an internationally known vocal advocate for the principles of self-ownership, non-aggression and a stateless society — in a word, *voluntaryism*. He can be found at TheRoseChannel.com.

The belief in "authority," which includes all belief in "government," is irrational and self-contradictory; it is contrary to civilization and morality, and constitutes the most dangerous, destructive superstition that has ever existed. Rather than being a force for order and justice, the belief in "authority" is the arch-enemy of humanity. (p. 3)

If human beings are so careless, stupid and malicious that they cannot be trusted to do the right thing on their own, how would the situation be improved by taking a subset of those very same careless, stupid and malicious human beings and giving them societal permission to forcibly control all the others? (p. 26)

Perhaps most telling is that if you suggest to the average person that maybe God does not exist, he will likely respond with less emotion and hostility than if you bring up the idea of life without "government." This indicates which religion people are more deeply emotionally attached to, and which religion they actually believe in more firmly. In fact, they believe so deeply in "government" that they do not even recognize it as being a belief at all. (p. 29)

If, for example, someone has a "right" to housing, and housing comes only from the knowledge, skills and efforts of other people, it means that one person has the right to force another person to build him a house. (p. 117)

All statists believe that the people who make up "government" have an exemption from basic human morality, and not only may do things which others have no right to do, but should and must do such things, for the (supposed) good of society. The type and degree of aggression varies, but all statists advocate aggression. (p. 121)

To quickly review, people cannot delegate rights they do not have, which makes it impossible for anyone to acquire the right to rule ("authority").

People cannot alter morality, which makes the "laws" of "government" devoid of any inherent "authority." Ergo, "authority" — the right to rule — cannot logically exist. (p. 144)

29
Can Anarcho-Capitalism Work?

Llewellyn H. Rockwell, Jr.

Lew Rockwell is founder and chairman of the Ludwig von Mises Institute, editor of LewRockwell.com, and author of *Fascism vs. Capitalism*. This talk was delivered at the Costa Mesa Mises Circle on "Society Without the State," on November 8, 2014.

The term "anarcho-capitalism" has, we might say, rather an arresting quality. But while the term itself may jolt the newcomer, the ideas it embodies are compelling and attractive, and represent the culmination of a long development of thought.

If I had to boil it down to a handful of insights, they would be these: (1) each human being, to use John Locke's formulation, "has a property in his own person"; (2) there ought to be a single moral code binding all people, whether they are employed by the State or not; and (3) society can run itself without central direction.

From the original property one enjoys in his own person we can derive individual rights, including property rights. When taken to its proper Rothbardian conclusion, this insight actually invalidates the State, since the State functions and survives on the basis of systematic violation of individual rights. Were it not to do so, it would cease to be the State.

In violating individual rights, the State tries to claim exemption from the moral laws we take for granted in all other areas of life. What would be called theft if carried out by a private individual is taxation for the State. What would be called kidnapping is the military draft for the State. What would be called mass murder for anyone else is war for the State. In each case, the State gets away with moral enormities because the public has been conditioned to believe that the State is a law unto itself, and can't be held to the same moral standards we apply to ourselves.

But it's the third of these ideas I'd like to develop at greater length. In those passages of their moral treatises dealing with economics, the Late Scholastics, particularly in the sixteenth and seventeenth centuries, had been groping toward the idea of laws that govern the social order. They discovered necessary cause-and-effect relationships. There was a clear connection, for example, between the flow of precious metals entering Spain from the New World on the one hand, and the phenomenon of price inflation on the other.

They began to understand that these social regularities were brute facts that could not be defied by the political authority.

This insight developed into fuller maturity with the classical liberals of the eighteenth century, and the gradual emergence of economics as a full-fledged, independent discipline. This, said Ludwig von Mises, is why dictators hate the economists. True economists tell the ruler that there are limits to what he can accomplish by his sheer force of will, and that he cannot override economic law.

In the nineteenth century, Frédéric Bastiat placed great emphasis on this insight. If these laws exist, then we must study them and understand them, but certainly not be so foolish as to defy them. Conversely, he said, if there are no such laws, then men are merely inert matter upon which the State will be all too glad to impose its imprint. He wrote:

> For if there are general laws that act independently of written laws, and whose action needs merely to be regularized by the latter, we must study these general laws; they can be the object of scientific investigation, and therefore there is such a thing as the science of political economy. If, on the contrary, society is a human invention, if men are only inert matter to which a great genius, as Rousseau says, must impart feeling and will, movement and life, then there is no such science as political economy: there is only an indefinite number of possible and contingent arrangements, and the fate of nations depends on the *founding father* to whom chance has entrusted their destiny.

The next step in the development of what would later become anarcho-capitalism was the radical one taken by Gustave de Molinari, in his essay "The Private Production of Security." Molinari asked if the production of defense services, which even the classical liberals took for granted had to be carried out by the State, might be accomplished by private firms under market competition. Molinari made express reference to the insight we have been developing thus far, that society operates according to fixed, intelligible laws. If this is so, he said, then the provision of this service ought to be subject to the same laws of free competition that govern the production of all other goods. Wouldn't the problems of monopoly exist with any monopoly, even the State's that we have been conditioned to believe is unavoidable and benign?

> It offends reason to believe that a well-established natural law can admit of exceptions. A natural law must hold everywhere and always, or be invalid. I cannot believe, for example, that the universal law of gravitation, which governs the physical world, is ever suspended in any instance or at any point of the universe. Now I consider economic laws comparable to natural laws, and I have just as much faith in the principle of the division of labor as I have in the universal law of gravitation. I

believe that while these principles can be *disturbed*, they admit of no exceptions.

But, if this is the case, the production of security should not be removed from the jurisdiction of free competition; and if it is removed, society as a whole suffers a loss.

It was Murray N. Rothbard who developed the coherent, consistent, and rigorous system of thought — out of classical liberalism, American individualist anarchism, and Austrian economics — that he called anarcho-capitalism. In a career of dozens of books and thousands of articles, Rothbard subjected the State to an incisive, withering analysis, unlike anything seen before. I dedicated *Against the State* to this great pioneer, and dear friend.

But can it work? It is all very well to raise moral and philosophical objections to the State, but we are going to need a plausible scenario by which society regulates itself in the absence of the State, even in the areas of law and defense. These are serious and difficult questions, and glib answers will naturally be inadequate, but I want to propose at least a few suggestive ideas.

The conventional wisdom, of course, is that without a monopoly provider of these services, we will revert to the Hobbesian state of nature, in which everyone is at war with everyone else and life is "solitary, poor, nasty, brutish, and short." A ceaseless series of assaults of one person against another ensues, and society sinks ever deeper into barbarism.

For one thing, it's not even clear that the logic behind Thomas Hobbes's fears really makes any sense. As Michael Huemer points out, Hobbes posits a rough equality among human beings in that none of us is totally invulnerable. We are all potential murder victims at the hands of anyone else, he says. He likewise insists that human beings are motivated by, and indeed altogether obsessed with, self-interest.

Now suppose that were true: all we care about is our own self-interest, our own well-being, our own security. Would it make sense for us to rush out and attack other people, if we have a 50 percent chance of being killed ourselves? Even if we happen to be skilled in battle, there is still a significant chance that any attack we launch will end in our death. How does this advance our self-interest?

Hobbes likewise speaks of pre-emptive attacks, that people will attack others out of a fear that those others may first attack them. If this is true, then it's even more irrational for people to go around attacking others: if their fellows are inclined to preemptively attack people they fear, whom would they fear more than people who go around indiscriminately attacking people? In other words, the more you attack people, the more you open yourself up to preemptive attacks by others. So here we see another reason that it makes no sense, from the point of view of the very self-interest

Hobbes insists everyone is motivated by, for people to behave the way he insists they must.

As for law, history affords an abundance of examples of what we might call trickle-up law, in which legal norms develop through the course of normal human interaction and the accumulation of a body of general principles. We are inclined to think of law as by nature a top-down institution, because we confuse law with the modern phenomenon of legislation. Every year the world's legislative bodies pour forth a staggering number of new rules, regulations, and prohibitions. We have come to accept this as normal, when in fact it is, historically speaking, an anomaly.

It was once common to conceive of law as something *discovered* rather than made. In other words, the principles that constitute justice and by which people live harmoniously together are derived from a combination of reflection on eternal principles and the practical application of those principles to particular cases. The idea that a legislative body could overturn the laws of contract and declare that, say, a landlord had to limit rents to amounts deemed acceptable by the State, would have seemed incredible.

The English common law, for example, was a bottom-up system. In the Middle Ages, merchant law developed without the State at all. And in the U.S. today, private arbitration services have exploded as people and firms seek out alternatives to a government court system, staffed in many cases by political appointees, that everyone knows to be inefficient, time-consuming, and frequently unjust.

PayPal is an excellent example of how the private, entrepreneurial sector devises creative ways around the State's incompetence in guaranteeing the inviolability of property and contract. For a long time, PayPal had to deal with anonymous perpetrators of fraud all over the world. The company would track down the wrongdoers and report them to the FBI. And nothing ever happened.

Despairing of any government solution, PayPal came up with an ingenious approach: it devised a system for preemptively determining whether a given transaction was likely to be fraudulent. This way, there would be no bad guys to be tracked down, since their criminal activity would be prevented before it could do any harm.

Small miracles like this take place all the time in the free sector of society, not that we're encouraged to learn much about them. Recall that as the Centers for Disease Control issued false statements and inadequate protocols for dealing with Ebola, it was a Firestone company town in Liberia that did more than any public authority in Africa to provide safety and health for the local population.

There is a great deal more to be said about law and defense provision in a free society, and I discuss some of this literature at the end of *Against the State*. But the reason we focus on these issues in the first place is that we realize the State cannot be reformed. The State is a monopolist of aggressive violence and a massive wealth-transfer mechanism, and it is doing precisely what is in its nature to do. The utopian dream of "limited government" cannot be realized, since government has no interest in remaining limited. A smaller version of what we have now, while preferable, cannot be a stable, long-term solution. So we need to conceive of how we could live without the State or its parasitism at all.

The point of this book is to speak frankly — at times perhaps even shockingly so — in order to jolt readers out of the intellectual torpor in which the ruling class and its system of youth indoctrination have lulled them. We might have a fighting chance if most people were aware of the ideas in this book, and in our intellectual tradition generally. They would never fall for the State's propaganda line, its apologias, its moral double standards. They would be insulted by these distortions and dissimulations.

And that's what we do at the Mises Institute. We don't publish "policy reports" in the vain hope that Congress will defy its own nature and pursue freedom. Every one of those policy reports winds up in the trash can. They are used to dupe the gullible into thinking the Washington think-tanks they support have influence in Washington.

Instead, we set forth the truth about the State without compromise or apology. The reason Ron Paul attracted so many young people was that they could see he was speaking to them in plain English, not politicalese. He was speaking frankly and truthfully, without regard for the lectures and hectoring he'd get for it at the hands of the media.

We've tried to emulate Ron's approach — and of course, we've been delighted to have Ron as a Distinguished Counselor to the Institute since its inception, and as a member of our board as well. The stakes are too high for us to do anything other than speak frankly and directly about what we know to be true. It's easy to publish toothless essays about public policy. It is harder to focus on war, the Federal Reserve, and the true nature of the State itself. But that is the path we have willingly chosen.

We hope you'll join us.

30
Chaos Theory (Excerpts)

Robert P. Murphy, Ph.D.

Robert P. Murphy, Ph.D. is a Senior Fellow at the Ludwig von Mises Institute and author of *Choice: Cooperation, Enterprise, and Human Action*.

First, we must abandon the idea of a mythical "law of the land." There doesn't need to be a single set of laws binding everyone. In any event, such a system never existed. The laws in each of the fifty states are different, and the difference in legal systems between countries is even more pronounced. Yet we go about our daily lives, and even visit and do business with foreign nations, without too much trouble. (p. 14)

Stripped to its essentials, a system of private law means that people who can't come to an agreement on their own will literally seek the opinion of a third party. Of course, in a modern Western economy, truly private legal systems would lead to specialized training and contractual codifications of the judge's role in rendering opinions on the cases brought before him or her. (p. 8)

Just because an arbitration agency ruled a certain way, wouldn't make everyone agree with it, just as people complain about outrageous court rulings by government judges. The press would pick up on the unfair rulings, and people would lose faith in the objectivity of Agency X's decisions. Potential employees would think twice before working for the big firm, as long as it required (in its work contracts) that people submitted to the suspect Agency X. (p. 15)

It's true, some people would still commit crimes and would have no insurance company to pay damages, but such cases are going to occur under any legal system. (p. 22)

Critics often dismiss private law by alleging that disputes between enforcement agencies would lead to combat — even though this happens between governments all the time! In truth, the incentives for peaceful resolution of disputes would be far greater in market anarchy than the present system. Combat is very expensive, and private companies take much better care of their assets than government officials take care of their subjects' lives and property. (p. 22)

"Won't the Mafia take over?"

Chaos Theory (Excerpts)

It is paradoxical that the fear of rule by organized crime families causes people to support the State, which is the most "organized" and criminal association in human history. Even if it were true that under market anarchy, people had to pay protection money and occasionally get whacked, this would be a drop in the bucket compared to the taxation and wartime deaths caused by governments. But even this concedes too much. For the mob derives its strength from government, not the free market. All of the businesses traditionally associated with organized crime — gambling, prostitution, loan sharking, drug dealing — are prohibited or heavily regulated by the State. In market anarchy, true professionals would drive out such unscrupulous competitors. (p. 23)

"Your insurance companies would become the State!"

On the contrary, the private companies providing legal services would have far less power under market anarchy than the government currently possesses. Most obvious, there would be no power to tax or to monopolize "service." If a particular insurance company were reluctant to pay legitimate claims, this would become quickly known, and people would take this into account when dealing with clients of this disreputable firm. (p. 23)

The fear of rogue agencies, unilaterally declaring themselves "owner" of everything, is completely unfounded. In market anarchy, the companies publicizing property rights would not be the same as the companies enforcing those rights. More important, competition between firms would provide true "checks and balances." If one firm began flouting the community norms established and codified on the market, it would go out of business, just as surely as a manufacturer of dictionaries would go broke if its books contained improper definitions. (p. 27)

This essay has outlined the mechanics of purely voluntary, market law. The main theme running throughout is that competition and accountability would force true experts to handle the important decisions that must be made in any legal system. It is a statist myth that justice must be produced by a monopoly institution of organized violence. (p. 39)

Apples and Oranges

This theoretical discussion is sure to provoke the cynic to remark, "I'd like to see what your insurance companies would do if they met a Panzer division." But such a question misses the point. We have demonstrated that a private defense system is the most effective, not that it is invulnerable. Yes, a small society of anarchists would be unable to repel the total might of Nazi Germany. But a small society of statists would fare even worse — and in fact, plenty of government militaries were obliterated by Hitler's armies. (p. 56)

31
The "Power Vacuum" Argument

Larken Rose

Larken Rose is an internationally known vocal advocate for the principles of self-ownership, non-aggression and a stateless society — in a word, *voluntaryism*. He can be found at TheRoseChannel.com.

As I explained in my previous article, when confronted about the inherent immorality and illegitimacy of "government," statists often fall back on making dire predictions of chaos and mayhem. Of course, this is logically irrelevant to philosophical principles. Reality doesn't change itself to avoid bad things happening.

> A: "Dude, don't jump out of the plane, you don't have a parachute!"
> B: "Yes, I do, because if I didn't, this would kill me! Aaaaaaah..."

Or...

> A: "People can't delegate rights they don't have."
> B: "Yes, they can, because otherwise there would be chaos!"

But there is something else worth noting about one of the most common dire predictions that statists fling around. They basically argue that if there were no government, the horrendous, chaotic, violent result would be... government. "Warlords would take over and build armies and rule us all!" In other words, the worst-case scenario that statists predict for anarchism is... statism. And that's pretty damn funny. ("I'm gonna advocate this bad thing — a big, powerful ruling class — because otherwise we would end up with the thing I'm advocating!")

Statists love to proclaim that if a certain regime or ruling class collapsed, was overthrown, or just disappeared, it would create a "power vacuum" and a new ruling class would magically appear.

Actually, in one way they are quite right about that. But in another way, they are dead wrong. The only reason "power vacuums" exist is because most people think there *should* be — and *has* to be — a ruling class, a supreme set of "law-makers," a "government." If, for example, Washington, D.C. just fell into the Atlantic today, a new "government" *would* regrow, but not because of magic, or human nature, or because the universe makes them appear, but because *people who believe in authority* will keep creating new ruling classes.

That's why I constantly emphasize the fact that the *belief* in "authority" (including all belief in "government") is the problem. Whatever particular regime is doing the evil crap right now is never the actual problem. The problem resides between several billion pairs of ears. As long as most people believe that having rulers is legitimate and necessary, they will keep putting narcissistic sociopaths on thrones.

So yes, as long as the general population is stuck in the authoritarian mindset (*"Someone has to be in charge! We neeeeeeed a leader!"*), then when one regime falls, another will be built in its place — often one even worse than the one before. And yes, this is why violent revolution is utterly pointless without there first being a revolution of how people think.

HOWEVER, once people outgrow the superstition of "authority" and escape the statist indoctrination they've been programmed with, there will be no "power vacuum" to fill. A society of voluntaryists is not going to suddenly decide that what they really need is to be violently dominated by a new group of politicians.

Statists often talk about how some tyrant or warlord would just "take over," while completely missing the fact that *their own belief system* is the *only* reason anyone can "take over." They seem to believe in the existence of Hollywood villains, who are so diabolical that they can just make power magically appear. They don't seem to know that every successful tyrant has to dupe the general public into seeing him as a *savior*, so that they gladly and eagerly give him control over their lives, and over everyone else's. Mao, Stalin, Hitler, they were all cheered into power by adoring masses. Masses of... you guessed it... *STATISTS* — people who believed in "authority," and thought "government" is what makes society and civilization work.

So in one sense, when a statist warns of the "power vacuum" thing, he is right, while failing to notice that he and his fellow statists are the *only reason* his dire prediction holds any truth. If the people don't perceive the new gang to have the right to rule — don't perceive it to be "authority" — then they don't cheer for it. They shoot at it. And it dies.

And that brings up the whole silly "warlord" thing. "If we didn't have government protecting us, warlords would take over!" Such an argument ignores the fact that warlords (and street gangs and the Mafia, too) are almost always funded by black markets *created* by "government" (*e.g.*, the "illegal" drug trade). Without a ruling class, they wouldn't exist to begin with.

But the "warlords" argument also shows a profound ignorance of human nature. It basically implies that, in the statist's mind, the ability to rule doesn't at all depend upon the *legitimacy* of those in power, in the eyes of the people. In reality, it has *everything* to do with that. Especially in a place where *a hundred million people* possess their own firearms, the idea of "warlords" ruling by brute force is just ridiculous.

An example of private gun ownership in the U.S.:

Would you want to try to rule those people by brute force? I wouldn't (and not just because I have moral principles). An example I like to use is this: imagine that you are an organized crime boss, and your goal is to extort a hundred million people of a large chunk of what they earn, every year. You have 100,000 loyal underlings. However, only two thousand of them are armed; the rest are paper-pushers. Do you think you could successfully rob those people, when they outnumber (and outgun) your armed enforcers *fifty-thousand*-to-one?

Guess what. The IRS does it. How? Most of their *victims* imagine the extortion to be "legal," and legitimate, and necessary. The victims feel an *obligation* to obey and pay tribute. If tomorrow they all stopped feeling that obligation, there would be no IRS by the end of the day. That shows how much *perceptions* determine power, and how much political "authority" depends completely on the mentality of those being controlled.

In conclusion, there is only *one* gang with the ability to continually extort and control the American people, and that is the one that the American people imagine to be "authority." In other words, the one gang that can dominate us is *already doing it*, and the only reason it is able to do so is because of the belief in "authority" infecting the minds of the general public.

We already *are* dominated by evil warlords. We already have been taken over by a violent gang. And, Mr. and Mrs. Statist, *you* are the cause; *your* belief system is what gives politicians all of their power. So when you whine at voluntaryists about how nasty gangs of crooks might take over, keep in mind that *they already did*, that *you* are condoning that, that *you* are making it happen, and that *your* crappy belief system is the only reason it continues to happen, or is able to happen at all. Way to go.

32
So, Tell Me, 'Do You Hate the State?'

Peter R. Quiñones

Peter R. Quiñones hosts the "Pete Quiñones Show" podcast.

This is a simple question. One you should ask yourself often (some of us ask and answer it every day). Murray Rothbard's short article[1] quoted in the title is a masterpiece, but was written in 1977. The last remnants of the gold standard had just been done away with and the remaining soldier/diplomats in Vietnam had come home a couple years prior. We are living in a different world but the question is as relevant today as it was in 1977, maybe a little more so.

Afghanistan is the longest war in American history and is responsible for the death, maiming and torture of countless tens of thousands of Afghans. That number could be over 100,000 and the people who started it, and refuse to end it, will make sure we never know the real total. The Americans who are sent to fight in Afghanistan suffer the same fate — killed, maimed and sometimes tortured. Oftentimes that torture is mental, in some cases caused by "following orders" of the State, and has resulted in 22 veterans a day committing suicide. Of course those veterans not only served in Afghanistan but also Iraq, Syria, Somalia, Ethiopia and on and on. No matter what you've been told, soldiers aren't peacekeepers. They serve one purpose. Expansion of elitists' power. By defending and supporting the State, you defend what soldiers are sent there to do.

Many Americans continue to be locked down in their homes. Businesses have been forced to close or operate using guidelines that make it impossible to remain open. ("It's a private business, bro, they can do what they want!" Except open, I guess.) Wealth has been decimated. Stores that have been open for generations are gone. And if you point this out, people run to default responses like "You don't care that people are dying," or "You want to see my grandma dead!" But when peer-reviewed studies[2] disputing that lockdowns had any effect are highlighted by "Cathedral" news outlets, they are ignored. The experts are telling you they got it wrong, but they're not apologizing. Why? Because they don't care that you lost your nest egg, home, business or loved one to suicide. By defending and supporting the State, you defend the "experts" who did this.

So, they got the lockdowns wrong, the masks are shown to be

ineffective,³ and it has been ten months of a two-week lockdown to "flatten the curve." After all of the chaos and guessing on their part, after governors sent the infected back into nursing homes to spread the virus to the demographic most affected by it, after every measure they took harmed people more than it helped, they expect us to trust a rushed to market vaccine developed by companies who suffer no liability if it's ineffective or harmful. And this is where libertarians/anarchists/whatever drop the ball. Medical freedom is one of the most important issues to sovereign individuals and so many are afraid to advocate for it lest they be called kooks or "anti-vaxxers." If you do not have the ability to decide when and what can be put in your body, are you free? Please stop and answer the question. I don't care that the State exists and claims ownership over the commons. That's just autistic, Libertarian B.S.! Are you really free if you can be forced to accept something into your body you don't want there? Maybe ask a rape victim? "bUt iT's A pRiVaTe cOrPoRaTioN rEqUiRiNg it!" Shut the hell up! By defending and supporting the State, you defend its ability to force anything it wishes into your body and use "private companies" to do it.

I could go on and on with examples but I hope these hit close enough to home. Most people know someone lost, hurt or traumatized by the "terror wars." Many know, or are themselves, the people destroyed financially and/or emotionally by the lockdowns. And I hope most of you are questioning a vaccine that would almost assuredly have gone through several more trials and tests even in a "libertarian society." Again, do you hate the State? Do you see costumed morons running around the Capitol building where all of these horrors are planned and clutch at your pearls? If you do, if that's your first impulse, you're on the side of the blood-soaked monsters. Why would you want to be there?

NOTES

1. Rothbard, Murray N. "Do You Hate the State?" Libertarian Forum, Vol. 10, No. 7, July 1977.
2. Colarossi, Natalie. "COVID Lockdowns May Have No Clear Benefit vs. Other Voluntary Measures." Newsweek, Jan. 2021.
3. Woods, Thomas E. "The Covid Cult." (mises.org/library/covid-cult).

33
Government Itself Is Immoral

James Corbett

James Corbett is the founder of *The Corbett Report*, an independent, listener-supported alternative news source. Find his work at CorbettReport.com. The following passage is an excerpt from "5 Important Lessons Absolutely No One Will Learn from Iowa."

No, I do not want better elections. I do not want to "clean up the system." I do not want to "get the money out of politics" and "make sure every vote is counted" and "drain the swamp" so we can "Make America [or any other geographical area] Great Again."

The state is not a benevolent force, despite what the most brainwashed of statists believe. It is not even a neutral tool that can be used for good or ill, as those who consider themselves pragmatists believe. It is violence. It is force. It is aggression. It is people believing that what is wrong for any individual to do is perfectly OK if an agent of the state does it.

If I steal, it is theft. If the state steals, it is taxation. If I kill, it is murder. If the state kills, it is warfare. If I force someone to work for me involuntarily, it is slavery. If the state does it, it is conscription. If I confine someone against their will, it is kidnapping. If the state does it, it is incarceration. Nothing has changed but the label.

What binds us to the state is the belief that there is a different morality for anything that has been sanctified through the political process. "Oh, 50%+1 of the population voted for forced vaccinations? Then I guess we have to comply." If you scoff at that sentence, how about if the vote were 100%-1? Would that change the morality of resistance? How about if forced vaccinations were mandated by the constitution? Then would you be compelled to submit?

Does the ballot box transform the unethical into the ethical? Of course not. But I'll tell you what it does do: It makes everyone who casts their ballot a part of the process that legitimizes the murder and violence committed by agents of the state.

No, I am not an efficiency manager for the state. I do not want to help it do its job of inflicting aggression and violence on peaceful people. I want the state to perish, not through violence or bloodshed, but by removing the mystical superstition from the minds of the general public that makes them believe that "government" is anything other than a gang of thugs with a fancy title.

This is the point that — in my experience as a communicator of voluntaryist ideas — I start butting up against a brick wall of incomprehension when talking to the normies in the crowd. They start having mental breakdowns, frothing at the mouth that "votes need to happen."

As if voting, elections, positions of responsibility and other things that exist under statism could not exist under voluntary associations. As if voluntary association itself were such an arcane and bewildering concept that no one could possibly wrap their head around it (let alone, heaven forbid, read a book[1] or two[2] to see if some of their questions on the subject have already been answered).

No, much easier to go back to the comforting political wrestling match. "Red vs. Blue? Now that I can get behind!"

That's a travesty, really. Because the truth is that this is not a complicated message. It's actually remarkably simple, and remarkably hopeful. The truth is that...

There Is Only One Vote That Matters

You'd think that a column like this would be all doom and gloom.

"Oh sure, James," say the statists in the crowd, twirling their handlebar moustaches and fingering the "I Voted" sticker proudly displayed on their chest, "but what's your solution? Sitting around and not voting is not going to change anything!"

Now I'm tempted to say, "Why ask for one solution when I've provided dozens?"[3]

But, more seriously, I would say: You're right.

No, really. You're right. Sitting around and not voting is not going to change anything. Yes, by all means, let's vote!...

...But (and you knew there was a "but" coming) I'm not talking about voting in some phony baloney (s)election to anoint some political puppet as President of this geographical location. I'm talking about the only vote that matters.

Hmmm... if only I had a way to explain this to the normies.

Oh, wait! I do...[4]

For the rest of us, there is the realization that the political system itself is just another form of enslavement. An enslavement that is all the more insidious, because it asks us to buy into it. All we have to do is push a button or pull a lever or touch a screen once every four years and we are now absolved from our moral responsibility.

Ironically, this realization is in itself liberating and puts the world into focus with crystal clarity. We are not cogs in some machine called "society" to be dictated to by some nebulous entity we have been taught to call "the government" or "the authorities." We are free individuals freely interacting with those around us, bound by the moral injunction not to initiate force against others or take things from others against their will. We are responsible for our actions and their consequences, both positive and negative. We are responsible for what we do or don't do to help those in our community, and to make this world better or leave it to rot. There is no political messiah that will descend from the heavens to tell us what to do or to protect us from the bad men. All we have is our self and our choices.

We vote every day, not in some meaningless election, but in whom we choose to associate with, what we choose to spend our money on, what we choose to invest our time and energy doing. This is the essence of freedom.

For us, it is painful to watch our brothers and sisters getting swept up in the election-cycle hype. We watch the sad spectacle not with a sense of scorn or derision, but with sadness for those who have not yet woken up to the reality of their mental enslavement. That sadness, however, is tempered by hope: hope that one day, those poor voters who are trudging off to that booth to pull that lever will realize that all they are really doing is voting for which slavemaster they will allow to put the chains around their neck.

Beautiful. I couldn't have said it better myself.

NOTES

1. *An Agorist Primer* by Samuel Edward Konkin III.
2. *Chaos Theory* by Robert P. Murphy, Ph.D.
3. "Solutions Watch" on CorbettReport.com.
4. *The Last Word on Voting* by James Corbett, September 13, 2012.

34
The Obviousness of Anarchy

John Hasnas, Ph.D.

John Hasnas[1] is a Professor of Law at Georgetown University Law Center, a Professor of Business at Georgetown's McDonough School of Business, and the executive director of the Georgetown Institute for the Study of Markets and Ethics.

"You see, but you do not observe."
— Sherlock Holmes to Dr. John Watson in *A Scandal in Bohemia*

Introduction

In this chapter, I have been asked to present an argument for anarchy. This is an absurdly easy thing to do. In fact, it is a task that can be discharged in two words — look around. However, because most of us, like Dr. Watson, see without observing the significance of what we see, some commentary is required.

Anarchy refers to a society without a central political authority. But it is also used to refer to disorder or chaos. This constitutes a textbook example of Orwellian newspeak in which assigning the same name to two different concepts effectively narrows the range of thought. For if lack of government is identified with the lack of order, no one will ask whether lack of government actually results in a lack of order. And this uninquisitive mental attitude is absolutely essential to the case for the state. For if people were ever to seriously question whether government is really productive of order, popular support for government would almost instantly collapse.

The identification of anarchy with disorder is not a trivial matter. The power of our conceptions to blind us to the facts of the world around us cannot be gainsaid. I myself have had the experience of eating lunch just outside Temple University's law school in North Philadelphia with a brilliant law professor who was declaiming upon the absolute necessity of the state provision of police services. He did this just as one of Temple's uniformed private armed guards passed by escorting a female student to the Metro stop in this crime-ridden neighborhood that is vastly underserved by the Philadelphia police force.

A wise man once told me that the best way to prove that something is possible is to show that it exists. This is the strategy I shall adopt in this chapter. I intend to show that a stable, successful society without government can exist by showing that it has, and to a large extent, still does.

Defining Terms and Limitations

I am presenting an argument for anarchy in the true sense of the term; that is, a society without government, not a society without governance. There is no such thing as a society without governance. A society with no mechanism for bringing order to human existence is oxymoronic; it is not "society" at all.

One way to bring order to society is to invest some people with the exclusive power to create and coercively enforce rules which all members of society must follow; that is, to create a government. Another way to bring order to society is to allow people to follow rules that spontaneously evolve through human interaction with no guiding intelligence and may be enforced by diverse agencies. This chapter presents an argument for the latter approach; that is, for a spontaneously ordered rather than a centrally planned society.

In arguing for anarchy, I am arguing that a society without a central political authority is not only possible but desirable. That is all I am doing, however. I am not arguing for a society without coercion. I am not arguing for a society that abides by the libertarian non-aggression principle or any other principle of justice. I am not arguing for the morally ideal organisation of society. I am not arguing for utopia. What constitutes ideal justice and the perfectly just society is a fascinating philosophical question, but it is one that is irrelevant to the current pursuit. I am arguing only that human beings can live together successfully and prosper in the absence of a centralised coercive authority. To make the case for anarchy, that is all that is required.

An additional limitation on my argument is that I do not address the question of national defense. There are two reasons for this. One is the logical one that a society without government is a society without nations. In this context, "national" defense is a meaningless concept. If you wish, you may see this as an assertion that an argument for anarchy is necessarily an argument for global anarchy. I prefer to see it merely as the recognition that human beings, not nations, need defense. The more significant reason, however, is that I regard the problem of national defense as trivial for reasons I will expand upon subsequently.[2]

The Question

Whether government is necessary is not an abstract metaphysical question. It is an entirely practical question concerning the delivery of goods and services. The defenders of government argue that certain goods or services that are essential to human life in society can be supplied only by a government. Anarchists deny this. The question, then, is whether there are any essential goods or services that can be supplied only through the conscious actions of human beings invested with the power to enforce rules on all members of society.

Note that the question is *not* whether the "market" can supply all necessary goods and services, at least not the market as it is usually defined by economists. Some anarchists argue that the free market can supply all necessary goods and services. But the case for anarchy does not require that one assert this claim, and I do not. Anarchy requires, and I argue, only that no essential good or service must be supplied through the conscious actions of the agents of a coercively maintained monopoly. Properly understood, the question is whether there are some essential goods and services that must be provided politically or whether all such goods and services can be provided by non-political means.³

Many political theorists argue that there is a wide array of goods and services that must be provided by the state. In the present context, however, there is no need to consider whether the government must provide postal service, elementary schooling, or universal health insurance. The debate between anarchists and the supporters of a classical liberal, night watchman state concerns the core functions of government. The question thus resolves itself into whether these core functions can be supplied through non-political means.

The Answer

Rules of Law

CREATION

Supporters of government claim that government is necessary to provide the fundamental rules that bring order to human life in society. Without government to create rules of law, they contend, human beings are unable to banish violence and coordinate their actions sufficiently to produce a peaceful and prosperous society, and hence, are doomed to a Hobbesian existence that is "solitary, poor, nasty, brutish, and short."⁴

The proper response to this is: look around. Those of us residing in the United States or any of the British Commonwealth countries live under an extremely sophisticated and subtle scheme of rules, very few of which were created by government. Since almost none of the rules that bring peace and order to our existence were created by government, little argument should be required to establish that government is not necessary to create such rules. On the contrary, it is precisely the rules that *were* created by government that tend to undermine peace and order.

The Anglo-American legal system is often referred to as a common law legal system. This is unfortunate, given the anachronistic contemporary understanding of the term "common law." Currently, common law is associated with "judge-made" law. For most of the formative period of the common law, however, judges did not make the law, but merely presided over proceedings where disputes were resolved according to the accepted principles of customary law. Hence, describing the English common law as judge-made law is akin to describing the market as something created by economists.

English common law is, in fact, case-generated law; that is, law that spontaneously evolves from the settlement of actual disputes. Almost all of the law that provides the infrastructure of our contemporary society was created in this way. Tort law, which provides protection against personal injury; property law, which demarcates property rights; contract law, which provides the grounding for exchange; commercial law, which facilitates complex business transactions; and even criminal law, which punishes harmful behavior, all arose through this evolutionary process. It is true that most of our current law exists in the form of statutes. This is because much of the common law has been codified through legislation. But the fact that politicians recognised the wisdom of the common law by enacting it into statutes, hardly proves that government is necessary to create rules of law. Indeed, it proves precisely the opposite.

English law provides a nice illustration of how law evolves when not preempted by government. When people live together in society, disputes inevitably arise. There are only two ways to resolve these disputes: violently or peacefully. Because violence has high costs and produces unpredictable results, human beings naturally seek peaceful alternatives. The most obvious such alternative is negotiation. Hence, in Anglo-Saxon times, the practice arose of holding violent self-redress in abeyance while attempts were made to reach a negotiated settlement. This was done by bringing the dispute before the communal public assembly, the *moot*, whose members, much like present-day mediators, attempted to facilitate an accommodation that the opposing parties found acceptable. When reached, such accommodations resolved the dispute in a way that preserved the peace of the community.

The virtue of settling disputes in this way was that the moot had an institutional memory. When parties brought a dispute before the moot that was similar to ones that had been resolved in the past, someone would remember the previous efforts at settlement. Accommodations that had failed in the past would not be repeated; those that had succeeded would be. Because the moot was a public forum, the repetition of successful methods of composing disputes gave rise to expectations in the community as to what the moot would recommend in the future, which in turn gave the members of the community advance notice of how they must behave. As the members of the community conformed their behavior to these expectations and took them into consideration in the process of negotiating subsequent accommodations, rules of behavior gradually evolved. This, in turn, allowed for the transformation of the dispute settlement procedure from one dominated by negotiation to one consisting primarily in the application of rules. The repetition of this process over time eventually produced an extensive body of customary law that forms the basis of English common law.[5]

It is true that, beginning in the late twelfth century, the common law developed in the royal courts, but this does not imply that either the king or his judges made the law. On the contrary, for most of its history, the common law was entirely procedural in nature. Almost all of the issues of concern to the lawyers and judges of the king's courts related to matters of jurisdiction or pleading; that is, whether the matter was properly before the court, and if it was, whether the issues to be submitted to the jury were properly specified. The rules that were applied were supplied by the customary law. As Harold Berman explains:

> [T]he common law of England is usually said to be itself a customary law... What is meant, no doubt, is that the royal enactments established procedures in the royal courts for the enforcement of rules and principles and standards and concepts that took their meaning from custom and usage. The rules and principles and standards and concepts to be enforced... were derived from informal, unwritten, unenacted norms and patterns of behavior.[6]

Thus, as late as 1765, Blackstone identified the common law with "general customs; which are the universal rule of the whole kingdom, and form the common law, in its stricter and more usual signification."[7] Indeed, modern commercial law is derived almost entirely from the customary law merchant that Lord Mansfield engrafted onto the common law wholesale in the eighteenth century.[8]

The interesting thing about the common law process is that it creates law only where it is actually needed to allow human beings to live together peacefully. Consider the torts of assault and battery. Battery forbids one from intentionally making "harmful or offensive contact" with another. This prohibits not only direct blows, but snatching a plate out of someone's hand or blowing smoke in his or her face. Assault forbids one from intentionally causing another to fear he or she is about to be battered, but it does not prohibit attempts at battery of which the victim is unaware or threats to batter someone in the future. These torts protect individuals against not only physically harmful contact, but against all offensive physical contact as well as the fear that such contact will be immediately forthcoming.

When I teach Torts, I ask the students to account for these rules. Being products of the legislative age, they inevitably launch into some theory of justice or moral desert or human rights, which invariably fails to account for the contours of the law. After all, attempting to batter someone is morally blameworthy whether or not the intended victim is aware of it, and one hardly has the right not to be offended.

The students fail because they think of the law as created by conscious human agency to serve an intended end. Thus, they miss the simpler evolutionary explanation. In earlier centuries, one of the most urgent social needs was to reduce the level of violence in society. This meant discouraging people from taking the kind of actions that were likely to provoke an immediate violent response. Quite naturally, then, when disputes arising out of violent clashes were settled, the resolutions tended to penalise those who had taken such actions. But what type of actions are these? Direct physical attacks on one's person are obviously included. But affronts to one's dignity or other attacks on one's honor are equally if not more likely to provoke violence.

Hence, the law of battery evolved to forbid not merely harmful contacts, but offensive ones as well. Furthermore, an attack that failed was just as likely to provoke violence as one that succeeded, and thus gave rise to liability. But if the intended victim was not aware of the attack, it could not provoke a violent response, and if the threat was not immediate, the threatened party had time to escape, enlist the aid of others, or otherwise respond in a nonviolent manner. Hence, the law of assault evolved to forbid only threats of immediate battery of which the target was aware.

This example shows how the common law creates the rules necessary for a peaceful society with minimal infringement upon individual freedom. Law that arises from the settlement of actual conflicts, settles conflicts. It does not create a mechanism for social control. Common law is law that is created by non-political forces. As such, it can give us rules that establish property rights, ground the power to make contracts, and create the duty to exercise reasonable care not to injure our fellows, but not those that impose a state religion, segregate races, prohibit consensual sexual activity, or force people to sell their homes to developers. Only government legislation, which is law that is consciously created by [whoever] constitutes the politically dominant interest, can give us rules that restrict the freedom of some to advance the interests or personal beliefs of others.

The unenacted common law provides us with rules that facilitate peace and cooperative activities. Government legislation provides us with rules that facilitate the exploitation of the politically powerless by the politically dominant. The former bring order to society; the latter tend to produce strife. Hence, not only is government not necessary to create the basic rules of social order, it is precisely the rules that the government does create that tend to undermine that order.

UNIFORMITY
Supporters of government claim that government is necessary to ensure that

there is one law for all and that the law applies equally to all citizens. If the government does not make the law, they contend, there would be no uniform code of laws. People in different locations or with different cultural backgrounds or levels of wealth would be subject to different rules of law.

The proper response to this is probably the one Woody Allen made to Diane Keaton in *Annie Hall* when she complained that her apartment had bad plumbing and bugs, which was: "You say that as though it is a negative thing." How persuasive is the following argument? Government is necessary to ensure that there is one style of dress for all and that all citizens are equally clothed. If the government does not provide clothes, there would be no uniform mode of dress. People in different locations or with different cultural backgrounds or levels of wealth would be clothed in garments of different styles and quality.

Why would anyone think that uniformity in law is any more desirable than uniformity in dress? The quest for uniformity leads us to treat the loving husband who kills his terminally ill wife to relieve her suffering the same way we treat Charles Manson, to apply the same rules of contracting to sophisticated business executives purchasing corporations and semi-literate consumers entering into installment contracts, and to act as though the slum lord in the Bronx and the family letting their spare room in Utica should be governed by the same rules of property law.

There are, of course, certain rules that must apply to all people; those that provide the basic conditions that make cooperative behavior possible. Thus, rules prohibiting murder, assault, theft, and other forms of coercion must be equally binding on all members of a society. But we hardly need government to ensure that this is the case. These rules always evolve first in any community; you would not even have a community if this were not the case.

The idea that we need government to ensure a uniform rule of law is especially crazy in the United States, in which the federal structure of the state and national governments is designed to permit legal diversity. To the extent that the law of the United States can claim any superiority to that produced by other nations, it is at least partially due to the fact that it was generated by the common law process in the "laboratory of the states."[9] Allowing the development of different rules in different states teaches us which rules most effectively resolve disputes. To the extent that the conditions that give rise to disputes are the same across the country, the successful rules tend to be copied by other jurisdictions and spread. This creates a fairly uniform body of law.[10] To the extent that the conditions that give rise to disputes are peculiar to a particular location or milieu, they do not spread. This creates a patchwork of rules that are useful where applied, but would be irrelevant or disruptive if applied in other settings.

One of the beauties of the common law process is that it creates a body of law that is uniform where uniformity is useful and diverse where it is not.

This is the optimal outcome.

Government legislation, in contrast, creates uniformity by imposing ill-fitting, one-size-fits-all rules upon a geographically and ethnically diverse population. Once again, not only is government not necessary to the creation of a well-functioning body of law, it is a significant impediment to it. Please consider this the next time you find yourself wondering why all businesses must be closed on Sunday [sic] in the Orthodox Jewish sections of Brooklyn.

ACCESSIBILITY

Supporters of government claim that government must make the law in order for it to be accessible to the citizens to be governed by it. The government promulgates its legislation in statute books that are available to all citizens. The unenacted rules of common law, they claim, are unintelligible to the lay person. Consisting of rules abstracted from cases over long periods of time, the common law is known only to the judges and lawyers who deal with it as part of their profession. A system of law that requires citizens to hire attorneys merely to find out what the law is is obviously unacceptable.

The proper response to this is: Are you serious? Look around. Please! Can any human being possibly be aware of the myriad arcane government regulations to which he or she is subject? Have you ever seen the Code of Federal Regulations? When was the last time you tried to prepare your income tax return? Critics of the common law contend that lay people would need professionals to tell them what the law is. Yet, year after year, studies demonstrate that even most professional tax preparers *and IRS employees* cannot understand what the United States tax code requires. The common law rule that protects citizens against unintentional injury is the requirement to exercise the degree of care a reasonable person would employ to avoid causing harm to others. This is hardly inaccessible. Does anyone know what all the rules are that the Federal Trade Commission, the Consumer Product Safety Commission, and the National Highway Traffic Safety Administration have issued to accomplish the same end?

The common law consists of rules that have proven over time to be successful in resolving disputes. Only rules that are both intelligible to the ordinary person and correspond to the ordinary person's sense of fairness can achieve this status. Rules which are inaccessible to those to be governed by them cannot be effective. This is why, for example, the common law rules of contract and commercial law specifically incorporate references to customary business practice and the duty to act in good faith. It is also why no legal expertise is required to know that the law of self-defense permits one to use deadly force to repel a life-threatening attack, but not to shoot the aggressor after the immediate danger has passed. Understanding the traditional rules of common law requires only that one be a member of the relevant community to which the rules apply, not that one be an attorney.

Government legislation, in contrast, need have no relationship to either the understanding or the moral sensibility of the ordinary person. Legislation is law created through the political process. As such, it is inherently responsive to political considerations. Such considerations can, and frequently do, produce rules that are not intelligible to the ordinary person. This is not merely because special interests can skew the legislative process. Even if legislators were selflessly devoted to the common good, they would still need some principle of justice or moral ideal to guide their law-making. But there is no guarantee that the measures necessary to effectuate such principles or ideals will correspond to the understanding of the ordinary person. The Civil Rights Act of 1964 may have been the noblest legislative effort of our age, but the ordinary person is unlikely to understand why requiring pizza delivery men to be clean shaven constitutes illegal racial discrimination[11] or how a company with a work force consisting of almost all minorities can nevertheless be guilty of discrimination.[12]

Fraud, as it evolved at common law, consists of intentionally misrepresenting a material fact that another relies upon in parting with his or her property. It is not difficult for the ordinary person to appreciate that such action may be against the law. Fraud, as defined by federal legislation, consists of any scheme or artifice to defraud. It does not require a misrepresentation of fact. Any misleading statement or non-disclosure will do. It does not require that anyone actually be misled or rely on the statement or non-disclosure. It does not require that anyone suffer any loss.[13] Martha Stewart was recently put on trial for securities fraud for the act of publicly declaring her innocence of insider trading.[14] It is probably fair to say that the ordinary person would not know that Stewart's comments to the media constituted a federal crime.

I understand the argument that if we had a night watchman state whose legislation was limited to simple, clear rules that are designed to secure individual rights, the law would be perfectly accessible. There are only two problems with this argument. The first is that in such a case, the legislation would merely reproduce the basic rules of common law. There is no need to create a government merely to publicise such rules. This can be, and is, done privately. The "restatements" of the common law are currently privately produced, easily accessible, and widely cited. The second is that it is impossible. The idea that there is a concise set of simple, clear rules that can preserve a peaceful, free society is a fantasy.[15] This becomes apparent even with regard to the fundamental rules barring aggression as soon as one attempts to specify the conditions under which force may be used in self-defense or for the defense of others, or is excused by mistaken belief or insanity. And that is without considering that these fundamental rules must be supplemented by the rules of contract, property, and tort law that are necessary for people to coordinate their behavior well enough to engage in peaceful cooperation.

Legislation, even libertarian legislation, will either reproduce the common law or depart from it to gratify a political interest or realise some conception of justice. In the former case, it is precisely as accessible or inaccessible as the common law. In the latter, it will diverge from the common-sense morality of the ordinary person producing rules that are less accessible than the common law. Not only is government not necessary to ensure that the rules of law are accessible, it inevitably renders them less so.

Courts

Now that we have eliminated the legislature, what about the judiciary? Supporters of government claim that government is necessary to provide a system of courts for settling disputes. In the absence of the government provision of "a known and indifferent judge,"[16] human beings would have no way to peacefully resolve interpersonal disputes. For "men being partial to themselves,"[17] adverse parties would inevitably seek to employ judges who would favor their interests; and judges, who would receive their fees from the litigants, would naturally favor those who could pay the most. Hence, they would not be impartial. Because parties would be unable to agree on a neutral arbiter, they would be forced to resort to violence to resolve their disputes. Thus, without government courts, peaceful coexistence is impossible.

I know this is getting boring, but the proper response to this is: look around. This is the age of globalisation. Business is contracted around the world among parties from virtually all countries. Although there is neither a world government nor world court, businesses do not go to war with each other over contract disputes. News is almost always the news of violent conflict. The very lack of reporting on international business disputes is evidence that international commercial disputes are effectively resolved without the government provision of courts. How can this be?

The answer is simplicity itself. The parties to international transactions select, usually in advance, the dispute settlement mechanism they prefer from among the many options available to them. Few choose trial by combat. It is too expensive and unpredictable. Many elect to submit their disputes to the London Commercial Court, a British court known for the commercial expertise of its judges and its speedy resolution of cases that non-British parties may use for a fee.[18] Others subscribe to companies such as JAMS/Endispute or the American Arbitration Association that provide mediation and arbitration services. Most do whatever they can to avoid becoming enmeshed in the coils of the courts provided by the federal and state governments of the United States, which move at a glacial pace and provide relatively unpredictable results. The evidence suggests that international commercial law not only functions quite well without government courts, it functions better because of their absence.

But there is no need to focus on the international scene to observe that human beings do not need government courts to settle disputes peacefully. Labor contracts not only specify wage rates and working conditions; they create their own workplace judiciary, complete with due process guarantees and appellate procedures. Universities regularly provide their own judicial processes, as do homeowner associations. Stockbrokers agree to submit employment disputes to binding arbitration as a condition of employment.[19]

Religious groups regularly settle disputes among congregants by appeal to priest or rabbi. Disfavored groups, for whom prejudice makes trial in government courts a mockery, readily devise alternative mechanisms for settling disputes without violence.[20] Insurance companies provide not only compensation for personal injury and property damage, but liability insurance, by which they assume the responsibility for resolving conflicts between their clients and those of other insurance companies according to antecedently specified agreements that allow them to avoid the morass of the government judicial system. And empirical evidence demonstrates that when potential litigants in the government court system are directed into mediation, a significant portion of the lawsuits are resolved without trial.[21]

But don't just look around. Look back. Tax supported courts of general jurisdiction are an entirely modern phenomenon. Anglo-American law evolved in the context of a richly diverse set of competing jurisdictions. The royal courts, once they developed, existed in parallel with the antecedently extant hundred, shire, manorial, urban, ecclesiastical, and mercantile courts.[22] These court systems had fluid jurisdictional boundaries, and because the courts collected their fees from the litigants, they competed with each other for business. Indeed, the law of contracts and trusts, which evolved in the ecclesiastical courts, and commercial law, which evolved in the mercantile courts, entered the common law as a result of this competition. Further, the royal courts themselves consisted of four different and competing courts: king's bench, common pleas, exchequer, and chancery. These courts, like the others, collected their fees from the litigants, and hence, competed among themselves for clients. It was only with the Judicature Act of 1873 and the Appellate Jurisdiction Act of 1876 that the British government assembled its courts into its present monolithic, hierarchical structure, with American courts following suit at varying intervals thereafter.

Further, focusing on the competition among the common law courts misleadingly underestimates the diversity of the dispute settlement mechanisms that were actually employed. Because the cost of utilising the common law courts was too great for the typical working man, those courts were virtually irrelevant to the majority of the population. Most citizens resolved their disputes according to informal, customary procedures that varied with the location (urban or rural) and class of those employing them.[23]

Since our present relatively non-violent, capitalistic society evolved in the context of a diverse and competitive system of courts and dispute settlement mechanisms, it cannot be the case that government provision of courts is necessary for peaceful settlement of disputes. In fact, a comparison of the amount of rancorous dissatisfaction produced by the contemporary government-supplied judiciary (consider the tort reform movement) with that associated with the more variegated traditional system of resolving disputes suggests that the government provision of courts reduces rather than augments social peace.

Police

Regardless of whether a state is needed to supply law and courts, supporters of government are adamant that police must be supplied exclusively by government. It may be true that the market can adequately supply most goods and services, but police services are unique in that they inherently involve the use of coercion. Obviously, no civilised society can permit competition in the use of violence. Civil society is formed precisely to escape from that situation. Unless government brings the use of violence under its monopolistic control, peaceful coexistence is impossible, and life is indeed as "nasty, brutish, and short"[24] as Hobbes contended.

Before I respond to this by suggesting that you look around, reflect for a moment on the silliness of this argument. For if civil society cannot exist without a government monopoly over the use of coercion, then civil society does not exist. Societies do not spring into existence complete with government police forces. Once a group of people has figured out how to reduce the level of interpersonal violence sufficiently to allow them to live together, entities that are recognisable as governments often develop and take over the policing function. Even a marauding band that imposes government on others through conquest must have first reduced internal strife sufficiently to allow it to organize itself for effective military operations. Both historically and logically, it is always peaceful coexistence first, government services second. If civil society is impossible without government police, then there are no civil societies.

In the 1960s Broadway musical *Oliver*, there is a song called "Be Back Soon" in which Fagin's boys sing the line "We know the Bow Street Runners." The Bow Street Runners were famous because they were London's first government sponsored police force, organised in the latter half of the eighteenth century by the magistrates of the Bow Street court, Henry and John Fielding. I think it is fair to say that the formation of the Bow Street Runners does not represent the moment that London was transformed from a Hobbesian state of nature to a civil society.

Note also the conflation of police services with coercion. Coercion may be employed aggressively for purposes of predation or defensively to repel attempts at predation. Police services involve the use of coercion for defensive purposes only. Competition among aggressors is, indeed, a bad thing that is antithetical to the existence of civil society. But it is not competition for the provision of police services. If competition among those offering the defensive use of coercion inevitably resulted in the equivalent of aggressive gang warfare, then we would want to eschew such competition. But whether this occurs is the very question under consideration. Identifying competition among providers of police services with competition among aggressors is entirely question-begging. It is avoiding, rather than making, an argument.

But I digress. The proper response to the claim that government must provide police services is: look around. I work at a University that supplies its own campus police force. On my drive in, I pass a privately operated armored car that transports currency and other valuable items for banks and businesses. When I go downtown, I enter buildings that are serviced by private security companies that require me to sign in before entering. I shop at malls and department stores patrolled by their own private guards. While in the mall, I occasionally browse in the Security Zone store that sells personal and home protection equipment. I converse with attorneys and, once in a while with a disgruntled spouse or worried parent, who employ private detective agencies to perform investigations for them. I write books about how the United States Federal government coerces private corporations into performing criminal investigations for it.[25] When I was younger, I frequented nightclubs and bars that employed "bouncers." Although it has never happened to me personally, I know people who have been contacted by private debt collection agencies or have been visited by repo men. Once in a while, I meet people who are almost as important as rock stars and travel with their own bodyguards. At the end of the day, I return home to my community that has its own neighborhood watch. I may be missing something, but I haven't noticed any of these agencies engaging in acts of violent aggression to eliminate their competitors.

Ah, but that is because the government police force is in the background making sure that none of these private agencies step out of line, the supporters of government contend. Really? How does that explain London before the Bow Street Runners? The New York City police force was not created until 1845. The Boston Police Department, which describes itself as "the first paid, professional public safety department in the country,"[26] traces its history back only to 1838. What kept the non-political police services in line before these dates?

Regardless of Hobbes's and Locke's philosophical musings, for most of English history, there was little government provision of police services.[27] It is true that as the kings of England learned how to collect revenue by declaring all violence and sinful activity a breach of the King's peace for which they were owed payment, they began to develop an administrative machinery to facilitate the collection of fines for "criminal" activity. Thus, the local representative of the Crown, the shire reeve (later sheriff), became tasked with reporting and eventually apprehending offenders. But since the sheriffs were only interested in pursuing offenders with the means to pay the amercement, this never represented a significant portion of the police activity within the realm. The customary, non-political methods of policing provided security for most of the population of England until quite recently.

My father's oldest brother, who was born in 1902, often told me about the tontine insurance arrangement my grandfather participated in through his fraternal organisation that provided both term life insurance and an old age annuity. Since the advent of the federal social security program, you don't hear much about tontine insurance. Most residents of New York City, who assume that only the government can provide and maintain the city's subway system, are puzzled as to why part of the system is named the BMT and part the IRT. They have no idea that in 1940, the City of New York purchased the privately built and operated Brooklyn-Manhattan Transit Corporation and the Interborough Rapid Transit Company to create the city-run Metropolitan Transportation Authority. When government begins providing services formerly provided non-politically, people soon forget that the services were ever provided non-politically and assume that only government can provide them. But just as this is not true for old age annuities and subway service, it is not true for police services. Traditionally, police services were not provided by government and, to a large extent, they still are not. Therefore, government is not necessary to provide police services.

Advocates of government can still argue that because of the special nature of police services, a government monopoly can provide such services more efficiently than non-political entities can. I must concede that there is nothing *a priori* wrong with this argument. It is certainly possible that when it comes to police services, a miracle occurs and investing a single politically directed agency with the power to supply the desired services by exacting involuntary payment from all members of society actually produces a better result than allowing the services to be supplied by non-political means. I can, however, find no evidence for this in the real world. To all outward appearances, when police services are supplied by a politically controlled monopoly, the public receives police services driven by political, rather than efficiency, considerations. Thus, disfavored, politically powerless groups are typically underserved, police resources are frequently directed toward politically favored ends (*e.g.*, suppression of victimless crimes) rather than their most productive use (*e.g.*, suppression of violence), and the nature of the service is determined by political budgetary concerns rather than actual need (*e.g.*, SWAT teams in Wisconsin). Further, because government police are not dependent on voluntary contributions for their revenue, they are less likely to be responsive to the concerns of the public (*e.g.*, police brutality) and more susceptible to corruption (see *e.g.*, the Knapp Commission Report[28] or just watch the movie *Serpico*).

Supporters of government often point to the high inner-city crime rate, the profusion of violent gangs, and the persistence of organised crime and drug cartels to argue that we dare not abandon the government monopoly on police services. I confess to being perplexed by this argument. How can highlighting the utter failure of the government system of policing possibly be an argument for its necessity?

It is worth noting that the contemporary crime problem is most severe where non-political methods of policing have been most completely displaced by government. The inner cities are the areas most dependent on government policing. Arguing that the high rate of inner-city crime and the presence of gangs implies that we must maintain a government monopoly on police services is a bit like arguing that the abysmal quality of inner-city public schools implies that we should not permit parents to use their tax money to send their children to private schools. And it can hardly be surprising that it is difficult to suppress the violent organisations that exist to exploit the black markets created by government prohibitions on the legal marketing of drugs, prostitution, gambling, and other "vices." But how any of this demonstrates the necessity of government provision of police is beyond me.

If a visitor from Mars were asked to identify the least effective method for securing individuals' persons and property, he might well respond that it would be to select one group of people, give them guns, require all members of society to pay them regardless of the quality of service they render, and invest them with the discretion to employ resources and determine law enforcement priorities however they see fit subject only to the whims of their political paymasters. If asked why he thought that, he might simply point to the Los Angeles or the New Orleans or any other big city police department. Are government police really necessary for a peaceful, secure society? Look around. Could a non-political, non-monopolistic system of supplying police services really do worse than its government-supplied counterpart?

Internalising Externalities

Supporters of government often argue that government is essential to provide needed regulation of market activities. Individuals contracting with each other in a market often act in ways that impose harm or unconsented to costs on others. Manufacturers make and consumers purchase products whose use imposes an unacceptable risk of injury on third parties. For example, automobile companies can produce and drivers will purchase cars that can move at speeds or have handling properties that create an unreasonable risk of injury to pedestrians. Oil companies can ship oil to consumers in ways that create an unreasonable risk of spills that would pollute the land or body of water over which the oil is transported. More generally, because people do not bear the costs their activities impose on others, they will often act in ways that impose greater costs on society than are justified by the personal benefits they realise. These unconsidered costs to others are the social costs of market activity; what economists call negative externalities. Supporters of government contend that only government can regulate market activity to ensure that private contractors consider the social costs of their transactions. Thus, even if rules of law, courts, and police services could be supplied non-politically, government would nevertheless be essential to internalise externalities.

I must confess that I am at a loss as to how to respond to this argument. Look around is not enough. That this argument has any plausibility at all is a testament to how completely oblivious people can be to the world around them. In a world in which one of the dominant political issues is tort reform; in which businesses are continually complaining to Congress that they are over-regulated by the common law of tort and begging government to protect them from this non-political method of internalising externalities, how can anyone seriously assert that government regulation is needed to deal with the problem of social costs?

It is true that economists posit a fictitious realm in which human beings engage in voluntary transactions free from all forms of regulation. But they do so because such an idealised conception of the market is useful to their exploration of the science of human interaction in much the same way that the concept of a perfect vacuum is useful to physicists exploring the laws of nature; not because they think it corresponds to anything in reality. In the real world, human interaction is always subject to regulation; by custom, by people's ethical and religious beliefs, and, in our legal system, by the common law. Tort law is precisely that portion of the law that evolved to protect individuals' persons and property from the ill-considered actions of their fellows; that is, to internalise externalities. It is only by ignoring the existence of these forms of non-political regulation; that is, only by believing that the economists' model of the market is a description of reality, that one could possibly believe that government is necessary to address the problem of social costs. Of course, one should never underestimate the power of a conceptual model to blind intellectuals to what is going on in the real world.

But, supporters of government claim, common law can never be an adequate regulatory mechanism because it is necessarily retroactive in operation. Lawsuits arise only after harm is done. Therefore, civil liability could never provide the type of proactive regulation necessary to prevent serious harm from occurring. Really? The basic rules of tort law prohibit individuals from intentionally harming others and require them to act with reasonable care to avoid causing harm inadvertently. There is nothing retroactive about this. It is true that precisely what constitutes reasonable care may have to be determined on a case by case basis, but in this respect, the common law is no different than government legislation that announces a general rule and then leaves it up to the courts to determine how it applies in particular cases. Furthermore, the common law can act prospectively in appropriate cases. The injunction, an order not to engage in a specified activity, evolved precisely to handle those cases in which one party's conduct poses a high risk of irreparable harm to others.[29] And by the way, government legislation is almost always retroactive as well. Limitations on human knowledge (not to mention public choice considerations) mean that legislators are rarely able to accurately anticipate future harm. Megan's law required public notification when a known sex offender moves into a community. It is called Megan's law because it was enacted after Megan was killed by a repeat sex offender who lived in her community. If I remember correctly, Sarbanes-Oxley was passed after Enron collapsed. And when was the USA Patriot Act passed? Oh, yes, after 9/11.

Until 1992, fast food restaurants served coffee at between 180 and 190°F, a temperature at which the coffee can cause third degree burns in two to seven seconds if brought into contact with human skin. This posed a considerable risk of serious injury, given how often coffee served in styrofoam cups is spilled. I did not notice any proactive legislative regulation designed to internalise this externality. In 1992, Stella Liebeck won a judgment against McDonald's for injuries received when she spilled coffee on herself equal to her medical expenses plus the amount of profit McDonald's earned in two days from knowingly selling coffee at a dangerously high temperature.[30] The next day every fast food restaurant in the United States served its coffee at 158°F, a temperature at which it takes 60 seconds to cause third degree burns; a sufficient amount of time for customers to brush the coffee off their clothes or skin. There may be many things wrong with contemporary tort law,[31] but being ineffective at internalising externalities is most assuredly not among them. The only way to believe that government is necessary to resolve the problem of social costs is to be studiously blind to the nature of both common law and government legislation.

Public Goods

Supporters of government claim that government is necessary to produce "public goods": goods that are important for human well-being but either cannot be produced or will be under-produced by the market. Public goods are goods that are both non-rivalrous in consumption; that is, its use by one person does not interfere with its use by others, and nonexclusive; that is, if the good is available to one person, it is available to all whether they help produce it or not. Supporters of government argue that such goods cannot be produced without government because, due to the free rider and assurance problems, individuals will not voluntarily contribute the capital necessary for their production. The free rider problem refers to the fact that because people can enjoy public goods without paying for them, many will withhold their contribution to the goods' production and attempt to free ride on the contribution of others. The assurance problem refers to the fact that in the absence of some assurance that others will contribute enough to produce the good, people are more likely to regard their own contribution as a waste of money and withhold it. Therefore, government is necessary to ensure the production of important public goods.

The proper response to the argument that government is necessary to produce public goods is: Like what? Like lighthouses? The light they provide is available to all ships and its use by one does not impair its value to others. But wait, lighthouses can be and have been supplied privately.[32] Like radio and television? A wag I know likes to say that he does something impossible every night by watching commercial television. After all, television signals are non-rivalrous in consumption and nonexclusive. Therefore, they cannot be produced by the market. Like the internet? But wait, that is privately funded also.

Perhaps like police and courts? Theorists frequently argue that police services and courts are public goods that must be supplied by government. With regard to police services, for example, the argument is made that:

> Security of person is to a large degree a collective good. ... [A]n important part of the service provided by public police and systems of criminal justice generally is to deter potential violators from harming people. And this deterrence is an indivisible nonexcludable good to neighbors and visitors... In addition to deterrence, there may be the benefits that follow from incarceration of the thief — namely, incapacitation — benefits that are also indivisible and nonexcludable. Social order, at least security of persons and possessions, then, is to a considerable degree a collective good. Accordingly, to the degree that this is the case, social order may not be efficiently provided in the absence of a state.[33]

Similarly, with regard to courts, it is argued that because the existence of definite and widely known rules of behavior provides a nonexcludable benefit to all, private courts lack an incentive to establish the clear precedents that give rise to rules. Indeed, because clear precedents "would confer an external, an uncompensated benefit, not only on future parties, but also on competing judges, ...judges might deliberately avoid explaining their results because the demand for their services would be reduced by rules that, by clarifying the meaning of the law, reduce the incidence of disputes."[34] Hence, government courts are necessary for the development of rules of law.

These are perfectly logical theoretical arguments belied only by the facts of reality. The evidence that police services and courts are not public goods is that, like lighthouses, television, and the internet, they have been supplied non-politically for most of human history. It is true, of course, that if government exists and creates areas of unowned, politically controlled property that no private party has an interest in maintaining, police services are likely to be under-produced in these locations. Policing of this "public" property may indeed have to be supplied by the government. However, this is not because police services are a public good that cannot be supplied by the market, but because police services will not be supplied when the market has been suppressed by the government. And although it is certainly true that private police services produce an uncompensated positive externality in that their deterrent effects make even those who have not paid for them more secure, this can hardly be a reason for believing that such services will not be produced. It is actually quite difficult to think of any useful activity that does not produce some uncompensated positive externality. My using deodorant and going about clothed certainly do, but government is not required to pay me to induce me to bathe and dress. Further, it is at least odd to argue that a system of competitive courts will not produce rules of law when the rules on which our civilisation rests actually arose out of just such a system.[35]

Like national defense? National defense is perhaps the archetypical public good. The security it provides is both non-rivalrous in consumption and benefits all members of society whether they pay for it or not. Can national defense be adequately supplied without government?

If "national defense" refers to the type of military expenditures associated with contemporary national governments, the answer is an obvious "no." Once a state becomes invested with the power to expropriate the wealth of its citizenry to provide for national defense, almost any desired expenditure begins to look like a requirement of national defense. Before long propping up Southeast Asian dictators and overthrowing Middle Eastern ones are being characterised as urgent national defense concerns. The fact that there is no non-governmental way to raise sufficient capital to realise this conception of national defense proves nothing about the viability of anarchy, and, in fact, serves as one more argument in favor of markets.

However, if "national defense" refers to only what is strictly necessary to protect the citizens of a nation against outside aggression, I am willing to admit that I do not know the answer to this question. I am not discomforted by this admission, however, because as I said at the outset, the question of national defense is, as a practical matter, a trivial one. No one believes that we can transition from a world of states to anarchy instantaneously. No reasonable anarchist advocates the total dissolution of government tomorrow. Once we turn our attention to the question of how to move incrementally from government to anarchy, it becomes apparent that national defense would be one of the last governmental functions to be de-politicised. If my argument for anarchy is flawed and anarchy is not a viable method of social organisation, this will undoubtedly be revealed long before doing away with national defense becomes an issue. On the other hand, to the extent that the gradual transition from government to anarchy is successful, the need for national defense continually lessens.

Consider what it would mean for a nation to seriously undertake a process of de-politicisation. Every reduction in the size and scope of government releases more of the creative energy of the population. The economic effects of this are well known and are currently being demonstrated in China. As economists point out, revolutionary change can be wrought by marginal effects. Even a slow process of liberalisation *that is sustained over time* will produce massively accelerated economic and technological growth. And the increase in freedom and prosperity in the liberalising nation would have profound external effects as well. Many of the bravest and most industrious residents of more repressive nations would attempt to immigrate to the liberalising one, and some other nations would learn by the liberalising nation's example and begin to copy its policies.

As the economic and technological gap between the liberalising nation and the rest of world widens, as the rest of the world becomes more dependent upon the goods and services manufactured and supplied by that nation, and as a greater number of other nations are moved to adopt liberalising policies themselves, the threat the rest of the world poses to the liberalising nation decreases. Evidence of this is supplied by the demise of the Soviet Union. Radical regimes and terrorist organisations may constitute a serious and continuing threat, but consider it in historical context. Such a threat is considerably less serious and less expensive to address than the threat of thermonuclear war.

Recall that we are considering the cost only of protecting citizens against aggression, not the cost of foreign adventures or "pre-emptive" warfare. How significant a threat of foreign invasion does the United States currently face? How much of its "national defense" spending is actually devoted to preventing such invasion? After years or decades of continual and sustained reduction in the size of government, how much wider will the economic and technological gap between the prenatal anarchy and the more repressive nations be? How much more sophisticated its defensive technology? How much more dependent will the repressive nations be on its goods and services? Let a nation begin to tread the path toward anarchy and by the time the question of whether national defense is a public good that must be supplied by government becomes relevant, it is very likely to be moot.

Conclusion

Aristotle called man the rational animal, identifying human beings' ability to reason as their essential defining characteristic. I think this is a mistake. I think man is the imaginative animal. Human beings undoubtedly have the ability to reason, but they also have the ability to imagine that the world is different than it is, and the latter is a far more powerful force. People root for the Chicago Cubs because they can imagine the Cubs winning the World Series, despite all evidence to the contrary. People regularly get married because they can imagine that they will change their obviously incompatible partner into the ideal husband or wife. People devote their time, effort, and money to political campaigns because they can imagine that if only Bill Clinton or Bob Dole or George W. Bush or John Kerry were elected, Washington, D.C. would be transformed into Camelot. And more significantly, people volunteer to fight wars because they can imagine themselves running through a field of machine-gun fire unscathed. Only the ability to imagine an afterlife for which they have absolutely no evidence can explain why human beings would strap explosives to themselves and blow themselves up in an effort to kill as many innocent people as possible.

Do you ever wonder why people believed in the divine right of kings, despite the fact that the monarchs of their time were patently not the type of individuals an all-knowing, all-good god would choose to reign over them? They believed in it because they were taught to believe in it and because they could imagine that it was so, regardless of all evidence to the contrary. We no longer believe in such silly things as the divine right of kings. We believe that government is necessary for an orderly peaceful society and that it can be made to function according to the rule of law. We believe this because we have been taught to believe it from infancy and because we can imagine that it is so, regardless of all evidence to the contrary.

One should never underestimate the power of abstract concepts to shape how human beings see the world. Once one accepts the idea that government is necessary for peace and order and that it can function objectively, one's imagination will allow one to see the hand of government wherever there is law, police, and courts, and render the non-political provision of these services invisible. But if you lay aside this conceptual framework long enough to ask where these services originated and where, to a large extent, they still come from, the world assumes a different aspect. If you want the strongest argument for anarchy, simply remove your self-imposed blinders and look around.

NOTES

1. Associate Professor, Georgetown University, J.D., Ph.D., LL.M. The author wishes to thank Ann C. Tunstall of SciLucent, LLC for her insightful comments and literary advice and Annette Hasnas of the Montessori School of Northern Virginia for a real-world illustration of how rules evolve in the absence of centralised authority. The author also wishes to thank Ava Hasnas of Falls Church, Virginia for her invaluable help with his time management skills.

2. See *infra* p. 129.

3. In this chapter, the term "political" will be used to refer to the output of government, and "non-political" to the product of all other forms of action.

4. T. Hobbes, *Leviathan* 107 (H. Schneider, ed., 1958) (1651).

5. For a fuller account of this process, see John Hasnas, *Toward a Theory of Empirical Natural Rights* 22, Social Philosophy and Policy 111 (2005) and John Hasnas, *Hayek, the Common Law, and Fluid Drive* 1, New York University Journal of Law & Liberty 79 (2005). See also Arthur R. Hogue, *Origins of the Common Law*, ch. 8 (1966).

6. Harold Berman, *Law and Revolution* 81 (1983).

7. William Blackstone, *Commentaries on the Laws of England* 67 (1765). See also Frederick Pollock, *First Book of Jurisprudence* 254 (6th ed. 1929): "[T]he common law is a customary law if, in the course of about six centuries, the undoubting belief and uniform language of everybody who had occasion to consider the matter were able to make it so."

8. See Leon E. Trakman, *The Law Merchant: The Evolution of Commercial Law* 27 (1983). The story of the evolution of modern commercial law from the customary law merchant is an often told tale. In addition to Trakman's account, see also Harold Berman, *Law and Revolution* ch. 11 (1983); Bruce Benson, *The Enterprise of Law* 30–35 (1990); and John Hasnas, *Toward a Theory of Empirical Natural Rights*, 22 Social Philosophy and Policy 111, 130–31 (2005). For a useful account of the customary nature of the English common law see, Todd Zywicki, *The Rise and Fall of Efficiency in the Common Law: A Supply-Side Analysis*, 97 Nw. U. L. Rev. 1551 (2003). See also J.H. Baker, *An Introduction to English Legal History* 72–74 (4th ed. 2002) and John Hasnas, *Hayek, Common Law, and Fluid Drive* 1, New York University Journal of Law & Liberty 79 (2005).

9. See *New State Ice Co. v. Liebmann*, 285 U.S. 262, 311 (1932) (Brandeis, J., dissenting).

10. Fairly, but not fetishistically. The law against homicide functions quite effectively despite the fact that the definitions of first and second degree murder and voluntary and involuntary manslaughter differ from state to state.

11. See *Bradley v. Pizzaco of Nebraska, Inc.*, 7 F.3d 795 (8th Cir. 1993).

12. See *Connecticut v. Teal*, 457 U.S. 440 (1982).

13. For a fuller account of the federal fraud statutes, see John Hasnas, *Ethics and the Problem of White Collar Crime*, 54 American University Law Review 579 (2005).

14. See Indictment, *United States v. Stewart* 37 (S.D.N.Y. 2003) (No. 03 Cr. 717).

15. For more on this, see John Hasnas, *The Myth of the Rule of Law*, 1995 Wisconsin Law Review 199 (1995).

16. John Locke, *Second Treatise of Government* 66 (C.B. Macpherson, ed. 1980) (1690).

17. Id.

18. See Mark Heaney, "Where Business is King: London's Commercial Court Hears International Clashes," *Nat'l L.J.*, June 5, 1995, at C1; Campbell McLachlan, "London Court Reigns as an International Forum: Parties in Cross-Border Disputes Welcome the Commercial Court's Expertise, Neutrality, and Speed," *Nat'l L.J.*, June 5, 1995, at C4.

19. Of course, this is mainly a measure designed to allow financial firms to escape from the quagmire of United States employment litigation.

20. See Yaffa Eliach, "Social Protest in the Synagogue: The Delaying of the Torah Reading," in *There Once Was a World* 84–86.

21. See Joshua D. Rosenberg and H. Jay Folberg, "Alternative Dispute Resolution: An Empirical Analysis," 46 *Stan. L. Rev.* 1487 (1994).

22. See Harold Berman, *Law and Revolution* (1983).

23. See E.P. Thompson, *Customs in Common: Studies in Traditional Popular Culture* (1993).

24. T. Hobbes, *Leviathan* 107 (H. Schneider, ed., 1958) (1651).

25. See John Hasnas, *Trapped: When Acting Ethically Is Against the Law* (2006).

26. See Boston Police Department website at: http://www.cityofboston.gov/police/glance.asp.

27. See Bruce Benson, *The Enterprise of Law* 73–74 (1990).

28. See Knapp Commission, *The Knapp Commission Report on Police Corruption* (1973).

29. Note that to obtain an injunction at common law and thereby curtail another citizen's freedom, one must meet a very high evidentiary threshold by establishing a high likelihood of irreparable harm. This is in contrast to government legislation that can curtail citizens' freedom whenever the politically dominant faction of the legislature deems it necessary, even if only to effectuate the "precautionary principle." I leave it to the reader to decide which is the superior standard for addressing potential future harm.

30. The judgment was reduced by 20 per cent to take account of Ms. Liebeck's contributory negligence with regard to how she opened the cup. This amount was further reduced on appeal.

31. Almost all of which are attributable not the way it evolved at common law, but to twentieth-century efforts to improve upon the outcome of this evolution. See John Hasnas, "What's Wrong with a Little Tort Reform?" 32 *Idaho Law Review* 557 (1996).

32. See Ronald H. Coase, "The Lighthouse in Economics," 17 *Journal of Law and Economics* 357 (1974).

33. Christopher W. Morris, *An Essay on the Modern State* 60–61 (1998).

34. See William M. Landes and Richard A. Posner, "Adjudication as a

Private Good," 6 *Journal of Legal Studies* 235 (1979).

35. For the true intellectuals among my readers who simply cannot accept that facts should be allowed to undermine a perfectly good theoretical model, I refer you to David Schmidtz, *The Limits of Government: An Essay on the Public Goods Argument* (1991). Schmidtz explains how the assurance problem can be handled by the assurance contract or money back guarantee and how the free rider problem can be cabined to a relatively small number of cases in which using coercion to produce the public good is ethically questionable.

35
Economics in One Lesson (Excerpts)

Henry Hazlitt
1946

Henry Hazlitt (1894–1993) was a journalist who wrote on economic affairs for *The New York Times*, *The Wall Street Journal*, and *Newsweek*, among many other publications.

The art of economics consists in looking not merely at the immediate but at the longer effects of any act or policy; it consists in tracing the consequences of that policy not merely for one group but for all groups. (p. 5)

But there is a decisive difference between the loans supplied by private lenders and the loans supplied by a government agency. Each private lender risks his own funds. (A banker, it is true, risks the funds of others that have been entrusted to him; but if money is lost he must either make good out of his own funds or be forced out of business.) When people risk their own funds they are usually careful in their investigations to determine the adequacy of the assets pledged and the business acumen and honesty of the borrower. (p. 27)

Machines may be said to have given birth to this increased population; for without the machines, the world would not have been able to support it. Two out of every three of us, therefore, may be said to owe not only our jobs but our very lives to machines. Yet it is a misconception to think of the function or result of machines as primarily one of creating jobs. The real result of the machine is to increase production, to raise the standard of living, to increase economic welfare. It is no trick to employ everybody, even (or especially) in the most primitive economy. Full employment — very full employment; long, weary, back-breaking employment — is characteristic of precisely the nations that are most retarded industrially. Where full employment already exists, new machines, inventions, and discoveries cannot — until there has been time for an increase in population — bring more employment. They are likely to bring more unemployment (but this time I am speaking of voluntary and not involuntary unemployment) because people can now afford to work fewer hours, while children and the overaged no longer need to work. (p. 41)

There is no limit to the amount of work to be done as long as any human need or wish that work could fill remains unsatisfied. (pp. 49–50)

This "purchasing power" argument is, when one considers it seriously, fantastic. It could just as well apply to a racketeer or a thief who robs you. After he takes your money he has more purchasing power. He supports with it bars, restaurants, nightclubs, tailors, perhaps automobile workers. But for every job his spending provides, your own spending must provide one less, because you have that much less to spend. Just so the taxpayers provide one less job for every job supplied by the spending of officeholders. (p. 53)

The economic goal of any nation, as of any individual, is to get the greatest results with the least effort. The whole economic progress of mankind has consisted in getting more production with the same labor. (p. 55)

The progress of civilization has meant the reduction of employment, not its increase. It is because we have become increasingly wealthy as a nation that we have been able to virtually eliminate child labor... (p. 56)

Because the American consumer had to pay $5 more for the same quality of sweater he would have just that much less left over to buy anything else. He would have to reduce his expenditures by $5 somewhere else. (p. 63)

Real wealth, of course, consists in what is produced and consumed: the food we eat, the clothes we wear, the houses we live in. It is railways and roads and motor cars; ships and planes and factories; schools and churches and theaters; pianos, paintings, and books. Yet so powerful is the verbal ambiguity that confuses money with wealth, that even those who at times recognize the confusion will slide back into it in the course of their reasoning. (p. 146)

Economics, as we have now seen again and again, is a science of recognizing secondary consequences. It is also a science of seeing general consequences. It is the science of tracing the effects of some proposed or existing policy not only on some special interest in the short run, but on the general interest in the long run. (p. 175)

36
How Markets Have Delivered More Economic Equality

Antony Sammeroff

Antony Sammeroff co-hosts the "Scottish Liberty Podcast" and is the author of *Universal Basic Income – For and Against*.

I recently attended the Soho Forum debate between (democratic socialist) Ben Burgis and (libertarian) Gene Epstein on the question of whether capitalism or socialism would lead to the most prosperity, equality, and liberty.

Ben took it for granted that a socialist economy would be more equal, and Gene did not fight hard on this point; indeed, libertarians were once fond of saying, "While capitalism may yield the unequal distribution of wealth, socialism yields only the equal distribution of poverty."

Well, let's look at the facts.

We are told that capitalism creates large disparities in income and wealth, and inequality might seem like a real issue if we only train our attention on dollar values.

More Equal Than Ever

In the material sense, however, we are the most equal society that has ever been.

A billionaire has a Maserati or Rolls Royce, but he can't drive the streets much faster than you or I can. Yet there was a time when the rich were carted around in horse-drawn carriages while most people walked. The former is a form of equality.

Pineapples and other tropical fruits were once were rare and highly valued exotic items. In fact, Charles II of England is seen being presented a pineapple (surely worth thousands of pounds) in a seventeenth-century painting. Nowadays, the rich frequent swanky restaurants, but most people in Western countries have access to more calories of quality food than they could ever eat.

That's not all. The richest person in the world can't get that much better of a broadband connection than you can, or a much comfier pair of shoes, bed, or couch.

How Markets Have Delivered More Economic Equality

In terms of the operations of day-to-day life we are becoming more equal. Increasingly everyone — even those in third world countries — have access to a smart phone which can reach the internet and all the education, art, music, culture, and social media that everyone else has access to.

A rich person has a flush toilet. You have a flush toilet. A rich person has water coming out of his taps. You have water that comes out of your taps. A rich person has electricity. You have electricity. You can afford soap. You can eat fruit that is flown in from all over the world, in every season. The richest lord in the world a couple hundred years ago couldn't even dream of the luxury that people who are considered impoverished in first world countries live in.

Competing for Resources Under a Socialist Regime

Burgis admits to wanting to place institutions like banking and finance, utilities, healthcare, and lord knows how many others under so-called democratic control, in the name of egalitarianism, but we have to wonder how the masses are going to vote on *how* the public gets access to telecommunications while still *serving the user*. Ultimately, private business owners are answerable to the consumer. It might look like they get to boss everyone around and make decisions, but if someone does it better, they are out of luck. They will be replaced by a competitor.

Removing the market does not solve the problem of "competition" (if this is indeed a competition). There will still be plenty of competition for government contracts and favored positions even once institutions are under democratic control. Ultimately, someone is going to have to make decisions when it comes to who gets what, and they will wield a disproportionate — dare I say "unequal" — amount of power, and likely will "get" rather a lot more than most people.

Ultimately, it is true that the more dollars you have on a free market, the more votes on what is produced and by whom you get. But, as I've explained, the "excessive wealth" of the rich is not stored under a mattress. The only way they can keep it is if they invest it in things that serve the public by creating better products and services. If they invest in lines of production no one wants, they will lose the investment. In this way, the market — to the extent that it is indeed a free market with only mutually agreed upon exchanges — forces an alignment of the interests of those who possess the wealth with those of the consumers. The consumers decide what the rich have to invest in to stay rich with their "votes." Gene mentioned over and over in the debate that those who make up the ranks of the "working class" control a disproportionate amount of consumer spending and therefore have a more equal say in how our society functions than most people would think.

The Issue of Healthcare

We can pit the market against socialism in the most seemingly inegalitarian case, which is the economics of life and death, namely, healthcare. In a debate with me, Burgis expressed horror that on a free market a rich person could buy their way to the front of a queue for life-saving treatments and said it would be better if the state rationed these things. This seems to make sense if we take a steady-state view of the economy, but economies are not fixed.* Supposing there was only one surgeon who could perform the operation, allowing the highest bidder to get first access to the surgeon would bring so much money in that it would be possible to calculate how much time the surgeon should be performing operations for the very wealthy and how much time he should spend teaching others to perform the same procedures. It would send out a signal to all other surgeons that this is a desperately needed specialization and that they should stop what they are doing immediately to train up in the new style of operation. In the long term far more people would have access to the procedure at an affordable price than if the state merely rationed out access to places. In the latter case, waiting lists would be huge and people would die for want of qualified surgeons. A strange form of equalization tends to occur over time whenever the market is allowed to function. Is access to healthcare in the USA unequal at the moment? You bet! But that is only because the market *is not* allowed to function.

The market creates an upward pressure on the quality of products and a downward pressure on their prices, because consumers want the best product at the best price. This means "production for us" *is* "production for profit." What is only accessible to the rich today becomes more equally accessible to everyone tomorrow.

That is why at first hardly anyone could afford a computer. But because the "greedy rich" opted for exuberance rather than charity, buying expensive computers rather than giving away their money to the poor, the companies that made those computers could afford to fund the research that led to the relative "supercomputer" that you are reading this article on today, affordable to you.

* With the exception in Mises's conception of the "evenly rotation economy," which he uses as a thought experiment to demonstrate how real-world markets actually function.

37
The State Is Too Dangerous to Tolerate (Excerpts)

Robert Higgs, Ph.D.

> Robert Higgs has been a Senior Fellow in Political Economy for the Independent Institute since 1994, serving also as Editor (and Editor at Large, since 2013) of *The Independent Review*. He is a former Senior Fellow at the Ludwig von Mises Institute. Archived from the live Mises.tv broadcast, this lecture was presented by Higgs at the 2013 Mises University, hosted by the Mises Institute in Auburn, Alabama, on July 27, 2013.

Defending the continued existence of the state, despite having absolute certainty of a corresponding continuation of its intrinsic engagement in extortion, robbery, willful destruction of wealth, assault, kidnapping, murder, and countless other crimes, requires that one imagine nonstate chaos, disorder, and death on a scale that nonstate actors seem incapable of causing.

If a population acts to serve its common interests, it will never choose the state. In reaching this conclusion, we need not deny the countless problems that will plague people living in a society without a state. Any anarchical society being peopled in normal proportions by vile and corruptible individuals will have crimes and miseries aplenty. *But everything that makes life without a state undesirable makes life with a state even more undesirable.* The idea that the antisocial tendencies that afflict people in every society can be cured or even ameliorated by giving a few persons great discretionary power over all the others is upon serious reflection seen to be a wildly mistaken notion.

Perhaps it is needless to add that the structural checks and balances on which Madison relied to restrain the government's abuses have proven to be increasingly unavailing, and bearing in mind the expansive claims and actions under the present U.S. regime, these checks and balances are almost wholly superseded by a form of executive caesars in which the branches of government that were supposed to check and balance each other have instead coalesced into a mutually supporting design to plunder the people and reduce them to absolute domination by the state.

Anarchists did not try to carry out genocide against the Armenians in Turkey; they did not deliberately starve to death millions of Ukrainians; they did not create a system of death camps to kill Jews, gypsies, and Slavs in Europe; they did not fire-bomb scores of large German and Japanese cities and drop nuclear bombs on two of them; they did not carry out a "Great Leap Forward" that killed scores of millions of Chinese people... they did not attempt to kill everybody with any appreciable education in Cambodia... they did not launch one aggressive war after another; they did not implement trade sanctions that killed perhaps 500,000 Iraqi children. In debates between anarchists and statists, the burden of proof clearly should rest on those who place their trust in the state. Anarchy's mayhem is wholly conjectural; the state's mayhem is undeniably, factually horrendous.

Although I admit that the outcome in a stateless society will be bad, because not only are people not angels, but many of them are irredeemably vicious in the extreme, I conjecture that the outcome in a society under a state will be worse, indeed much worse, because, first, the most vicious people in society will tend to gain control of the state[1] and, second, by virtue of this control over the state's powerful engines of death and destruction, they will wreak vastly more harm than they ever could have caused outside the state.[2] It is unfortunate that some individuals commit crimes, but it is stunningly worse when such criminally inclined individuals wield state powers... The lesson of the precautionary principle is plain: because people are vile and corruptible, the state, which holds by far the greatest potential for harm and tends to be captured by the worst of the worst, is much too risky for anyone to justify its continuation. To tolerate it is not simply to play with fire, but to chance the total destruction of the human race.[3]

NOTES

1. Hayek 1944, pp. 134–52; Bailey 1988; Higgs 2004, pp. 33–56.
2. Higgs 2004, pp. 101–05.
3. Higgs, Ph.D., Robert. "If Men Were Angels: The Basic Analytics of the State Versus Self-Government." *Journal of Libertarian Studies*, Vol. 21, No. 4 (Winter 2007): 55–68.

38
An Invisible Enemy Turned Inward

Clint Russell
"Liberty Lockdown" Podcast

Clint Russell is a former private mortgage broker and entrepreneur, who retired at 37 when he turned radical liberty advocate during the lockdowns of 2020.

With rare exception, war has been fought by the poor and powerless on behalf of the wealthy and powerful. No war in my lifetime has broken this pattern. Young men go overseas under false pretenses, wrapped in the United States flag to propagate a message which the flag does not represent. Far too many return covered in that very flag.

I've witnessed firsthand the mental toll taken upon those who realize the atrocities they committed, only when it was too late. Hands trembling, crippled with guilt, reaching for whatever substance might soothe their moral aches. Left uncared-for and unhealed, all too often they replace that substance eventually with a revolver. My opposition to future wars, at its heart, lies in the devastation the state has wrought both upon the soldiers who were destroyed internally by these acts of aggression and upon the million-plus external victims left in their overseas-wake.

Today, having learned none of the lessons the War on Terror made plain, it has been turned inward.

A new invisible enemy has arisen, morphing from an amorphous "extremist religious terrorism" into a respiratory virus and then back into a new label of "biological terrorism." No liberty is left unmolested when war is afoot and these wars are eternal, intentionally so. The apparatuses foolishly allowed for and established under the War on Terror — namely the NSA, DHS, TSA, plus a newly enriched FBI — are now ramping up to be wielded against those who demand that their bodily autonomy and medical privacy be respected.

Libertarians, the peaceful live-and-let-live, just-leave-me-alone types, have been added to the list of potential homegrown domestic terrorism threats, according to the former director of the CIA, no less. We all know what this label entails: endless war, endless persecution and prosecution without due process, that no rights will be respected, and that if you demand that they be so, your life will be very much in jeopardy. There now exists a fascistic alliance of employer-mandated vaccine compliance, in which millions are now left with the brutal choice of either injecting — under duress — a substance for which long-term side effects cannot be known, or being *de facto* excommunicated from society for fear of a virus which was in all likelihood created with tax money stolen from these very victims.

War has been declared on the American people by the very government which, at least on paper, had sworn to protect them.

39
A Right-Wing Critique of the Police State

Llewellyn H. Rockwell, Jr.

Lew Rockwell is founder and chairman of the Ludwig von Mises Institute, editor of LewRockwell.com, and author of *Fascism vs. Capitalism*. The following passage is an excerpt from *The Left, the Right, and the State*.

The American Right has long held a casual view toward the police power, viewing it as the thin blue line that stands between freedom and chaos. And while it is true that law itself is critical to freedom, and police can defend rights of life and property, it does not follow that any tax-paid fellow bearing official arms and sporting jackboots is on the side of good. Every government regulation and tax is ultimately backed by the police power, so free-market advocates have every reason to be as suspicious of socialist-style police power as anyone on the left.

Uncritical attitudes toward the police lead, in the end, to the support of the police state. And to those who doubt that, I would invite a look at the U.S.-backed regime in Iraq, which has been enforcing martial law since the invasion, even while most conservatives have been glad to believe that these methods constitute steps toward freedom.

The problem of police power is hitting Americans very close to home. It is the police, much militarized and federalized, that are charged with enforcing the on-again-off-again states of emergency that characterize American civilian life. It is the police that confiscated guns from New Orleans residents during the flood, kept residents away from their homes, refused to let the kids go home in the Alabama tornado last month, and will be the enforcers of the curfews, checkpoints, and speech controls that the politicians want during the next national emergency. If we want to see the way the police power could treat U.S. citizens, look carefully at how the U.S. troops in Iraq are treating the civilians there, or how prisoners in Guantánamo Bay are treated.

A related problem with the conservative view toward law and justice concerns the issue of prisons. The United States now incarcerates 730 people per 100,000, which means that the U.S. leads the world in the number of people it keeps in jails. We have vaulted ahead of Russia in this regard.

Building and maintaining jails is a leading expense by government at all levels. We lock up citizens at rates as high as eight times the rest of the industrialized world. Is it because we have more crime? No. You are more likely to be burglarized in London and Sydney than in New York or Los Angeles. Is this precisely because we jail so many people? Apparently not. Crime explains about 12 percent of the prison rise, while changes in sentencing practices, mostly for drug-related offenses, account for 88 percent.

Overall, spending on prisons, police, and other items related to justice is completely out of control. According to the Bureau of Justice Statistics, in the twenty years ending in 2003, prison spending has soared 423 percent, judicial spending is up 321 percent, and police spending shot up 241 percent. When current data become available, I think we will all be in for a shock, with total spending around a quarter of a trillion dollars per year. And what do we get for it? More justice, more safety, better protection? No, we are buying the chains of our own slavery.

We might think of prisons as miniature socialist societies, where government is in full control. For that reason, they are a complete failure for everyone but those who get the contracts to build the jails and those who work in them. Many inmates are there for drug offenses, supposedly being punished for their behavior, but meanwhile drug markets thrive in prison. If that isn't the very definition of failure, I don't know what is. In prison, nothing takes place outside the government's purview. The people therein are wholly and completely controlled by state managers, which means that they have no value. And yet it is a place of monstrous chaos, abuse, and corruption. Is it any wonder that people coming out of prison are no better off than before they went in, and are often worse, and scarred for life?

In the U.S. prison and justice system, there is no emphasis at all on the idea of restitution, which is not only an important part of the idea of justice but, truly, its very essence. What justice is achieved by robbing the victim again to pay for the victimizer's total dehumanization? As Rothbard writes:

> The victim not only loses his money, but pays more money besides for the dubious thrill of catching, convicting, and then supporting the criminal; and the criminal is still enslaved, but not to the good purpose of recompensing his victim.

Free-market advocates have long put up with jails on grounds that the state needs to maintain a monopoly on justice. But where in the world is the justice here? And how many jails are too many? How many prisoners must there be before the government has overreached? We hear virtually nothing about this problem from conservatives. Far from it, we hear only the celebration of the expansion of prison socialism, as if the application of ever more force were capable of solving any social problem. (p. 247)

40
The Only Police Reform That Matters

Jason Brennan, Ph.D.

Jason Brennan is the Robert J. and Elizabeth Flanagan Family Chair and Professor of Strategy, Economics, Ethics, and Public Policy at the McDonough School of Business at Georgetown University. He specializes in political philosophy and applied ethics. The following is a partial transcript taken from an episode (dated May 6, 2020) of the podcast "Don't Tread on Anyone," hosted by Keith Knight.

Keith Knight: I want to talk about your most recent work, a book called *When All Else Fails: The Ethics of Resistance to State Injustice*. What is the "moral parity thesis"?

Jason Brennan, Ph.D.: The moral parity thesis is the claim that the conditions under which you are able to resist injustice conducted by a government official, even when acting in the capacity of their office, are exactly the same as the conditions under which you're allowed to resist me. So basically, there's one set of rules of self-defense and one set of rules for when you're allowed to use violence or subterfuge or deceit or other things to defend other people from injustice, and that same set of rules applies to government agents as it does to defendants against civilians — they are one and the same. So the reverse of this thesis, or the thing I'm arguing against, is what you might call the "special immunity thesis," which says that government agents, either when they're working within their office or not, or maybe just democratic government agents but some government agents, enjoy a kind of special immunity against resistance and actions to resist their injustice. So, like, if I were to try to kill you right now just for the hell of it because I'm having a bad day and I'm misbehaving, everyone thinks that you'd be allowed to defend yourself against me and that other people will be allowed to intervene to defend you against me. But most people think that if a police officer has a bad day and starts beating the crap out of somebody, that you just have to stop and let them do it. You can complain later, you can file, maybe there should be a formal investigation — but you're not permitted to intervene violently. You're not permitted to lie to the government, you're not permitted to resist them except in really extreme circumstances. And so the book [*When All Else Fails*], the simple claim is: just whatever you can do in self-defense or defense of others against anything that I, J. Brennan do, you can do against the U.S. president.

41
Welfare Before the Welfare State

Joshua Fulton, B.A.

Joshua Fulton holds a B.A. from NYU, and an MFA in Creative Writing from UNC, Wilmington. He also co-organized the first successful citizens' ballot initiative in North Carolina in the last 10 years. His website is AbsorbYourHealth.com.

Many people think life without the welfare state would be chaos. In their minds, nobody would help support the less fortunate, and there would be riots in the streets. Little do they know that people found innovative ways of supporting each other before the welfare state existed. One of the most important of these ways was the mutual-aid society.

Mutual aid, also known as fraternalism, refers to social organizations that gathered dues and paid benefits to members facing hardship. According to David Beito in *From Mutual Aid to the Welfare State*, there was a "great stigma" attached to accepting government aid or private charity during the late 18th and early 19th centuries.[1] Mutual aid, on the other hand, did not carry the same stigma. It was based on reciprocity: today's mutual-aid recipient could be tomorrow's donor, and vice versa.

Mutual aid was particularly popular among the poor and the working class. For instance, in New York City in 1909, 40 percent of families earning less than $1,000 a year, little more than the "living wage," had members who were in mutual-aid societies.[2] Ethnicity, however, was an even greater predictor of mutual-aid membership than income. The "new immigrants," such as the Germans, Bohemians, and Russians, many of whom were Jews, participated in mutual-aid societies at approximately twice the rate of native whites and six times the rate of the Irish.[3] This may have been due to new immigrants' need for an enhanced social safety net.

By the 1920s, at least one out of every three males was a member of a mutual-aid society.[4] Members of societies carried over $9 billion worth of life insurance by 1920. During the same period, "lodges dominated the field of health insurance."[5] Numerous lodges offered unemployment benefits. Some black fraternal lodges, taking note of the sporadic nature of African-American employment at the time, allowed members to receive unemployment benefits even if they were up to six months behind in dues.[6]

Under lodge medicine, the price for healthcare was low. Members typically paid $2, about a day's wage, to have yearly access to a doctor's care (minor surgery was frequently included in this fee). Non-lodge members typically paid about $2 every doctor's visit during this time period.[7]

Low prices for lodges did not, however, necessarily translate to low quality. The Independent Order of Foresters, one of the largest mutual-aid societies, frequently touted that the mortality rate of its members was 6.66 per thousand, much lower than the 9.3 per thousand for the general population.[8]

Lodges also had incentives to keep down costs. For instance, the Ladies Friends of Faith Benevolent Association, a black-female society, would pay members taken ill $2 a week if they saw the lodge doctor, and $3 if they didn't. A visiting committee also checked on the claimant to guard against false claims. Members who failed to visit the claimant were fined $1.[9]

Mutual-aid societies also enforced moral codes. In 1892, the Connecticut Bureau of Labor Statistics found that societies followed the "invariable rule" of denying benefits "for any sickness or other disability originating from intemperance, vicious or immoral conduct." Many societies refused to pay benefits for any injury sustained in the "participation in a riot."[10] Some lodges even denied membership to people who manufactured explosives or played professional football.[11]

Many mutual-aid societies branched out and founded their own hospitals and sanitariums. The Securities Benefit Association, or SBA, charged $21 for an 11-day stay at their hospital in Kansas, while the average at 100 private hospitals was $72.[12] Again, quality was not necessarily sacrificed for price. At the SBA's sanitarium, the mortality rate was 4.5 percent, while the historical average for sanitariums was 25 percent. This is especially impressive considering that 30 to 50 percent of all cases admitted to the SBA's sanitarium were "advanced."[13]

A large number of African-American societies also created their own hospitals. In the early 20th century, it was not a given that African-Americans would be admitted into many hospitals. If they were, they frequently had to face such indignities as being forced to bring their own eating utensils, sheets, and toothbrushes and to pay for a black nurse if none was on staff.[14] When the Knights and Daughters of Tabor in Mississippi, a black fraternal society with a reach across only a few counties, opened Taborian Hospital in 1942, membership nearly doubled in three years to 47,000.[15]

Mutual-aid societies also founded 71 orphanages between 1890 and 1922, almost all without government subsidy.[16] Perhaps the largest of these was Mooseheart, founded by the Loyal Order of Moose in 1913. Hundreds of children lived there at a time. It had a student newspaper, two debate teams, three theatrical organizations, and a small radio station. The success of Mooseheart alumni was remarkable. Alumni were four times more likely than the general population to have attended institutions of higher learning. Male alumni earned 71 percent more than the national average, and female alumni earned 63 percent more.[17]

Of course, with so many services being supplied by mutual aid, many groups had reason to lobby government for its destruction.

The first major blow against fraternalism occurred when the American Medical Association gained control of the licensing of medical schools. In 1912, a number of state medical boards formed the Federation of State Medical Boards, which accepted the AMA's ratings of medical schools as authoritative. The AMA quickly rated many schools as "unacceptable." Consequentially, the number of medical schools in America dropped from 166 in 1904 to 81 in 1918, a 51 percent drop.[18] The increased price of medical services made it impractical for many lodges to retain the services of a doctor. Medical boards also threatened many doctors with being stripped of their licenses if they practiced lodge medicine.[19]

The next most damaging piece of legislation was the Mobile Law. The Mobile Law required that mutual aid societies show a gradual improvement in reserves. Until this time, societies had tended to keep low reserves in order to pay the maximum benefits possible to members. High reserve requirements made it difficult for societies to undercut traditional insurance companies. The Mobile Law also required a doctor's examination for all lodge members and forbade all "speculative" enterprises such as the extension of credit to members. By 1919, the Mobile Law had been enacted in 40 states.[20]

The requirement that all members undergo a medical examination effectively barred mutual-aid societies from the growing group-insurance market. Group insurance is insurance offered to a large group of people, such as all the employees at a company, without a medical examination. From 1915 to 1920, the number of people insured under group policies rose from 99,000 to 1.6 million.[21] Some lodges, such as the Arkansas Grand Lodge of the Ancient Order of Workmen, tried to get around the medical examination requirement by offering group insurance at a higher price than normal lodge coverage, but this put them at a competitive disadvantage.[22]

Mutual aid was hindered in other ways. Lodges were prohibited from providing coverage for children. This opened the door for commercial companies to offer industrial policies in which children's coverage was standard. The number of industrial policies rose from 1.4 million in 1900 to 7.1 million in 1920. By 1925, industrial policies surpassed the number of fraternal policies.[23] Group medical insurance also eventually became tax deductible, while private plans such as those purchased through a lodge did not.[24]

Fraternal hospitals also came under attack. During the 1960s, the regulation of hospitals increased. Taborian Hospital in Mississippi was cited for "inadequate storage and bed space, failure to install doors that could swing in either direction, and excessive reliance on uncertified personnel." A state hospital regulator said of the Taborian Hospital, "We are constantly told that you do not have funds to do these things [make improvements], yet if you are to operate a hospital, something has to be done to meet the Minimum Standards of Operation for Mississippi Hospitals."[25]

The Hill-Burton Hospital Construction Act of 1946 also hurt many fraternal hospitals, especially black hospitals. The act required that hospitals receiving federal funds use a portion for indigent care and that services be offered "without discrimination on account of race, creed, or color." Although this enabled many blacks to get free service at hospitals previously unavailable to them, it also cut into the membership base for black fraternal hospitals. Additionally, some hospitals, such as Taborian Hospital and the Friendship Clinic in Mississippi, received no funds, while their nearby competitors received millions.[26]

The advent of Medicare also hastened the decline of fraternal hospitals. MIT economist Amy Finkelstein estimated that Medicare drove a 28 percent increase in hospital spending between 1965 and 1970 by encouraging hospitals to adopt new medical technologies. Smaller hospitals, such as many fraternal hospitals, were not able adopt new technologies as quickly as larger hospitals and were driven out of the market, another finding supported by Finkelstein.[27]

Some fraternal societies escaped the attack of the state by converting into traditional insurance corporations. Both Prudential and Metropolitan Life have their origins in fraternalism.[28] Many societies, however, simply died off.

Although millions of Americans are still members of fraternal societies such as the Masons or Oddfellows, the organizations no longer have the importance in society that they once did. The history of fraternalism serves as a reminder of the power of human cooperation in a free society.

NOTES

1. David Beito, *From Mutual Aid to the Welfare State: Fraternal Societies and Social Services, 1890–1967* (University of North Carolina, 2000), p. 3.
2. Ibid., p. 21.
3. Ibid., p. 22.
4. Ibid., p. 2.
5. Ibid.
6. Ibid., p. 52.
7. Ibid., p. 117.
8. Ibid., p. 119.
9. Ibid., p. 115.
10. Ibid., p. 45.
11. Ibid., p. 44.
12. Ibid., p. 175.

13. Ibid., p. 164.
14. Ibid., p. 183.
15. Ibid., p. 185.
16. Ibid., p. 63.
17. Ibid., p. 86.
18. Dale Steinreich, "100 Years of U.S. Medical Fascism," *Mises Daily*, April 16, 2010.
19. Beito, p. 177.
20. Ibid, p. 142.
21. Ibid, p. 212.
22. Ibid, p. 213.
23. Ibid, p. 211.
24. Ibid, p. 214.
25. Ibid, p. 196.
26. Ibid, p. 197.
27. Amy Finkelstein, "The Aggregate Effects of Health Insurance: Evidence from the Introduction of Medicare," *The Quarterly Journal of Economics* (2007) 122 (1): p. 137.
28. Beito, p. 24.

42
Fallacies You Need to Be Told About

Michael Huemer, Ph.D.

Michael Huemer is a Professor of Philosophy at the University of Colorado, Boulder.

Now I'm going to tell you about some more interesting errors that human beings are prone to. If you're like most people, you probably actually need to be told about these things.

Anecdotal Evidence

Often, people try to support generalizations by citing a single case, or a few cases that support the generalization. Scientists call this "anecdotal evidence." Example: You try to show that immigrants are dangerous by citing a few examples of immigrants who committed Crimes.

Anecdotal evidence has two problems. First, usually, when people do this, they don't pick a case randomly; they search for a case that supports their conclusion while ignoring cases that don't. (See: Cherry Picking.) Second, random variation: Even if you picked the cases randomly, it can easily happen just by chance that you picked a few atypical cases. In the immigration example, what you should actually do is look up the statistics on crime rates for immigrants compared with native-born citizens.

Assumptions

One of the major ways we go wrong is that we simply assume things that we don't know. Unfortunately, when you assume things, you go wrong a lot more often than you expect. (You should assume that most of your assumptions are wrong!) It is hard to combat this, because we often don't notice what we're assuming, and it doesn't even occur to us to question it.

Here are a couple of examples. Suppose you hear a statistic about how common intimate partner violence is in the United States (this is where someone physically abuses their girlfriend, boyfriend, or spouse). You naturally assume that the vast majority of these cases are men beating up women, and you might just go on reasoning from that implicit assumption. In reality, though, survey evidence suggests that men and women suffer this kind of abuse about equally often.

Or suppose you hear a statistic stating that most murder victims are killed by a family member or someone they knew. You naturally assume that most murders result from domestic disagreements, and that the murders are committed by ordinary people who lost control during an argument with a family member, or something like that. In fact, it turns out that almost everyone who commits a murder has a prior criminal record. Also, the vast majority of the victims are also criminals. (The category "a family member or someone they knew" includes such people as the victim's drug dealer, the victim's criminal partner, the victim's fellow gang members, and so on.) You just assumed that these were ordinary people, but the original statistic didn't say that.

I can't really properly convey to you just how often assuming things leads you astray — you need to experience being wrong over and over again, in order to appreciate the point. Unfortunately, most people never come to appreciate the point, because they never check on their assumptions to find out how many are wrong.

Base Rate Neglect

A "base rate" is the frequency with which some type of phenomenon happens in general. E.g., the base rate for heart disease is the percentage of people in the general population who have heart disease. The base rate for war is the percentage of the time that a country is at war. Etc.

When you want to know whether some kind of event is going to happen (or has happened, etc.), the best place to start is with the base rate. If you want to know whether you have a certain disease, first find out how common the disease is in general. If 1% of the population has it, then a good initial estimate is that you have a 1% chance of having it. From there, you should adjust that estimate up or down according to any special risk factors (or low-risk factors) that you have.

Most people don't do this; people commonly ignore base rates. Example: Suppose there is a rare disease that afflicts 1 in a million people. There is a test for the disease that's 90% accurate. Suppose you took the test, and you tested positive (the test says you have the disease). Question: Given all this information, what is the probability that you have the disease?

Many people think it is 90%. Even doctors sometimes get this wrong (which is disturbing). The correct answer is about 0.0009% (less than one in a hundred thousand). Explanation: Say there are 300 million people in the country. Of these, 300 (one millionth) have the disease, and 299,999,700 don't. The test is 90% accurate, so 270 of the 300 people who have the disease would test positive (that's 90%), and 29,999,970 of the 299,999,700 who don't have the disease would also test positive (that's 10%). So, out of all the people who test positive, the proportion who actually have the disease is $270/(270+29,999,970) \approx 0.000009$.

Cherry Picking

"Cherry picking" refers to the practice of sifting through evidence and selecting out only the bits that support a particular conclusion, ignoring the rest. Simple example: I have a bag of marbles. I want to convince you that most of the marbles in the bag are black. I look inside the bag, which is full of many colors of marbles — black, red, teal, chartreuse, and so on. I pick out five black ones, show them to you, and say, "See, these marbles came from this bag." I don't show you any of the other colored marbles that were in the bag. You might be misled into concluding that the bag is full of black marbles.

That's like what people do in political debate. If I want to convince you, say, that affirmative action is bad, I might search for cases where affirmative action was tried and it didn't work or it had harmful effects. If I want to convince you that it's good, I search for cases where it really helped someone. Of course both kinds of cases exist — it's a big society, full of millions of people! Almost any policy is going to benefit some people and harm others. Because of this, you should be suspicious when someone tells you stories designed to support a conclusion — always ask yourself whether they have a bias that might have caused them to cherry pick the data.

Confirmation Bias

When asked to evaluate a theory, people have a systematic tendency to look for evidence supporting the theory and not look for evidence against it. (This happens especially for theories that we already believe, but can also happen for theories we initially have no opinion about.) *E.g.*, if asked whether liberal politicians are more corrupt than conservative politicians, a conservative would search through his memory for any cases of a liberal doing something corrupt, and he would not search through his memory for cases of conservatives being corrupt. A liberal, on the other hand, would do the reverse. Each just looks for cases that support his existing belief, and does not look for evidence against it. This is called "confirmation bias."

To combat this, it is necessary to make a conscious effort to think of exceptions to the generalizations that you accept, and to look for evidence against your existing beliefs. Whenever you feel inclined to cite some examples supporting belief A, stop and ask yourself whether you can also think of similar examples supporting $\sim A$.

Credulity

Humans are born credulous — we instinctively believe what people tell us, even with no corroboration. We are especially credulous about statistics or other information that sounds like objective facts. Unfortunately, we are not so scrupulous when it comes to accurately and non-misleadingly reporting facts. There is an enormous amount of disinformation in the world, particularly about politics and other matters of public interest. If the public is interested in it, there is bullshit about it.

I have noticed that this bullshit tends to fall into three main categories. First, ideological propaganda. If you "learn" about an issue from a partisan source — for instance, you read about gun control on a gun control advocacy website, or you hear the day's news from a conservative radio show — you will get pretty much 100% propaganda. Facts will be exaggerated, cherry picked, deceptively phrased, or otherwise misleading. Normally, you will have no way of guessing the specific way in which the information is deceptive, making the information essentially worthless for drawing inferences.

Second, sensationalism. Mainstream news sources make money by getting as many people as possible to watch their shows, read their articles, and so on. To do that, they try to make everything sound as scary, exciting, outrageous, or otherwise dramatic as possible. Third, laziness. Most people who write for public consumption are lazy and lack expertise about the things they write about. If a story has some technical aspect (*e.g.*, science news), journalists probably won't understand it, and they may get basic facts backwards. Also, they often just talk to one or a few sources and print whatever those sources say, even if the sources have obvious biases.

I can't give you adequate evidence for all that right now. But here's an anecdote that illustrates what I mean. I once heard a story on NPR (National Public Radio, a left-leaning radio news source). It was about a man on death row who was about to be executed. From the story, it appeared that the man was innocent. New evidence had emerged after the trial, several of the witnesses had recanted their testimony, yet the courts had refused to grant a new trial. The only remaining hope was for the governor to grant a stay of execution. There was an online petition that listeners could sign.

Usually, I just accept news stories and then go on with my day. But on that occasion, I decided to look into the story before signing the petition. With a little googling, I found the court decision from the convict's most recent appeal, which had been denied. I read the decision, which contained a summary of the facts of the case and an explanation of the judge's decision.

What it revealed was that the NPR story was bullshit. What NPR said was basically just what the defendant's lawyer had claimed. The court carefully explained why each of those claims was bogus and provided no basis for an appeal. The most striking claim (which had initially made me think the defendant was probably innocent) was that multiple witnesses had "recanted" their testimony. What had actually happened was this: The defense lawyer went back to the witnesses many years after the original trial and questioned them on details of the case. Several of them either couldn't remember the details, or reported details slightly differently (*e.g.*, what color shirt someone was wearing). The lawyer described this as "recanting their testimony." But none of them had changed their mind about the defendant being guilty.

The NPR journalists had apparently just credulously reported what the lawyer told them, without bothering to look up the court documents from the case. Why would they do that? Three reasons: (i) Ideological bias: The story painted the death penalty in a bad light, which a left-leaning news outlet would like. (ii) Sensationalism: The story of an innocent man about to be executed grabbed the audience's attention and inflamed their passions. (iii) Laziness: Checking on the story would have required work. Why put in that work when you know that almost all of your audience will just accept whatever you say? Long experience has led me to think that that case was not unusual; this is the way news media work.

Lesson: Popular media stories are untrustworthy. (By the way, it's no good checking them against other popular news sources, because they basically all copy from each other.) That also goes for, *e.g.*, most bloggers, your next door neighbor, and other casual information sources. For relatively reliable information, look at academic books and articles and government reports (*e.g.*, Census Bureau reports, FBI crime reports).

Dogmatism and Overconfidence
People who study rationality have a notion called "calibration." Your beliefs are said to be well-calibrated when your level of confidence matches the probability of your being correct. For example, for all the beliefs that you hold with 90% confidence, about 90% of them should be true. When you're 100% confident of things, they should be true 100% of the time. Etc.

Most people are badly calibrated. In fact, almost everyone errs in a particular direction: Almost everyone's beliefs are too confident. People say they are "100% certain" of a bunch of things, but then it turns out that only, say, 85% of those things are actually true. (There are psychological studies of this.) This is the problem of overconfidence. Almost everyone has it, and almost no one has the opposite problem (underconfidence), so you should assume that you are probably overconfident too. You should therefore try to reduce your confidence in your beliefs, particularly about controversial things, and particularly for speculative and subjective claims.

Ideological "Cause" Judgments
Back in 2008–2009, America suffered a severe economic recession. A lot of people lost money, lost their jobs, and were generally unhappy. What set it off was problems in real estate. Home prices had gotten very high, then they dropped, a lot of people started defaulting on (not repaying) their home loans, banks were in a lot of trouble, and other investors and financial companies were in trouble because they'd made investments that depended on home prices staying high and home loans getting repaid.

In the wake of the crisis, many people tried to explain why it had all happened. This included people with opposing ideologies. Roughly, there were people with pro-government and people with anti-government ideologies, and both tried to explain the crisis. Can you guess what the two sides said? The pro-government people said the recession happened "because" there wasn't enough regulation — and they listed regulations that, if they had been in place, would probably have prevented the crisis. The anti-government people said the recession happened "because" there was too much government intervention — and they listed existing government policies that, if they hadn't been in place, the crisis probably wouldn't have happened.

Notice that the basic factual claims of both sides are perfectly consistent: It's perfectly possible that there were some actions the government took such that, if the government hadn't taken them, the crisis wouldn't have happened, and also there were some actions the government failed to take such that, if it had taken them, the crisis wouldn't have happened. It's perfectly plausible that the crisis could have been averted in more than one way: either by adding certain government interventions, or by removing some other government interventions. Which alternative you focus on depends on your initial ideology.

Both sides took the episode to further support their ideology: "We have too much government," or "We need more government." These conclusions were supported by their respective causal interpretations: "The recession was caused by government interventions," or "The recession was caused by government failure to intervene."

Who was right? Assume the facts are as stated (that some additional interventions would have prevented the recession and the repeal of some other interventions would have prevented the recession). In that case, we should either accept both causal claims or reject both causal claims, depending on what we mean by "cause." If we mean "sole cause," then we should reject both causal claims (*i.e.*, we should say the recession was not caused either by government intervention or by failure to intervene). If we just mean "factor such that, if it were changed, the effect wouldn't have happened," then we should accept both causal claims (the recession was caused by intervention and by failure to intervene).

It's okay to say that x was caused by y, provided that you also recognize all the other things that caused x in the same sense. If there are many different causes, then you need additional evidence or arguments to establish which one of those causes is the best one to change. In the recession case, we would need independent arguments to establish which cause of the recession (intervention or failure to intervene) it would have been better to change.

Oversimplification

People very often oversimplify philosophical issues. Say you're thinking about the morality of abortion. A tempting simplification would be to say that there are two positions: pro-choice and pro-life (or pro- and anti-abortion). Either fetuses are people and killing them is murder, or fetuses aren't people and killing them is perfectly fine.

But this overlooks the possibility that late-term fetuses are people but early-term fetuses are not; or maybe personhood comes in degrees and fetuses become progressively more personlike as they develop; or maybe fetuses are persons in some senses but non-persons in other senses. So there is a range of possible positions, not just two.

Viewing things in black-and-white terms is a common oversimplification. We look at two simple positions rather than considering a spectrum of possibilities. The problem is that often, the truth is a more subtle position that doesn't clearly fall under either of the two simplest categories of view.

p-hacking

Similar to cherry picking, "p-hacking" or "data mining" sometimes happens in science. A scientist has a large amount of statistical data, with different variables. Even if all the data is completely random, any complex set of data is going to show some patterns that look significant. Essentially, one can take the data and use it to test many different possible hypotheses. Even if all the hypotheses are false, eventually, just by chance (due to random variations in the data), one of the hypotheses will pass a test for "statistical significance." This is one reason why many published research results, especially in medicine, psychology, and social science, are false. *E.g.*, a study will find that some food increases the risk of cancer for non-smoking, middle-aged men; but then someone tries to replicate it, and they don't get the same result, because the original result was just due to chance.

Speculation

Speculative claims are essentially guesses about things that we lack the evidence to establish as yet. Claims about the future, or claims about what would have happened in hypothetical alternative possibilities, are good examples of speculative claims.

Example: You're arguing about whether it's good for government to try to stimulate the economy by spending money. You say this is good because, *e.g.*, if the government hadn't stimulated the economy back in 2009, the recession would have continued much longer. This is speculative — we don't know what would have happened, because in fact the government did pass a stimulus plan, and we can't now go back in time and change that to see what would have happened if they hadn't.

The problem with speculative claims is that people with different philosophical (or political, religious, etc.) beliefs tend to find very different speculations plausible. *E.g.*, people who are suspicious of government will find it more plausible that, without government stimulus, the recession would have been shorter. So arguments that start from speculative premises are typically not rationally persuasive.

Advice: If you want to rationally persuade people of something, try to avoid speculation.

Subjective Claims

Roughly, a "subjective" claim is one that requires a judgment call, so it can't just be straightforwardly and decisively established. For example, the judgment that political candidate A is "unqualified" for the office; the judgment that it's worse to be unjustly imprisoned for 5 years than to be prevented from migrating to the country one wants to live in; the judgment that Louis CK's jokes are "offensive"; etc. (This differs from speculative claims, because in the case of speculation, there might be ways that the claim could in principle be decisively verified; it just hasn't in fact been verified.)

Note: I am not saying that there is "no fact" or "no answer" as to whether these things are the case, or that they are dependent on people's "opinions." What I am saying is that there are not clear, established criteria for these claims, so it is difficult to verify them. Maybe it's true that Louis is offensive, but if someone doesn't find him offensive, there is no decisive way of proving that he is.

People often rely on subjective premises when arguing about controversial issues. The problem with this is that subjective claims are more open to bias than relatively objective (that's the opposite of "subjective") claims. So people with different philosophical (or political, or religious) views will tend to disagree a lot about subjective claims. And for that reason, they are ill suited to serve as premises in philosophical, political, or religious arguments. Advice: Try to base your arguments, as much as possible, on relatively objective claims.

Treatment Effects vs. Selection Effects

Let's say you have created a new educational program for pre-school children. You want to know whether it improves learning or not. What you would do is look at kids after they've had your program, and compare them to kids of the same age who didn't have your program, and see if the first group perform better on tests. Let's say kids who had your special program perform 10% better on later tests, on average. Then you'd probably conclude that your program works.

But wait. Here is another possibility. Suppose (as would usually be the case) that the kids who entered your special educational program were the kids whose parents chose to enroll them in that program. The rest were kids whose parents did not decide to enroll them. Furthermore, maybe the parents who enroll their kids in special programs are on average smarter and value education more than the parents who don't do that. Furthermore, maybe intelligence and value placed on learning are partly genetic, and so these parents passed those traits on to their kids. So the children who went into your program were already, on average, smarter and more interested in learning than the children who didn't go into the program. And maybe that explains why they did 10% better on tests after the program. Maybe your program has no effect at all; it's just that you got the smart kids in it, and that made the program look good.

That is an example of a "selection effect" — a case where it looks like A causes B, but it's actually just that the instances of A that you tested were already more likely to be B's for other reasons. Selection effects are contrasted with "treatment effects" — cases where the thing you're testing really causes the effect that it's thought to cause. In the education example, academic success is correlated with taking the special program. This could be due to a treatment effect (meaning the program causes kids to learn more), or due to a selection effect (meaning the program selects students who are already good at learning).

Selection effects are very often mistaken for treatment effects. Another example: You want to know if some vitamin improves people's health. So you look at people who take supplements of that vitamin regularly, and you find that they are healthier than the people who don't take it. You think this shows that the vitamin supplements are good for people... but actually, it's more likely a selection effect: People who take vitamins are more likely to also be exercising, eating healthy foods, and so on, which is why they would be healthier than average, even if the vitamins did absolutely nothing.

Whataboutism

Similar to *tu quoque*, whataboutism occurs when someone criticizes something bad, and you respond with, "What about x?", where x is some other bad thing. Example: Someone complains that the current President's proposed budget has a very high deficit. You say, "What about the previous President? He had high deficits too!" Or: Someone complains that the President just murdered a child. You respond that some other political figure, from an opposing party, also murdered children. "What about that?" you demand.

The reason people engage in whataboutism is that, rather than being interested in practical issues about what should be done in our current situation, they instead see political discussion as a kind of tribal contest, a competition between "their side" and "the other side," where whoever makes their side look better wins. So they don't want attention focused on any flaws in one of their side's people (*e.g.*, a politician from their own political party). So they try to divert attention to something that's bad about someone on the other side.

    The problem is that this practice systematically prevents evils from being addressed. For any evil in the world (unless it's literally the worst thing in the world), one can always identify some other, even worse evil, and say "What about that?" For any evil done by any political leader, it will virtually always be true that some other leader from another party has some time committed a similar evil (and also that members of that person's party didn't do anything about it). If your response when you hear about any evil currently happening is to deflect attention to some past evil committed by another person or group, that means that evils never get addressed. Attention always gets deflected away by whataboutism. The next time someone else is doing something evil, that won't be addressed either, because people will say "what about" the present evil that wasn't properly addressed.

43
The Anti-Capitalist Ideology of Slavery

Phillip W. Magness, Ph.D.

Phillip W. Magness is Senior Research Faculty and Interim Research and Education Director at the American Institute for Economic Research. The following article was published by the American Institute for Economic Research in August of 2019.

What is capitalism's view toward slavery? It seems like a crazy question, but not so much actually, not in these times. So let us begin with the opening line of the first chapter of George Fitzhugh's *Sociology for the South*, first published in 1854:

> Political economy is the science of free society. Its theory and its history alike establish this position. Its fundamental maxim Laissez-faire and "Pas trop gouverner," are at war with all kinds of slavery, for they in fact assert that individuals and peoples prosper most when governed least.

Fizhugh's point was to inveigh against economic freedom and in defense of slavery. His radical tract sought to make out an elaborate ideological case for slave labor and indeed all aspects of social ordering. Such a system, he announced, would resolve the posited state of perpetual conflict between labor and the owners of capital by supplanting it with the paternalistic hierarchy of slavery — a model he advocated not only for the plantations of the South but also for adaptation to the factories of the Northeast.

In total, Fitzhugh presented a horrifying vision of a national society reordered around the principle of chattel slavery. And as his introductory remarks announced, attainment of that society required the defeat of its remaining obstacle, the free market.

Although rightly rejected today, the Virginia-born Fitzhugh attained national prominence in the late antebellum period as one of the most widely read defenders of a slave-based economy. Charles Sumner called him a "leading writer among Slave-masters," and his regular contributions to the pro-South magazine *DeBow's Review* gained him a national readership in the 1850s.

In 1855 Fitzhugh embarked on a publicity tour of the Northeast, jousting with abolitionist Wendell Phillips in a series of back-to-back lectures on the slavery question. By 1861, he had added his voice to the cause of southern secessionism and began mapping out an elaborate slave-based industrialization policy for the Confederacy's wartime economy.

Fitzhugh was also an avowed anti-capitalist. Slavery's greatest threat came from the free market economic doctrines of Europe, which were "tainted with abolition, and at war with our institutions." To survive, he declared, the South must "throw Adam Smith, Say, Ricardo & Co., in the fire."

Such rhetoric presents an under-acknowledged conundrum for modern historians. It is academically trendy at the moment to depict plantation slavery as an integral component of American capitalism.

A new multipart feature series in the *New York Times* advances this thesis, depicting modern free market capitalism as an inherently "racist" institution and a direct lineal descendant of plantation slavery, still exhibiting the brutality of that system. This characterization draws heavily from the so-called "New History of Capitalism" (NHC) — a genre of historical writing that swept through the academy in the last decade and that aggressively promotes the thesis that free market capitalism and slavery are inextricably linked.

Many leading examples of NHC scholarship in the academy today are plagued by shoddy economic analysis and documented misuse of historical evidence. These works often present historically implausible arguments, such as the notion that modern double-entry accounting emerged from plantation ledger books (the practice actually traces to the banking economies of Renaissance Italy), or that its use by slave owners is distinctively capitalistic (even the Soviets employed modern accounting practices, despite attempting to centrally plan their entire economy). Indeed, it was NHC historian Ed Baptist who produced an unambiguously false statistic purporting to show that cotton production accounted for a full half of the antebellum American economy (it actually comprised about 5 percent of GDP).

Despite the deep empirical and historical deficiencies of this literature, NHC arguments are still widely enlisted not only as historical analysis of slavery's economics but as an ideological attack on modern capitalism itself. If capitalism is historically tainted by its links to slavery, they reason, then the effects of slavery's stain persist in modern American capitalism today. In its most extreme iterations, these same historians then advocate a political reordering of the American economy to remove that stain. In other words, to reconcile our society to its history and atone for the sins of slavery, we must abandon what remains of American capitalism.

The NHC literature's use of the term "capitalism" is plagued by its own definitional fluidity, which, at times, encompasses everything from laissez-faire non-intervention to protectionist mercantilism to state-ordered central planning. Most economic historians take care to differentiate between the features of these widely varying systems; however, the NHC literature has adopted a habit of simply relabeling everything as "capitalism." A command-and-control wartime industrial policy thus becomes "war capitalism," while a slave-oriented mercantilist regime of protective tariffs and industrial subsidies becomes "racial slave capitalism," and so forth.

When brandished in modern politics, it quickly becomes clear that the same scholars have only one "capitalism" in mind. The NHC genre's own economic inclinations veer unambiguously in a leftward direction, suggesting their real ire is toward the classical liberal free market variety of capitalism. Wealth redistribution, the nationalization of health care and other entire economic sectors, socialistic central planning of industries around labor activism, and even a plethora of climate change policies thereby become necessary acts of "social justice" to correct for capitalism's supposed slavery-infused legacy.

We therefore arrive at the curious position wherein "atonement" for slavery, as presented by the NHC historians, involves politically repudiating the same free market doctrines that Fitzhugh deemed the greatest danger to slavery itself in the decade before the Civil War.

Returning to Fitzhugh's defense of slavery, we find deep similarities to anti-capitalist rhetoric today. The economic doctrines of laissez-faire, he wrote in 1857, foster "a system of unmitigated selfishness." They subject nominally free labor to the "despotism of capital" wherein the capitalist class extracts an "exploitation of skill" from wage laborers, as found in the difference between the value of what they create and the much lower compensation they receive.

As Fitzhugh argued, by way of the example of a wealthy acquaintance who had "ceased work" and lived off of his fortune, the capitalist's "capital was but the accumulation of the results of their labor; for common labor creates all capital." He then succinctly explained the result by noting "the capitalist, living on his income, gives nothing to his subjects. He lives by mere exploitation." As Fitzhugh continued:

> It is the interest of the capitalist and the skillful to allow free laborers the least possible portion of the fruits of their own labor; for all capital is created by labor, and the smaller the allowance of the free laborer, the greater the gains of his employer. To treat free laborers badly and unfairly, is universally inculcated as a moral duty, and the selfishness of man's nature prompts him to the most rigorous performance of this cannibalish duty. We appeal to political economy; the ethical, social, political and economic philosophy of free society, to prove the truth of our doctrines. As an ethical and social guide, that philosophy teaches, that social, individual and national competition, is a moral duty, and we have attempted to prove all competition is but the effort to enslave others, without being encumbered with their support.

The difference between the value of the laborer's product and this substantially lower wage, Fitzhugh explained, provided a measure of the exploited share of his work.

If this line of reasoning sounds familiar, it is due to a very real parallel between Fitzhugh's formulation of the capital-labor relationship and that of another famous contemporary. Fitzhugh had effectively worked out the Marxian theory of "surplus value" over a decade before the publication of Marx's own *Capital* (1867), and derived it from the same sweeping indictment of the free-labor capitalism.

The two thinkers would only diverge in their next steps, the prescriptive solution. Whereas Marx rejected chattel slavery and extrapolated a long historical march to an eventual socialist reordering through revolutionary upheaval, Fitzhugh saw a readily available alternative. "Slavery is a form, and the very best form, of socialism," he explained. Wage labor, he predicted, would be forever insufficient to meet the needs of the laborer due to deprivation of his products from his skill. Slavery, to Fitzhugh's convenience, could step in and fill the gap through the paternalistic provision of necessities for the enslaved, allegedly removing the "greed" of wage exploitation from the process.

Since slaves became the charge of the slave master and were placed under his care for food and shelter, Fitzhugh reasoned that "slaves consume more of the results of their own labor than laborers at the North." Plantation slavery, according to this contorted line of thinking, thereby mitigated the "exploitation" of wage labor capitalism and returned a greater portion of the posited surplus value. In the Marxian counterpart, a socialist state fulfills a similar function.

Fitzhugh's eccentric extrapolation from what are essentially Marxian doctrines has the effect of turning Marx's own untenable "solution" to capital ownership on its head. But the two thinkers unite in their grievances: a shared enmity toward market capitalism, and a desire to cast free market allocation of resources aside through coercive social reordering to achieve their respective ideal societies — mass enslavement or global communism.

These similarities between Fitzhugh and socialism, and indeed the aggressive anti-capitalist rhetoric of proslavery ideology, are seldom examined in the NHC literature. In its quest to politically tar modern capitalism with the horrors of slavery, these historians have adopted a practice of evidentiary negligence that conveniently excludes the explicit anti-capitalist ideological tenets of the very same slave system that they rebrand as a foundation of the modern capitalist economy.

Fitzhugh was not alone in adopting and adapting anti-capitalist ideology to the defense of slavery. Indeed, he heavily extrapolated it from Thomas Carlyle's own racist attacks upon the "dismal science" of economics on account of its close historical ties to abolitionism. That these proslavery thinkers found a parallel rationale in socialism and deployed it to attack a common enemy of free markets, irrespective of their otherwise-divergent claims, is indicative of a shared illiberalism between the two. In practice, unfortunately, the immiserating historical records of each reveal that the only remaining distinction between their political outcomes consists of the choice between the slavery of the plantation and the slavery of the gulag.

44
From Marine to Voluntaryist

Shane Hazel

> Shane Hazel is a former United States Marine and is now the host of the podcast "Radical."

In early 2004, had somebody told me that by 2021, I would be promoting voluntaryism as a podcaster in the Liberty movement with runs for the U.S. House and U.S. Senate under my belt, as well as a governor race on the horizon, I would have told him he was high.

So how does one go from being a neocon in the United States Marine Corps legendary 1st Force Recon Co. to a voluntaryist? Knowledge and Experience.

One book opened my mind to the idea that everything I had ever been forced to learn was a lie for the sake of manipulation to serve the most senior government officials, bankers, and corporations, which I have since affectionately named "The Murder Cult." That book was John Taylor Gatto's *The Underground History of American Education*. (Read everything Gatto.)

It was the end of November 2004, and I had just come off the front lines of the bloody house-to-house battle of Fallujah. Earlier that year, in August, I had witnessed the battle of Najaf in the same fashion, but at the end of it, we Marines were ordered to stand down and watch the "enemy" walk out of the Imam Ali Shrine under a ceasefire brokered by some far-off politicians. It was then that the thought occurred to me: "What the fuck are we doing here, if we're not destroying our enemies?"

Luckily for me, my answer was just a few months and a giant battle away. Gatto explained that the American education system was designed and initially implemented by Prussian Fabian socialists in the 1700s, before being brought to America in the 1800s by Horace Mann. Its intent, according to Gatto, was: "1) Obedient soldiers to the army; 2) Obedient workers for mines, factories, and farms; 3) Well-subordinated civil servants, trained in their function; 4) Well-subordinated clerks for industry; 5) Citizens who thought alike on most issues; 6) National uniformity in thought, word, and deed."

And there I was, lying on my rack, in a shitty tent, halfway around the world, being a good number 1. I was in shock, but I could not deny Gatto's teachings. At that moment, I was more determined than ever to get out of the Marine Corps as fast as I could.

Luckily, I survived my final months in Iraq. From there, I went back to bedrock, or at least what Government youth indoctrination had told me was bedrock. In 2008, I found Ron Paul and his crowd, and I began to devour information. I memorized the Constitution and its mechanics by studying *The Federalist*. Then I found *The Anti-Federalist*, which destroyed the fiction of *The Federalist* and moreover exposed their Coup. "Coup," you say, Shane? Yes, the Federalists were power-hungry bastards. The Constitution was a successful coup of the "aristocratic combination" (a.k.a. The Murder Cult) to take control from the newly Free States in order to centralize and grow power. Lysander Spooner came along later for me, but he emphasized the question... What contract did you sign? "None," I said aloud.

It wasn't until 2012 that I was introduced to the Mises Institute by my cousin Greg. Like most people, I was extremely intimidated by economics, and moreover I had a perceived economics as boring. I started with *Economics in One Lesson*, and I was hooked. Economics wasn't dull or boring. Economics was, I soon discovered, the study of the root of how history's most powerful people moved people and ideas around the world. To say the least, Rothbard, Mises, Hayek, and Hazlitt taught me as much as I ever wanted to know about economics.

In terms of literature, the latest question I've evolved on has been spirituality, thanks to Brian Muraresku. Specifically, the omission and lies of the Church. Warning: Brian's book *The Immorality Key* is damning for the Church and State.

45
The Law (Excerpts)

Frédéric Bastiat
1850

Claude-Frédéric Bastiat (1801–1850) was a French economist and writer. He was a prominent member of the French Liberal School.

If every person has the right to defend — even by force — his person, his liberty, and his property, then it follows that a group of men have the right to organize and support a common force to protect these rights constantly. (p. 4)

Since an individual cannot lawfully use force against the person, liberty, or property of another individual, then the common force — for the same reason — cannot lawfully be used to destroy the person, liberty, or property of individuals or groups. (p. 4)

When a portion of wealth is transferred from the person who owns it — without his consent and without compensation, and whether by force or by fraud — to anyone who does not own it, then I say that property is violated; that an act of plunder is committed. I say that this act is exactly what the law is supposed to suppress, always and everywhere. (p. 17)

According to their degree of enlightenment, these plundered classes may propose one of two entirely different purposes when they attempt to attain political power: Either they may wish to stop lawful plunder, or they may wish to share in it. (p. 6)

The Results of Legal Plunder

It is impossible to introduce into society a greater change and a greater evil than this: the conversion of the law into an instrument of plunder. What are the consequences of such a perversion? It would require volumes to describe them all. Thus, we must content ourselves with pointing out the most striking. In the first place, it erases from everyone's conscience the distinction between justice and injustice. No society can exist unless the laws are respected to a certain degree. The safest way to make laws respected is to make them respectable. When law and morality contradict each other, the citizen has the cruel alternative of either losing his moral sense or losing his respect for the law. These two evils are of equal consequence, and it would be difficult for a person to choose between them. The nature of law is to maintain justice. This is so much the case that, in the minds of the people, law and justice are one and the same thing. There is in all of us a strong disposition to believe that anything lawful is also legitimate. This belief is so widespread that many persons have erroneously held that things are "just" because law makes them so. Thus, in order to make plunder appear just and sacred to many consciences, it is only necessary for the law to decree and sanction it. Slavery, restrictions, and monopoly find defenders not only among those who profit from them but also among those who suffer from them. If you suggest a doubt as to the morality of these institutions, it is boldly said that "You are a dangerous innovator, a utopian, a theorist, a subversive; you would shatter the foundation upon which society rests." (p. 7)

Slavery is a violation, by law, of liberty. The protective tariff is a violation, by law, of property. (p. 12)

But how is this legal plunder to be identified? Quite simply. See if the law takes from some persons what belongs to them, and gives it to other persons to whom it does not belong. See if the law benefits one citizen at the expense of another by doing what the citizen himself cannot do without committing a crime. (p. 13)

Legal plunder has two roots: One of them, as I have said before, is in human greed; the other is in false philanthropy. (p. 17)

When a politician views society from the seclusion of his office, he is struck by the spectacle of the inequality that he sees. He deplores the deprivations which are the lot of so many of our brothers, deprivations which appear to be even sadder when contrasted with luxury and wealth. Perhaps the politician should ask himself whether this state of affairs has not been caused by old conquests and lootings, and by more recent legal plunder. Perhaps he should consider this proposition: Since all persons seek well-being and perfection, would not a condition of justice be sufficient to cause the greatest efforts toward progress, and the greatest possible equality that is compatible with individual responsibility? (p. 20)

But what do the socialists do? They cleverly disguise this legal plunder from others — and even from themselves — under the seductive names of fraternity, unity, organization, and association... But we assure the socialists that we repudiate only forced organization, not natural organization. (p. 22)

A Confusion of Terms

Socialism, like the ancient ideas from which it springs, confuses the distinction between government and society. As a result of this, every time we object to a thing being done by government, the socialists conclude that we object to its being done at all. We disapprove of state education. Then the socialists say that we are opposed to any education. We object to a state religion. Then the socialists say that we want no religion at all. We object to

The Law (Excerpts)

a state-enforced equality. Then they say that we are against equality. And so on, and so on. It is as if the socialists were to accuse us of not wanting persons to eat because we do not want the state to raise grain. (p. 22)

If people are as incapable, as immoral, and as ignorant as the politicians indicate, then why is the right of these same people to vote defended with such passionate insistence?... If the natural tendencies of mankind are so bad that it is not safe to permit people to be free, how is it that the tendencies of these organizers are always good? Do not the legislators and their appointed agents also belong to the human race? Or do they believe that they themselves are made of a finer clay than the rest of mankind? (p. 48)

Please understand that I do not dispute their right to invent social combinations, to advertise them, to advocate them, and to try them upon themselves, at their own expense and risk. But I do dispute their right to impose these plans upon us by law — by force — and to compel us to pay for them with our taxes. (p. 49)

They need only to give up the idea of forcing us to acquiesce to their groups and series, their socialized projects, their free-credit banks, their Graeco-Roman concept of morality, and their commercial regulations. I ask only that we be permitted to decide upon these plans for ourselves; that we not be forced to accept them, directly or indirectly, if we find them to be contrary to our best interests or repugnant to our consciences... But, again, if persons are incompetent to judge for themselves, then why all this talk about universal suffrage? (p. 49)

Essentially, economics is the science of determining whether the interests of human beings are harmonious or antagonistic. (p. 51)

...I invariably reach this one conclusion: The solution to the problems of human relationships is to be found in liberty. (p. 56)

[I]n short, the happiest, most moral, and most peaceful people are those who most nearly follow this principle: Although mankind is not perfect, still, all hope rests upon the free and voluntary actions of persons within the limits of right... (p. 57)

46

How Government Solved the Health Care Crisis

Roderick T. Long, Ph.D.

Roderick Long is a Professor of Philosophy at Auburn University. This article was published in the Winter 1993–94 issue of *Formulations* by the Free Nation Foundation.

Today, we are constantly being told, the United States faces a health care crisis. Medical costs are too high, and health insurance is out of reach of the poor. The cause of this crisis is never made very clear, but the cure is obvious to nearly everybody: government must step in to solve the problem.

Eighty years ago, Americans were also told that their nation was facing a health care crisis. Then, however, the complaint was that medical costs were too *low*, and that health insurance was too *accessible*. But in that era, too, government stepped forward to solve the problem. And boy, did it solve it!

In the late 19th and early 20th centuries, one of the primary sources of health care and health insurance for the working poor in Britain, Australia, and the United States was the fraternal society. Fraternal societies (called "friendly societies" in Britain and Australia) were voluntary mutual-aid associations. Their descendants survive among us today in the form of the Shriners, Elks, Masons, and similar organizations, but these no longer play the central role in American life they formerly did. As recently as 1920, over one-quarter of all adult Americans were members of fraternal societies. (The figure was still higher in Britain and Australia.) Fraternal societies were particularly popular among blacks and immigrants. (Indeed, Teddy Roosevelt's famous attack on "hyphenated Americans" was motivated in part by hostility to the immigrants' fraternal societies; he and other Progressives sought to "Americanize" immigrants by making them dependent for support on the democratic state, rather than on their own independent ethnic communities.)

The principle behind the fraternal societies was simple. A group of working-class people would form an association (or join a local branch, or "lodge," of an existing association) and pay monthly fees into the association's treasury; individual members would then be able to draw on the pooled resources in time of need. The fraternal societies thus operated as a form of self-help insurance company.

Turn-of-the-century America offered a dizzying array of fraternal societies to choose from. Some catered to a particular ethnic or religious group; others did not. Many offered entertainment and social life to their members, or engaged in community service. Some "fraternal" societies were run entirely by and for women. The kinds of services from which members could choose often varied as well, though the most commonly offered were life insurance, disability insurance, and "lodge practice."

"Lodge practice" refers to an arrangement, reminiscent of today's HMOs, whereby a particular society or lodge would contract with a doctor to provide medical care to its members. The doctor received a regular salary on a retainer basis, rather than charging per item; members would pay a yearly fee and then call on the doctor's services as needed. If medical services were found unsatisfactory, the doctor would be penalized, and the contract might not be renewed. Lodge members reportedly enjoyed the degree of customer control this system afforded them. And the tendency to overuse the physician's services was kept in check by the fraternal society's own "self-policing"; lodge members who wanted to avoid future increases in premiums were motivated to make sure that their fellow members were not abusing the system.

Most remarkable was the low cost at which these medical services were provided. At the turn of the century, the average cost of "lodge practice" to an individual member was between *one and two dollars a year*. A day's wage would pay for a year's worth of medical care. By contrast, the average cost of medical service on the regular market was between one and two dollars *per visit*. Yet licensed physicians, particularly those who did not come from "big name" medical schools, competed vigorously for lodge contracts, perhaps because of the security they offered; and this competition continued to keep costs low.

The response of the medical establishment, both in America and in Britain, was one of outrage; the institution of lodge practice was denounced in harsh language and apocalyptic tones. Such low fees, many doctors charged, were bankrupting the medical profession. Moreover, many saw it as a blow to the dignity of the profession that trained physicians should be eagerly bidding for the chance to serve as the hirelings of lower-class tradesmen. It was particularly detestable that such uneducated and socially inferior people should be permitted to set fees for the physicians' services, or to sit in judgment on professionals to determine whether their services had been satisfactory. The government, they demanded, must do something.

And so it did. In Britain, the state put an end to the "evil" of lodge practice by bringing health care under political control. Physicians' fees would now be determined by panels of trained professionals (*i.e.*, the physicians themselves) rather than by ignorant patients. State-financed medical care edged out lodge practice; those who were being forced to pay taxes for "free" health care whether they wanted it or not had little incentive to pay extra for health care through the fraternal societies, rather than using the government care they had already paid for.

In America, it took longer for the nation's health care system to be socialized, so the medical establishment had to achieve its ends more indirectly; but the essential result was the same. Medical societies like the AMA imposed sanctions on doctors who dared to sign lodge practice contracts. This might have been less effective if such medical societies had not had access to government power; but in fact, thanks to governmental grants of privilege, they controlled the medical licensure procedure, thus ensuring that those in their disfavor would be denied the right to practice medicine.

Such licensure laws also offered the medical establishment a less overt way of combating lodge practice. It was during this period that the AMA made the requirements for medical licensure far more strict than they had previously been. Their reason, they claimed, was to raise the quality of medical care. But the result was that the number of physicians fell, competition dwindled, and medical fees rose; the vast pool of physicians bidding for lodge practice contracts had been abolished. As with any market good, artificial restrictions on supply created higher prices — a particular hardship for the working-class members of fraternal societies.

The final death blow to lodge practice was struck by the fraternal societies themselves. The National Fraternal Congress — attempting, like the AMA, to reap the benefits of cartelization — lobbied for laws decreeing a legal minimum on the rates fraternal societies could charge. Unfortunately for the lobbyists, the lobbying effort was successful; the unintended consequence was that the minimum rates laws made the services of fraternal societies no longer competitive. Thus the National Fraternal Congress' lobbying efforts, rather than creating a formidable mutual-aid cartel, simply destroyed the fraternal societies' market niche — and with it the opportunity for low-cost health care for the working poor.

Why do we have a crisis in health care costs today? *Because government "solved" the last one.*

Bibliography

Beito, David T. "Mutual Aid for Social Welfare: The Case of American Fraternal Societies." *Critical Review*, Vol. 4, no. 4 (Fall 1990).

Beito, David T. "The 'Lodge Practice Evil' Reconsidered: Medical Care Through Fraternal Societies, 1900–1930." (unpublished)

Gosden, P. *Self-Help: Voluntary Associations in the 19th Century*. Batsford Press, London, 1973.

Gosden, P. *The Friendly Societies in England, 1815–1875*. Manchester University Press, Manchester, 1961.

Green, David. *Reinventing Civil Society: The Rediscovery of Welfare Without Politics*. Institute of Economic Affairs, London, 1993.

Green, David. *Working Class Patients and the Medical Establishment: Self-Help in Britain from the Mid-Nineteenth Century to 1948*. St. Martin's Press, New York, 1985.

Green, David & Lawrence Cromwell. *Mutual Aid or Welfare State: Australia's Friendly Societies*. Allen & Unwin, Sydney, 1984.

Loan, Albert. "Institutional Bases of the Spontaneous Order: Surety and Assurance." *Humane Studies Review*, Vol. 7, no. 1, 1991/92.

Siddeley, Leslie. "The Rise and Fall of Fraternal Insurance Organizations." *Humane Studies Review*, Vol. 7, no. 2, 1992.

Young, S. David. *The Rule of Experts: Occupational Licensing in America*. Cato Institute, Washington, 1987.

47
The Imposers and the Imposed Upon

Jeff Deist

Jeff Deist is president of the Ludwig von Mises Institute, where he serves as a writer, public speaker, and advocate for property, markets, and civil society. The following is an excerpt from a talk delivered on October 9, 2020, at the Mises Institute's Annual Supporters Summit, Jekyll Island, Georgia.

I'd like to talk to you this afternoon about two classes of Americans, and it may not be the two classes you think of, but nonetheless, there are two distinct classes in America, and we have to break up, and we have to break up sooner rather than later.

A nation that believes in itself and its future, a nation that means to stress the sure feeling that its members are bound to one another not merely by accident of birth but also by the common possession of a culture that is valuable above all to each of them, would necessarily be able to remain unperturbed when it saw individual persons shift to other nations. A people conscious of its own worth would refrain from forcibly detaining those who wanted to move away and from forcibly incorporating into the national community those who were not joining it of their own free will. To let the attractive force of its own culture prove itself in free competition with other peoples — that alone is worthy of a proud nation, that alone would be true national and cultural policy. The means of power and of political rule were in no way necessary for that.

Ludwig von Mises wrote this about a hundred years ago, and it rings absolutely as true today as the day he wrote it, and it's all about the idea of letting people go if they want to form a different political union or political entity. At the end he mentions true national and cultural policy. And so I would ask all of you today to consider: Is America a nation at this point? I would argue no. Is it even a country? Barely. Or is it, as Ilana Mercer calls it, Walmart with nukes? And that's what America feels like very much today. It feels like we're all living in one big federal subdivision, doesn't it?

Last night I mentioned that about a hundred years ago in the interwar period Mises wrote his great trilogy, three books, remarkable books: *Nation, State, and Economy* first, then *Socialism*, then *Liberalism*, all within a ten-year span. These three remarkable books basically laid out a blueprint for both organizing society in a prosperous and peaceful way and also a warning in *Socialism* about how to destroy it. Turns out it's a lot easier to destroy than build.

Mises lays out his conception of what a liberal nationhood might look like. It's rooted in property, of course, and rigorous self-determination at home, and what this means is that he's always stressing the right of secession, back then, for political, linguistic, ethnic, economic minorities. They always have the right to secede, and of course, coming out of the patchwork of the former Austro-Hungarian Empire and in Europe, he understood what it meant to be a linguistic minority in particular. So, for Mises, any kind of nation, any kind of real nationalism, liberal nationalism, requires *laissez-faire* at home, of course. It requires free trade with your neighbors, to avoid a tendency toward war and autarchy, and it requires a noninterventionist foreign policy to avoid war and empire.

When we think of these three books, we can only imagine what the West and what America might look like today if these books had been read and absorbed broadly at the time. If Western governments had been even somewhat reasonable, let's say over the past century, consuming, let's say, only 10 or 15 percent of private wealth in taxes, maintaining just somewhat reasonable currencies backed by gold, mostly staying out of education and banking and medicine, and most of all avoiding supernational wars and military entanglements. If governments had just been somewhat reasonable in the West, we might still live in a more gilded era, like Mises once enjoyed in Vienna, but with all the unimaginable benefits of our technology and material advances today.

The truth is that liberalism didn't hold and we have to be honest with ourselves about it. It didn't hold in the West, and it never took root in the full Misesian sense anywhere, at least not for long, and that's why all of us are here today. If the world had listened to Mises even somewhat, if Western states had committed to the prescription of sound money, markets, peace, all of our libertarian anarcho-capitalist theory might have been completely unnecessary. We might be sitting here today just sort of grumbling about potholes and local property taxes and local schools. Instead, we're here talking about the state as an existential threat to civilization. So, two very different scenarios. But again, the world didn't listen to Mises; that's why it got Rothbard and Hoppe, by the way.

One of the great progressive achievements of the last hundred years, which goes almost totally unremarked today, goes to the title of my talk: the degree to which the Imposers, we can call them, have been able to portray themselves as the Imposed Upon. It's absolutely uncanny. We see it in every aspect of American society and every aspect of our politics today. We see it in the presidential election; we see it with the culture wars; we see it in academia in spades; we see it with Antifa in the streets. If we think about just the last hundred years since Mises wrote these three books — the past century in America — progressives of all stripes, of all political parties, I want to add, what have they given us? They've given us two world wars, quagmires in Korea and Vietnam, endless Middle East wars in Iraq, Afghanistan — Yemen maybe is coming soon, Iran, who knows? They imposed these enormous welfare schemes that Amity Shlaes has written so much about in the form of the New Deal and Great Society programs, which have ruined how many untold lives? They created all these alphabet soup federal agencies and departments to spy on us, tax us infinitely, regulate every aspect of our lives. And they built the military-industrial complex and the state media complex and the state education complex. They legislated violations of basic human property rights, which would absolutely shock our great-grandfathers if they were alive, all with the courts nodding along in their acquiescence. And to pay for it all, they gave us central banking — the Federal Reserve System hatched up, schemed right here on this island, in November of 1910. What do they, the Imposers, call this? They call it liberalism. If you oppose it, they call you a reactionary.

To be a libertarian today is to be a reactionary against the state degradations and depredations and impositions of the twentieth century. The political class, either the Imposers themselves or their agents, what has the political class gotten us? Well, they managed to ruin peace, they managed to ruin diplomacy, money, banking, education, medicine, not to mention, along the way, culture, civility, and goodwill. And if you oppose the Imposers and the elites, they call you a populist for it. So, call me a populist.

All of this, of course, flows from the Imposers, from their positive rights worldview which animates them. It animates everything they do and that's why they're able to scream at Rand Paul, for example, for denying them healthcare. Once you accept a positive rights view of the world, then anyone who doesn't go along with your program is taking from you, and this is how they see the world, the Imposers. If the twentieth century represents a triumph of liberalism, I'd hate to see illiberalism.

We all know what the Imposers have in store for us now in the fledgling twenty-first century. And I would add, as an aside, a good way to tell a Beltway person from a Rothbardian is to ask them the simple question of whether they consider the twentieth century in the West a triumph of liberalism or not. I think most Rothbardians would say it was not, and I think most Beltway types would say it was. They consider the twentieth century some sort of victory for liberalism.

So, what that got us, along with all of these other problems is, of course, a huge divide in society. What they've gotten us is an almost unbelievable and epic divide in society between the Imposers and the Imposed Upon. How divided are we and along what kind of lines?

This was a nice little vignette, which took place the other day on Twitter.

The Imposers and the Imposed Upon

We have Chris Hayes, from MSNBC, who says, Well, you know with Covid, "the most responsible way to deal with all these people" — that sounds like Seinfeld, "those people" — "if we survive this, is some kind of truth and reconciliation commission." Wow, that sounds fun. I suspect many of us in the room would be candidates for that. I don't know if there's boxcars outside. So he represents the progressive left in America today. And then along comes our friend from the neoconservative right, the great Bill Kristol, with whom we've all had enough but we always get more. I mean, this guy does not go away. He's like when you take the fish oil capsule at seven in the morning, and then at noon, that's Bill Kristol. So, he says, "How about truth and no reconciliation?"

The degree of open contempt and hatred that these lunatics have for us has in part been exposed by Trump and Trumpism. And to that extent we owe Trump a degree of gratitude for letting us see them for what they truly are. I would ask either one of these gentlemen: If you truly believe, let's say, 40 percent of the United States is beyond redemption, irredeemable, what does that mean? What do you propose doing with them? Does that mean some sort of reeducation camp? Presumably it means that either you separate from them somehow or you vanquish them, and by vanquish, that could be economically, politically, or, in the horrific scenario which we've seen repeated throughout history, even physically.

The divide we have in this country today is not so simple as saying blue and red states or counties, Republicans and Democrats, or liberals and conservatives, or even by class. It's a little more complicated than that. There's a company out there called Survey Monkey, which took in a lot of data after the 2016 election between Hillary Clinton and Donald Trump. There was a big *Washington Post* story using this, and they grouped it in a bunch of very interesting ways. I wonder how many people in this room were aware of some of these divides in American culture.

Sadly, there's a huge divide along racial lines in voting patterns. If only white people had voted in the 2016 election, Trump would have won forty-one states and if only nonwhite people had voted, Hillary Clinton would have won forty-seven states. I view this as basically a testament to the Democrat's ability to sell some kind of sick victimhood and dependency and to the Republican's failure to sell any sense of real ownership or opportunity or capitalism. But nonetheless, that's the divide. It's real.

How about union members? If only union member households — in other words, a household with at least one union member — had voted, Hillary Clinton would have won forty states. And if no union members, Donald Trump would have won thirty-seven.

When we get into religion, things get even more stark. What about households that claim that the inhabitants are either atheists or no particular religion? Hillary Clinton would have won at least forty-six states, if only nonreligious people had voted. How about if households which claim Protestant or Catholic membership would have been the sole voters? Trump would have won forty-five states. Evangelical voters only, Trump would have won forty-seven states. People who attend church weekly, Trump would have won forty-eight states. People who seldom or never attend church or synagogue, Hillary Clinton would have won forty-three states.

It strikes me as we go through some of these numbers that these divides are awfully hard to overcome politically. I'm not sure how you do that. How about unmarried people? Hillary Clinton would have won thirty-nine states if only unmarried people had voted. Trump would have won forty-three states if only married people had voted, another huge quiet cultural and political gap in this country.

You've heard a lot about urban versus rural voters; it's a motif which keeps coming up again and again. For purposes of the Survey Monkey data, an urban county is one with greater than 530 voters per square mile and a rural county is one with fewer than ninety voters per square mile. Again, only urban counties vote, Hillary Clinton wins forty states. Only rural voters vote, Donald Trump wins forty-seven states.

The last stat I'll throw out is gun-owning households. (I know that none of you own firearms, but there are people who do. They lock them up and just shoot deer with them. They don't have Uzis, or modified weapons… And I know there's no weapons in this room today; I feel comfortable with that statement.) If only gun-owning households voted, Donald Trump wins forty-nine states. Guess which one he loses? The only one he loses is Bernie Sanders's Vermont, because I think up there you just have a gun anyway just because you're in Vermont but you vote for Bernie. So, if households with no firearms of any kind were the sole voters in America, Hillary Clinton also wins forty-nine states and guess which one she loses? West Virginia, another anomaly.

The point here is that these kinds of divides and problems cannot be neatly solved by politics, especially national politics, and if you think about them, they don't cleave neatly along geographic lines. This isn't the Mason-Dixon line. These kinds of divides exist in every state, they exist within counties. If you go to California, which we all think of as a deep blue state, then go twenty miles inland. You know what it is? It's Trump flags, it's country music, and it's Mexican rancheros. That's what it is. We don't have the Mason-Dixon line in America in 2020. And more importantly, what we have to understand is: even if you could win some national election, if you could somehow get 51 percent of the voters to vote for a candidate like a Rand Paul, it doesn't really matter, because hearts and minds haven't changed. Politically vanquished people never really go away. This is what we have to understand; this is why we have to break up.

A couple of years ago, Bloomberg did some polling in the former Soviet

Union, now Russia. There are millions of Russians, especially elderly Russians, who still absolutely pine for the Soviet days when they knew what their job was, they didn't have to pay for their apartment, etc. Seventy percent of those people have overall a generally beneficial view about Stalin, in 2019. They view him as the great reformer who helped save their country from the Nazis, etc. In other words, despite all the historical examples that the twentieth century provided us, despite the fall and the collapse of the Soviet Union, despite all of the obvious benefits of capitalism, there is still a significant amount of nostalgia for the old system. Politically vanquished people don't just go away. And the Hillary Clinton people thought that the deplorables were going to do just that. They thought they were dying, they thought they were aging out, and they thought there were fewer of them than there were, and that's what happened in 2016 and that sent the entire country into basically some kind of psychosis, which we're still suffering under today.

I know the concept of decentralization is one that's obvious and clear to all of you. I know secession seems like a tough go, but I want to just throw out to you some happy facts, things that are happening slowly right under our noses, some very decentralist impulses which are at work. Of course, they have been absolutely intensified by the Covid issue and by these terrible riots which have been roiling across the United States this summer and now into the fall. As it turns out, all crises happen to be local. What do I mean by that?

One beautiful thing about Covid is that it has done further damage to our sort of credulousness when it comes to so-called authorities. Neither the UN nor the World Health Organization nor our own CDC has been able to project any sort of authority whatsoever amongst people. They have been able to [[[drive]]] no consensus. As a result, we've had vastly different approaches to Covid across international lines and even within our fifty states, and even within some areas within various cities.

No central authority was able to sort of seize it and boss everyone around and tell everyone what to do. Of course, outlets like the *New York Times* tried to do that, but that's just in the United States. It's been absolutely fascinating to watch how places like Singapore and Hong Kong and Sweden have been relatively open and places like the province in China where it happened were drastically locked down. Some places like San Francisco have been drastically locked down, so there've been different approaches in this decentralized effort. And none of this is because people woke up one day and said ideologically, "Wow, maybe we should try a more decentralized approach." No, it's just what naturally happens in crises.

Even the vaunted Schengen Area Agreement in Europe, which allows free travel between the member countries, immediately broke down. All of a sudden, a German is a German again and a Frenchman is a Frenchman, and you can't even drive across. I don't think that Americans can drive or fly into

Canada right now, even as we speak, with the liberal — supposedly liberal — Trudeau administration up there.

It turns out that when it comes to a crisis, things really get local very, very quickly. No matter who you are, even if you're Bill Gates and you can buy ten vacation houses and go to New Zealand on your yacht, you have to be somewhere physically; you have to exist in an analog world, and that means you need calories, you need kilowatts of energy and air conditioning coming into your home or your abode, you might need some healthcare or some prescription drugs, and all of this becomes unavoidable in a crisis. You have to be somewhere. Even Jeff Bezos had a bunch of protestors surrounding his house, his swanky house in D.C. Now I don't know if he happened to be there at the time, but the point is even Jeff Bezos could conceivably be contained in his home by a mob that you can't escape. This idea that we're now on this sort of new global happy plane is being sorely tested, I think, by Covid. I think that the idea of political globalism — the bad kind of globalism — is showing its strain. I think it's cracking very badly.

Let's talk about the great relocation that's happening in America, this incredible movement of people out of cities. What's the charm of a New York, a Manhattan, or a Chicago without the restaurants, and the theaters, and the food, and the museums? High rent, high crime, no fun? We find that a lot of younger people are starting to rethink things. I think this form of *de facto* secession away from these big cities, which tend to be very, very left-wing in orientation, is a wonderful development to see, because some of that political power that the big cities tend to hold is going to be attenuated. Atlanta tends to control Georgia; Nashville increasingly controls Tennessee. We see this in a lot of states. Las Vegas controls Nevada. But if people start to move away from these big cities, then some of that political power similarly is going to go with them.

This decentralist impulse is really the untold story of the twenty-first century: we see it in companies in the way they organize and manage their teams. Now we see all kinds of teleworking (which I think is a mixed bag, but nonetheless it's happening, one way or another). Look at distribution systems, what used to be the old hub-and-spoke model of getting your products, like the JCPenney catalogue, or how you got a sweater forty years ago. We're now looking at companies like Amazon that have a very decentralized system of spider webs. The distribution of goods and services is becoming radically decentralized.

How do we obtain information? It wasn't that long ago, thirty years or so, you had to go to your local mall and they might have Milton Friedman's *Free to Choose* or John Kenneth Galbraith's *Affluent Society*. They didn't have Rothbard. So, libraries and universities and professors were almost kind of like the new versions of monks. They were the literate ones, and you had to go to them to get information. But that's no longer the case. You have something in your pocket the size of a deck of cards that has basically all of human history on it. That's hugely decentralizing.

What we're seeing right now in the education revolution is just absolutely phenomenal. Even before Covid came along, we had Khan Academy and all kinds of new platforms springing up. We had the student loan debt crisis. We had parents questioning the value of sending their kids to school for $40,000 a year so that they can get a degree which doesn't get them a job and then, when they come home after those four years, they hate your guts. It turns out that that's not such a good value proposition.

Money and banking itself is becoming increasingly decentralized. We have all kinds of payment gateways now. We have systems like PayPal, we have bitcoin, and so really, it's just that top layer of banking that is happening at major banks.

All of these things are happy facts and we ought to be celebrating and thinking about them when we consider the political landscape.

I'm not so sure that what matters for our immediate future is whether Trump or Biden wins. We all know what Biden is and what he will do. We don't know what the hell Trump is or what he will do. That's what it means to be Trump. But nonetheless, I think some of these impulses which are happening are inexorable. I'm not sure that even a Kamala Harris or a Joe Biden can stop them. We ought to celebrate that.

What's interesting is that the one thing which still seems awfully centralized in our world is the political world. In other words, in all these other areas of life, all these things I've just been mentioning, decentralization is something that's happening naturally, it's happening by market force, it's happening inexorably, and it's happening by free choice of people. But the one area out of our lives where we still accept gross centralization, and all the inefficiencies it brings, is government.

Many things that used to be decided at the city level are now decided at the regional or the state level. Things that used to be decided at the state level, decided at the federal level — and then sometimes even at the international level. That's really the political story of the twentieth century, the centralization of politics at higher and higher levels, which is of course antidemocratic, even though all of these people are telling us about our sacred democracy. Every level of government that's further removed from you is attenuated by definition, is less democratic, because your input and your consent, so-called, is less and less meaningful. But I wonder if there aren't even some hopeful signs when it comes to politics and the decentralization of political power.

At an event last fall in Vienna, Austria, Hans-Hermann Hoppe was on a panel, and one thing that struck me about what he said was, if you look at the nationalist impulses of the nineteenth and twentieth centuries, the patchwork of former Europe came together — if you think of Germany as all these principalities and regions, and Bavaria and Prussia, these areas came together. He said nationalism in the nineteenth and twentieth century was mostly a centralizing impulse. That's what nationalism meant. When it becomes belligerent and spills over its borders, you get aggressive, you get Nazi Germany. But he said in the twenty-first century, from his perspective, nationalist movements tend to be decentralist. In other words, they're moving away from this sort of global government model which we all thought was going to be our future in the late twentieth century.

Hoppe says, if we look at things like the Brexit vote, if we look at what's happening in countries like Poland and Hungary, if we look at Catalonia — the Catalonian secession movement in Barcelona in the Catalonian region of Spain — these tend to be breakaway decentralist secessionist movements. That's the difference between some of the national movements of today versus yesteryear. And I think this is coming soon to a city near you in the United States.

This kind of talk is really becoming reality. Ryan McMaken, who is the editor of Mises.org, just wrote an article about how even the mainstream publications now are talking quite openly and seriously about secession, and I think that's because on some level, nervously, they still think Trump could win. I think that's what's driving it.

There have been very serious people on both left and right, not wild-eyed radicals like me, who have been talking about this for the last several years. Frank Buckley, a law professor at George Mason University — oh, we can't say that anymore, sorry; it's GMU. It turns out George Mason had a slave or two. Buckley wrote a very serious book about what secession might look like just a year ago. And this is a sober conservative guy. Similarly, Angelo Codevilla, who writes for the Claremont Institute, a retired political science professor at Boston University, wrote an article back in 2016 called "The Cold Civil War." You can find it at Claremont.org. Again, a very sober, serious conservative, the kind of guy who still uses the lexicon and things like *statecraft*; you know what I mean. And they're talking about this. Similarly, people at places on the left, at places like *The New Republic* and *The Nation*, are talking about this like never before. Gavin Newsom, governor of California, has applied the term nation-state to his own state.

What happens in the fall, in a month, if somehow, some way Trump manages to win this election — I don't know what that's going to look like. I think we are going to see, first of all, an outpouring of grief and psychosis and outright violence from a significant portion of the country that we're just not prepared for. But when that subsides, you're going to simply see blue state governors saying, "No, we're walking away." The sanctuary-city talk will become more and more pronounced, and I think that'll be a beautiful and helpful thing for this country.

Now, the flip side — and when I say who wins, I should say who's actually installed in January; we don't know anything about these ballots and postal delivery carriers dropping them in sewers or whatever it might be. But whoever wins — if Joe Biden and Kamala Harris are installed — I think what you're going to see is nothing short of a new Reconstruction in America. I think you are going to see outright and open attempts, gleeful attempts in the media class to impose themselves on the red states and punish them. Not only for having the audacity to put Donald Trump in the White House instead of Hillary Clinton — who we all knew was going to win — but more importantly on a more macro level, for coming along and interrupting that arc of history that progressives believe in so deeply; that we're always improving and that we're always getting better, the past is always bad and retrograde. To have that upended by Trump is a sin which they still haven't gotten over.

If Biden and Kamala Harris win, the sales tax deduction for state taxes will be immediately reintroduced so that those blue states can start deducting things again. I think you'll see it in myriad ways. You will see sort of an outpouring, a collective outpouring from the Left that wants to use the state as sort of a laser focus, you know, to bludgeon us, the rest of us. And that, in turn, will cause the red state folks and the red state voters to be thinking very seriously about an exit strategy. I wish I could give you something more hopeful than that, because as I mentioned before, the problem here is that nothing goes along neat geographic lines. But the lines are there nonetheless, and we can't ignore them.

I'll close with this: Tom Woods, our friend who spoke earlier, he reminds us political arrangements exist to serve us, not the other way around. Who the hell said that we have to put up with all of this? Can we change ours without bloodshed? That's the question of the twenty-first century. I think the question of the twentieth century was socialism versus property. I think the question of the twenty-first century is centralized versus decentralized. So, in post-persuasion America, where we seem to live, it's not just a matter of intellectual error. There's more to it than that. It's not just about convincing academics and journalists and politicians that our cause is right and you should agree with us. Because it's also about self-interest and power. They don't see for themselves a path to greater self-interest and a path to greater power in the kind of society which all of us in this room would prefer to live in, and they're not just going to let us have it without some effort on our part. And I hope very strongly that that path does not involve bloodshed.

There is reason for optimism: there is a decentralist impulse that is working its way across the world. It's coming to America, and I think that is where we have to put our hopes and our efforts.

48
Agorism (Quotes)

This chapter and the next are dedicated to considering what we should do once we acknowledge that the state is merely a criminal gang writ large. Here is a collection of quotes pertaining to Agorism, the attempt to subvert the state by means of black and gray markets to lessen the state's ability to impose its edicts.

Agorism can be defined simply: it is thought and action consistent with freedom... Agorism is the consistent integration of libertarian theory with counter-economic practice; an agorist is one who acts consistently for freedom and in freedom.
– Samuel Edward Konkin III, "An Agorist Primer" (2009, KoPubCo), pp. 12–13.

Counter-Economics is the study and practice of the human action in the Counter-Economy. The Counter-Economy is all human action not sanctioned by the State.

Just as Quantum Mechanics arose by theoretical chemists and physicists refusing to ignore the paradigm-breaking experiments, and Relativity arose from Einstein's acceptance of the Michelson Morley results, Counter-Economics arose as a theory by taking into account what all standard economics either ignored or downplayed. Just as light tunneled out of Hawking's black holes, human action tunneled under the control of the state. And this underground economy, black market, *nalevo* Russia turned out to be far, far too vast to ignore as a minor correction...

The Counter-Economic alternative gave the agorists a devastating weapon. Rather than slowly amass votes until some critical mass would allow state retreat (if the new statists did not change sides to protect their new vested interests), one could commit civil disobedience profitably, dodging taxes and regulations, having lower costs and (potentially) greater efficiency than one's statist competitors — if any. For many goods and services could only arise or be provided counter-economically.
– Samuel Edward Konkin III, "The Last, Whole Introduction to Agorism," *The Agorist Quarterly*, Fall 1995, Vol. 1, No. 1.

Whereas the LP & small government types couldn't even get an audit of the Fed passed, in 2008, Satoshi Nakamoto's White Paper [https://bitcoin.org/bitcoin.pdf] brought an end to the Fed's counterfeiting operation & currency controls in one, irreversible, fell swoop. Then in 2011, Ross Ulbricht combined Satoshi's work with J. Neil Schulman's agorist manifesto, *Alongside Night*, to give us the first truly free market mankind has ever known — a feat the unelectable, wannabe warlords from the Libertarian Party could only ever dream of accomplishing. A couple years later, in 2013, Cody Wilson did with his 3D printer what hundreds of millions of dollars in donations to "small government" politicians & gun-rights interest groups could never do: bring decisive & irreversible closure to the gun control debate.

Not to mention, in 2008, entrepreneurs successfully disintermediated the cartelized hotel industry when they created AirBNB. A year later the state was sent into a similar frenzy when other entrepreneurs did the same to the taxi cartels & founded Uber. And of course, lest we forget, during this same time, massive waves of non-compliance & civil disobedience forced western states to ease drug laws.

And we're not done.

Soon, privacy coins & decentralized exchanges will free us from the burden of taxation altogether. Agorists will fix the broken health care system using medical tokens. We will eliminate the SEC's cartel of brokers, FINRA, using tokenized securities & assets, unleashing a wave of capital and innovation unlike anything the world has ever seen.

– Sal Mayweather, "Against the LP," *New Libertarian*, Dec. 2020.

Abstract: A purely peer-to-peer version of electronic cash would allow online payments to be sent directly from one party to another without going through a financial institution. Digital signatures provide part of the solution, but the main benefits are lost if a trusted third party is still required to prevent double-spending. We propose a solution to the double-spending problem using a peer-to-peer network. The network timestamps transactions by hashing them into an ongoing chain of hash-based proof-of-work, forming a record that cannot be changed without redoing the proof-of-work. The longest chain not only serves as proof of the sequence of events witnessed, but proof that it came from the largest pool of CPU power. As long as a majority of CPU power is controlled by nodes that are not cooperating to attack the network, they'll generate the longest chain and outpace attackers. The network itself requires minimal structure. Messages are broadcast on a best effort basis, and nodes can leave and rejoin the network at will, accepting the longest proof-of-work chain as proof of what happened while they were gone.

– Satoshi Nakamoto,
"Bitcoin: A Peer-to-Peer Electronic Cash System" (Oct. 2008).

Only the agorist truly recognizes that no grant of authority was ever given. He, and not the sheriff, determine the extent to which the State intrudes on his life. If he finds such intrusion to be tolerable, he tolerates it. If not, he disregards their imposition. The agorist confidently answers to a higher, natural law — one that empowers the self, and not the parasite.

Finally, when enough resources are relegated to the counter-economy, private defense agencies will arise from the market like a phoenix. These PDAs will not only quickly outcompete the State's "police," but will be tasked with defending private property *from* the State. In time, they will do exactly that, thus defenestrating the political class & liberating man from the tyranny of government.

The key to this story is understanding that liberation from the State only comes *after* and *through* individual, self-liberation. Freedom is something inherent within all of us. It's not something one can "take" or "be given," rather it must be recognized, claimed, nourished & guarded with fervent jealousy.

– Sal Mayweather, author of "Anti-Politics: A Collection of Agorist Essays."

So, this is an exciting time for Bitcoin isn't it? When I first learned about it, it was trading for 6 cents or so. It's incredible to see something increase 300,000 fold in value... wow!... Let us stay grounded in the principles that Bitcoin was incubated in: decentralization, a focus on empowering individuals, and a community of love and respect.

– Ross Ulbricht,
"Letter from Ross to the Bitcoin Superconference" (Feb. 2018).

49
What Must Be Done (Excerpt)

Hans-Hermann Hoppe, Ph.D.

Hans-Hermann Hoppe is an Austrian School economist, a libertarian and anarcho-capitalist philosopher, and Professor Emeritus of Economics at the University of Nevada, Las Vegas.

Strategy: Stopping the Statist Disease

How can the State and the statist disease be stopped? Now I will come to my strategic considerations. First off, three fundamental insights or guiding principles must be recognized. First: that the protection of private property and of law, justice, and law enforcement, is essential to any human society. But there is no reason whatsoever why this task must be taken on by one single agency, by a monopolist. As a matter of fact, it is precisely the case that as soon as you have a monopolist taking on this task, he will with necessity destroy justice and render us defenseless against foreign as well as domestic invaders and aggressors.

It is then one's ultimate goal which one has to keep in mind is the demonopolization of protection and justice. Protection, security, defense, law, order, and arbitration in conflicts can and must be supplied competitively — that is, entry into the field of being a judge must be free.

Second, because a monopoly of protection is the root of all evil, any territorial expansion of such a monopoly is *per se* evil too. Every political centralization must be on principle grounds rejected. In turn, every attempt at political decentralization — segregation, separation, secession and so forth — must be supported.

The third basic insight is that a democratic protection monopoly in particular must be rejected as a moral and economic perversity. Majority rule and private property protection are incompatible. The idea of democracy must be ridiculed: it is nothing else but mob rule parading as justice. To be labeled a democrat must be considered the worst of all possible compliments! This does not mean that one may not participate in democratic policies; I will come to that a little bit later.

But one must use democratic means only for defensive purposes; that is, one may use an anti-democratic platform to be elected by an anti-democratic constituency to implement anti-democratic — that is, anti-egalitarian and pro-private property — policies. Or, to put it differently, a person is not honorable because he is democratically elected. If anything, this makes him a suspect. Despite the fact that a person has been elected democratically, he may still be a decent and honorable man; we have heard one before.

From these principles we now come to the problem of application. The basic insights — that is: monopolized protection, a State, will inevitably become an aggressor and lead to defenselessness; and political centralization and democracy are means of extensifying and intensifying exploitation and aggression — while these basic insights give us a general direction in the goal, they are obviously not yet sufficient to define our actions and tell us how to get there.

How can the goal of demonopolized protection and justice possibly be implemented given the present circumstances of centralized — almost world democracy — as at least temporarily our starting point from which we have to begin. Let me try to develop an answer to this question by elaborating first in what respect the problem, and also the solution to it, has changed in the course of the last 150 years — that is, since around the middle of the 19th century.

Top-Down Reform: Converting the King

The problem up to 1914 was comparatively small and the possible solution was comparatively easy then; and today as we will see, matters are more difficult and the solution is far more complicated. By mid-19th century, in Europe as well as in the United States, not only was the degree of political centralization far less pronounced than it is now; the Southern War of Independence had not yet taken place, and neither Germany nor Italy existed as unified States.

But in particular, the age of mass democracy had hardly begun at this time. In Europe, after the defeat of Napoleon, countries were still ruled by kings and princes, and elections and parliaments played small roles and were in addition restricted to extremely small numbers of major property owners. Similarly, in the United States, government was run by small aristocratic elites, and the vote was restricted by severe property requirements. After all, only those people who have something to be protected should be running those agencies that do the protection.

One hundred and fifty or even 100 years ago, only the following thing was essentially necessary in order to solve the problem. It would have been necessary only to force the king to declare that from now on, every citizen would be free to choose his own protector, and pledge allegiance to any government that he wanted. That is, the king would no longer presume to be anyone's protector, unless this person had asked him, and met his prize that the king would have asked for such service.

Now what would have happened in this case? What would have

What Must Be Done (Excerpt)

happened, let's say, if the Austrian emperor had made such a declaration in 1900? Let me try to give a brief sketch or scenario of what I think would likely have happened in this situation.

First, everyone, upon this declaration, would have regained his unrestricted right to self-defense, and would have been free to decide if he wanted more or better protection than that afforded by self-defense, and if so, where and from whom to secure this protection. Most people in this situation undoubtedly would have chosen to take advantage of the division of labor, and rely, in addition to self-defense, also on specialized protectors.

Second, on the lookout for protectors, almost everyone would have looked to persons or agencies who own or are able to acquire the means to assure the task of protection — that is, who have themselves a stake in the to-be protected territory in the form of substantial property holdings — and who possess an established reputation as reliable, prudent, honorable, and just.

It is safe to say that no one would have considered an elected parliament up to this task. Instead, almost everyone would have turned for help to one or more of three places: either the king himself, who is now no longer a monopolist; or a regional or local noble, magnate, or aristocrat; or a regional, national, or even international operating insurance company.

Obviously, the king himself would fulfill these requirements that I just mentioned, and many people would have voluntarily chosen him as their protector. At the same time, however, many people also would have seceded from the king; of these, a large proportion would have likely turned to various regional nobles or magnates, who are now natural instead of hereditary nobility. And on a smaller territorial scale these local nobles would be able to offer the same advantages as protectors as the king himself would be able to offer. And this shift to regional protectors would bring about a significant decentralization in the organization and structure of the security industry. And this decentralization would only be reflective of, and in accordance with, private or subjective protection interests — that is, the centralization tendency that I mentioned before has also led to an overcentralization of the protection business.

Lastly, nearly everyone else, especially in the cities, would have turned for protection to commercial insurance companies, such as fire insurers. Insurance and private property protection are obviously very closely related matters. Better protection leads to lower insurance payoffs. And by insurers entering the protection market, quickly protection contracts, rather than unspecified promises, would have become the standard product form in which protection would have been offered.

Further, by virtue of the nature of insurance, the competition and cooperation between various protection insurers would promote the development of universal rules of procedure, evidence, conflict resolution, and arbitration. As well, it would promote the simultaneous homogenization and dehomogenization of the population into various classes of individuals with different group risks regarding their property protection, and accordingly, different protection insurance premiums. All systematic and predictable income and wealth redistribution between different groups within the population as it existed under monopolistic conditions would be immediately eliminated. And this would of course make for peace.

Most importantly, the nature of protection and defense would have been fundamentally altered. Under monopolistic conditions, there is only one protector; whether it is monarchical or democratic makes no difference in this respect, a government is invariably conceived of as defending and protecting a fixed and contiguous territory. Yet this feature is the outcome of a compulsory protection monopoly. With the abolition of a monopoly, this feature would immediately disappear as highly unnatural or even artificial. There might have been a few local protectors who defended just one contiguous territory. But there would have also been other protectors, such as the king or insurance agencies, whose protection territory consisted of widespread patchworks of discontiguous bits and pieces and stretches. And the "borders" of every government would be in constant flux. In cities in particular, it would not be more unusual for two neighbors to have different protection agencies, than it is to have different fire insurers.

This patchwork structure of protection and defense improves protection. Monopolistic, contiguous defense presumes that the security interests of the entire population living in a given territory are somehow homogeneous. That is, that all people in a given territory have the same sort of defense interests. But this is a highly unrealistic and actually untrue assumption. Actually, peoples' security needs are highly heterogeneous. People may just own property in one location, or numerous territorially widely dispersed locations, or they may be largely self-sufficient, or only dependent on a very few people in their economic dealings; or on the other hand, they may be deeply integrated into the market and dependent economically on thousands and thousands of people strewn out over large territories.

The patchwork structure of the security industry would merely reflect this reality of highly diversified security needs that exist for various people. As well, this structure would in turn stimulate the development of a corresponding protective weaponry. Rather than producing and developing weapons and instruments of large-scale bombing, instruments would be developed for protecting small-scale territories without collateral damage.

In addition, because all interregional redistribution of income and wealth would be eliminated in a competitive system, the patchwork structure would also offer the best assurance of interterritorial peace. The likelihood and the extent of interterritorial conflict would be reduced if there are patchworks. And because every foreign invader, so to speak, would almost instantly, even

What Must Be Done (Excerpt)

if he invaded only a small piece of land, run into the opposition and military and economic counterattacks by several independent protecting agencies, likewise the danger of foreign invasions would be reduced.

Indirectly, it is already clear at least partially how and why it has become so much more difficult to reach this solution in the course of the last 150 years. Let me point out some of the fundamental changes that have occurred which make all of these problems far bigger. First, it is no longer possible to carry out the reforms from the top-down. Classical liberals, during the old monarchical days, could and did in fact frequently think and could actually realistically believe in simply converting the king to their view, and ask him to abdicate his power, and everything else would have almost automatically fallen into place.

Today, the State's protection monopoly is considered public instead of private property, and government rule is no longer tied to any particular individual, but to specified functions, exercised by unnamed or anonymous individuals as members of a democratic government. Hence, the one or few men conversion strategy does no longer work. It doesn't matter if one converts a few top government officials — the president and a handful of senators — because, within the rules of democratic government, no single individual has the personal power of abdicating the government's monopoly of protection. Kings had this power; presidents don't.

The president can only resign from his position, only to be taken over by someone else. But he cannot dissolve the government protection monopoly, because supposedly the people own the government, and not the president himself. Under democratic rule then, the abolition of the government's monopoly of justice and protection requires either that a majority of the public and of their elected representatives would have to declare the government's protection monopoly and accordingly all compulsory taxes abolished, or even more restrictive, that literally no one would vote and the voter turnout would be zero. Only in this case could the democratic protection monopoly be said to be effectively abolished. But this would essentially mean that it was impossible to ever rid ourselves of an economic and moral perversion. Because nowadays it is a given that everyone, including the mob, does participate in politics, and it is inconceivable, that the mob should ever, in its majority or even in its entirety, should renounce or abstain from exercising its right to vote, which is nothing else than exercising the opportunity to loot the property of others.

Moreover, even if one assumes against all odds that this was achieved, the problems do not end. Because another fundamental sociological truth in the age of modern egalitarian mass democracy is the almost complete destruction of natural elites. The king could abdicate his monopoly and the security needs of the public still would have been almost automatically taken care of because there existed for mostly the king himself, and also regional and local nobles and major entrepreneurial personalities, a clearly visible and established natural, voluntarily acknowledged elite and a multilayered structure of hierarchies, and rank orders to which people could turn with their desire to be protected.

The Disappearance of Natural Elites

Today, after less than one century of mass democracy, there exists no such natural elites and social hierarchies to which one could immediately turn for protection. Natural elites and hierarchical social orders and organizations, that is people and institutions commanding an authority and respect independent of the State, are even more intolerable and unacceptable to a democrat and more incompatible with the democratic spirit of egalitarianism than they were a threat to any king or to any prince. And because of that, under the democratic rules of the game, all independent authorities, all independent institutions have been systematically wiped or diminished through economic measures to insignificance. Today, no one person or institution outside of government itself possesses genuine national or even regional authority. Rather than people of independent authority we now merely have an abundance of people who are prominent: sports and movie stars, pop stars, and of course, politicians. But these people, while they may be able to set trends and shape fashions, do not possess any such thing as natural personal social authority.

This is true in particular of politicians: they may be great stars now, every day they are on TV and the subject of public debate, but this is almost entirely due to the fact that they are a part of the current State apparatus with its monopolistic powers. Once this monopoly was dissolved, these "stars" of politics would become non-entities, because in real life they are mostly nothing, hacks, and half-wits. And only democracy allows them to rise to these elevated positions. Left to their own devices, left to their own personal achievements, they are, with almost no exception, complete nobodies. Put bluntly, once the democratic government — Congress — had declared that from now on everyone would be free to choose his own judge and protector, such that he still can but no longer must choose the government for protection, who in his right mind would ever choose them?! That is, the current members of Congress and the federal government: who would choose them voluntarily as their judge and protector?! To raise this question is to answer it. Kings and princes possessed real authority; there was coercion involved, no question whatsoever, but they received a significant amount of voluntary support.

In contrast, democratic politicians are generally held in contempt, even by their own mob constituency. But then there is also no one else to whom one might turn for protection. Local and regional politicians are basically posing the same sort of problem, and with the abolition of their monopoly powers, they obviously do not offer an attractive alternative to this problem either. Nor are there any great entrepreneurial personalities standing in the wings, and insurance companies in particular, have become almost entirely creatures of the egalitarian democratic state, and thus appear as little trustworthy as anybody else to take over this particularly important task of protection and justice.

Thus, if one did today what the king could have done a hundred years ago, there would be the immediate danger of having in fact social chaos, or of "anarchy" in the bad sense. People would indeed at least temporarily become highly vulnerable and defenseless. So then the question becomes: is there no way out? Let me sum up the answer in advance: Yes, but rather than by means of the top-down reform, one's strategy must now be that of a bottom-up revolution. And instead of one battle, on a single front, a liberal-libertarian revolution now will have to involve many battles on many fronts. That is, we want guerrilla warfare rather than conventional warfare.

The Role of Intellectuals

Before explaining this answer as another step in the direction of this goal, a second sociological fact has to be recognized: the change of the role of intellectuals, of education, and of ideology. As soon as the protection agency becomes a territorial monopolist — that is, a State — it is turned from a genuine protector into a protection racket. And in light of resistance on the part of the victims of this protection racket, a State is in need of legitimacy, of intellectual justification for what it does. The more the State turns from a protector to a protection racket — that is, with every additional increase in taxes and regulation — the greater does this need for legitimacy become.

In order to assure correct statist thinking, a protection monopolist will employ its privileged position as the protection racket to quickly establish an education monopoly. Even during the 19th century under decidedly undemocratic monarchical conditions, education, at least on the level of elementary schooling and university education, was already largely monopolistically organized and compulsorily funded. And it was largely from the ranks of the royal government teachers and professors, that is, those people who had been employed as intellectual bodyguards of kings and princes, from where the monarchical rule and the privileges of kings and nobles was ideologically undermined and instead egalitarian ideas were promoted, in the form of democracy and socialism.

This was with good reason from the point of view of the intellectuals. Because democracy and socialism in fact multiply the number of educators and intellectuals, and this expansion of the system of government public education in turn has led to an ever greater flood of intellectual waste and pollution. The price of education, as the price of protection and justice, has gone up dramatically under monopolistic administration, all the while the quality of education, just as the quality of justice, has continuously declined. Today, we are as unprotected as we are uneducated.

Without the continued existence of the democratic system and of publicly funded education and research, however, most current teachers and intellectuals would be unemployed or their income would fall to a small fraction of its present level. Instead of researching the syntax of Ebonics, the love life of mosquitoes, or the relationship between poverty and crime for $100 grand a year, they would research the science of potato growing or the technology of gas pump operation for $20 grand.

The monopolized education system is by now as much of a problem as the monopolized protection and justice system. In fact, government education and research and development is the central instrument by which the State protects itself from public resistance. Today, intellectuals are as important or even more so, from the point of view of the government, for the preservation of the status quo, than are judges, policemen, and soldiers.

And just as one cannot convert the democratic system from the political top-down, so it also cannot be expected that this conversion will come down from within the established system of public education and public universities. This system cannot be reformed. It is impossible for liberal-libertarians to infiltrate and take over the public education system, as the democrats and socialists could when they replaced the monarchists.

From the point of view of classical liberalism, the entire system of publicly, or tax-funded education must go, root and branch. And with this conviction, it is obviously impossible for anyone to make a career within these conditions. I will not ever be able to become the president of the university. My views bar me from making a career like this. Now this is not to say that education and intellectuals do not play a role in bringing about a libertarian revolution. To the contrary, as I explained before, everything hinges ultimately on the question of whether or not we will succeed in delegitimizing and exposing as an economic and moral perversity, democracy and the democratic monopoly of justice and protection.

This is obviously nothing but an ideological battle. But it would be wrongheaded to assume that official academia will be of any help in this endeavor. On the government dole, educators and intellectuals will tend to be statists. Intellectual ammunition and ideological direction and coordination can only come from outside of established academia, from centers of intellectual resistance — from an intellectual counterculture outside and independent of, and in fundamental opposition to the government monopoly of protection as well as of education, such as the Mises Institute.

A Bottom-Up Revolution

At last to the detailed explanation of the meaning of this bottom-up revolutionary strategy. For this, let me turn to my earlier remarks about the defensive use of democracy, that is, the use of democratic means for non-democratic, libertarian pro-private property ends. Two preliminary insights I have already reached here.

First, from the impossibility of a top-down strategy, it follows that one should expend little or no energy, time, and money on nationwide political contests, such as presidential elections. And also not on contests for central government, in particular, less effort on senatorial races than on house races, for instance.

Second, from the insight into the role of intellectuals, in the preservation of the current system, the current protection racket, it follows that one should likewise expend little or no energy, time, or money trying to reform education and academia from the inside. By endowing free enterprise or private property chairs within the established university system, for instance, one only helps to lend legitimacy to the very idea that one wishes to oppose. The official education and research institutions must be systematically defunded and dried up. And to do so all support of intellectual work, as an essential task of this overall task in front of us, should of course be given to institutions and centers determined to do precisely this.

The reasons for both of these pieces of advice are straightforward: Neither the population as a whole nor all educators and intellectuals in particular are ideologically completely homogeneous. And even if it is impossible to win a majority for a decidedly anti-democratic platform on a nationwide scale, there appears to be no insurmountable difficulty in winning such a majority in sufficiently small districts, and for local or regional functions within the overall democratic government structure. In fact, there seems to be nothing unrealistic in assuming that such majorities exist at thousands of locations. That is, locations dispersed all over the country but not evenly dispersed. Likewise, even though the intellectual class must be by and large regarded as natural enemies of justice and protection, there exists at various locations isolated anti-intellectual intellectuals, and as the Mises Institute proves, it is very well possible to assemble these isolated figures around an intellectual center, and give them unity and strength, and a national or even an international audience.

But what then? Everything else falls almost automatically from the ultimate goal, which must be kept permanently in mind, in all of one's activities: the restoration from the bottom-up of private property and the right to property protection; the right to self-defense, to exclude or include, and to freedom of contract. And the answer can be broken down into two parts.

First, what to do within these very small districts, where a pro-private property candidate and anti-majoritarian personality can win. And second, how to deal with the higher levels of government, and especially with the central federal government. First, as an initial step, and I'm referring now to what should be done on the local level, the first central plank of one's platform should be: one must attempt to restrict the right to vote on local taxes, in particular on property taxes and regulations, to property and real estate owners. Only property owners must be permitted to vote, and their vote is not equal, but in accordance with the value of the equity owned, and the amount of taxes paid. That is, similar to what Lew Rockwell already explained has happened in some places in California.

Further, all public employees — teachers, judges, policemen — and all welfare recipients, must be excluded from voting on local taxes and local regulation matters. These people are being paid out of taxes and should have no say whatsoever how high these taxes are. With this platform one cannot of course win everywhere; you cannot win in Washington, D.C. with a platform like this, but I dare say that in many locations this can be easily done. The locations have to be small enough and have to have a good number of decent people.

Consequently, local taxes and rates as well as local tax revenue will inevitably decrease. Property values and most local incomes would increase whereas the number and payment of public employees would fall. Now, and this is the most decisive step, the following thing must be done, and always keep in mind that I am talking about very small territorial districts, villages.

In this government funding crisis which breaks out once the right to vote has been taken away from the mob, as a way out of this crisis, all local government assets must be privatized. An inventory of all public buildings, and on the local level that is not that much — schools, fire houses, police stations, courthouses, roads, and so forth — and then property shares or stock should be distributed to the local private property owners in accordance with the total lifetime amount of taxes — property taxes — that these people have paid. After all, it is theirs, they paid for these things.

These shares should be freely tradeable, sold and bought, and with this local government would essentially be abolished. If it were not for the continued existence of higher superior levels of government, this village or city would now be a free or liberated territory. What would consequently happen to education and more importantly, what would happen to property protection and justice?

On the small local level, we can be as certain, or even more so than we could have been 100 years ago about what would have happened if the king abdicated, that what would happen is roughly this: all material resources that were previously devoted to these functions — schools, police stations, courthouses — still exist, and so does the manpower. The only difference is that they are now privately owned, or temporarily unemployed in the case of public employees. Under the realistic assumption that there continues to be a local demand for education and protection and justice, the schools, police stations, and courthouses will be still used for the very same purposes. And many former teachers, policemen, and judges would be rehired or resume their former position on their own account as self-employed individuals, except that they would be operated or employed by local "bigshots" or elites who own these things, all of whom are personally known figures. Either as for-profit enterprises, or as, and what seems to be more likely, some mixture of charitable and economic organization. Local "bigshots" frequently provide public goods out of their own private pocket; and they obviously have the greatest interest in the preservation of local justice and peace.

And this is all easy enough to see to work for schools and policemen, but what about judges and justice? Recall that the root of all evil is compulsory monopolization of justice, that is one person says this is right. Accordingly judges must be freely financed, and free entry into judgeship positions must be assured. Judges are not elected by vote, but chosen by the effective demand of justice seekers. Also don't forget that on the small local level under consideration, one is talking actually about a demand for one or very few judges only. Whether this or these judges are then employed by the private courthouse association or stock company, or are self-employed individuals who rent these facilities or offices, it should be clear that only a handful of local people, and only widely known and respected local personalities — that is, members of the natural local elite — would have any chance whatsoever of being so selected as judges of local peace.

Only as members of the natural elite will their decision possess any authority and become enforceable. And if they come up with judgments that are considered to be ridiculous, they will be immediately displaced by other local authorities that are more respectable. If you proceed along these lines on the local level, of course, it cannot be avoided that one will come into direct conflict with the upper and especially the federal level of government power. How to deal with this problem? Wouldn't the *federales* simply crush any such attempt?

They would surely like to, but whether or not they can actually do so is an entirely different question, and to recognize this, it is only necessary to recognize that the members of the governmental apparatus always represent, even under conditions of democracy, merely a tiny proportion of the total population. And even smaller is the proportion of central government employees.

This implies that a central government cannot possibly enforce its legislative will, or perverted law, upon the entire population unless it finds widespread local support and cooperation in doing so. This becomes particularly obvious if one imagines a large number of free cities or villages as I described them before. It is practically impossible, manpower-wise, as well as from a public relations standpoint, to take over thousands of territorially widely dispersed localities and impose direct federal rule on them.

Without local enforcement, by compliant local authorities, the will of the central government is not much more than hot air. Yet this local support and cooperation is precisely what needs to be missing. To be sure, so long as the number of liberated communities is still small, matters seem to be somewhat dangerous. However, even during this initial phase in the liberation struggle, one can be quite confident.

It would appear to be prudent during this phase to avoid a direct confrontation with the central government and not openly denounce its authority or even abjure the realm. Rather, it seems advisable to engage in a policy of passive resistance and non-cooperation. One simply stops to help in the enforcement in each and every federal law. One assumes the following attitude: "Such are your rules, and you enforce them. I cannot hinder you, but I will not help you either, as my only obligation is to my local constituents."

Consistently applied, no cooperation, no assistance whatsoever on any level, the central government's power would be severely diminished or even evaporate. And in light of the general public opinion, it would appear highly unlikely that the federal government would dare to occupy a territory whose inhabitants did nothing else than trying to mind their own business. Waco, a tiny group of freaks, is one thing. But to occupy, or to wipe out a significantly large group of normal, accomplished, upstanding citizens is quite another, and quite a more difficult thing.

Once the number of implicitly seceded territories has reached a critical mass, and every success in one little location promotes and feeds on the next one, it will become inevitably further radicalized to a nationwide municipalization movement, with explicitly secessionist local policies and openly and contemptuously displayed non-compliance with federal authority.

And it is in this situation then, when the central government will be forced to abdicate its protection monopoly and the relationship between the local authorities that reemerge and the central authorities, who are about to lose their power, can be put on a purely contractual level, and one might regain the power to defend one's own property again.

50
Quotes

In lieu of a "Further Reading" list, the following is a collection of my favorite quotes on the subjects of voluntaryism and economics, from authors whose works would have been included in such a list.

Taxes are... at no level of taxation consistent with individual freedom and property rights. Taxes are theft. The thieves — the state and its agents and allies — try their very best to conceal this fact, of course, but there is simply no way around it. Obviously, taxes are not normal, voluntary payments for goods and services, because you are not allowed to stop such payments if you are not satisfied with the product. You are not punished if you no longer buy Renault cars or Chanel perfume, but you are thrown into jail if you stop paying for government schools or universities or for Mr. Sarkozy and his pomp. Nor is it possible to construe taxes as normal rent-payments, as they are made by a renter to his landlord... because the French state is not the landlord of all of France and all Frenchmen. To be the landlord, the French state would have to be able to prove two things: first, that the state, and no one else, owns every inch of France, and second, that it has a rental contract with every single Frenchman concerning the use, and the price for this use, of its property. No state — not the French, not the German, not the U.S.-American or any other state — can prove this. They have no documents to this effect and they cannot present any rental contract. Thus, there is only one conclusion: taxation is theft and robbery by which one segment of the population, the ruling class, enriches itself at the expense of another, the ruled.

– Hans-Hermann Hoppe, Ph.D., The Great Fiction
(2021, Mises Institute), p. 519.

For a minority cannot lastingly rule a majority solely by brute force. It must rule by "opinion." The majority of the population must be brought to *voluntarily* accept your rule. This is not to say that the majority must agree with every one of your measures. Indeed, it may well believe that many of your policies are mistaken. However, it must believe in the legitimacy of the institution of the state *as such*, and hence that even if a particular policy may be wrong, such a mistake is an "accident" that one must tolerate in view of some greater good provided by the state.

Quotes

– Hans-Hermann Hoppe, Ph.D., *The Great Fiction*
(2021, Mises Institute), p. 4.

As widespread as the standard view regarding the necessity of the institution of a state as the provider of law and order is, it stands in clear contradiction to elementary economic and moral laws and principles.

First of all, among economists and philosophers two near-universally accepted propositions exist:

1. Every "monopoly" is "bad" from the viewpoint of consumers. Monopoly is here understood in its classic meaning as an exclusive *privilege* granted to a single producer of a commodity or service, or as the absence of "free entry" into a particular line of production. Only one agency, A, may produce a given good or service, X. Such a monopoly is "bad" for consumers, because, shielded from potential new entrants into a given area of production, the price of the product will be higher and its quality lower than otherwise, under free competition.

2. The production of law and order, *i.e.*, of security, is the primary function of the state (as just defined). Security is here understood in the wide sense adopted in the American Declaration of Independence: as the protection of life, property, and the pursuit of happiness from domestic violence (crime) as well as external (foreign) aggression (war).

– Hans-Hermann Hoppe, Ph.D., *The Great Fiction*
(2021, Mises Institute), p. 190.

It was to a large extent the inflated price of justice and the perversions of ancient law by the kings which motivated the historical opposition to monarchy. However, confusion as to the causes of this phenomenon prevailed. There were those who recognized correctly that the problem lay with *monopoly*, not with elites or nobility. But they were far outnumbered by those who erroneously blamed it on the elitist character of the rulers instead, and who accordingly strove to maintain the monopoly of law and law enforcement and merely replace the king and the visible royal pomp by the "people" and the presumed modesty and decency of the "common man." Hence the historic success of democracy.

– Hans-Hermann Hoppe, Ph.D., *Democracy: The God That Failed*
(2001 [2017] Routledge), p. 72.

Once the premise of government is accepted, liberals are left without argument when socialists pursue this premise to its logical end. If monopoly is just, then centralization is just. If taxation is just, then more taxation is also just. And if democratic equality is just, then the expropriation of private property owners is just, too (while private property is not). Indeed, what can a liberal say in favor of *less* taxation and redistribution?...

Without moral argument at his disposal, a liberal is left only with the tool of cost-benefit analysis, but any such analysis must involve an interpersonal comparison of utility, and such a comparison is impossible (scientifically impermissible)...

Liberals will have to recognize that no government can be contractually justified...

Private property anarchism is simply consistent liberalism; liberalism thought through to its ultimate conclusion, or liberalism restored to its original intent.

– Hans-Hermann Hoppe, Ph.D., *Democracy: The God That Failed* (2001 [2017] Routledge), pp. 234–236.

...[W]e human beings, as social animals, need individual freedom to fully flourish. The equation is simple: individual freedom = social cooperation = individual and social flourishing. Many corollaries follow. To pick one, the freedom to choose with whom we will cooperate entails competition among those who wish to cooperate with any given individual.

– Sheldon Richman, *What Social Animals Owe to Each Other* (2020, Libertarian Institute).

When you see that trading is done, not by consent, but by compulsion — when you see that in order to produce, you need to obtain permission from men who produce nothing — when you see that money is flowing to those who deal, not in goods, but in favors — when you see that men get richer by graft and by pull than by work, and your laws don't protect you against them, but protect them against you — when you see corruption being rewarded and honesty becoming a self-sacrifice — you may know that your society is doomed.

– Ayn Rand, *Atlas Shrugged* (1957, Random House), p. 413.

Anyone who initiates the use of force against another human being is in that moment, acting like a dictator.

– Ayn Rand, on "The Phil Donahue Show."

Capitalism has been called a system of greed — yet it is the system that raised the standard of living of its poorest citizens to heights no collectivist system has ever begun to equal, and no tribal gang can conceive of.

– Ayn Rand, "Global Balkanization," from a lecture given at Boston's Ford Hall Forum, Apr. 1977.

When I say "capitalism," I mean a full, pure, uncontrolled, unregulated laissez-faire capitalism — with a separation of state and economics, in the same way and for the same reasons as the separation of state and church.

– Ayn Rand, "The Objectivist Ethics,"

from a lecture given at the University of Wisconsin, Feb. 1961.

America's abundance was not created by public sacrifices to "the common good," but by the productive genius of free men who pursued their own personal interests and the making of their own private fortunes. They did not starve the people to pay for America's industrialization. They gave the people better jobs, higher wages, and cheaper goods with every new machine they invented, with every scientific discovery or technological advance — and thus the whole country was moving forward and profiting, not suffering, every step of the way.

– Ayn Rand, "What Is Capitalism?"
in *Capitalism: The Unknown Ideal* (1966, New American Library), p. 29.

The smallest minority on earth is the individual. Those who deny individual rights, cannot claim to be defenders of minorities.

– Ayn Rand, "America's Persecuted Minority: Big Business,"
in *Capitalism: The Unknown Ideal* (1966, New American Library), p. 61.

A businessman cannot force you to buy his product; if he makes a mistake, he suffers the consequences; if he fails, he takes the loss. A bureaucrat forces you to obey his decisions, whether you agree with him or not — and the more advanced the stage of a country's statism, the wider and more discretionary the powers wielded by a bureaucrat. If he makes a mistake, you suffer the consequences; if he fails, he passes the loss on to you, in the form of heavier taxes.

– Ayn Rand, "From My 'Future File,'"
in *The Ayn Rand Lexicon* (1988, Penguin).

Free trade in labor, like trade in goods and services, frees existing Americans to do what's in their comparative advantage. In fact, the basic economic case for free trade in labor really isn't different than that for trade in goods and services. Economists are in nearly universal agreement that free trade promotes national wealth.

– Benjamin Powell, Ph.D., "An Economic Case for Immigration,"
EconLib, June 2010.

The libertarian insists that whether or not such practices are supported by the majority of the population is not germane to their nature: that, regardless of popular sanction, War is Mass Murder, Conscription is Slavery, and Taxation is Robbery.

– Murray N. Rothbard, Ph.D., *For a New Liberty*
(1973 [2006], Mises Institute), p. 29.

The rapid economic advance that we have come to expect seems in a large measure to be the result of this inequality and to be impossible without it. Progress at such a fast rate cannot proceed on a uniform front but must take place in echelon fashion...

At any stage of this process there will always be many things we already know how to produce but which are still too expensive to provide for more than a few...

All the conveniences of a comfortable home, of our means of transportation and communication, of entertainment and enjoyment, we could produce at first only in limited quantities; but it was in doing this that we gradually learned to make them or similar things at a much smaller outlay of resources and thus became able to supply them to the great majority. A large part of the expenditure of the rich, though not intended for that end, thus serves to defray the cost of the experimentation with the new things that, as a result, can later be made available to the poor.

– Friedrich A. Hayek, Ph.D., *The Constitution of Liberty* (1978 [2011], University of Chicago Press), pp. 96–97.

In order for the state to function, the mass of the people has to believe in its legitimacy. To that end, the state employs a class of professional apologists and controls the means of propaganda, often through dominance of the education system. The task of the State apologist is "...to convince the public that what the State does is not... crime on a gigantic scale, but something necessary and vital that must be supported and obeyed." In return for their services, the apologists are rewarded with power and status and allowed to share in the booty obtained from the masses.

– Gerard Casey, Ph.D., *Libertarian Anarchy: Against the State* (2012, Continuum International Publishing Group), p. 27.

If all human beings are intrinsically power-hungry and savage, how can we solve our problems by giving ultimate law-making and law-enforcing authority to one particular group of such appalling animals?... The libertarian anarchist contention is not that under anarchy things would be perfect, but that they would be better than they now are.

– Gerard Casey, Ph.D., *Libertarian Anarchy: Against the State* (2012, Continuum International Publishing Group), pp. 74–75.

The heart of the liberal philosophy is a belief in the dignity of the individual, in his freedom to make the most of his capacities and opportunities according to his own lights, subject only to the proviso that he not interfere with the freedom of other individuals to do the same. This implies a belief in the equality of men in one sense; in their inequality in another. Each man has an equal right to freedom. This is an important and fundamental right precisely because men are different, because one man will want to do different things with his freedom than another, and in the process can contribute more than another to the general culture of the society in which many men live.

– Milton Friedman, Ph.D., *Capitalism and Freedom*
(1962 [2002], University of Chicago Press), p. 195.

I'm not scared of the Maos and the Stalins and the Hitlers. I'm scared of the thousands or millions of people that hallucinate them to be "authority," and so do their bidding, and pay for their empires, and carry out their orders. I don't care if there's one looney with a stupid moustache. He's not a threat if the people do not believe in authority.

– Larken Rose, author of *The Most Dangerous Superstition*.

Over the years I've realized that the best measure of someone's political beliefs is what makes their blood boil. What do they demonstrate that they care the most about? If it's evil tyranny, they are usually an ally. If it's nonsense, then they are usually useless.

– Dave Smith, host of the "Part of the Problem" podcast.

What are presented as the strongest arguments against anarchism are invariably descriptions of the status quo.

– Michael Malice, author of *The New Right*.

The Moral Parity Thesis
The conditions under which a person may, in self-defense or the defense of others, deceive, lie to, sabotage, attack, or kill a fellow civilian, or destroy private property, are also conditions under which a civilian may do the same to a government agent (acting *ex officio*) or government property. The moral parity thesis holds that justifying self-defense or the defense of others against government agents is on par with justifying self-defense or the defense of others against civilians.

– Jason Brennan, Ph.D.,
When All Else Fails: The Ethics of Resistance to State Injustice
(2019, Princeton University Press), p. 11.

This book addresses the foundational problem of political philosophy: the problem of accounting for the authority of government. This authority has always struck me as puzzling and problematic. Why should 535 people in Washington be entitled to issue commands to 300 million others? And why should the others obey?

– Michael Huemer, Ph.D., *The Problem of Political Authority:*
An Examination of the Right to Coerce and the Duty to Obey
(2013, Palgrave Macmillan), p. xxvii.

The illegitimacy of the state rests on the fact that it exercises control over resources that its agents never acquired through original appropriation or voluntary exchange, and it does so without the consent of the rightful owners of said resources.

– Christopher Chase Rachels,
Spontaneous Order: The Capitalist Case for a Stateless Society
(2015, CreateSpace Independent Publishing Platform), p. 15.

This is one of the places that the people who are pro-socialist go very wrong, in thinking that profit is a thing that you find in capitalism, and it's not a thing you find in socialism. Profit-seeking is a function of the human being. As long as you have human beings, you're going to have profit-seeking behavior. The difference between capitalism and socialism isn't that one has profit and the other doesn't. They both have profit; it's just that socialism pretends that it doesn't by preventing you from measuring it, but it's still there... I think it's important here — and this applies to both systems, socialism or capitalism — to make a distinction between voluntary and involuntary profit. Voluntary profit is what comes about when I, a business, offer you a product that you like so much you're willing voluntarily to hand over your money in exchange for the product.

Now if you're willing to do that and I'm willing to offer the product, by definition we're both better off; and so, the profit that I make is a sign that I have made you better off. How do I know I've made you better off? because if I hadn't made you better off, you wouldn't have given me the money in the first place. That's *voluntary* profit.

Involuntary profit is when I co-opt the government to take the money from you and give it to me. Now here I have an accumulation of dollars — it's the same pile of dollars that you have with voluntary profit — but I came about them in a very different way. I came about them not by providing you with something that makes you happy; I came about them because I could cause somebody else to strongarm you to give it to me. Involuntary profit is a big problem.

– Antony Davies, Ph.D., Professor of Economics at Duquesne University, from an episode of Keith Knight's "Don't Tread on Anyone" podcast.

What causes poverty? Nothing. It's the original state, the default and starting point. The real question is: What causes prosperity?

– Per Bylund, Ph.D.,
Professor of Entrepreneurship at Oklahoma State University.

Capitalism puts human creativity to the service of humanity by respecting and encouraging entrepreneurial innovation, that elusive factor that explains the difference between the way we live now and how generation after generation after generation of our ancestors lived prior to the nineteenth century...

Capitalism is not just about people trading butter for eggs in local markets, which has gone on for millennia. It's about adding value through the mobilization of human energy and ingenuity on a scale never seen before in human history, to create wealth for common people that would have dazzled and astonished the richest and most powerful kings, sultans, and emperors of the past. It's about the erosion of long-entrenched systems of power, domination, and privilege, and the opening of "careers to talent." It's about the replacement of force by persuasion. It's about the replacement of envy by accomplishment. It's about what has made my life possible, and yours.

Free markets, understood as systems of free exchange among persons with well-defined, legally secure, and transferable rights in scarce resources, are a necessary condition for the wealth of the modern world. But as economic historians, most notably Deirdre McCloskey, have convincingly shown, they are not sufficient. Something else is needed: an ethics of free exchange and of wealth production through innovation.

– Tom G. Palmer, Ph.D.,
The Morality of Capitalism: What Your Professors Won't Tell You
(2011; Jameson Books, Inc.), pp. 2, 4.

It is not from the benevolence of the butcher, the brewer, or the baker, that we expect our dinner, but from their regard to their own interest. We address ourselves, not to their humanity but to their self-love, and never talk to them of our necessities but of their advantages.

– Adam Smith, *The Wealth of Nations*, Book IV, Chapter II (1776).

The norm required to reach the above conclusion is this: whenever it can somehow be proven that the production of a particular good or service has a positive effect on someone but would not be produced at all, or would not be produced in a definite quantity or quality unless others participated in its financing, then the use of aggressive violence against these persons is allowed, either directly or indirectly with the help of the state, and these persons may be forced to share in the necessary financial burden.

– Hans-Hermann Hoppe, Ph.D., *A Theory of Socialism and Capitalism*
(2010, Mises Institute), p. 233.

Unfortunately, in the case of politics the information problem is much worse than it is in the market. Consider the following example of individual behavioral incentives in a private market choice. In purchasing an automobile, I invest a certain amount of time and resources in learning about new cars, for the simple reason that I know a mistake will directly affect me and my wallet, convenience, and comfort.

...[C]ustomers will be, if not perfectly informed, at least better informed than the voter.

We must accept that in government, as in any form of commerce, people will pursue their private interests, and they will achieve goals reasonably closely related to those of company stockholders or of citizens only if it is in their private interest to do so.

– G. Tullock, A. Seldon, and G. Brady,
Government Failure: A Primer in Public Choice
(2002, Cato Institute), pp. 6, 10.

A growing number of scholars contend that government should have no role whatever in crime protection or dispute resolution. Their argument is an appealing one, stressing the advantages of freedom of choice and competition, the cost-minimizing incentives of profit-seekers, the avoidance of the commons problem, and the benefits of specialization. This point of view stresses the efficiency and effectiveness of *supply* by private producers *relative* to supply by public producers.

– Bruce L. Benson, Ph.D., *The Enterprise of Law*
(1990 [2011], Independent Institute), p. 252.

...[P]olitical behavior is largely driven by coalition loyalty... wanting to appear loyal to the groups around us... It's also in many ways a performance.

...[P]olitics (like religion) is a team sport.

...[S]ome treat expressive voting as an act of *consumption* — something we do in order to feel good, without concern for external benefits. In this view, voting is seen as providing a psychological reward, like getting to "affirm one's identity" or "feel a sense of belonging."

...[B]enefits come not from voting *per se*, but rather from all the activities surrounding the election, like attending rallies, posting to social media, and watching election coverage with friends and family.

– Robin Hanson, Ph.D. and Kevin Simler, *The Elephant in the Brain*
(2020, Oxford University Press), pp. 292, 295.

A change in how people honored markets and innovation caused the Industrial Revolution, and then the modern world. The old conventional wisdom, by contrast, has no place for attitudes about trade and innovation, and no place for liberal thought.

People had to start liking "creative destruction," the new idea that replaces the old.

It was ideas, or "rhetoric," that caused our enrichment...

– Deirdre N. McCloskey, Ph.D.,

Quotes

"Liberty and Dignity Explain the Modern World,"
in Tom G. Palmer, ed., *The Morality of Capitalism*
(2011, Jameson Books), pp. 27–30.

The soul-crushing misery, the mass exodus to get out, the endless broken promises so endemic to socialism simply cannot be dismissed as the failures of a few bad people. There's something rotten in the system itself. Indeed, the very ideas from which it springs are rotten. At socialism's core is end-justifies-the-means, moral relativist, anti-individual and collectivist rubbish. Bad people are everywhere, but nothing brings them forth and licenses them to do evil more thoroughly than concentrated power and the subordination of morality to the service of a statist ideology. That is the essence of the socialist vision, the iron fist within the velvet glove that belies all the happy talk to the contrary.

– Lawrence W. Reed, economist, historian, and think tank president.

The Jimmy Dore type of leftist (the ones who are anti-state but also support social safety nets) could have most to everything they want in an anarchist society in the form of mutual aid societies. Those are the types of leftists that are worth reaching out to, unlike neoliberals.

– Ace Archist, guest speaker at the Libertarian Institute.

As long as the state exists, you will never properly be able to answer "Who watches the Watchmen?"

– Ace Archist.

The transformation of charity into legal entitlement has produced donors without love and recipients without gratitude.

– Antonin Scalia, United States Supreme Court Justice.

One of the great non sequiturs of the left is that if the free market doesn't work perfectly, then it doesn't work at all — and the government should step in.

– Thomas Sowell, Ph.D., Professor of Economics at Cornell University.

The first lesson of economics is scarcity. There's never enough of anything to satisfy all those who want it. The first lesson of politics is to disregard the first lesson of economics.

– Thomas Sowell, Ph.D.

The reason so many people misunderstand so many issues, is not that these issues are so complex, but that people do not want a factual or analytical explanation that leaves them emotionally unsatisfied. They want villains to hate and heroes to cheer — and they don't explanations that don't give them that.

– Thomas Sowell, Ph.D.

Competition does a much more effective job than government at protecting consumers.

– Thomas Sowell, Ph.D.

If a foreigner wants to accept a job offer from a willing employer... or rent an apartment from a willing landlord... what moral right does anyone have to stop them? These are contracts between consenting adults, not welfare programs!

– Bryan Caplan, Ph.D., *Open Borders: The Science and Ethics of Immigration*
(2019, First Second Books), p. 16.

The socialist society would have to forbid capitalist acts between consenting adults.

– Robert Nozick, Ph.D., *Anarchy, State, and Utopia*
(1974 [2013] Basic Books), p. 163.

From each as they choose, to each as they are chosen.

– Robert Nozick, Ph.D., *Anarchy, State, and Utopia*
(1974 [2013] Basic Books), p. 158.

It is true that in the beginning men submit under constraint and by force; but those who come after them obey without regret and perform willingly what their predecessors had done because they had to. This is why men born under the yoke and then nourished and reared in slavery are content, without further effort, to live in their native circumstance, unaware of any other state or right, and considering as quite natural the condition into which they are born... the powerful influence of custom is in no respect more compelling than in this, namely, habituation to subjection.

– Étienne de La Boétie,
The Politics of Obedience: The Discourse on Voluntary Servitude
(1577 [1975], Mises Institute), p. 54.

Briefly, the State is that organization in society which attempts to maintain a monopoly of the use of force and violence in a given territorial area; in particular, it is the only organization in society that obtains its revenue not by voluntary contribution or payment for services rendered but by coercion. While other individuals or institutions obtain their income by production of goods and services and by the peaceful and voluntary sale of these goods and services to others, the State obtains its revenue by the use of compulsion; that is, by the use and the threat of the jailhouse and the bayonet.

– Murray N. Rothbard, Ph.D., *Anatomy of the State*

(1974 [2009], Mises Institute), pp. 11–12.

The problem with political decisions isn't that most of us don't get our own way. It's also that these decisions are usually imposed on us against our will, by threats of violence...

Democracy, as we practice it, is unjust. We expose innocent people to high degrees of risk because we put their fate in the hands of ignorant, misinformed, irrational, biased, and sometimes immoral decision makers.

– Jason Brennan, Ph.D., *Against Democracy*
(2016, Princeton University Press), pp. 230, 240.

Someone asked me the other day if I believe in conspiracies. Well sure, here's one. It is called the political system. It is nothing if not a giant conspiracy to rob, trick and subjugate the population.

– Jeffrey A. Tucker,
Founder and President of the Brownstone Institute.

Unobtainable Perfection
When the arguments for and against courses of action are assessed, it is important to remember that the choice has to be made from the available alternatives. All of them might be criticized for their imperfections, as might the status quo. Unless one of the options is perfect, the imperfections of the others are insufficient grounds for rejection. The fallacy of unobtainable perfection is committed when lack of perfection is urged as a basis for rejection, even though none of the alternatives is perfect either.

– Madsen Pirie, Ph.D., *How to Win Every Argument: The Use and Abuse of Logic*
(2006, Continuum International Publishing Group), p. 171.

What is considered theft in the private sector is "taxation" when done by the state. What is kidnapping in the private sector is "selective service" in the public sector. What is counterfeiting when done in the private sector is "monetary policy" when done by the public sector. What is mass murder in the private sector is "foreign policy" in the public sector.

– Llewellyn H. Rockwell, Jr., *The Left, the Right, and the State*
(2008, Mises Institute), p. 42.

Free markets are not just about generating profits, productivity, and efficiency. They aren't just about spurring innovation and competition. They are about the right of individuals to make autonomous choices and contracts, to pursue lives that fulfill their dreams even if these dreams are not approved by their government masters.

– Llewellyn H. Rockwell, Jr., *The Left, the Right, and the State*
(2008, Mises Institute), p. 30.

There will always be those who claim to have special rights over the rest of society, and the state is the most organized attempt to get away with it. To focus on these people as a unique problem is not an obsession, but the working out of intellectual responsibility.
— Llewellyn H. Rockwell, Jr., *The Left, the Right, and the State*
(2008, Mises Institute), p. 43.

What is the state? It is the group within society that claims for itself the exclusive right to rule everyone under a special set of laws that permit it to do to others what everyone else is rightly prohibited from doing, namely aggressing against person and property.
— Llewellyn H. Rockwell, Jr., *The Left, the Right, and the State*
(2008, Mises Institute), p. xiii.

...[T]here can be no more blatant case of involuntary servitude than our entire system of conscription... What else is involuntary servitude if not the draft?
— Murray N. Rothbard, Ph.D., *For a New Liberty*
(1973 [2006], Mises Institute), p. 98.

So, this is the essential paradox of regulation: To favor increasing regulation, you have to think the unorganized mass of consumers, taxpayers, and common public will generally be more effective in lobbying for their interests than organized, highly motivated special interest groups who keep offices in Washington, D.C. You have to think that the people who enjoy concentrated benefits and can spread their costs onto others will be less effective than the masses who suffer from diffused costs.
— Jason Brennan, Ph.D., *Why It's Okay to Want to Be Rich*
(2021, Routledge), p. 100.

The term "property rights" is used to refer to a bundle of rights that could include rights to sell, lend, bequeath, and so on. In what follows, I use the phrase to refer primarily to the right of owners to exclude nonowners. Private owners have the right to exclude nonowners, but the right to exclude is a feature of property rights in general rather than the defining feature of private ownership in particular. The National Park Service claims a right to exclude. Communes claim a right to exclude nonmembers.
— David Schmidtz, Ph.D., "The Institution of Property,"
Social Philosophy & Policy 11 (1994), pp. 42–62.

Political authority (hereafter, just "authority") is the hypothesized moral property in virtue of which governments may coerce people in certain ways not permitted to anyone else and in virtue of which citizens must obey governments in situations in which they would not be obligated to obey anyone else. Authority, then, has two aspects:

(i) Political legitimacy: the right, on the part of a government, to make certain sorts of laws and enforce them by coercion against the members of its society — in short, the right to rule.

(ii) Political obligation: the obligation on the part of citizens to obey their government, even in circumstances in which one would not be obligated to obey similar commands issued by a nongovernmental agent.

> – Michael Huemer, Ph.D., *The Problem of Political Authority: An Examination of the Right to Coerce and the Duty to Obey* (2013, Palgrave Macmillan), p. 5.

The scientific problem in explaining modern economic growth is its astonishing magnitude — anywhere from a 3,000 to a 10,000 percent increase in real income, a "Great Enrichment." Investment, reallocation, property rights, exploitation cannot explain it. Only the bettering of betterment can, the stunning increase in new ideas, such as the screw propeller on ships or the ball bearing in machines, the modern university for the masses and careers open to talent. Why, then, the new and trade-tested ideas? Because liberty to have a go, as the English say, and a dignity to the wigmakers and telegraph operators having the go made the mass of people bold. Equal liberty and dignity for ordinary people is called "liberalism," and it was new to Europe in the eighteenth century, against old hierarchies. Why the liberalism? It was not deep European superiorities, but the accidents of the Four R's of (German) Reformation, (Dutch) Revolt, (American and French) Revolution, and (Scottish and Scandinavian) Reading. It could have gone the other way, leaving, say, China to have the Great Enrichment, much later. Europe, and then the world, was lucky after 1900. Now China and India have adopted liberalism (in the Chinese case only in the economy), and are catching up.

> – Deirdre N. McCloskey, Ph.D., "The Great Enrichment: A Humanistic and Social Scientific Account" (2016, *Scandinavian Economic History Review*), p. 1.

Advocates for capitalism claim that — unlike in politics — markets "work" even if people are self-interested, because the dynamics of competition limit bad actions.

The reason that we tolerate, or in some cases celebrate, capitalism is that entrepreneurs find ways to produce new products, new services, or new ways of making things that make consumers better off. Many of us would pay far more than the store price for clean water, wholesome food, cars that run for 200,000 miles, or cell phones that connect us to the entire world. Entrepreneurs think up the new goods or services, and competition drives down the price. The result is that many products not available even to the very wealthy in 1900 are now owned by all but the poorest among us.

> – Michael Munger, Ph.D., "Is Capitalism Sustainable?"

(2019, American Institute for Economic Research).

The impetus for this book is Libertarianism. The basic premise of this philosophy is that it is illegitimate to engage in aggression against nonaggressors. What is meant by aggression is not assertiveness, argumentativeness, competitiveness, adventurousness, quarrelsomeness, or antagonism. What is meant by aggression is the use of violence, such as that which takes place in murder, rape, robbery, or kidnapping. Libertarianism does not imply pacifism; it does not forbid the use of violence in defense or even in retaliation against violence. Libertarian philosophy condemns only the initiation of violence — the use of violence against a nonviolent person or his property.

– Walter Block, Ph.D., *Defending the Undefendable* (1976 [2018], Mises Institute), p. xiii.

What voters don't know could fill a university library. In the last few decades, economists who study politics have thrown fuel on the fire by pointing out that — selfishly speaking — voters are not making a mistake. One vote has so small a probability of affecting electoral outcomes that a realistic egoist pays no attention to politics; he chooses to be, in economic jargon, *rationally ignorant*.

– Bryan Caplan, Ph.D.,
"The Myth of the Rational Voter: Why Democracies Choose Bad Policies"
(2007, Cato Institute), p. 3.

In theory, democracy is a bulwark against socially harmful policies. In practice, however, democracies frequently adopt and maintain policies that are damaging. How can this paradox be explained?

The influence of special interests and voter ignorance are two leading explanations. I offer an alternative story of how and why democracy fails. The central idea is that voters are worse than ignorant; they are, in a word, *irrational* — and they vote accordingly. Despite their lack of knowledge, voters are not humble agnostics; instead, they confidently embrace a long list of misconceptions.

Economic policy is the primary activity of the modern state. And if there is one thing that the public deeply misunderstands, it is economics.

People do not grasp the "invisible hand" of the market, with its ability to harmonize private greed and the public interest. I call this *anti-market* bias. They underestimate the benefits of interaction with foreigners. I call this *anti-foreign* bias. They equate prosperity not with production, but with employment. I call this *make-work* bias. Finally, they are overly prone to think that economic conditions are bad and getting worse. I call this *pessimistic* bias.

In the minds of many, Winston Churchill's famous aphorism cuts the conversation short: "Democracy is the worst form of government, except all those other forms that have been tried from time to time." But this saying overlooks the fact that governments vary in scope as well as form. In democracies the main alternative to majority rule is not dictatorship, but markets. A better understanding of voter irrationality advises us to rely less on democracy and more on the market.

– Bryan Caplan, Ph.D.,
"The Myth of the Rational Voter: Why Democracies Choose Bad Policies"
(2007, Cato Institute), p. 1.

Socialism... must be conceptualized as an institutionalized interference with or aggression against private property and private property claims. Capitalism, on the other hand, is a social system based on the explicit recognition of private property and of nonaggressive, contractual exchanges between private property owners.

– Hans-Hermann Hoppe, Ph.D., *A Theory of Socialism and Capitalism*
(2010, Mises Institute), p. 10.

This idea that individuals can be and should be sacrificed for the "greater good" is the essence of the fascist/socialist/collectivist philosophy...

For many intellectuals, the attractiveness of socialism is that it is "rational"; it is a "planned" economy, planned by people like them.

– Thomas J. DiLorenzo, Ph.D., *The Problem with Socialism*
(2016, Regnery Publishing), pp. 68, 121.

One of the great virtues of an economic order that directs "self-seeking" individuals to discover and pursue profitable relations with "strangers" is that the resulting wider net of economic relations systematically undercuts the hostility that almost all of us initially feel towards members of different clans, castes, nationalities or religions. Mutually beneficial economic interaction among self-seeking individuals enhances tolerance — at least by shifting attention away from differences that people find hard to tolerate. This point about how trade relationships foster tolerant cosmopolitanism was, of course, most famously conveyed in Voltaire's description of the London Stock Exchange:

> ...[E]nter the Exchange of London, that place more respectable than many a court, and you will see there agents from all nations assembled for the utility of mankind. There the Jew, the Mohammedan, and the Christian deal with one another as if they were the same religion, and give the name of infidel only to those who go bankrupt.

– Eric Mack, Ph.D., "In Defense of Individualism,"
in *Ethical Theory and Moral Practice* (1999).

The direct use of physical force is so poor a solution to the problem of limited resources that it is commonly employed only by small children and great nations... Cooperation occurs either when several individuals perceive that they more easily can achieve a common end jointly than individually or when they find that they more easily can achieve their different ends by cooperating through trade, each helping the others achieve their ends in exchange for their helping him achieve his.

– David D. Friedman, Ph.D.,
The Machinery of Freedom: Guide to a Radical Capitalism
(1973 [2015], CreateSpace Independent Publishing Platform), p. 4.

Capitalism is essentially a system of mass production for the satisfaction of the needs of the masses. It pours a horn of plenty upon the common man. It has raised the average standard of living to a height never dreamed of in earlier ages. It has made accessible to millions of people enjoyments which a few generations ago were only within the reach of a small elite.

– Ludwig von Mises, Ph.D., *The Anti-Capitalist Mentality*
(1956 [2008], Mises Institute), p. 49.

The religion of "authority" is based on the illusion and falsehood that some are masters who may set arbitrary dictates which are not based in morality and enforced by violence, while others are slaves who have a moral obligation to obey the arbitrary dictates set by the masters... And the biggest manifestation of this universal world religion called the "belief in authority" is "government."

– Mark Passio, Founder of WhatOnEarthIsHappening.com.

The Painful Truth: The order follower always bears MORE moral culpability than the order giver, because the order-follower is the one who actually performed the action, and in taking that action, actually brought the resultant harm into physical manifestation.

– Mark Passio.

"Why do we owe it to others not to aggress against them," I would respond along these lines: because we individually should treat other persons respectfully, that is, as ends in themselves and not merely as means to our own ends... Nonaggression is an implication of the obligation to treat persons respectfully, as ends in themselves and not merely as means... Long concludes, "A truly human life, then, will be a life characterized by reason and intelligent cooperation."

– Sheldon Richman, *What Social Animals Owe to Each Other*
(2020, Libertarian Institute).

There are several ways to prove that government cannot possibly be legitimate — never has been, and never will be.

For example, people obviously cannot delegate rights they do NOT have themselves. If you do not have the right to rob your neighbor on your own, then you can't possibly give such a right to some public official, nor can anyone else.

No election, no constitution, no political process can make robbery and extortion moral and righteous; even if politicians first do a bunch of complicated pseudo religious rituals, and then call the robbery law and taxation.

– Larken Rose, author of *The Most Dangerous Superstition*.

Once you accept the principle of government, namely that there must be a judicial monopoly and the power to tax, once you accept this principle incorrectly as a just principle, then any idea or any notion of restraining or limiting government power and safeguarding individual liberty and property becomes illusory. Rather, under monopolistic auspices, the price of justice and protection will continually rise, and the quality of justice and protection will continually fall. A tax-funded protection agency is a contradiction in terms. That is, it is an expropriating property protector.

-- Hans-Hermann Hoppe, Ph.D., *Economy, Society, and History* (2021, Mises Institute), p. 174.

One thing people miss about market competition is competition to cooperate. The landscaping companies that advertise in my neighborhood are competing against each other, sure. Yet what they compete for is the opportunity to cooperate — to make mutually beneficial, reciprocal trades with people in my neighborhood. It's a contest to decide who gets to serve others.

– Jason Brennan, Ph.D., *Why It's Okay to Want to Be Rich* (2021, Routledge), p. 86.

If there is one well-established truth in political economy, it is this: That in all cases, for all commodities that serve to provide for the tangible or intangible needs of the consumer, it is in the consumer's best interest that labor and trade remain free, because the freedom of labor and of trade have as their necessary and permanent result the maximum reduction of price. And this: That the interests of the consumer of any commodity whatsoever should always prevail over the interests of the producer. Now in pursuing these principles, one arrives at this rigorous conclusion: That the production of security should, in the interests of the consumers of this intangible commodity, remain subject to the law of free competition. Whence it follows: That no government should have the right to prevent another government from going into competition with it, or to require consumers of security to come exclusively to it for this commodity.

— Gustav de Molnari, *The Production of Security*
(1849 [2009], Mises Institute), p. 23.

We don't oppose the state's wars because they'll be counterproductive or overextend the state's forces. We oppose them because mass murder based on lies can never be morally acceptable.

— Llewellyn H. Rockwell, Jr.

To kill one man is to be guilty of a capital crime, to kill ten men is to increase the guilt tenfold, to kill a hundred men is to increase it a hundredfold. This the rulers of the earth all recognize, and yet when it comes to the greatest crime — waging war on another state — they praise it!... If a man on seeing a little black were to say it is black, but on seeing a lot of black were to say it is white, it would be clear that such a man could not distinguish black and white... So those who recognize a small crime as such, but do not recognize the wickedness of the greatest crime of all... cannot distinguish right and wrong.

— Mozi (470–391 B.C.), *Condemnation of Offensive War I*, Book V.

...[T]here's no such thing as "objective news." ...When I choose to do a story — you choose to do a story — we do so for a particular reason. There is a near infinity of stories that you could do at any point during the day. And the ones that you choose are because it fits your particular goal.

— Stefan Molyneux, M.A.,
in Mike Cernovich's *Hoaxed: Everything They Told You Is a Lie*
(2018, R.R. Bowker LLC).

There is no such thing as gun control. There is only centralizing gun ownership in the hands of a small political elite and their minions.

— Stefan Molyneux, M.A.

FORMULATION 1. Justice is respect for the rights of individuals and associations.

(1) The right of several property specifies a right to acquire, possess, use, and dispose of scarce physical resources — including their own bodies. Resources may be used in any way that does not physically interfere with other persons' use and enjoyment of their resources. While most property rights are freely alienable, the right to one's person is inalienable.

(2) The right of first possession specifies that property rights to unowned resources are acquired by being the first to establish control over them.

(3) The right of freedom of contract specifies that a right-holder's consent is both necessary (freedom from contract) and sufficient (freedom to contract) to transfer alienable property rights.

— Randy Barnett, J.D., *The Structure of Liberty: Justice and the Rule of Law*

(1998 [2014] Oxford University Press), p. 83.

Falsehood is a recognized and extremely useful weapon in warfare, and every country uses it quite deliberately to deceive its own people, to attract neutrals, and mislead the enemy. The ignorant and innocent masses in each country are unaware at the time that they are being misled, and when it is all over only here and there are the falsehoods discovered and exposed... [T]he authorities in each country do, and indeed must, resort to this practice and in order, first, to justify themselves by depicting the enemy as an undiluted criminal; and secondly to inflame popular passion sufficiently to secure recruits for the continuance of the struggle... People must never be allowed to become despondent; so victories must be exaggerated and defeats, if not concealed, at any rate minimized, and the stimulus of indignation, horror, and hatred must be assiduously and continuously pumped into the public mind by means of "propaganda"... The Public can be worked up emotionally by sham ideals. A sort of collective hysteria spreads and rises until finally it gets the better of sober people and reputable newspapers.

— Arthur Ponsonby, *Falsehood in War-time*
(1928, Unwin Brothers Ltd.), pp. 13–14.

Protectionism is a misnomer. The only people protected by tariffs, quotas and trade restrictions are those engaged in uneconomic and wasteful activity. Free trade is the only philosophy compatible with international peace and prosperity.

— Walter Block, Ph.D.

Once admit any right of secession whatever, and there is no logical stopping-point short of the right of individual secession, which logically entails anarchism, since then individuals may secede and patronize their own defense agencies, and the State has crumbled.

— Murray N. Rothbard, Ph.D., *The Ethics of Liberty*
(1982 [2016], New York University Press), p. 182.

Prior to capitalism, the way people amassed great wealth was by looting, plundering and enslaving their fellow man. Capitalism made it possible to become wealthy by serving your fellow man.

— Walter E. Williams, Ph.D., "I Love Greed,"
(Jan. 2012, Creators.com).

All initiation of force is a violation of someone else's rights, whether initiated by an individual or the state, for the benefit of an individual or group of individuals.

— Congressman Ron Paul.

Is it really a surprise that as the government gets bigger and bigger and bigger, everything in life becomes more and more hyper-political?

When you think about it, right, there are such profound differences that people have... you will have right now in this audience... a Christian sitting next to an atheist, the most profound difference in belief: one person believes that the person next to them is going to burn in a pit of Hell forever, and that atheist looks over at you and believes you are delusional.

But you're fine. Like, you're not going to war, because it's separated from politics. Now if tomorrow there was going to be a vote over whether the government is Christian or atheist, those people start going to war, because they're warring over... who rules over you, and so, the problem with all of this, with comedy and with everything else online — it's not that we have differences; it's that we have political differences.

Politics is poison, and that's why you want to reduce the size of government...

– Dave Smith, host of "Part of the Problem" podcast,
in a panel discussion at FreedomFest in Rapid City, SD on July 22, 2021.

Government should never be able to do anything you can't do.

– Congressman Ron Paul.

...[W]hen we're truly free, it doesn't mean there won't be any evil in the world. In fact, a stateless society is a recognition of the fact that evil exists and the first place that evil doers go is to the state, to gain control over the state.

...[I]f human beings are all good we don't need a state. If human beings are all evil we can't afford the state. If human beings are mostly evil and only somewhat good then the mostly evil people vote for democratic policies that overwhelm and subjugate the good people. If people are mostly good and only somewhat evil, which is my belief, then the good people become the tax livestock controlled by the evil people who swarm to the state to gain control over the good. There was no scenario of any admixture of good and evil which justifies the existence of the state. The state is a giant magnet for monsters in human form.

– Stefan Molyneux, M.A.

Here's the difference: In capitalism, people have risked their lives to save their dogs; in socialism, people kill their dogs to save their own lives... that's why people risk their lives to migrate to the United States of America. And that's why people risked their lives to migrate from Venezuela, North Korea, and Cuba.

– Johan Norberg, "Lesson from Sweden"
(2018, The Fund for American Studies).

Half the harm that is done in this world is due to people who want to feel important. They don't mean to do harm — but the harm does not interest them. Or they do not see it, or they justify it because they are absorbed in the endless struggle to think well of themselves.

– T.S. Eliot, *The Cocktail Party*
(1950 [1974], Faber and Faber), p. 111.

I don't think people understand how severely outdated and therefore overpriced "education" is in this country (and really everywhere).

If this was not the most State-subsidized industry, what we traditionally understand as K–12 or higher education would be completely eliminated. Right now, it is just traditional bullshit that is propped up by way of the taxpayer and doesn't function as an actual market. Which is why, despite accessibility to information and communication being at an all-time high... so is the cost/spending on said "education." As an example, if the Department of Education was abolished alongside the elimination of government grants and loans, you'd see the entire industry of "education" changed in ways you couldn't even personally perceive.

– Eric July, host of "For Canon Sake."

It must also be remembered that, unless men are left to their own resources, they do not know what is or what is not possible for them. If government half a century ago had provided us all with dinners and breakfasts, it would be the practice of our orators to-day to assume the impossibility of our providing for ourselves.

– Auberon Herbert, "State Education: A Help or Hindrance" (1880).

What We Voluntaryists Believe:
The self-owner is owner of his own mind and body and his own property... No peaceful, nonaggressive citizen can be submitted to the control of others, apart from his own consent... The moral rights of a delegated body, such as a government, can never be greater than the moral rights of the individuals who delegated to it its power. Force can only be used (whether by an individual or by a government makes no difference) for defensive purposes — never for aggressive purposes.

– Auberon Herbert, "The Principles of Voluntaryism and Free Life" (1885).

We voluntaryists believe that no true progress can be made until we frankly recognize the great truth that every individual, who lives within the sphere of his own rights, as a self-owner, and has not himself first aggressed upon others by employing force or fraud in his dealings with them (and thus deprived himself of his own rights of self-ownership by aggressing upon these same rights of others), is the only one true owner of his own faculties, and his own property... Because free countries have affirmed many years ago that a compulsory church rate is immoral and oppressive, for the sake of the burden laid upon individual consciences; and in affirming this truth they have unconsciously affirmed the wider truth, that every tax or rate, forcibly taken from an unwilling person, is immoral and oppressive. The human conscience knows no distinction between church rates and other compulsory rates and taxes. The sin lies in the disregarding of each other's convictions, and is not affected by the subject matter of the tax.

– Auberon Herbert, "The Principles of Voluntaryism and Free Life" (1885).

There is one and only one principle, on which you can build a true, rightful, enduring and progressive civilization, which can give peace and friendliness and contentment to all differing groups and sects into which we are divided — and that principle is that every man and woman should be held by us all sacredly and religiously to be the one true owner of his or her faculties, of his or her body and mind, and of all property, inherited or — honestly acquired. There is no other possible foundation — seek it wherever you will — on which you can build, if you honestly mean to make this world a place of peace and friendship, where progress of every kind, like a full river fed by its many streams, may flow on its happy fertilizing course, with ever broadening and deepening volume. Deny that self-ownership, that self-guidance of the individual, and however fine our professed motives may be, we must sooner or later, in a world without rights, become like animals who prey on each other. Deny human rights, and however little you may wish to do so, you will find yourself abjectly kneeling at the feet of that old-world god, Force — that grimmest and ugliest of gods that men have ever carved for themselves out of the lusts of their hearts; you will find yourselves hating and dreading all other men who differ from you; you will find yourselves obliged by the law of conflict into which you have plunged, to use every means in your power to crush them before they are able to crush you; you will find yourselves day by day growing more unscrupulous and intolerant, more and more compelled by the fear of those opposed to you, to commit harsh and violent actions, of which you would once have said, "Is thy servant a dog that he should do these things?"; you will find yourselves clinging to and welcoming force, as the one and only form of protection left to you, when you have destroyed the rule of the great principles.

– Auberon Herbert, "A Plea for Voluntaryism" (1908).

Hence my complaint against copyright: it violates the natural and common-law rights that we would otherwise enjoy to freely use our voices, pens, and presses.

– Tom W. Bell, J.D.,
Intellectual Privilege: Copyright, Common Law, and the Common Good

(2014, Mercatus Center at George Mason University), p. 2.

Do you like having options when you look for a new bank, dry cleaner, or veterinarian? Of course you do. You want to find the service that will best satisfy your particular demands, after all, and you know that when banks, cleaners, and vets have to compete they have a powerful incentive to make you happy. A monopoly, in contrast, can take its customers for granted. Polycentric law simply extends that observation from commercial services to government ones. Just as competition makes life better for those who seek banking, cleaning, and pet care services, it can benefit those seeking fair and efficient legal systems. Competition helps consumers and citizens alike.

– Tom W. Bell, J.D. "What is Polycentric Law?"
(2014, Foundation for Economic Education).

Hobbes was wrong — on both counts. Individuals have secured property protection and social cooperation without government and still do. Moreover, in much of the world, government has proved to be the greatest depredator of property rights, creator of conflict, and instigator of chaos, rather than an innocuous antidote to anarchic afflictions. Governance — social rules that protect individuals' property and institutions of their enforcement — doesn't require government, which is but one means of supplying governance. Hobbes overlooked the possibility of self-governance: privately created social rules and institutions of their enforcement. He also underestimated the possibility of truly horrible governments.

– Peter T. Leeson, Ph.D.,
Anarchy Unbound: Why Self Governance Works Better Than You Think
(2014, Cambridge University Press), p. 1.

They'll think that it's a real comeback against us to say, "Hey you, don't forget we live in a society"... Of course we know we live in a society; that's *why* we're against the state, because the state disrupts the normal, healthy interactions of human beings that comprise society; because the state by its nature pits society against itself... now we're pitted against each other because some people wear masks and some don't; and now we're yelling, "You don't listen to science!" This wouldn't have happened if that hadn't been politicized. Or then they'll say, "Well, this group gets a special subsidy, and this industry gets this," so now we're pitted against each other because of that... So it's *because* we like society — we like peace and normal human interaction — that we're against the state; it's not that we're against society. Of course these schmucks want to confuse society and the state, because the state wants to take credit for all the good things we have in society, but I refuse to give them that credit. The state is a parasite that shows up later. Society is all the good things that we do spontaneously, and then the state takes credit for it, and then we're told if we're against the state we're against society!

– Thomas E. Woods, Jr., Ph.D.
on "Kibbe on Liberty" with Matt Kibbe.

Christianity, with its doctrine of humility, of forgiveness, of love, is incompatible with the state, with its haughtiness, its violence, its punishment, its wars.

– Leo Tolstoy, a Christian anarchist and pacifist.

I have never understood how the religion whose heart is that God is love and that we are to love our neighbors as ourselves can give rise to wars that are absolutely unjustifiable and unacceptable relative to the revelation of Jesus.

– Jacques Ellul, a French philosopher and Christian anarchist.

The logic of the market is predicated on the pervasive and glorious inequality of man. No two people have the same scales of values, talents, or ambitions. It is this radical inequality, and the freedom to choose our own lot in life, that makes possible the division of labor and exchange. Through money and contracts, markets allow us to settle differences to our mutual advantage. The result — and here is why people call the market miraculous — is a vast, productive system of international cooperation that meets an incomprehensibly huge range of human needs, and finds a special role for everyone to participate in building prosperity.

– Llewellyn H. Rockwell, Jr., *The Left, the Right, and the State*
(2008, Mises Institute), p. 69.

The government exists outside the matrix of exchange. There are no market prices for the goods and services it endeavors to produce. The revenue it receives is not a reward for social service but rather money extracted from the public by force. It is not spent with an eye to return on investment. As a result there is no means for the government to calculate its own profits and losses. Its inability to calculate with attention to economic rationality is the downfall of governments everywhere. Its decision-making is ultimately economically arbitrary and politically motivated.

– Llewellyn H. Rockwell, Jr., *The Left, the Right, and the State*
(2008, Mises Institute), pp. 64–65.

Lasting prosperity can only come about through a system that allows people to cooperate to their mutual advantage, innovate and invest in an environment of freedom, retain earnings as private property, and save generation to generation without fear of having estates looted through taxation and inflation. Human effort in the framework of a market economy:

this is the source of wealth; this is the means by which a rising population is fed, clothed, and housed; this is the method by which even the poorest country can become rich.

– Llewellyn H. Rockwell, Jr., *The Left, the Right, and the State* (2008, Mises Institute), p. 53.

What all these moral crusades have in common is their moral exaltation of the anointed above others, who are to have their very different views nullified and superseded by the views of the anointed, imposed via the power of government. Despite the great variety of issues in a series of crusading movements among the intelligentsia during the twentieth century, several key elements have been common to most of them:

Assertions of a great danger to the whole of society, a danger to which the masses of people are oblivious.

An urgent need for action to avert impending catastrophe.

A need for government to drastically curtail the dangerous behavior of the many, in response to the prescient conclusions of the few.

A disdainful dismissal of arguments to the contrary as either uninformed, irresponsible, or motivated by unworthy purposes.

– Thomas Sowell, Ph.D., *The Vision of the Anointed: Self-Congratulations as a Basis for Social Policy* (1995, Basic Books), p. 5.

The battle is won when the average American regards a corporate journalist exactly as they regard a tobacco executive.

– Michael Malice, author of *Dear Reader: The Unauthorized Biography of Kim Jong Il.*

"Authority" can be summed up as *the right to rule*... Do not complicate things. Don't have a laundry list of different things you want the statist to believe and agree with you about. Accomplish the one thing of helping him give up the belief in "authority," and over time he will extrapolate most of the other things that matter.

– Larken Rose, "Candles in the Dark" Seminar (2017).

Even if we do not see our ideas triumph during our lifetime, we will know and be eternally proud that we gave it our all, and that we did what every honest and noble person had to do.

– Hans-Hermann Hoppe, Ph.D.

Were it necessary to bring a majority into a comprehension of the libertarian philosophy, the cause of liberty would be utterly hopeless. Every significant movement in history has been led by one or just a few individuals with a small minority of energetic supporters.

— Leonard E. Read, "How to Advance Liberty,"
from a lecture given on March 10, 1965.

The case against anarchism is also subject to a powerful *reductio ad absurdum*. If the U.S. is needed to keep Smith and Jones from creating mayhem against each other, then what about governments themselves? Must they not be kept apart from one another? At present, Albania and Argentina are in a state of anarchy with each other. That is, there is no World Government to act as a referee between them. The exact same situation applies to Bolivia and Burundi; to Canada and Chile, to Denmark and the Dominican Republic, to Egypt and Ecuador, to France and Finland, to Greece and Ghana, to Haiti and Hungary, to Ireland and Israel, to Japan and Jamaica, to Korea and Kenya, to Luxembourg and Liberia, to Mexico and Morocco, to Netherlands and New Zealand...

— Walter Block, Ph.D., Defending the Undefendable III
(2021, Springer Nature), p. ix.

Special-interest legislation is inherent in the very nature of government. On the free market, the network of voluntary exchanges, all activity is based on individual liberty and results in mutually beneficial outcomes. The competitive profit and loss mechanism incentivizes individuals to produce goods and services that consumers desire. However, the government, the legitimated monopoly of power, lacks this mechanism and produces outcomes that are harmful to society. The incentive structure is different: unlike the Invisible Hand of the market, individuals that control the coercive Visible Hand are encouraged to pass legislation that benefits themselves at the expense of others. The stronger the government, the more lucrative the rewards. To control the government machinery is to control the levers of cronyism.

— Patrick Newman, Ph.D., Cronyism: Liberty vs. Power in America, 1607–1849
(2021, Mises Institute), p. 13.

We should compare the outcome of some event or policy to the alternative timeline in which that event never happened or that policy was never put in place. We should not compare before and after only. This alternative timeline, the "what would have been," is called counterfactual. Economics is all about counterfactuals because economics is all about choices. A choice is choosing one course of action over all others. The next-best course of action is the counterfactual (and the value of that next-best course of action is called the opportunity cost of the choice)... Moreover, taxes and inflation do not bring about new resources — they only increase the amount of our resources that are consumed according to politicians' and bureaucrats' preferences.

— Jonathan Newman, Ph.D., The Broken Window (2021).

The "private sector" of the economy is, in fact, the voluntary sector; and... the "public sector" is, in fact, the coercive sector. The voluntary sector is made up of goods and services for which people voluntarily spend the money they have earned. The coercive sector is made up of the goods and services that are provided, regardless of the wishes of the individual, out of taxes that are seized from him.
– Henry Hazlitt, Journalist and author of *Economics in One Lesson*.

Free association... the only true form of society.
– Pierre-Joseph Proudhon, founder of the mutualist philosophy.

A democratic vote is like the captain of a ship having to consult every passenger about the best course to chart through an approaching storm.
– The School of Life, *Philosophy in 40 Ideas* (2020), p. 13.

It is absurd to believe that an agency which may tax without consent can be a property protector. Likewise, it is absurd to believe that an agency with legislative powers can preserve law and order.
– Hans-Hermann Hoppe, Ph.D., *Democracy: The God That Failed* (2001 [2017] Routledge), p. 279.

To many people, even today, high profits are often attributed to high prices charged by those motivated by "greed." In reality, most of the great fortunes in American history have resulted from someone's figuring out how to reduce costs, so as to be able to charge lower prices and therefore gain a mass market for the product. Henry Ford did this with automobiles, Rockefeller with oil, Carnegie with steel, and Sears, Penney, Walton and other department store chain founders with a variety of products. A supermarket chain in a capitalist economy can be very successful charging prices that allow about a penny of clear profit on each dollar of sales.
– Thomas Sowell, Ph.D., *Basic Economics* (2015, Basic Books), p. 165.

Human beings really only have two organizing principles, right? We either cooperate with each other, and that's exactly what it sounds like — we all find a way to negotiate our way through life day to day; or we use the force of government to coerce one another.
– James R. Harrigan, Ph.D., author of *Cooperation and Coercion: How Busybodies Became Busybullies and What That Means for Economics and Politics*.

War not only destroys the lives and limbs of the soldiery, but, by progressively consuming the accumulated capital stock of the belligerent nations, eventually shortens and coarsens the lives and shrivels the limbs of the civilian population. The enormous destruction of productive wealth that war entails would become immediately evident if governments had no

recourse but to raise taxes immediately upon the advent of hostilities; their ability to inflate the money supply at will permits them to conceal such destruction behind a veil of rising prices, profits, and wages, stable interest rates, and a booming stock market.
> – Joseph Salerno, Ph.D., "War and the Money Machine: Concealing the Costs of War Beneath the Veil of Inflation" (Aug. 2021, Mises.org).

[Carl] Menger sought to explain prices as the outcome of the purposeful, voluntary interactions of buyers and sellers, each guided by their own, subjective evaluations of the usefulness of various goods and services in satisfying their objectives (what we now call marginal utility, a term later coined by Friedrich von Wieser). Trade is thus the result of people's deliberate attempts to improve their well-being, not an innate "propensity to truck, barter, and exchange," as suggested by Adam Smith. The exact quantities of goods exchanged — their prices, in other words — are determined by the values individuals attach to marginal units of these goods. With a single buyer and seller, goods are exchanged as long as participants can agree on an exchange ratio that leaves each better off than he was before.
> – Peter G. Klein, Ph.D., "Menger the Revolutionary" (Nov. 2021, Mises.org).

In one sense, anarchism is nothing more than the declaration that "You do not speak for me." Everything else is just implementation... outsourcing the delivery of security is no different than outsourcing the delivery of food... Anarchism is not a location. Anarchism is a relationship, one in which none of the parties has authority over the other.
> – Michael Malice, *The Anarchist Handbook* (2021), pp. 1–2.

I call this the three-axes model of political communication. A progressive will communicate along the oppressor-oppressed axis, framing issues in terms of the (P) dichotomy. A conservative will communicate along the civilization-barbarism axis, framing issues in terms of the (C) dichotomy. A libertarian will communicate along the liberty-coercion axis, framing issues in terms of the (L) dichotomy.
> – Arnold Kling, Ph.D.,
> *The Three Languages of Politics: Talking Across the Political Divides*
> (2017, Cato Institute), p. 5.

In the private sector, firms must attract voluntary customers or they fail; and if they fail, investors lose their money, and managers and employees lose their jobs. The possibility of failure, therefore, is a powerful incentive to find out what customers want and to deliver it efficiently. But in the government sector, failures are not punished, they are rewarded. If a government agency is set up to deal with a problem and the problem gets worse, the agency is rewarded with more money and more staff — because, after all, its task is now bigger. An agency that fails year after year, that does not simply fail to solve the problem but actually makes it worse, will be rewarded with an ever-increasing budget.

– David Boaz, *Liberating Schools: Education in the Inner City* (1991, Cato Institute).

Rather, I only want to shed some light on the principal strategy that all statists, from the late Middle Ages on until today, have pursued to reach their statist ends, so as to also gain (if only indirectly) some insight into any possible counterstrategy that could lead us out of the current predicament. Not back to the Middle Ages, of course, because too many permanent and irreversible changes have taken place since, both in regard to our mental and our material conditions and capacities, but to a new society that takes its cues from the study of the Middle Ages and understands and knows of the principal reason for its demise.

The strategy was dictated by the quasi-libertarian, stateless medieval starting point, and it suggested itself "naturally," first and foremost to the top ranks of social authority, in particular to feudal kings. In a nutshell, it boils down to this rule: instead of remaining a mere *primus inter pares*, you must become a *solus primus*, and to do this you must undermine, weaken, and ultimately eliminate all competing authorities and hierarchies of social authority. Beginning at the highest levels of authority, with your most immediate competitors, and from there on down, ultimately, to the most elementary and decentralized level of social authority invested in the heads of individual family households, you (every statist) must use your own initial authority to undermine each and every rival authority and strip away its right to independently judge, discriminate, sentence, and punish within its own territorially limited realm of authority.

Kings other than you must no longer be allowed to freely determine who is another or the next king, who is to be included or excluded from the rank of kings, or who may come before them for justice and assistance. And likewise for all other levels of social authority, for noble lords and vassals as well as all separate local communities, orders, associations, and ultimately all individual family households. No one must be free to autonomously determine his own rules of admission and exclusion. That is, to determine who is supposed to be "in" or "out," the conduct to expect of those who are "in" and want to remain in good standing, and what member conduct instead results in various sanctions, ranging from disapproval, censure, and fines to expulsion and corporal punishment.

And how to accomplish this and centralize and consolidate all authority in the hands of a single territorial monopolist, first an absolute monarch and subsequently a democratic state? By enlisting the support of everyone resentful of not being included or promoted in some particular community, association, or social rank, or of being expelled from them and "unfairly" punished. Against this "unfair discrimination" you, the state or would-be state, promise to get the excluded "victims" in and help them get a "fair" and "nondiscriminating" treatment in return for their binding commitment to and affiliation with you. On every level of social authority, whenever and wherever the opportunity arises, you encourage and promote "deviant behavior" and "deviants" and enlist their support in order to expand and strengthen your own authority at the expense of all others.

Accordingly, the principal counterstrategy of *recivilization*, then, must be a return to "normality" by means of decentralization. The process of territorial expansion that went hand in hand with the centralization of all authority in one monopolistic hand must be reversed. Each and every secessionist tendency and movement, then, should be supported and promoted, because with every territorial separation from the central state another separate and rival center of authority and adjudication is created. And the same tendency should be promoted within the framework of any newly created separate and independent territory and center of authority. That is, any voluntary membership organization, association, order, club, or even household within the new territory should be free to independently determine its own house rules, *i.e.*, its rules of inclusion, of sanctions, and of exclusion, so as to successively replace the current statist system of forced territorial and legal integration and uniformation with a natural, quasi-organic social order of voluntary territorial and legal-customary association and dissociation.

Moreover, as an important addition, in order to safeguard this order of increasingly decentralized centers, ranks, and hierarchies of natural social authority from internal corruption or external (foreign) attack, each newly (re)emerging social authority should be encouraged to build as wide as possible a network with similarly placed and like-minded authorities in other, "foreign" territories and jurisdictions for the purpose of mutual assistance in case of need.

– Hans-Hermann Hoppe, Ph.D., *The Great Fiction*
(2021, Mises Institute), pp. 484–486.

Let me explain why I am convinced that these questions must be answered in the negative. That is why we have some reason to be optimistic. First off, it should be noticed that what we see in front of our very own eyes — that is, social democracy and welfare-warfare statism — is itself the result of a revolution. Someone who, around the mid-19th century, would have advocated the policies, laws, and institutions that our Democratic Republican rulers, the mass media, our so-called intellectual elites, and much of public opinion [would] nowadays regard as normal and self-evident, would then 150 years ago have been regarded as a dangerous revolutionary. More precisely, he would have been considered a communist. Just take a look for instance at the *Communist Manifesto* of 1848 and the political planks that are contained in this manifesto. Most of what was then considered to be the agenda of nuts has in the meantime become political reality, and what would have been called then as three-quarters communism is nowadays called liberalism. Now surely this change must be called a revolution? And just as surely then, if a socialist revolution is possible, why not also a classical liberal, libertarian revolution?

Now, indeed, as Murray Rothbard has shown in his historical writings, the original American Revolution was, to a large extent, a classical liberal, libertarian revolution, and such a thing, then, that has happened in the past can hardly be considered an impossibility.

– Hans-Hermann Hoppe, Ph.D., "How America Can Be Saved,"
from a lecture at the Mises Institute Supporters Summit,
San Francisco, Feb. 1996.

Afterword

One need look no further than to the examples of North and South Korea or East and West Germany to see that the freer people are, the wealthier they can become through mutually beneficial voluntary exchange. These two controlled experiments, where mostly free markets competed against mostly state-controlled economies, have yielded an undeniable result: the more free, the more prosperous.

Maybe that was then, and this is now, and things are totally different, which is why we need a big government? Maybe we just haven't found the right person or group of people to lead the government, and when they get the right idea, we can give them the right to rule everyone else through coercion?

That is the solipsistic, poisonous mindset that grants tyranny the leeway it needs to take hold of the minds of good people. "Let's see if it works" is so profoundly ridiculous that it could only have been thought up by academics. Because there are so many different metrics to measure success and data can always be cherry picked, the media can always be relied upon to deceive the public. Anything but a principled rejection of the initiation of aggression — with no exemptions for state actors — can be our only way to success.

As the late Dr. Murray N. Rothbard once said: "To use the phrases of the New Left of the late 1960s, the ruling elite must be 'demystified,' 'delegitimated,' and 'desanctified.'" Imagine someone saying: "The Catholic Church should have the right to rule you for a while, and we'll see if that works. Then maybe Amazon should rule over Africa, and we'll see if that works. Then Asians should enslave Hispanics, and we'll see if that works. Then Russia should rule America until the region is stabilized."

All moral relativism and initiations of aggression should be unapologetically and unequivocally rejected as the attempts of one person or group to rule over another by claiming ownership over their bodies (*i.e.*, enslaving them).

Self-Ownership and Its Implications
The proposition that people own their own bodies implies that no one is entitled to your money or your time, and you are not entitled to anyone else's, either. Now that you understand that you are morally justified in disassociating from bad actors both in your personal and economic life, guilt shakedowns will no longer hold irrational sway over you. The freedom to associate or disassociate is the ultimate check and balance against the immoral actors who invariably exist in every society.

In addition to establishing your own standards using your human faculties, you'll be incentivizing good behavior, and you'll be happier. You will be happier because you know that since you are not entitled to anyone's time, labor, money, resources, etc., anything you have justly acquired is a blessing and a testament to your own value.

Many ideas compete against the abolitionist idea that people own their own bodies. Alternatives include rule by deliberative democracy, rule by kings, rule by tradition, rule by oligarchy, rule by the wisest, rule by the wealthiest, rule by the oldest — the list goes on.

The truth is that you either believe in *self-ownership* or you believe in *slavery*. You have one life, so live it to the fullest, using your faculties and reason, while respecting the same rights of others.

As every right comes with a corresponding obligation, in this case you have a moral obligation to achieve your goals in life through the use of reason and persuasion, rejecting the *initiation* of violence. Honoring this obligation grants the greatest number of people the opportunity to pursue their happiness.

Human life and private property are far too precious to be surrendered to the primitive minds who seek to bring violence into peaceful cooperation.

Permissions

The following chapters were reprinted with permission from the authors:

Chap. 15
Stringham, Edward P. 2015. "How Private Governance Made the Modern World Possible." Cato Unbound. https://www.cato-unbound.org/2015/10/05/edward-peter-stringham/how-private-governance-made-modern-world-possible.

Chap. 16
Woods, Thomas E., Jr. 2012. "The Misplaced Fear of 'Monopoly.'" The Future of Freedom Foundation. https://www.fff.org/explore-freedom/article/the-misplaced-fear-of-monopoly.

Chap. 22
Long, Roderick T. 2004. "Libertarian Anarchism: Responses to Ten Objections." Mises Institute. https://mises.org/library/libertarian-anarchism-responses-ten-objections.

Chap. 23
Sobran, Joseph. 2015. Subtracting Christianity: Essays on American Culture and Society. FGF Books.

Chap. 27
Skousen, Mark, and Jo Ann Skousen. 1992. "Persuasion vs. Force." MSkousen.Com. http://mskousen.com/articles/politics-and-liberty/persuasion-vs-force-by-mark-skousen.

Chap. 34 (© INFORMA UK LIMITED)
Hasnas, John. 2008. "The Obviousness of Anarchy." In *Anarchism/Minarchism: Is a Government Part of a Free Country?*, 111–31. Ashgate.

Chap. 42
Huemer, Michael. 2021. Knowledge, Reality, and Value: A Mostly Common Sense Guide to Philosophy. Independently published.

Chap. 46
Long, Roderick T. 1993. "How Government Solved the Health Care Crisis." *Formulations* 1 (2). https://praxeology.net/libertariannation/a/f12l3.html.

Acknowledgements

Thank you very much to my copy editor Ben Parker.

Thank you also to TopLobsta for designing the cover art.

Many thanks also to Mike Dworski and Grant F. Smith for their assistance in preparing this book for publication.

Thank you to Scott Horton and my colleagues at the Libertarian Institute for sharing their expertise.

Thank you to Michael Malice, organizer of *The Anarchist Handbook*, for the inspiration behind this project.

Above all else, thank you to all listeners of the "Don't Tread on Anyone" podcast.